D0382929

A
Season
in
Spain

ANN AND LARRY
WALKER

Simon & Schuster

NEW YORK LONDON TORONTO
SYDNEY TOKYO SINGAPORE

SIMON & SCHUSTER
SIMON & SCHUSTER BUILDING
ROCKEFELLER CENTER
1230 AVENUE OF THE AMERICAS
NEW YORK, NEW YORK 10020

DESIGNED BY EVE METZ
DECORATIONS AND MAPS BY MICHAEL HALBERT
MANUFACTURED IN THE UNITED STATES OF AMERICA

1   3   5   7   9   10   8   6   4   2

LIBRARY OF CONGRESS CATALOGING IN PUBLICATION DATA
WALKER, ANN, 1944–
A SEASON IN SPAIN/ANN AND LARRY WALKER.
P.   CM.
INCLUDES BIBLIOGRAPHICAL REFERENCES AND INDEX.
ISBN 0-671-69662-9
1. COOKERY, SPANISH.   2. WINE AND WINE MAKING—SPAIN.
3. SPAIN—SOCIAL LIFE AND CUSTOMS.   4. SPAIN—DESCRIPTION
AND TRAVEL—1981–   .
I. WALKER, LARRY, 1936–   .   II. TITLE.
TX723.5.S7W33   1992
394.1′2′0946—DC20   91-38749
                                                             CIP

To our sons—David, Jude, and Morgan—
who shared many of our seasons in Spain
and were always ready with knife, fork, and wineglass.
In the name of research they tirelessly
explored countless tapas bars and bodegas,
and the sometimes confusing byways of the Spanish soul.

ACKNOWLEDGMENTS

Our deepest thanks go to our literary agent, Martha Casselman— she had the courage to take on this book, which doesn't really fit any of the usual categories. We also want to thank Carole Lalli, for seeing the potential of the idea. Our very special thanks go to Kerri Conan, our editor, who has played a very important role in giving the book its focus and direction. And a very big thank you to a dear friend and sometime traveling companion, Marimar Torres, whose two books *The Spanish Table* and *The Catalan Country Kitchen* are milestones in the development of Spanish cuisine. Finally, thanks to Ron Scherl, a good and loving friend, who helped in the early planning for the book.

What this book is about is Spain. Spanish days and Spanish nights. Spain is unknown territory to many otherwise experienced travelers. Even though the pace has recently quickened a bit, Spain is not to be taken at full gallop; it is not to be rushed, either, at the table or elsewhere. An example: Rarely—except in Madrid and Barcelona, which are being internationalized to a degree—does one see people eating while walking down the sidewalk. Even American-style fast-food establishments in Spain have had to add more seating space to radically change our industrial do-it-fast-and-get-it-over-with approach. The McDonald's- and Pizza Hut–style restaurants have been adapted to Spanish attitudes by taking on more of the ambience of a café. They stay open later at night, serve much more coffee and more pastries, and often have mini–tapas bars.

It is a pace, a style of life that many fear is being swallowed up as Spain moves rapidly into a newly integrated Europe. And because it is true that Spanish industry has become more efficient, the Spanish businessman is more aware of the dreadful scrip called time is money that is paid out in solemn misery all over the industrial and postindustrial world. Regular visitors to Spain can see changes almost from month to month as the country pushes more confidently into modern Europe.

No one can really expect Spain to stand still just so it can offer charming, quaint vistas to tourists. It has, at any rate, been the "Mexico of Europe" –used as a playground for the more affluent— for far too long; post-Franco, it seems at times too intent on becoming the "Florida of Europe."

There are a number of encouraging signs, however, that Spain—as always—will remain Spain, even while learning to hustle a bit. At best, many Spaniards have found a way to fit the hustle into a traditional, more graceful style of life.

A *Season in Spain* is not quite a cookbook, or a wine book, nor is it a travel guide. It's a little of all three, with a smattering of history and culture to boot. We trace a Spanish season based roughly on the cycle of the vine. For those of you who want recipes, you will find them. For those of you curious about the wine, you will come away with a better understanding of the range and exceptional quality of Spanish wine. For those of you who want to know where to stay and where to dine, you will find travel guidelines in each section. These journeys are completely personal in nature and are in a few cases very scanty. They make no pretense of presenting a "complete" guide to Spain. The serious traveler should refer to the bibliography for a list of travel guides.

The history and cultural bits are arranged so that they can be easily ignored by those in a hurry to get to the dining table, although we believe they will add to your understanding of the food and wine.

One of the great attractions of Spain for the modern traveler is the feeling that something a little out of the ordinary might happen at any time. This is because Spain is not quite Europe, not quite Africa, but altogether something else. In Spain, the unexpected is only a step or two away; life often takes a slightly bizarre, almost surreal twist, as if you were living on the extended set of a high-budget film noir.

We wish you a good journey.

A.W.
L.W.

CONTENTS

INTRODUCTION

Donde menos se piensa salta la liebre.
Where one least expects it, the hare leaps up.

—SPANISH PROVERB

We had been traveling in Bordeaux, researching some wine and food stories for magazines. We had landed in Paris in April with a light snow falling. After that, the weather had gotten bad. In Bordeaux it had alternated between sleet, hail, rain, thunder, and lightning with brief periods of pale sunshine. We had promised ourselves that when our work in France was finished, we would reward ourselves with a few days in Spain.

Not surprisingly, although the almond trees were flowering, it was snowing when we crossed the border at Puigcardà, after a harrowing drive over the mountain pass in heavy snow in our rented Renault with no chains. Sheer craziness.

The road dropped rapidly beyond the frontier and in a few miles we were in sunshine. We stopped at a truckdrivers' café, perhaps 10 kilometers into Spain.

At once, we felt at home. The counterman encouraged our rusty Spanish. We drank hearty red wine and ate slices of cured Valencia ham, rough bread, and olives. He made no fuss about accepting our francs (in our rush through the snow, we had neglected to exchange francs for pesetas). You can imagine what the French reaction would have been had we offered pesetas even a few kilometers north.

One of the truckdrivers came over to ask if we had driven over the pass. Was it still snowing? He had no chains. Should he wait? Others joined the conversation with advice, concern, a little friendly bantering, which became more friendly when we kept trying out our Spanish.

Very soon, someone bought another bottle of wine. Our benefactor had a cousin who worked in San Francisco. Would we take his cousin's name and address and call him when we returned to California? Perhaps buy this cousin a small brandy? Yes, yes, we could do all that.

It was wonderful. After weeks with the very proper, very correct, but never very friendly Bordelaise, it was like being greeted by a whole pack of warm, friendly puppies.

It was Spain. The wine was cheap and good. The food was abundant and tasty. The sun was shining.

History is often regarded as a linear affair, a stepping-stone series of dates leading in an orderly, reasonable fashion directly to now. It's best to shed that attitude completely when considering a historical atlas of Spain. It's a zigzag, a mosaic of time and people, moving sideways, inside out, and sometimes backward, like a rabbit in a field. Sometimes, again rabbitlike, it seems to come to a stop, to be frozen in midcourse.

In Spain, perhaps more than anywhere in Europe, the geography of the land has played a major role in the political, cultural, and culinary history of the people who have lived on the land. It has certainly played a role in what those people put in their cooking pots.

Spain is a bewildering patchwork of mountain ranges, dominated by huge rock outcroppings. With the exception of the Ebro and the Guadalquivir, the rivers are short and often dry. Alexandre Dumas and Washington Irving have both left us accounts of their disappointment at the size and water volume (or lack of it) of Spanish rivers. Yet, to the Moors, Spain was a land of rivers. Coming from the deserts of North Africa and the Middle East, they must have found even the short, scrawny rivers of Spain impressive.

The mountain ranges (and lack of navigable rivers) have always made communications difficult. No doubt these geographic features have played a major role in Spain's lack of national unity.

One enters Spanish cultural history about fourteen thousand years ago in Basque country in the north at the Cuevas de Altamira, with its remarkable animal paintings. There are other cave paintings scattered throughout northern Spain. They are haunting pieces of Spain's distant past. The Basques themselves may be the descendants of cave dwellers from the Pyrenees. Their origin and language remain a mystery.

People still live in the caves of Spain. Gypsies have been living for centuries in caves in the hills around Granada. In fact, there is a flourishing subculture there, with bars and music, cafés and handicraft shops. I have never heard of any modern wall paintings, however. But for the Gypsies of Granada, history stopped some time ago.

The next major group of people to arrive were the Iberians, a desert-dwelling tribal folk from North Africa who settled southern and Central Spain in slow waves of migration, starting perhaps as early as 3000 B.C. and continuing until the sixth century B.C. These are the people who gave their name to the entire peninsula. The word *Iber* is believed to be based on their word for "river," and the Ebro River is probably the northern limit of Iberian occupation. The center of Iberian culture was apparently around Valencia, on the Mediterranean coast, and north to Tarragona.

Early writers were impressed by the Iberian talent for war. In *A History of Spain and Portugal*, English historian William C. Atkinson quotes the early Roman writer Pompeius Trogus on the Iberians: "They prefer war to ease and, should they lack foes without, seek them within. Rather than betray a secret they will often die under torment, setting a silent reserve before life itself. Active of body, restless of spirit, they commonly set more store by their horses and fighting accoutrement than by the blood of their kin."

The Phoenicians were active in Spain by as early as the twelfth century B.C., probably calling in at Valencia to trade with the Iberians. They also founded the cities of Cádiz and Málaga in southern Spain. They were after the silver and gold from the Spanish mines, so very early in Spanish history the "treasure" motif is put into play. Spain is perhaps the semilegendary biblical country of Tarshish (Cádiz), so rich with mineral wealth that the Phoenician trading ships were said to have anchors made of silver.

About the same time, or a few centuries later, Celts from northern Europe began crossing the Pyrenees, often mingling with the Iberians in a cultural mix called Celt-Iberians. The Celts themselves are also a bit of a mystery, appearing out of northern and central Europe, worshiping (from the Mediterranean point of view) strange gods, including a kind of beer-swilling backwoods Dionysius. The Celtic influence is still dominant in Galicia and Asturias.

During any look at Mediterranean history, the Greeks always turn up sooner or later. Beginning in about the seventh century, they established trading posts in the Balearic Islands and along the southeast coast, in competition with the Phoenicians.

Then came the Carthaginians, who were actually just more Phoenicians; the city of Carthage in North Africa had originally been established as a Phoenician trading post. Carthage, under the leadership of Hamilcar Barca, seized most of Andalusia and the Valencian coastal area north to Barcelona in the lull following the First Punic War with Rome. (Remember Carthage lost that city and with it the Carthaginian settlements in Sicily.) The city of Barcelona was named after Barca. He also established Carthago Nova, today's Cartagena, as the capital of Spain. It was his son, Hannibal, who led an army, using elephants as a kind of armored division, over the Pyrenees and over the Alps into Italy, where he won every battle but lost the war, and his elephants as well.

How tangled early Spanish history is! It is even more remarkable that it stays that way right up to the day before yesterday. Everything seemed to be happening at the same time, with different groups of people arriving from all directions, sometimes trading with each other, sometimes killing each other.

Even the various names given Spain and the peninsula are difficult to sort out. The name Iberia has stuck pretty well, but the Greeks called Spain Hesperia, meaning something like "land of the setting sun." The Carthaginians called it Ispania, from their word *span*, or "rabbit," so Ispania means "land of the rabbits." When the Romans came in the third century, they kicked out the Carthaginans but kept the name, calling the country Hispania.

There are rabbits shown on early Iberian coins, and of course some variation on rabbit stew is one of the main—and often most tasty—dishes of the Spanish countryside. Considering that the erratic course of Spanish history could serve as a kind of ideograph of a rabbit running, the name fits.

There are those who say that España is actually a Basque word meaning frontier or boundary, and since no one knows anything for sure about the origins of the Basque, it is as reasonable as the next theory.

I believe Virginia Woolf, however—not noted as a Spanish scholar but strong on language—offers evidence for the rabbit theory in her book *Flush*, a biography of the English poet Elizabeth Barrett Browning's cocker spaniel.

Woolf wrote: "Many million years ago the country which is now called Spain seethed uneasily in the ferment of creation. Ages passed; vegetation appeared; where there is vegetation the law of Nature has decreed that there shall be rabbits; where there are rabbits, Providence has ordained there shall be dogs." (And if the dogs chase *spans*, or rabbits, they could be called spaniels. And the spaniel is, of course, of Spanish origin.)

Some authorities, according to Waverley Root in his book *Food*, believe that the rabbit originated in northwestern Africa and crossed into Spain, and from there to the rest of Europe, which would mean that the rabbit and the Iberians came from the same area, although the rabbit arrived several hundred thousand years before the Iberians, while there was still a land bridge between Africa and Spain and the Mediterranean was an inland sea.

We won't get into what is a rabbit and what is a hare, since it makes little difference once the animal is in the pot. But as Root also points out, "I do not suppose that this is the primary function of the rabbit, but it can serve as a touchstone to separate food snobs from those earthy characters who really like to eat. Hare is respectable, even distinguished; rabbit is common and vulgar, and it is good form to turn up the nose at it."

The Romans certainly appreciated rabbit, and there are many recipes for its preparation in the first-century Roman cookbook *De Re Coquinaria*, by Apicius. The Roman conquest of Spain began even as Hannibal and his elephant brigade were still in Italy. In 209 B.C. the chief Carthaginian base, Cartagena, fell to Rome, and in 205 B.C. the last Carthaginians were driven from Spain. The conquest of the peninsula was virtually completed in 133 B.C. with the fall of the Celt-Iberian city of Numantia, north of Madrid, although there were still holdouts in the mountains until the time of Augustus, almost a century later. The Pax Romana lasted in Spain for five centuries, with legions settled in for a good bit of serious road building, bridge construction, and general civilizing, although the country was hardly a wilderness when the Romans arrived.

The Phoenicians had, of course, been interested primarily in the rich mineral deposits—gold, silver, copper, and iron, which were found throughout the peninsula, although more abundantly in the south. The Greeks were not above taking an interest in silver and gold, but they also turned to agriculture. Olives, olive oil, wheat, and wine, along with wax, honey, fish, and wool, were all exported through the Greek settlements. Spanish olive oil was recognized then as now for superior quality. So when the Romans arrived, they found a functioning agricultural trading economy with connections all around the Mediterranean. And the center of that agricultural economy was—and to a large degree still is—the olive.

It is probably impossible for us to understand fully the importance of the olive in the ancient Mediterranean world. We are more accustomed to thinking of the olive as a green or black decorative flourish on the appetizer plate, often stuffed with this or that. Olive oil is somewhat more central to our kitchens, but it is still used by many people as simply one of several virtually interchangeable cooking oils.

To the Greeks and other Mediterranean people, however, the olive was central. Waverley Root wrote in *Food*: "It has thus, over a period of five thousand years or more, shaped the cuisines of the Middle East, Greece, Italy, Spain, and southern France as we know them today and as they are likely to remain."

The goddess Athene is said to have brought the olive tree to Greece at the time of the founding of the capital city. Athene struck the ground with her spear, and an olive tree sprang up. The grateful Greeks named the city Athens. (Athene would be an excellent candidate for anyone's kitchen goddess. According to the poet Robert Graves, she invented—along with many other useful items—the earthenware pot, an essential element in the Spanish kitchen, where it is called a *cazuela*.)

The olive tree itself is not native to Spain. The olive appears to have spread from somewhere in the eastern Mediterranean, where it has been cultivated since Neolithic times. Egypt, Syria, Palestine, and even Crete have been offered as the original home of the olive. No doubt, as with many other plants, it grew wild in a number of areas and was probably brought into domestic cultivation many times in many places. The olive gradually became widespread enough to enter into commerce by at least 2500 B.C., when there are Egyptian records of olive oil being imported from Crete.

For anyone who has driven for hours through the olive groves of Andalusia in the south of Spain, it is difficult to believe that the tree hasn't always been a part of the Spanish landscape. Indeed, it was introduced about the fourth or fifth century B.C. by both the Carthaginians and the Greeks. The olive played a part in many spring festivals throughout the Mediterranean, including the Ramos festivals in Spain. And it was, of course, an olive branch that the dove carried back to Noah after the Biblical flood.

Like the olive, wheat was everywhere in the Mediterranean. It was probably the first crop planted by man, perhaps about 10,000 years ago on the upper Tigris. There was evidence of wheat in Spain from Mesolithic sites, although it is impossible to know whether it was wild or cultivated wheat. Spring-ripening wheat would be perfectly adaptable to the often erratic and always sparse rainfall of much of Spain, since the little rain that does fall comes in late winter and spring. There are vestiges of terraced wheat fields in Catalonia, once an important wheat-exporting area.

Think of Mediterranean agriculture as a triad. If the olive and wheat are two legs of the triad, the grape is the third. The history of the vine is obscure. Or at least what we think of as the wine-producing vines, *Vitis vinifera*. It is *vinifera* that gives us Cabernet Sauvignon, Chardonnay, and all the other varietals we think of as wine grapes. Various forms of vines grow almost everywhere in the world, but few make wine worth bothering about. Generally, the home area of *vinifera* is thought to be somewhere between the Black Sea and the Caspian Sea.

There were undoubtedly vines in Spain in Neolithic times, but it is uncertain if they were *vinifera*. It is difficult enough to sort out just what vines are what in modern Spain, much less fifteen thousand years ago. We are certain that by the eighth or ninth century B.C. the Phoenicians were trading in wine from the Mediterranean coast of Spain, although it isn't clear exactly which grapes went into those Phoenician wines.

A few centuries later, the Greeks brought the Malvasia grape and planted it extensively along the Mediterranean coast south of Tarragona. By the time of the Romans, Malvasia was grown throughout much of Spain.

There is no way to know, of course, what these early wines tasted like. Plenty of written records address winemaking, however, which was well established in the Middle East, Egypt, and parts of China (where it never caught on, somehow) by 3000 B.C. There is an ancient Chinese text, dated 2285 B.C., that tells of a man being punished for blending grape wine and rice wine.

The Egyptians were the first (as far as we know) to vintage-date wine and to designate wine from selected vineyards. One Egyptian wine label from the time of Ramses III in the twelfth century B.C. reads: "In the year 30, good wine from the well-irrigated terrain of the temple of Ramses II in Per-amon. The chief of the wine-dressers, Tutmes." Like most wine writing today, that tells us quite a bit about the wine but not what it tasted like.

The wines of the classical Mediterranean world are universally described as being very sweet and very aromatic. Probably they were sweet because many of the grapes described from those times (and

the Roman writer Pliny listed over a hundred varieties) are grapes
that are naturally high in sugar at maturity. And many wines would
have fair amounts of residual sugar remaining because the inefficient wild yeasts would die or go dormant before converting all the
sugar to alcohol during the fermentation process.

Oxygen is the enemy of wine. In fact, a modern California winemaker has described his job as simply knowing when to intervene to
prevent fermented grape juice from turning into vinegar—as it will,
given too much exposure to oxygen. The ancient winemakers had
no way of completely sealing a vessel to prevent oxygen from reaching wine. At least no way inexpensive enough to use for mass-pro-
duced and shipped wines. So many strange things were added to
wine to keep oxygen out.

The Greeks sealed wine amphorae with resin plugs, for example,
and actually developed a taste for resined wines, which they drink to
this day. The Romans and others floated olive oil on top of wine.
Infusions of various herbs were also added to wine to mask the
vinegary flavors. For a time it was the fad in Rome to smoke wines;
open wine containers were placed in the chimneys or smoke holes
of houses to give the wine a smoky flavor and preserve it. We may
be better off not knowing just what wine did taste like.

The Greeks early on associated the spread of the vine with the
spread of civilization. Dionysius, the Greek god of wine, was much
more than the drunken lout the Romans made him as Bacchus.
Several of the cluster of stories surrounding Dionysius from early
Greek tradition identify him as the builder of libraries and the
founder of cities all across the Middle East and into India.

The god of wine also had his dark side, which Miguel Torres
captures well in *Wines and Vineyards of Spain:* "The Greeks had
explored the field of human psychology and created two gods, rep-
resenting the poles of human life. Apollo, the god of light, was cold,
temperate, and intellectual, and his code of conduct, inscribed in
the temple at Delphi, could be summarized as: 'Know thyself, and
do nothing to excess.' His counterpart, Dionysius, was the god of
the subconscious, of instinct, impulse and intoxication, and so came
to be known as the god of wine, for it is wine that sets men free from
cold reason and bares the inner being or, as the Romans said: *In
vino veritas.*"

The Romans, of course, mastered transportation—of people,
water, and commercial goods such as wine. It is estimated that the
Romans built at least 12,000 miles of highways in Spain. The roads
were built first for military use, but they later served well for traders.

Many modern highways follow the old Roman roads, and in some cases (notably the Roman bridges at Mérida in Extremadura) are still in use.

The Romans were particularly ingenious in transporting wine by sea. For reasons that began with ease of manufacture, the huge amphorae, or wine-bearing vessels, were shaped with pointed rather than flat bottoms. They were then set into prefabricated wooden frames that fit into the ships. These containers made it easy for one person to pour from a vessel holding several hundred gallons of wine.

Amphorae were probably first made by the Egyptians. They were made in sizes ranging from a few gallons to hundreds of gallons. Besides those built to fit into a wooden form, there were some that were made to sit upright in sand and others built to fit into a tripod.

For transportation by sea it was necessary to build holders for the amphorae. These were constructed of long beams placed side by side with enough space in between to form slots so that the amphorae would sit upright. Several of these Roman wine-transit ships have been found at the bottom of the Mediterranean. Some were the ancient equivalent of oil supertankers, holding up to ten thousand amphorae, while others might have held only three or four hundred. Each shipment also carried bottled and sealed samples so merchants could be sure upon arrival that the wine in the amphorae and the wine in the sample bottles were the same.

Besides improvements in the transportation of wine, the Romans vastly extended the vineyards of Spain. Although wine had been made (and traded) in the Rioja since the time of the Phoenicians, the Romans improved the vineyards by planting new varieties brought from Italy, as they did everywhere in Spain.

The Romans also brought Christianity, and with it the institution of the Catholic Church, one of the strongest influences—for better or worse—on the Spanish character. The Christian experience in Spain was quite different from what it was anywhere else in the world because of the long centuries of warfare against the Moors.

The entire experience of the Reconquest is very difficult for us to imagine today. Perhaps the nearest we could come to understanding it would be to imagine that the nineteenth-century Native American wars in North America had lasted eight centuries and that they had often been fought against a superior foe—both militarily and culturally—professing a hated religion. But even that falls short in a number of ways. The Reconquest was a war against an invader; the

ground fought over was regarded as Christian and sacred, not new
territory to be exploited.

Let's backtrack for a second and remember that between the Romans and the Moors stood the barbarians. Beginning in the early
years of the fifth century, three different Germanic tribes—the
Suevi, the Vandals, and the Alans—swept into Spain from the
north. The long-range impact of the barbarian tribes on Spain is
slight. Their impact on food and wine is nonexistent, so we will
banish them from history's kitchen and get right back to the Arabs.

The Moorish occupation is what makes Spanish cuisine so completely different from that of the other former Roman provinces of
the western Mediterranean. For although Spanish food is firmly
rooted in that broader Roman-Mediterranean cuisine, it has been
bent into some curious patterns and delicious detours by the Moors.

The development of a first-rate cuisine can really take place only
in a fairly stable political and social situation, which the Moors
maintained over much of Spain for several centuries. It is impossible, really, to overestimate the impact of the Arab kitchen on the
cuisine of Spain, and through that, the food of the entire western
Mediterranean basin.

As one small example, there is frumenty, a dish that has come
down to the present roughly defined as gruel. The *Larousse Gastronomique* (which most cooks have used, for good or ill, as the standard
encyclopedia/dictionary of the kitchen) defines frumenty as a "very
old country dish, consisting of a porridge or gruel made from wheat
boiled with milk, then sweetened and spiced. Originating in Touraine, it is mentioned as a dessert in *La Menagier de Paris* (1383),
being made with milk in which almonds have been boiled to give
flavor." The use of almonds is a dead giveaway that we are dealing
with an Arab dish, one that certainly did not originate in Touraine
but in Spain or North Africa.

Although the Moor invaders are often thought of as having been
all one people, they were actually even more disparate than the
Germanic tribes that replaced the Romans in Spain. The invading
army was composed of Arabs, Syrians, Egyptians, Berbers, and
other North Africans, but the unifying force was the Arab language
and religion—and an almost sensual love of food. The Arabs
brought the heavy, aromatic spices of the Mideast and the Far East
—cinnamon, cloves, nutmeg, and other goodies that the rest of
Europe would not see in any quantity for a few more centuries.
They brought cumin seeds and almonds. They brought the art of

drying fruits of all sorts; they brought the bitter orange. Arab traders brought sugar cane and rhubarb, quinces, apples, and quails, pomegranates and figs, saffron and rice.

Although the Arabs contributed rice to the cooking pots of Spain and Europe, the grain originated somewhere in southeast Asia, probably no later than 3000 B.C. One group of modern food scholars points to Thailand, while another school opts for China. Alexander the Great found rice growing in India, and while it is sometimes mentioned by classical writers, there is no evidence at all that it was ever grown in Europe until the Moors brought it to Andalusia and Valencia in the eighth century A.D.

Saffron, on the other hand, was well known to the Romans; it was widely cultivated in the eastern Mediterranean and an important element of Phoenician trade. Although it grew wild in Italy, Rome imported saffron from Greece. In classical times its chief use had been as a dye and a perfume and in certain rituals and ceremonies. The use of saffron in Europe died out after Rome fell. When the Arabs brought it to Spain as a kitchen herb, it was regarded as an entirely new condiment.

It takes between seventy and eighty thousand saffron flowers to make one pound of saffron. Given that the preparation of saffron is labor-intensive (and skilled labor at that), the production of culinary saffron is limited to those societies willing to divert more than the usual amount of labor, and therefore money, to the kitchen. Then as now, saffron is sold in small containers, by the ounce, in the south of France and in Spain. And a little goes a long way.

There occurred, then, in the eighth century, one of those times in the history of food when all the right materials were in the right place at the right time. Rice, saffron, and abundant seafood: From those three elements came the most well-known of all Spanish dishes, paella. The dish itself originated around seaside Valencia, a Catalan-speaking region. The name comes from the Catalan word for skillet or cooking pan, *paellera*.

Just where and when rice and saffron were first combined is impossible to say. Paella may have had an ancestor somewhere in the Middle East, even before the Arabs arrived in Spain. Besides paella, there is another legendary Mediterranean dish that combines rice and saffron—risotto alla Milanese. The year 1574 is cited by Root and others as the first mention of risotto alla Milanese, certainly several centuries after the creation of paella.

There are various herbs that can cast a yellow glow over a dish—

safflower and turmeric come immediately to mind—but none has quite the privileged place in the kitchen that saffron has. One occasionally comes across a substance called saffron powder or paella powder in the south of France and in Spain. This often has no saffron in it at all and is simply a slightly salty coloring agent that gives a somewhat garish cast to rice and fish dishes. Saffron's role in bouillabaisse (as well as risotto) must go back to the Moors in Spain. There is simply no other source for a culinary use of saffron in Europe.

But whatever the culinary treasures brought to Spain by the Arabs (and through Spain to other points in Europe), the Christians were not impressed. The Reconquest began in 722 at the battle of Covadonga deep in Basque country, only a few years after the Moorish invasion. Very soon, Christian armies emerged from the Pyrenees beginning the long march south, and the 800-year Reconquest began.

The frontier was always a patchwork of conflicting alliances. A Christian king might well be allied with a Moorish prince against other Moors. Or a Moor might fight beside Christians against other Moors. The Reconquest followed a back-and-forth rhythm but with the momentum always coming from the north.

So the incredible Byzantine zigzag of Spanish history continued, with rabbits popping up everywhere.

(It is interesting to speculate about the earlier history of Spain—and, indeed, of all of Europe. If the Moors had pressed their advantage and advanced into the mountains to wipe out the tiny pockets of Christian resistance, rather than falling back and giving the petty Christian kings a chance to regroup and strike back, we might have an Arab Spain today. Consider the impact that would have made on the history of Europe and the New World. There was a brief time in the early eighth century that it was a real possibility.)

By the mid-fifteenth century the balance had swung over to the Christians. It had been moving their way for some time. Spain was finally united under Ferdinand and Isabella with the conquest of Granada in 1492. This last Arab stronghold fell on January 2 of that year. Four months later, and hardly by coincidence, their Christian majesties issued the proclamation to expel the Jews from Spain.

Generally, the Moors had always been more tolerant of the Jews than the Christians, perhaps because they respected the intellectual achievements of many Jewish scholars, or perhaps because they felt the Jews offered no threat to their power.

But the Christians felt otherwise. There had been frequent sporadic outbreaks of Christian intolerance of the Jews. There was an infamous aggression against the Jews in Sevilla in 1391 on Ash Wednesday, when the Jewish quarter of the city was burned and hundreds of Jews were killed. What began as a local riot spread to other parts of Andalusia and then into Castile. In the end, thousands of Jews were killed and tens of thousands were forced to "convert" to Christianity. Although the Jews left strong cultural marks on the history of Spain, they had little influence in the Spanish kitchen and wine cellar.

The same is true of the Gypsies, another wandering and often persecuted people, who first reached Spain only a few decades before the Jews were expelled. No one knows for sure where the Gypsies came from. Perhaps they were fleeing Tamerlane, who invaded India in 1398. If so, they made their way fairly rapidly across the Middle East and North Africa, to reach Spain by 1440 at the latest.

The modern Spaniards simply consider the Gypsies leftovers of the Moors, and in most of Spain they are held in great contempt. The Gypsies in Barcelona, however, where money is the great equalizer and where there are wealthy Gypsies, have to some extent entered the mainstream of Spanish life. But to foreigners—who may be forgiven for being a bit more romantic about Spain than the residents themselves—the Gypsies convey part of the spirit of Spain.

Historical astrologers should take a close look at the year 1492 in Spain. The Moors were driven out, the Jews were expelled, and the New World was discovered.

And from the modest kitchens of the natives in South and North America, we may round out our Spanish kitchen. The list of foods brought back from the Americas is long. Yet it isn't just the number of foods that is impressive, but also the key role that the plants, such as the tomato, were to play in Europe's post-Columbian cuisine.

The Italians were the first to realize the full potential of the tomato, which most probably entered Italy through Naples. The city came under Spanish rule in 1522, just about the right time for the plant to have arrived from either Peru or Mexico, or both. It was present in both countries, though not as widely cultivated as potatoes, beans, and squash, which the Spanish also took to Europe.

It is curious that the Italian word for tomato—*pomodoro*—is similar to the Polish word for tomato, *pomodory*. Some food historians have reported that the potential of the tomato was first fully realized in Poland during Renaissance times, long before it was commonly accepted in southern Europe.

But we are getting far afield from the Spanish kitchen. Of all the foods brought from the New World, the potato is the one the Spanish most readily welcomed into the kitchen. The first potatoes encountered in the Americas were sweet potatoes, noted by Columbus on his first voyage. What early writers called the Virginia potato, and what we curiously call the Irish potato, was cultivated only in the high mountain valleys of the Andes in South America. It was cultivated in Peru as early as 3000 B.C.

The name Virginia potato was given the tuber by both English and French writers, who were under the impression that Sir Walter Raleigh was the first to bring the potato to Europe. An impression that came about, according to Waverley Root, because in 1586 Raleigh had provisioned one of his ships with potatoes at Cartagena, in South America, and taken them back to Virginia.

Spanish tradition has it that Pedro de Cieza de León first brought potatoes to Europe and that they were planted in the Hospital de la Sangre in Sevilla as early as 1539. They were immediately recognized as a cheap and filling food for the poor, for soldiers, and probably for prisoners.

In a curious historical parallel, potato farming became a specialty in Galicia, the most Celtic area of Spain, foreshadowing the dominance of the potato on the table of those other Celts, the Irish, a few centuries later. From Galicia, potatoes were shipped to Genoa. Italy was apparently the second country in Europe to cultivate the plant.

The potato is far from the image most people hold of modern Spanish food, but in fact it is present in just about every bar in Spain, usually in the form of a tortilla or *patatas bravas*. In the Spanish countryside the potato is found on almost any plate in ordinary restaurants. It will often be nestled beside some form of the haricot bean, another import from the Americas.

The name "haricot" is said to be based on the Aztec word *ayacotl*, but the *conquistadores* found them all over the New World. As with the tomato, the Italians took to them most rapidly. According to Root, they were a great favorite of the Medicis, who had got them as a gift from Pope Clement VII in 1528. The Pope, in turn, had got them from an unnamed Spaniard who had brought them from Mexico. In fact, the haricot became so popular in Tuscany that other Italians still call the Tuscans *mangiafagioli* or bean eaters. And it was the New World haricot that was the Tuscan favorite, since *fagioli* refers directly to the New World bean, not the fava bean of Europe.

Chocolate was another great find that the Spanish brought back from the Americas. Columbus sent cacao beans to Spain from Nicaragua in 1502, but no one knew quite what to do with them. In 1519, Cortez learned how the Aztecs made (and used) chocolate; Aztec chocolate was thick, almost like a paste, apparently, and was sometimes referred to as a soup, most probably the forerunner of today's molé sauces.

Spain tried to keep the method of preparation a secret and was successful for a time, until Jews, who had been expelled from Spain, settled in France and let the word out, although the French scorned chocolate in the beginning. The city of Bayonne would not allow chocolate to be made within the city limits.

The French attitude had changed considerably by 1846, when Alexandre Dumas wrote *From Paris to Cadiz*. Dumas described his first taste of Spanish chocolate: "A servant entered bearing a tray upon which were arranged five thimble-sized cups full of a thick black fluid, five glasses of clear water, and a little basket containing small sticks of bread, pink and white. From our earliest days we had heard of the wonderful chocolate one gets in Spain, and we hardly dared raise the cups to our lips, lest this impression should vanish like so many other illusions of childhood. But no! The chocolate was excellent. Unfortunately there was only just enough to taste."

The New World foods introduced by the Spanish to the European kitchen—chilies, squashes, corn, potatoes, and more—shine far more brightly than all the gold and silver the *conquistadores* brought back to Spain.

The gold is spent, the potatoes remain.

Across a hot, dusty plaza in a small Andalusian town, a swarm of children erupt from a shadowed street. They are perhaps five or six years old. A few of them have tattered cloths wrapped around their heads. They are in the lead, weaving and twisting, trying to avoid a much larger group of children. This larger group, many waving sticks in swordlike fashion, are shouting, Moros! Moros! Matamoros! *"Moors! Moors! Kill the Moors!"*

And soon they do. In a noisy, jumbled battle that swirls around the table where Larry sits having coffee and brandy in the sparse shade of an ancient olive tree, they gleefully reenact eight hundred years of Spanish history.

"Kill the Moors!"

As the battle sweeps on across the plaza, what Moors that do not lie sprawled and giggling dead on the stones are taken prisoner and marched away up a twisting street leading toward the church. Doubtless either to submit to instant baptism or to be put to the sword on the church steps.

Larry feels a tinge of sympathy and remembers that in his cowboy and Indian days in mid-America he was always the one who stuck the feather of a crow in his hair and ambushed the wagon train crossing the backyard.

THE FOOD

The recipes in this book are authentic Spanish recipes adapted for the American kitchen. Many—in fact, probably most—are almost identical to an original Spanish version. Others have been changed to simplify or (especially in the case of country dishes) to lighten them up a bit.

This adaptation was done to encourage the American cook to make these dishes everyday dishes on the family menu, not special-occasion dishes. Spanish food begins in the home kitchen; this fact is reflected in the large number of women—such as Montse Gillian, in Catalonia; Josefa Cores, in Galicia; and Toya Roqué, also in Catalonia—who have become well known as chefs in Spain and abroad. Home cooking, refined over centuries of isolation—not only from the rest of Europe but even from other regions of the Iberian Peninsula—maintains regional Spanish cuisines with strong local roots. A number of these recipes can easily become part of the standard repertory of the inquisitive, imaginative cook who wants to try new techniques and ingredients in the same way so many now cook Italian, French, and Asian dishes.

In short, the Spanish kitchen is not exotic terrain, to be entered on rare occasions only, with compass and map; it is standard Mediterranean territory (with, always, that touch of Africa and the Middle East from the Moors), where most of the culinary road signs will apply.

Treat the recipes here as a Spanish cook would—as a base to work from. They are simply the skeletal outline of the food they represent, able to crossbreed well with French (especially southern French) and northern Italian cuisine.

There is nothing sacred about the text. It exists only as a guide to what your imagination can produce. Perhaps the best thing to do is to take the approach that is used in translating poetry: Word for word is obviously impossible. We seek the feeling of the poem, the emotion, the "wholeness" of the verse. It is the same when trying to duplicate a dish from another cuisine. Even if the ingredients appear to be the same—two tomatoes, three onions, and so forth—of course they are not. No two tomatoes are ever alike, any more than any two fish are ever alike.

Recipes, even within the same cuisine, are always only a rough guide, a simple map of the territory, not to be taken for the territory itself. Just imagine, then, trying to duplicate a Chinese or Indian or Basque dish in an Anglo kitchen! That marvelous mystery writer Nicholas Freeling, who worked for many years in hotel kitchens, wrote one of the best food books of this century. It's called simply *The Kitchen*, and he makes very clear that recipes can often be fatal to anyone trying to cook.

So as the best translator regards the text of the poem as an indication of the direction the translation should take, a good cook will use a "foreign" recipe as a series of signs pointing toward the finished dish.

Even the most simple recipe exists only to serve the cook's needs. It should be interpreted in your kitchen so that when the dish reaches the table it is your own creation, or at least a variation on a theme.

Edward Espe Brown, the Zen chef who created the *Tassajara Bread Book*, wrote: "A recipe doesn't belong to anyone. Given to me, I give it back to you. Only a guide, only a skeletal framework. You must fill in the flesh according to your nature and desire. Your life, your love will bring these words into full creation. This cannot be taught. You already know. So please cook, love, feel, create."

The recipes here have been gathered from various sources—restaurants, the home kitchens of friends, winery kitchens, even from a monastery. Although there are a number of regional Spanish cuisines, there is a great deal of overlap from region to region, the same dish appearing in a slightly different version. For example, take *menestra*, a kind of vegetable soup or stew found everywhere, with the major differences being the regional food specialties. In these cases, the recipe presented in this book may be a synthesis of the several formulas. All dishes have been made successfully in our kitchen with easily available American ingredients.

WHAT YOU NEED IN THE KITCHEN

As food and wine educators, we have worked in a lot of kitchens. Sometimes we have had to create them on the spot from a closet without running water or in an outdoor courtyard with just a garden hose. So when people brag about how much space and how many things they have in their kitchens, it doesn't always impress us. All the gadgets money can buy will not necessarily add up to a good meal.

Granted, it is nice to have ample counter and cabinet space, but most important, have good, sharp carbon-steel knives and a sharpening steel. Keep your knives sharp and store them carefully. Don't just toss them in a drawer.

Spanish cooking requires very little in the way of special equipment. Here are just a few items that would be helpful, in addition to normal kitchen supplies.

• Clay casseroles (of assorted sizes). Called *cazuelas* in Spain, they are available in many shopping areas that cater to the Hispanic community in the United States and generally through good kitchen supply catalogs such as Williams-Sonoma. They can be used on top of the stove as well as in the oven and then taken directly to the table.

• Paella pan. There is really no substitute for a paella pan. It's a flat-bottomed, shallow metal pan with two handles. Paella pans should always be oiled before storage.

• Citrus zester. This handy little device allows you to remove just the colored part of the skin of the fruit in fine strips.

• Ceramic mortar and pestle. This should be of at least a three- to four-cup capacity. Any smaller is useless. It is important that it be of glazed ceramic; the rough stone mortars used in Mexico or Southeast Asia absorb odors and don't produce a fine consistency.

• Large fine-mesh strainer or *chinois*.

• Heavy-duty food processor.

• Easy-to-use pepper grinder.

• Twelve-inch pizza pan (at least one, if not more).

And that's it, unless you are really just starting to put your kitchen together. In that case, buy as you need and always buy good quality. Think carefully before buying too many gadgets. Storage can be a real problem.

THE WINE

If there is one image—one touchstone—that focuses and holds together the food of Spain, it is the vine. The vine is rooted in Spanish history from the time of the Phoenician traders forward. Each successive wave of people brought the vine—the Greeks, the Romans, the Moors (in the form of exotic table grapes), and modern viticulturists fresh from college in California or France. But the vine remains stubbornly Spanish, taking its nourishment from the Spanish earth.

The roots reach deep into Spanish soil and the branches extend into every province of Spain, helping shape the cultures that today make Spain a unique country. Its tough, light-seeking tendrils illuminate the heart of the Spanish soul.

Following the ancient rhythm of the vineyards, the recipes and events described here denote a circle: harvest, pruning, growth.

The harvest marks the climax of the vine's year, although not the end of the year, for in a circle there is no end. It starts first in the south of Spain, in Andalusia, in late August and ends in the far north in late October or early November. Everywhere there are harvest festivals, starting with the famous *vendimia* in Jerez de la Frontera, the heart of the sherry district. This is also where we will begin our journey into a season in Spain.

Pruning is that quiet time of year after harvest is finished and the young wines are safely tucked away into tanks or barrels. The vines look like dead sticks poking up from a bleak winter landscape. In the Basque north they may appear to be drowned in the heavy winter rains. In Catalonia the vines could be gray and black lines against a field of snow. Wherever they are, they will look shaggy and unkempt, each vine appearing a bit like a miniature brush pile all on its own. Then the pruners arrive, armed with knives and shears, to trim and shape the vines, preparing them for the new growth to come.

The period of growth begins in late spring, when tiny green buds all at once break through the brittle gray tips of the vines, and when each branch is charged with that energy the poet Dylan Thomas called "the force that through the green fuse drives the flower." Those tiny whispers of green will grow into the lavish green shouts of spring and summer, ending, finally, in the harvest. Which is where we came in.

During the vine's season, we will move geographically and culturally through that sometimes slightly askew state of mind that is
Spain, from the Moorish-influenced south, with its cooling, tiled
Arab palaces, through the seemingly barren high plateau of La Mancha, to the home of the Basques and the Celts in the green northwest. Along the way we pause to consider the urban delights at the
tables of Barcelona and Madrid, as well as the simpler pleasures of
the country kitchen.

Spain, with a memory going back before the Romans, plunges
with great style and verve toward the twenty-first century, holding
on, it seems, to those parts of the past that make the present bearable. Parts that certainly include the fruit of the vine.

Spain has more acreage planted to vineyards than any other nation in the world. In most of Spain it is impossible to travel more
than a few kilometers without seeing the vine. As in other Mediterranean countries, in Spain wine is regarded as simply part of the
meal. On those occasions when you might order a glass of wine,
almost surely food will be presented, even if it's only a small plate of
olives. There is very little wine snobbery in Spain, even though
Spain produces some of the world's greatest wines, from Jerez in the
south to the Rioja and Penedés in the north. Just as the Spanish
expect their food to be good, they expect their wine to be good. It
must be exceptional—either exceptionally good or exceptionally bad
—to bring forth any comment.

There is also an extraordinary range of older wines routinely available in restaurants and retail shops in Spain. This easy access gives
some insight, I believe, into the Spanish attitude toward wine. Wine
is not worshiped and locked away in a cellar, so there are more older
wines in ordinary commercial circulation than we are accustomed
to finding in New York or London.

Until recently, even white wines were not released until after they
had aged three to four years in the bottle, a practice that tends to
increase the range of older wines available. Even now, after the
Spanish have to some degree adopted the international trend of
drinking younger, fruitier wines, most bodegas continue with the
traditional wine programs. This means that a white wine will typically come on market four to five years from vintage, a red wine six
to eight years from vintage.

In California, in comparison, a Sauvignon Blanc is often put on
the market in the spring following the harvest, a Chardonnay only a
few months later. Even producers of "serious" Chardonnays seldom

hold the wine more than eight to twelve months in the bottle before its release. The better red wines in California usually go to market within two years of harvest, with reserves held an additional six to twelve months.

Besides making a great difference in cash flow, it also affects how a wine is made. A wine released early is going to be consumed early about 98 percent of the time. (Most wine purchased in the United States is drunk within forty-eight hours of purchase.) It must be made in a light, easy-to-drink style. Such wines are given minimal skin contact because the grape skin contains tannic elements that create a sensation of bitterness in young wine, but the skins also contain flavor elements that are lost when the fermenting juice is taken from the skins too early.

Wines made in the drink-me-now style are also less likely to barrel-age for any length of time. Barrel aging is an often-misunderstood aspect of winemaking. The barrel—generally made of oak, although redwood is still in use in some California wineries and chestnut in very traditional Italian wineries—imparts some flavor and tannin elements to the wine, particularly when it is new. The barrel's chief function is to contribute to the aging process.

Put quite simply, wine held in wooden barrels has some limited contact with oxygen. A winemaker walks a fine line. Too much oxygen and he is merrily on the way to vinegar; just the right touch and he adds a complexity to the finish of the wine, which perhaps will not even appear until after several more years in the bottle.

A number of other differences in winemaking techniques separate wine for early drinking and wine intended to reach a balance of bottle maturity. And balance is the key. It's quite true that the younger wines made in the past decade from Spain, and most of the rest of the world's winegrowing regions, have immediate taste appeal. The best are loaded with up-front fruit. They are what the British call quaffable, but their life expectancy is in doubt. Most of the time, age hardly matters. But at certain special times, it becomes obvious why people make such a fuss about older wines.

Probably the last major wine bargains in the world are the red wines from the Rioja district in the north of Spain. For anyone interested in laying down the foundations of a good wine cellar at a reasonable cost, this is exactly the place to begin. The wines of Rioja boast the longevity of the wines of Bordeaux. They maintain a remarkable freshness and youthfulness, even after fifty or sixty years in the bottle. Yet they sell for perhaps a tenth of the price of comparable French wines.

Those in the United States who are accustomed to varietal nomenclature—Chardonnay, Cabernet Sauvignon, Sauvignon Blanc, and so on—will find little familiar in Spanish wines. There is some experimentation with those familiar varietals, but most wine is identified by region—Rioja, Penedés, etc.—rather than by grape name. As we come to each region, we will be looking at the major varietals within that region.

The Spanish, quick to see the possibilities of tourism in other areas, have yet to grasp fully that there are growing numbers of people who like to visit wineries. Some wineries are beginning to move in that direction, especially those active in the export market. The smaller, strictly local wineries are usually friendly enough to the casual visitor, but call in advance unless you know for sure that the winery has a tasting room. You will find a selection of wineries that welcome visitors in the "Guidelines" sections.

Most Spanish restaurants that cater at all to tourists lean heavily on the Rioja wines, which is a pity, because the regional wines of Spain can be perfectly delightful with the regional dishes—indeed, they seem to have grown up together, perfect tablemates. For example, saffron can be difficult for wine, yet the light, high-acid rosés and red wines of Valencia go perfectly with the saffron-laced paella. The *fino* and *manzanilla* sherries of Andalusia are perfect tablemates for the grilled seafood and shellfish dishes of the south. And of course there is no better match for the lamb dishes of Rioja than the rich red wines from that area.

There have been volumes ill-written in the past few years about matching wine and food, as if they were alien creatures to one another and needed constant attention else they would react and explode. The truth is, wine and food are two aspects of the same thing —the total dining experience. They are naturally compatible and complement each other. If you want to prepare a Spanish dish, and a Spanish wine isn't at hand, don't hesitate to try a California or French or Italian wine. The grapes are cousins, after all. Likewise, a good bottle of Rioja does wonders for a standard American charcoaled steak.

Spain is a major brandy-producing country, and the Spanish drink a lot of brandy inevitably called "*coñac*," which drives the French into a frenzy. Anise-flavored liqueurs are also quite popular in Spain, as are *aguardientes*, the Spanish version of the French marc or Italian grappa, made by distilling the skins and seeds (pomace) left over from winemaking.

The producer of one of the best-known brands of Galician *aguardiente*, the Cooperativa del Ribeiro, has tried to set several little advertising tales in motion regarding the drink. One goes that it takes three men to drink a glass of *aguardiente*. One to drink it and two friends to hold him up. They also recommend that before drinking it you pin a card with your address to your jacket.

Good ad copy, but Galician *aguardiente* is no different from marc, grappa, or any of the other dozens of Spanish *aguardientes*. *Aguardientes* vary tremendously in quality, depending on the quality of the grape pomace. The better ones, like the better grappas in the United States, have become a very trendy drink in Madrid and Barcelona. They are made with quite a bit of the grape must (the young, just-fermenting grape juice) added back, which gives the *aguardiente* an intense fruitiness.

Many restaurants achieve a very agreeable substitute by adding fruits or berries to the base of common *aguardiente* and letting it simmer in the bottle for a few months. While it doesn't have the intensity of a first-rate grape grappa or *aguardiente*, it makes a nice finish to a meal and a good substitute for a heavier dessert. A restaurant-made *aguardiente* using a fruit called *pacharán*, a kind of wild cherry, is a favorite throughout Spain. There are also commercial fruit brandies that use the *pacharán*.

Finally, this being a food-and-wine-together book, it is perhaps unnecessary to point out that although there is much here about drinking, it is almost always as an accompaniment to food. Emotionally, intellectually, the Mediterranean is a "sea of wine," yet not a "sea of drunks." One rarely sees a person drunk in Spain (or in Mediterranean France or Italy for that matter). It is a great embarrassment, a thing of shame, for a man or woman to be drunk in public. Also, the drinking takes place over a longer period of time than the traditional American "happy hour," which is often so unhappy. Since one has more time to be sociable and to share a bottle of wine, a plate of food, both food and wine are consumed more slowly. There is no rush for "a last round before closing."

The consumption of wine seems to fit naturally into the pace of the Mediterranean life, as coffee consumption does in Northern Europe and the United States. In the book *The Mediterranean Diet: Wine, Pasta, Olive Oil, and a Long, Healthy Life,* Carol and Malcolm McConnell wrote: "Italians currently drink approximately ten times as much wine as Americans—that is, per capita wine consumption in Italy averages 24.2 gallons a year, compared with 2.4 gallons for Americans. But Italians have one of the lowest rates of alcoholism in the world. Indeed, the most traditionally Mediterranean countries—Greece, Italy, Spain, and Portugal—where low-alcohol table wine is traditionally consumed with meals, have the lowest rates of alcohol abuse and alcoholism in Europe."

Salud!

THE SPANISH AT TABLE

You may get the impression from this book that the Spanish eat a great deal. That is not exactly true. They spend a lot of time eating, but they don't eat a lot. Once, a young Spaniard of seventeen came to visit us in California. After a few days, we asked him what his strongest impression of America was up to that point.

"There are so many fat people," he replied at once.

His point was well taken. There are very few fat people in Spain, even though the Spanish put in a lot of time at table, beginning with a light breakfast in the morning, perhaps a roll, coffee, or chocolate, often taken standing at a bar.

For field workers, there will be a midmorning break for some kind of substantial snack, but in the city, most workers will take only a coffee break before lunch, which typically isn't until one-thirty or two in the afternoon. This is the most substantial meal of the day, both in terms of the amount of food consumed and the length of the lunch, which often lasts one and a half or two hours. There has been a ripple of a movement in Spain to have shorter "American-style" lunches, then back to work, but it hasn't made much headway.

The typical lunch break is from one o'clock until four o'clock or five o'clock. Stores and shops are closed, offices are closed or on skeleton staff. Business resumes from four or five o'clock until seven or eight o'clock, followed by tapas and dinner at ten or eleven at night. If dinner is at home, it is very light, perhaps no more than an extended tapas or a bowl of soup and bread. If one is dining out, dinner is a more elaborate affair of several courses, lasting until well past midnight.

THE REGIONS

While following the vine's season through Spain, we will also explore the regions of Spain. As we have seen, geographical features have kept the separate areas of Spain largely isolated until very recently. Added to the geographical isolation are political and linguistic differences—both ancient and modern—which have created a fierce regional pride. As we move through each of these regions, we will look in detail at the wines and food, but perhaps a hasty overview—as the rabbit runs—might be in order. Remember, this is a knife, fork, and wineglass tour.

We begin in Andalusia in southern Spain, where the Moorish influence is the strongest. There, a hasty traveler will find the Spain of Hollywood, of Gypsy dancers and handsome men and women on horseback; it is the Spain that probably comes the nearest to the media image of Spain with its bullfights, white towns, towering castles, and fountain-filled, tiled Moorish fantasy palaces. Oddly enough, it's all true. Behind this romantic, picture-postcard image of Andaluz, you can hear the Gypsy guitars, the wild staccato Gypsy clapping. You can see the beautiful horses, the bulls charging to their doom across the sands of the arena. It *is* a picture postcard, but it is also one of Spain's poorest regions. The sons and daughters of Andaluz families can often be found in Madrid or Barcelona, working in shops or factories. But they take Andalusia with them

The only region in Spain poorer than Andalusia is Extremadura, the land of the *conquistadores*. It's a harsh, unforgiving land of jagged mountain ranges and high meadows filled with cork trees and ubiquitous menacing storks. Extremadura lies between Madrid and the Portuguese border, an ancient battlefield, fought over for centuries by Christians and Moors; there is a certain lean grimness about the place that can be off-putting to the casual visitor. Although it is not a popular tourist destination (indeed, it is one of the most undervisited areas of Spain), for some there is a strange fascination about Extremadura. It is the mystic center of the hispanidad, the panhispanism that links Spain with Central and South America. This stark sheep and stork country invites us to view life under the eye of eternity.

La Mancha, the heart of the great central plateau of Spain, has the same brooding intensity as Extremadura, but it is somewhat easier. Life is lived not quite so near the bone. The climate can be as harsh as Extremadura's, but there is the occasional flash of Andaluz gaiety, laughter in the teeth of despair. It is difficult to travel in La Mancha and not think of Don Quixote, of past glories. Nothing wrong with that at all; it's a fairly pleasant occupation, perhaps while sitting in a rare patch of shade in a small pueblo plaza, and having a glass of the area's light red wine with a plate of olives and a slice of the famed *manchego* cheese. La Mancha can be puzzling, hard to get a handle on. It seems to be all cattle, sheep, and vines; a flat landscape fitfully punctuated by bits of village, then, suddenly, one looks up and there is Toledo, maybe wrapped in cloud as El Greco painted it or maybe just gleaming in sunlight. Toledo—about which more later on—is in some ways the spiritual heart of La Mancha, as La Mancha is the spiritual heart of Spain. Toledo has, like Florence, that rare urban ability to absorb uncounted tourists yet literally rise above it all. For all the difficulties—torrid summers and freezing winters—La Mancha repays a closer look.

In some ways, the northern region of Rioja-Navarre seems an extension of La Mancha. The high plains and long dry valleys, however, gradually give way to the rocky outlying riders of the Pyrenees. We have run right out of Moorish country across the Río Ebro. Although the Arabs occasionally raided north of the Ebro, they never really had a firm grip on this part of Spain. Rioja and Navarre (politically two distinct regions, but very similar at table) are "European" Spain, or at least seem to be. But dig a little deeper, wander out into the little hill towns outside Pamplona or the countryside around the great winemaking center of Logroño and you may fetch up in the Middle Ages. One of the great pilgrim routes of the Middle Ages, the Camino de Santiago de Compostela runs through northern Rioja, and one may still walk it today. I sometimes think of the small towns of Rioja as time machines, even if of somewhat limited scope. They are time machines especially in the food, where the traditional country fare has probably not changed since the tenth or eleventh century. Also, in Rioja one meets the Basques for the first time—people who take food with a playful seriousness.

For a closer look at these fascinating people and their cuisine, we must cross the Pyrenees into País Vasco, Basque country. There are two major Basque provinces: País Vasco, with the cities of Bilbao and San Sebastián, and Cantabria, with Santander. (A note for the purists and for my Basque friends: We're going to stick to Castilian nomenclature because we believe most readers will find it easier to deal with than the tongue-twisting Basque names.) If there was the occasional vestige of Moorish influence remaining in Rioja-Navarre, it is gone entirely here on the beaches of the Atlantic. In a certain sense, indeed, I would argue that when you cross the watershed of the Pyrenees, you leave Spain. On the south, with a few exceptions, the rivers flow toward the Mediterranean; on the north slope, toward the Atlantic. The climate changes abruptly. One could be in Wales or Ireland, it's that green—and damp. There is also a subtle change in the people. They truly become more European, a bit more abrupt; clocks suddenly become important. There are street signs everywhere and taxis whenever needed. (In contrast, taxis are hard to find in Madrid or even Barcelona.) Don't look for romance here, simply great food.

Recrossing the Pyrenees (skirting too close to the border of France for one who is a Francophobe), nip across the northern bit of Navarre, a land of pine forests, mountains, and clear trout streams that could be Colorado, except the truck stops have better food, and make a stop in Aragón. Welcome back to Spain. The Spain of castles and gaunt knights on horseback, their eyes fixed on a heavenly Virgin. You are also back in a drier land, a jumble of mountains and high plains, climbing into the Pyrenees. The flatland below looks like west Texas or eastern New Mexico, with scattered mesas rising abruptly, often topped with ancient Arab watchtowers. The city of Zaragoza on the Río Ebro is one of the underrated treasures of Spain: a modern metropolis with all the pleasing diversions of a city, yet small enough for a brisk walk-around, with outstanding restaurants and tapas bars. More later on Zaragoza.

Beyond Aragón lies Catalonia and the city of Barcelona. Catalonia is a complex region, not only culturally and gastronomically but geographically as well. From the dramatic beaches of the Costa Brava, to the high mountain passes in the north, to the rugged interior mountains that divide Catalonia from Aragón and País Valenciano and the Levante, Catalonia is an incredibly diverse land and that diversity is reflected in its people and its food and drink. We sometimes get impatient with Catalans, accusing them of not really being Spanish. Of course, they are delighted by that and cite centuries of Catalan history when it was one of the major Mediterranean powers. Perhaps, from the visitor's point of view, one great virtue of Catalonia is the marvelous cities: Barcelona is unarguably one of the most exciting cities in the world; the ancient Roman capital of Tarragona has managed to keep the past alive without making a museum of it; Lerida is a surprisingly cosmopolitan agricultural center with one of the best restaurants in Europe hiding unexpectedly in an old mansion near the rail station. The small towns and villages of Catalonia can hold one for days, peeling away layer after layer of pleasure. Yet I believe Catalonia in the end is not for the traveler who expects "Spain" in the travel-poster sense of Andalusia. Catalonia is industrial; it bustles (not as much as País Vasco, but it does bustle, there's no denying it) and it rarely looks back, or indeed sideways. The Catalans believe that they already have everything they need.

Turning to the south, follow the ancient Mediterranean coast into the "Garden of Spain," Valencia, Alicante, and Murcia, known collectively as the Levante. This is the land of orange groves, of big red wines and paella. Valencia itself is a Catalan-speaking area, but the Arabs have not left their mark in Catalonia proper, as they have in Valencia—in food, in architecture, and in the pace of life. Below Valencia, the coast curves in a gentle arc toward Africa. The Islas Baleares are just out of sight out there in the Mediterranean, and beyond them Sicily and Crete. We begin to look east and south. Europe is a cold dream somewhere in the north. In Alicante and Murcia, life begins to take on the pace of Andalusia, which borders Murcia to the west. Clocks have oddly disappeared again. You find bars with several barrels of sherry lined up, ready for tapping by barmen who keep your score with chalk marks on the wooden top. We've come full circle, and the grapes are heavy on the vine.

PART ONE

Harvest

The key to the wine in the bottle is when the grapes are picked. Although picking obviously takes place in the vineyard, it is a critical point during the winemaking process in the winery—perhaps the most critical point. There must be a fine balance in the wine grape between sugar and acids. If the sugar level of the grape is too low, the resulting wine can be thin, acidic; if it is too high, the wine will be too high in alcohol (roughly, the higher the sugar level, the higher the alcohol content) and will taste "hot" and unpleasant in the mouth. These are fairly simple equations. But then, factor in the acid, for there, too, a balance must be struck. Usually a wine high in acids is low in sugar; similarly, a wine with a high sugar level signals that the acid levels have fallen. Low-acid grapes produce a flabby, uninteresting wine, a wine without "bite."

To a large degree, sugar and acid levels are controlled by the weather. If the growing season is too hot, the grapes mature quickly, rapidly building high sugar levels—too high in relation to the lower acid levels. If the weather is too cool or rainy, the sugar levels fall and the acid levels rise too high. For the best grape balance the grower and winemaker are looking for long, slow ripening—cool weather but not too cool and certainly no rain during harvest. (Rain is a double enemy to the grape. It not only lowers the sugar level but stimulates the growth of rot and mildew.)

Balance is the key concept at harvest: harmony in the grape between sugars and acids and other elements (like tannin and fruit) and in the weather between hot and cold. Then, unless the wine is spoiled by a careless or incompetent winemaker, the result is a balanced wine, which simply means that when the wine is tasted, there is no single element that leaps out—you don't taste oak or tannin or acidity or sweetness, or even excessive fruit, you taste a harmony of all those elements.

The grapes at harvest are, of course, the product of a full season of growth. In fact, the process begins in midwinter, when the vines are a tangle of apparently dead sticks, gray and lifeless. Proper pruning of the vines in February and March leads directly to the harvest of September and October. A successful harvest also depends on the growth of the vines during the spring and summer—how were the young shoots positioned? What kind of fertilizer, if any, did the vines receive? Were they irrigated? Are they free of disease? Keep in mind that even though we are entering the year of the vine at harvest, which would appear to be the climax of the season, the season is really a round—a cycle—with each part depending on, and influencing, the following part. Where we begin is arbitrary.

Those who work the harvest are too often overlooked. The winemaker has become a superstar; he or she autographs wine labels and gives speeches before select groups, explaining this or that esoterica of the wine. Yet whether in California or Spain, there would be no wine without the people in the field, who put in ten or twelve hours a day of grinding, backbreaking labor. For the grape doesn't ripen on a forty-hour-workweek timetable—when ready, it must be picked. Here I come, ready or not.

That isn't to say that winemakers don't work hard as well. During the harvest, they probably put in a longer day than the field hands. I've known winemakers who simply put a cot and hotplate in the winery and move in for three or four weeks. Clearly, the romance of winemaking wears a bit thin at harvest time. The harvest is hard work all around, and it becomes very plain that wine is an agricultural product. Nature sets the schedule and refuses to conform to any sort of time-motion efficiency study.

We'll begin our journey into the season of the vine in Andalusia, at the sherry harvest, or *vendimia*, in early September. We begin here because the harvest season in Spain begins here, in the south, where the summers are hot and the grapes ripen early. We also begin in Andalusia because the harvest festivals there are among the best parties in the world.

We end this section in the Rioja in late October. We'll visit small towns that reek of wine, where the harvesters have watched the clouds anxiously, praying for a few more days of sunshine, sniffing the north wind in fear of rain.

ANDALUSIA

*Las niñas y las viñas difíciles
son de guardar.*
Girls and vineyards are
difficult to guard.

—OLD JEREZ PROVERB

IN FOCUS

Andalusia is one of Spain's largest regions, covering over two million acres. It is roughly the size of Portugal and stretches across the southern tier of the country from Portugal and the Atlantic on the west to the Mediterranean on the east. In the north, Andalusia reaches the plateau of La Mancha, and in the south, back to the coast, where one can catch a tantalizing glimpse of Africa. Throughout it is crossed and recrossed by mountain ranges, including the huge massif of the Sierra Nevada, with some of the highest mountains in Spain.

The region can be unbearably hot in the summer. Some of the highest temperatures ever recorded anywhere have been reached in Sevilla. In summer, follow the Spanish lead and take your walkabouts in the morning. Summer nights can also be warm, although they are more bearable. Winter temperatures are moderate, with light rainfall along the coast. In the mountains the temperatures can be quite cold, and sometimes there are brief snowstorms, but generally sweater weather prevails.

Andalusia was the site of the ancient, almost legendary, kingdom of Tartessos, centered at modern-day Sevilla. The gold and silver of Tartessos first attracted the Phoenicians and Greeks to the area. Both probably also brought vines, but the Phoenicians were already shipping wine from Cádiz by the ninth or tenth century B.C. The Phoenician town of Xera is most likely Jerez de la Frontera, today's capital of the sherry district.

After passing through the hands of the Carthaginians, Romans, and Vandals, Andalusia fell to the Moors in the famous battle of

Guadalete, near Jerez, in 711. Moorish influence is reflected everywhere in Andalusian architecture, and certainly in the cuisine.

Despite strictures in the Koran against alcohol, vineyards thrived under the Moors, and the long wine trade with England began as early as the fourteenth century under Moorish rule. Although the Moors themselves were forbidden wine, they had no objection to Christians living in their territories making it for their own use or even selling it. In either case, the Moors collected the taxes and let the Christians deal with their own God in the matter of alcohol.

Today, Andalusia is one of Spain's sixteen autonomous regions, governed by the Junta de Andalusia. However, the individual provinces of Andalusia—Almería, Cádiz, Córdoba, Granada, Jaén, Huelva, Málaga, and Sevilla—are also strongly independent, which reflects the political picture for all of Spain.

THE FOOD

The Andalusian kitchen has deep roots in basic Mediterranean (Greek and Roman) and Moorish cuisine. Visitors often come away thinking that Andalusian cooking is fairly light and delicate—despite an emphasis on frying—depending on where they've been. That is true in Jerez. In the mountains outside the major cities, however, you'll find a more basic peasant cooking—stews featuring lamb, rabbit, or fowl. And hams everywhere, especially the famous *Jabugo* hams from the mountains north of Huelva, near the border of Extremadura.

In an odd way, the very abundance of fresh seafood, fruit, and vegetables has kept Andalusian cuisine from developing the complexity that seems to be expected from a major cuisine, because the very abundance of fresh ingredients encourages a simple, uncomplicated cooking—viewed by some as lacking "weight." But this simplicity is slowly changing as Andalusian chefs learn how to keep the fresh purity of the raw ingredients while building more complex dishes. Fortunately, they are not abandoning the older ways, but combining and recombining the old with the new.

To this point, the Catalonia and Basque cuisines of the north have been Spain's major entries in the international food sweepstakes, but as Andalusian chefs gain more confidence dealing with the region's natural abundance of raw materials, we believe the regional cuisine will become more prominent.

As we've said, the roots of Andalusian cuisine are Moorish, perhaps more so than any other part of Spain. There are also strong Jewish influences, however, especially Sephardic, and there are remnants from other parts of Spain as well. But there is one characteristic of Andalusian food that is unvaried, and that is the illusion of simplicity. Perhaps one reason that people in the north of Spain dismiss the food of Andalusia and Jerez so quickly is that it appears to be more casual than it actually is.

(In other parts of Spain—particularly Catalonia—they will tell you there is no Andalusian cuisine, just as they will tell you that all Andalusians are lazy, sleep all day, and are quite happy living in caves. Spanish regionalism is a powerful thing.)

We think of fried seafood or boiled shellfish as "simple dishes." But in fact there is a baroque complexity of spices and flavorings for these types of dishes that the Andalusians call *fritos variados*.

Andalusian chefs, such as José María Solano at the Alboronia in Puerto de Santa María, a few miles from Jerez, are busily taking the seemingly simple Andalusian fare and developing a truly spectacular regional cuisine that deserves to stand as one of the major cuisines of Europe. Compare two dishes prepared by Solano at Alboronia. First, as an appetizer, we were served tiny brined anchovies on grilled, sliced baguettes, with a little top-quality olive oil just lightly drizzled over the top. It tasted delicious because the quality of the ingredients—fish, bread, olive oil, that's all—were absolutely first-rate. One of the entrées was a complex and beautifully presented dish of *pimientos de pequillo rellenos de chipirones en su tinta* (red peppers stuffed with tiny squid, also stuffed, and in their own ink). Served on a white plate, with a bit of rice on the *tinta*, the squid ink, the peppers looked as wonderful as they tasted. The red peppers were about the size of a double thumb on a large man; each contained three *chipirones*, which are very tiny squid, unfortunately not available in the United States. Each tiny squid was stuffed with finely diced ham and bits of their own tentacles. It would be feasible to substitute sliced rings of squid and chopped ham. Here, basic "peasant" ingredients were used to create a sophisticated dish.

Andalusia is also the heartland of the tapa, that small serving of food, that delicious morsel that defines a lifestyle as much as a culinary style. There is a faint and very distant relationship between "doing tapas" and "bar hopping," but bar hopping implies a serious commitment to drinking that is absent in the tapas scene.

"Doing tapas," although certainly accompanied by abundant

quantities of wine, is more about talking and eating than drinking. The wine is, perhaps, the adhesive that holds together the conversation, the friends, and the food. The primary purpose of tapas is to talk to friends, to share the gossip of the day, perhaps to discuss the latest follies of the politicians. Tapas are part of the shared communal life of the pueblo at the public level, a giggle between two good friends at a more private level. (The concept of tapas also involves that very Spanish social art form, the ability to "hang out." The Spanish are experts at hanging out, lingering for hours over a few glasses of sherry or coffees.)

The food is important, of course, but that goes without saying. An Andalusian would never even talk about the importance of food. It is as obvious as the importance of breath, of the heart beating. In fact, the quality and variety of food are so important to the Spanish, that they spend a higher percentage of their disposable income on food than any other industrial nation in the world. Food doesn't cost more in Spain than in France or Canada or Australia—the Spanish simply demand better food and a greater variety of food.

A serious evening of tapas will start at perhaps seven, a few short hours after the ending of lunch (which, remember, usually does not get under way until about two in the afternoon).

The Spaniards ordinarily follow an established route, beginning at the "local" tapas bar and moving on to several other tapas bars before dinner, which might start about eleven o'clock. The choice of where to go depends to some extent on where friends will be found and what special tapa may be on offer. Some tapas bars gain a reputation for a particular dish, and they are visited just for that; others are known for a wide selection, the kinds of places where you can settle in for the evening.

Tapas can be just about anything, but writ small. At their simplest, the tapas can be only a plate of olives, perhaps a few slices of ham, a bit of cheese, perhaps fried squid or grilled prawns. They also can be as elaborate as the cook's imagination and resources.

No one agrees about when or where the term first came into use. *Tapa* literally means a cover or a lid. The story goes that at the old coaching inns in the south of Spain, the innkeeper would have glasses of wine ready to offer travelers whose horses were being changed. The changing of horses was often a split-second affair, with one team unhitched and the other quickly put to the yoke. The innkeeper would rush the wine to the carriage in a kind of early fast-food take-out arrangement. What with all the dust, flies, and other unmentionable debris swirling around the courtyard in an unappetizing fashion, innkeepers, so it is said, began covering the wineglass with a thin slice of bread. A *tapa*, or cover.

As competition increased, some innkeepers began putting a slice of ham or cheese on the bread, as an inducement to the hungry traveler to urge the coachman to take a few minutes longer so they could order another glass of wine.

In many bars today, the basic tapas are still free. In fact, you can get some curious looks from bartenders if you turn down the offer of a plate of olives, especially in the countryside or the more traditional bars of Madrid or Sevilla. Remember that in Spain it is rare for anyone to drink without a bite of something.

Like the flamenco, the friendly pursuit of tapas has spread from the south all across Spain. Tapas bars can now be found in San Sebastián in the Basque country, in Catalonia, in Valencia, everywhere. In Barcelona the tapas bar is combined with that delightful Catalan institution the *xampanyería*. Instead of sherry, one can sample glasses of *cava* (the Spanish name for sparkling wine) with the tapas.

In Andalusia, Sevilla is especially famous for its tapas. Wander endlessly through the streets of the Old Quarter near the cathedral and beyond, sampling a bit of this and a bit of that. In most of the tapas bars in Sevilla, the tab is still marked with a piece of chalk on the surface of the bar, or sometimes it is just kept in the barman's head.

Each part of Sevilla has its own characteristic tapas bars with special dishes that are just a little different—or so the barman will say—from the place just a few blocks away.

There are countless tapas bars in the old Santa Cruz quarter near the Alcázar, the cathedral, and the Giralda, that fantastic Arab tower that gazes calmly across the Plaza del Triunfo at the Alcázar.

At some of the larger establishments, there will be two bars, one serving kitchen tapas (that is, tapas that require some preparation and are served warm) and a smaller bar serving cold tapas that require no last-minute preparation. Oddly enough, the best sherry can generally be found at the smaller bar, perhaps because the customers go there to concentrate on the wine, with the food secondary.

Some typical Sevilla tapas include *la pringa*, which is a stew of vegetables, salt pork, pork, and sausage. When the stew is finished, the meats are taken out and shredded, then stuffed into partially cooked rolls. The rolls are then baked until done. *Espinacas con garbanzos* is a spinach and refried-chick-pea tapa topped or garnished with a paste made of garlic, fried bread, vinegar, and salt. It is sometimes served with a dash of paprika. *La punta* is beef tenderloin that has been cooked in a sauce or sliced into thin fillets and grilled. *Pavias* are strips of salt cod that have been well soaked, then dipped into a batter of flour, saffron, baking soda, salt, and hot water and fried in olive oil until crisp. There are two different snail tapas, *caracoles* and *cabrillas*. The *caracoles* are very small and the *cabrillas* are somewhat larger. Both are cooked in sauce with various spices.

There are also dozens of tapas bars along the Guadalquivir—the river from which Columbus began his first voyage to America—especially along Betis street, which runs along the banks of the river between the San Telmo and Isabel II bridges. The street is filled with locals until far past midnight. Los Chorritos, which overlooks the river at number 28, is open only in the summer and serves only grilled sardines. The Primera del Puente at number 66 is famous for seafood tapas. Bar Diego at number 28 is the best place to sample the *espinacas con garbanzos* tapa.

In the heart of the Santa Cruz quarter the Casa Román in the Plaza de los Venerables Sacerdotes is a good stop for ham, while Alfaro in Plaza Alfaro is famous for its tortilla, a kind of hard Spanish omelet served hot or cold.

A dipping sauce, called *mojo-picón*, is slightly *picante*. It can be used on almost anything and is especially good with grilled pork. *Mojo-picón* is made of oregano, cumin, garlic, vinegar, water, salt, cayenne, pimiento, onions, and garlic.

These—and hundreds of other tapas—can be found all over Andalusia, not just in Sevilla. So when the crowds in Sevilla become overwhelming (as they can, at least during the summer tourist crush), remember that the road from Jerez to Sevilla leads back to Jerez.

One of the best of the tapas bars in Jerez is Tendido 6 (so named because it is just opposite the Gate 6 entrance to the Plaza de Toros). The regular lunch and dinner menus are also quite good. The service is friendly, relaxed, and welcoming. There are several good regional dishes on the menu. The restaurant looks the way a Spanish restaurant should—gleaming dark woods, brightly painted tiles. And in a rare meeting of decor and cuisine, the food also tastes the way it should taste.

If you have the misfortune to arrive in Jerez and find the older downtown hotels filled, you may end up as we once did at one of those modern establishments that inexplicably grow on the outskirts of cities. They look and feel exactly the same, whether they are in Munich, Rome, Honolulu, or Jerez. There is the same swimming pool, the same mattress, the same television, the same bar, and often it seems even the same somehow sad conventioners.

There is such a hotel (which shall go unnamed) on the Avenida Alcalde Alvaro Domecq, which is the old road to Sevilla. It is less than a mile from the central area, even closer to the Plaza de Toros. Just across the Alcalde is Las Botas, a tapas bar favored by the locals. The setting is unlikely, on the ground floor of a modern apartment building, but since we were directed there by a native *jerezano* who works at Harvey's sherry bodega, we settled in at an outside table anyway. To be sure you are at the right place, look for a very fat dog, who would be even fatter if someone didn't occasionally throw him a ball, which he is glad to chase all night long through the gardens of the apartment building. One of the tapas we had there, which we did not share with the dog, was a simple grilled squid (*sepia a la plancha*) superbly prepared with chopped garlic, parsley, and olive oil. Shrimp (*gambas*) can be prepared in much the same way. In Café Tango, our Spanish tapas bar in California, *gambas a la plancha* was always a big hit.

Obviously, almost everything you would want, as a cook or as an eater, is available in Andalusia. It's the only region of Spain with both an Atlantic and a Mediterranean coast. The seafood and shellfish are incredible and plentiful.

There are olives, avocados, citrus fruits, nuts, fresh berries, and vegetables of all sorts. Parts of Andalusia actually grow three crops of garden produce a year. The area around Huelva in western Andalusia, near Portugal, exports fresh vegetables year-round to northern Europe.

There is lamb, goat, some excellent beef, and, of course, rabbit and partridge, which are now raised commercially. Game—venison, pigeon, partridge, boar, and wild rabbit—plays an important part at the Andalusian table.

At the risk of belaboring an earlier point, all this richness would mean little if it were not properly spent—at the table. Luckily, the Andalusians do distinguish themselves in the kitchen and are beginning to gain international recognition for their foods.

Grazalema, a little-visited white town in the mountains on the seldom-traveled back road between Arcos de la Frontera and Ronda.

Stopped for early-morning coffee—with just a splash of brandy—at the parador in Arcos, sitting on the terrace watching the hawks drift down the deep canyon below, we are planning a late lunch in Ronda. A city built on an abyss, a stunning town.

The road, highway number 344 on some maps, plunges up and down through range after range of mountains. Why is wilderness so surprising in Spain? It shouldn't be. Spain has more wild areas than any country in Europe, save Scandinavia. There are wolves and bears in the north. In the white towns of the south, down many twisting streets or surprised in flower-filled plazas, there are lions. White stone lions flank the entry to a private courtyard in a street narrow enough for a passerby to touch both walls at the same time. At the end of a street filled with the scent of spring geraniums, a small square of light opens onto a plaza and beyond the plaza a range of jagged mountains falls away toward Ronda.

But Ronda had to wait for an unexpected stop in Grazalema, which was celebrating the Feast of Saint Carmen. The saint had taken her annual outing by donkey cart to the edge of town, just to the first fields, then back through the main plaza to the church. There was the usual wild Spanish confusion of horses, children, guitar players, dogs, and fireworks.

But in a small island of stillness, only yards behind the saint herself, walked a woman dressed in white. Her hair was braided high on her head, and from the braided coils long stalks of wheat and other grains spilled out. There were flowers woven into the hem of her dress and across her breast. Here was a goddess more familiar with the streets of Grazalema than the Christian upstart, Carmen.

After the sainted Carmen entered the church, the corn goddess turned away to a nearby bar, El Postigo, where we joined her for sherry and a few bites of loma manteca, a Spanish country dish that unfortunately will not translate into the modern American kitchen. (Think of sheep intestines and lard. Think no further.)

As the corn goddess sipped her sherry we exchanged news of the day with one of her acolytes, a wiry man who could have passed for a not-too-threatening bandit. He identified himself as a "pig-sticker" who traveled all about Andalusia and up into Extremadura during the butchering season. (Ordering the loma manteca was his idea.)

After another half-bottle of fino, he joined two friends at the bar, leaving the goddess to explain that he was an hombre loco. The three men at the bar stood in a semicircle, seemingly involved in a quiet conversation. Without warning, one of the men—the oldest, *with many gaps in his mouth*—*began singing. Singing the harsh, full-throated, deep song of the south of Spain.*

The words pushed and twisted from his body, throat muscles straining rigid. The man across from him answered in song, each word drawn out, syllables repeated, stretched seemingly to the breaking point of the human voice, the harsh tones rising and falling like an ancient, wordless prayer against the night. Then the third man came in and the trio began trading phrases, pushing and tugging at the rhythm.

We were utterly unprepared. This had to be the beginning of poetry, this rich, unrehearsed ritual of vocal give-and-take. Around the bar people continued to eat and drink, to order wine and talk to their friends, but the tone was quiet, with many glances at the trio of singers.

While the men were still singing, a modern sevillana band began playing in the square outside. The amplified music broke into El Postigo, jarring, unwelcome, like a fingernail drawn across a blackboard. The three singers, only moments before a weather-worn frieze on an ancient vase, returned to their wine and their loma manteca. The corn goddess got up and walked into the night and was seen no more.

THE WINES

A good sherris sack hath a twofold operation in it. It ascends me into the brain; dries me there all the foolish and dull and crudy vapours which environ it; makes it apprehensive, quick, forgetive, full of nimble, fiery and delectable shapes; which delivered o'er to the voice, the tongue, which is the birth, becomes excellent wit. The second property of your excellent sherris is the warming of the blood. . . . If I had a thousand sons, the first human principle I would teach them should be to forswear thin potations and to addict themselves to sherris sack.

—SIR JOHN FALSTAFF,
King Henry the Fourth, Part II,
Shakespeare

Sir John was in his prime near the end of the sixteenth century, but sherry is still the best-known wine of Andalusia, and certainly the best-known in the international wine market. Especially if Montilla and Málaga are included. Neither is really quite the same thing as sherry, although they are made in a like fashion.

There are also excellent local table wines all over Andalusia. First-rate wines from high-altitude vineyards boast a surprising array of grape varieties for a hot-weather area; we unexpectedly encountered Riesling, Cabernet Sauvignon, and even Pinot Noir. There is, for example, a flourishing table wine industry around Arcos de la Frontera, a few miles east of Jerez de la Frontera, started by French winemakers who settled in Spain during the French-Algerian war and later years.

But sherry is the signature wine of Andalusia. It's a pity that good, fresh sherry is so hard to find in the United States. We need some basic lessons in sherry drinking. Somehow, we have learned only half of the sherry equation—the sweet half.

There are really only two kinds of sherry—*fino* and *oloroso*. Everything else is simply a variation within those categories, even the sweet sherries. The light—and dry—*finos* and *manzanillas* are surely the most refreshing wines in the world. The intriguing nutty aroma mingles with slight scents of damp, cool earth; there is something green, almost vegetal in the nose of a good *fino* sherry, reminiscent of a fresh garden on a hot afternoon. *Fino* (or *manzanilla*) also gives an impression of coolness on the palate, followed by the tangy, spicy surprise of the finish, which lingers for almost a full minute after the first swallow. It's a wine of great complexity and a wine that matches very well with a number of foods.

Well-made sweet sherries—all variations on *oloroso*—are magnificent dessert wines, subtle and complex with, we believe, a greater range of flavors than any other dessert wine.

Perhaps to understand the wine in the glass well, it is necessary to understand how it is made. And the "how" of sherry is quite different from the "how" of table wines. There are two key elements to understanding sherry. The first element is the fermentation process, which is quite different from the process followed for table wines. The second key element is the blending process.

One of the best guides to unraveling the tangled mysteries of how sherry is made was drawn for us with chalk one morning on the side of a stainless steel tank by José Ignacio Domecq, Jr., of the famous sherry family in a Domecq bodega in Jerez.

After the grapes are picked and crushed, they go through a rapid fermentation in a stainless steel tank (exactly like the one Domecq was using as a chalk board, tracing the mysterious development of sherry). For there is still a bit of mystery remaining at the heart of sherry, even in these days of scientific winemaking, and it centers on the yeast bloom called *flor*, meaning "flower" in Spanish. The thin white film that grows over the sherry is not a flower, however, but a film of yeast cells.

Following fermentation, which lasts up to six weeks, the sherry *flor* develops first in small yellowish patches. Growing gradually, within three to four weeks it covers the whole surface of the wine in the sherry butt. This first (and strongest) bloom lasts about six months.

The growth of *flor* on sherry is much better understood than before. It is now believed to be a yeast "bloom" found in the final phase of fermentation. The *flor* is apparently related to a wild strain of the *saccharomyces*, a yeast that is associated worldwide with winemaking in the conversion of grape sugars into alcohol. This particular strain or bloom is seen in only two other places, however—the Jura region of France and the Russian Caucasus.

The *flor* bloom occurs spontaneously, so it is obviously a wild yeast strain. Despite many efforts by winemakers in California, Australia, and elsewhere, no one has been able to match it. In fact, *flor* taken from Spain to California mutates in a few generations and becomes an entirely different yeast, if it lives at all.

The process by which wine is made is pretty much the same all over the world, allowing for variations in technical skills and winemaking inclinations. Sherry is something else altogether. Unlike other wines, sherry is stored in partially filled barrels, in the presence of oxygen. For all other wines, oxygen is regarded as the enemy, and it will, in a very short time, turn the wine to vinegar.

Although sherry is intentionally a bit oxidized, the *flor* furnishes some protection. Unlike the yeasts that eat sugar and turn it into alcohol (the normal fermentation process), the *flor* eats oxygen, thus protecting the wine from harm in most cases. There are always a few butts that do begin to turn to vinegar; these are rushed from the sherry storage area of the bodega to the vinegar house—and very good vinegar they make.

Although fermenting *fino* sherry is never without some amount of *flor*, the *flor* is most active in the spring and again in September and October, and least active during summer and winter, the hottest and coldest times of the year. The *flor* thrives at temperatures between 65 and 75 degrees Fahrenheit and at a humidity of about 60 percent. During hot weather the floors of the bodegas are hosed down several times a week (depending on the temperature) to cool the air and create the proper humidity.

On the coast, at Sanlúcar de Barrameda and Puerto de Santa María, the temperature is more moderate and stable year-round and the *flor* bloom is thicker and more constant than in the more extreme temperatures of Jerez.

In the past, the *flor* even had a hand (or perhaps a pseudopod) in the selection of the kind of sherry each butt would produce. The cellar foreman would check the newly fermented butts of wine for *flor*. Those with a strong growth of *flor* were likely to be classified as *finos*; those with little or no *flor* would probably become *oloroso* or, in rare cases, *palos cortados*. The *palo cortado*, although often given a category of its own by sherry experts, is really a subdivision of *oloroso*. It has the flavor characteristics of an *oloroso*, but the aroma is as penetrating as an *amontillado*—a kind of *fino*.

This system of letting nature take its course is—for better or worse —no longer followed. Now, in most cases, the difference is simply that *fino* is made from free-run juice (that is, the grapes are crushed but not pressed) and the *oloroso* from the first and second pressing —which certainly simplifies the winemaking process.

In the case of *oloroso*, brandy is added as soon as fermentation is completed, stopping the growth of the *flor*, since no yeast can live if the alcohol content is above 16.4 percent. It is the addition of brandy, at least in the beginning, that gives *oloroso* that typical rounded feeling in the mouth. As *oloroso* ages (and it ages magnificently), it becomes truly mouth-filling and complex, with a very long finish.

Sometimes, of course, those wines preselected as *finos*, and therefore apparently living in a state of grace, stubbornly refuse to grow a decent crop of *flor*. These will eventually become *olorosos*.

At this stage, the sherry is dry, whether *fino* or *oloroso*. Sweet sherries are made by the addition of Moscatel or Pedro Ximénez juice to an *oloroso* base wine, with the amount of sweet juice controlling the sweetness of the sherry. Some sweet sherries are of very high quality and are some of the most long-lived wines in the world, but others, especially the almost generic cream sherries, are made from low-quality base wines, heavily sweetened to mask the wretchedness of the wine.

An *amontillado* is a kind of *fino* sherry that has been left in the cask to deepen in color. It takes on some of the character of an *oloroso*, because of the longer aging and oxidation, but retains much of the fresh quality of *fino* in the aroma. In its natural state, *amontillado* is always dry, but too often it is sweetened, especially for the export market.

Manzanilla, also a kind of *fino*, is made only at Sanlúcar de Barrameda. It is made exactly like *fino*, and quite inexplicably, if the young manzanilla is taken to Jerez to mature, it will take on the character of a pure *fino*.

On the palate, *manzanilla* differs from *fino* by having a faintly bitter, almost salty taste. It is usually lighter in color than fino, and the alcohol content is somewhat lower before the addition of brandy. A fresh *manzanilla* with a plate of simple fried fish at a beachfront restaurant in Sanlúcar is one of life's great delights. There are some traditionalists who claim that the peculiar tangy flavor of *manzanilla* is a result of the sea air at Sanlúcar. Anything is possible. It could also be, though, a peculiarity of the particular *flor* at Sanlúcar.

Freshness is essential for any *fino*, even though it is fortified at bottling to reach between 15.5 and 17 percent alcohol. Unlike other fortified wines (port or the sweet sherries), however, it fades quickly after opening and within twenty-four hours loses much of its charm and flavor.

If you do not intend to finish a standard bottle within a day, it is far better to buy half bottles. This is, perhaps, one of the reasons for the failure of sherry to capture more palate share of the American wine market, because as *fino* fades, the bitter quality of the wine becomes dominant and can be downright unpleasant.

In fact, *fino* begins to change and coarsen as soon as it is removed from the *solera* and bottled. We pity the consumer who buys a bottle of *fino* that has been sitting on a wine merchant's shelf for a year or more. The more reputable shippers—with Lustau in the lead—are beginning to date *fino* bottles. Look for the date of bottling somewhere on the paper foil around the cork.

Once the future of the sherry has been decided, the butts of new wine are moved into the bodegas. Here we truly enter the cathedral, the holy of holies, and the puzzling rituals and mysteries of the *solera* system.

Begin with the bodegas themselves. Although the interiors of the bodegas have often been compared to cathedrals, the exteriors look more utilitarian than sacred, more like a very well constructed storage building. That, of course, is exactly what they are. Since the total sherry stock hovers between 180 million and 200 million gallons of wine, concentrated in the hands of barely a dozen major houses in Jerez and Sanlúcar, the storage space has to be enormous. Each sherry butt contains roughly 500 gallons of wine, or about 400,000 casks of sherry. And that doesn't even take into account the brandy casks, which probably equal the sherry casks. It is a comforting thought.

Inside the bodega, with its high ceilings, high windows—usually of stained glass—the cathedral comparison is valid. Not much seems to be happening in the bodegas, just that rather arcane process called the *solera* system humming quietly along. On a minor and nameless hill on the outskirts of Jerez is the Domecq bodega called La Mezquita, or the mosque. It is based roughly on the great mosque in Córdoba, except in Córdoba the Christians ripped out the center of the mosque to make a church. As one stands among the 40,000 butts of sherry and brandy at Domecq's Mezquita, the great pillars stretch away in all directions, creating a seeming maze broken into intricate geometric patterns across the high white-washed walls and ceilings.

The patterns are broken only by draperies of a fine mold that in the oldest bodegas, such as Domecq's El Molino a few kilometers away, covers walls, ceilings, and barrels. The Spanish leave the mold alone, believing that it encourages the growth of the *flor*.

The *solera* year coincides roughly with the beginning of harvest. Each August 31, the regulatory agency that controls sherry production, El Consejo, determines the maximum amount of sherry that can be taken from the bodega. The number naturally changes somewhat, but in the late eighties it was about 29 percent.

To a certain extent, as far as wine quality is concerned, the *solera* system has freed sherry producers from the dangers of a poor harvest. In the case of a short harvest the producers would simply have to cut production, taking less wine from each *criadera*, so the supply would always be in balance.

It is also necessary to resist the temptation to push the *solera* to produce more sherry to meet increased demand. This happened in the 1960s, when there was an unexpected worldwide increase in the demand for sherry. A number of producers depleted stocks, bottling sherry that was not yet ready for the market. Today, bottlings are much more tightly controlled.

The *solera* system was established in the nineteenth century, partly in an effort to achieve a more uniform quality of wine. The system consists of several tiers of casks, each filled with a similar wine. The casks with the oldest wine are those on the ground. In fact, the word *solera* is probably derived from *suelo*, or ground. Resting on top of the lowest cask are the various tiers, known as *criaderas*. Each tier contains wine that is younger than the tier just below. The tier just above the oldest, or bottom, tier is the first *criadera*, followed by the second, third, fourth, and so on.

The number of *criaderas* varies somewhat with the different producers, but since the minimum aging period is three years, the *criadera* would have to be a maximum of four tiers high, the most weight that the bottom barrel can withstand. The new wines, naturally, would be at the top. If a producer wanted a longer *solera*, the younger wines would be stored in a separate area.

What happens is fairly simple and again varies somewhat from producer to producer. But for a common *fino*, a maximum of one-third of the wine in the bottom or the oldest tier of the criadera would be drawn out and bottled. Then, from each *criadera* one-third of the wine is drawn off—very carefully so as to disturb the *flor* as little as possible—and added to the *criadera* below. In practice, this is done four or five times a year, the one-third withdrawal being the total for the year, not each withdrawal. As the younger wines are blended with the older wines, each successive blend takes on the character of the lowest *criadera*, so that there is a uniformity of style and character. And that is the heart of the sherry mystery!

THE VINEYARDS

The vineyards near Jerez de la Frontera, the center of the sherry triangle, are as dazzling white as the famous "white towns" of the Andalusian coast a few kilometers away. Long ago, the area was covered by a shallow sea, which has left the soil about 40 percent chalk, as white as the cliffs of Dover but not so vertical. A walk through the vineyards may turn up ancient seashells that don't look a great deal different from those that will turn up a bit later on your plate at lunch. (You might even flush a partridge. If the season is right and luck is with you, that will be dinner.) But whatever you have for lunch or dinner, it's a safe bet that the wine will be sherry.

That vast sweep of vineyards to the north and east of Jerez is generally considered to be the most important—in both size and quality—of the sherry district. Of the 46,000 total acres of grapes in the area, about 30,000 are in the Jerez district. The view from the Domecq vineyards, which lie in the center of the area, is down toward the coast and Sanlúcar, row after row of vines, soft green waves breaking over the dazzling white soil.

Over 95 percent of the vines are planted to the Palomino grape, although only two hundred years ago there were literally hundreds of varieties of grapes grown near Jerez. No doubt many dated back to classical times. Even as late as the 1870s there were still about forty varieties under cultivation, but by the end of the nineteenth century, the Palomino had become dominant, mainly because of the efforts of the Domecq family. They took the lead in the planting of quality grapes and the general upgrading of the vineyards in Jerez.

It seems that nothing is ever simple in Spain, from the rabbit tracks of its history to its tumbled geography. This certainly holds true when it comes to the Palomino grape, which is found all over southern Spain (including the Canary Islands). The several cousins of the present Palomino include the Palomino de Jerez, which is believed to have been introduced by the Moors, possibly as a table grape. Other authorities trace the fruit to Oriental origins and introduction by the Phoenicians.

The current Palomino is called Palomino Fino. The vines have a higher yield and are more resistant to disease, and the sherry producers believe the grape makes a base wine more suitable for sherry production, because it is fairly neutral in taste and can be easily manipulated.

The grape is named after Fernán Yanes Palomino, a knight in the service of King Alfonso X in the thirteenth century. A Palomino family still exists in Jerez and they are (or until very recently were) in the sherry business. The family firm, Palomino y Vergara, was part of the giant Rumasa operation in the 1960s, and it was finally taken over by Harvey's in 1985, after the Spanish government broke up Rumasa.

One of the common names for the Palomino is Tempranilla, interesting because the Tempranillo—a red grape—is the chief grape of Rioja. (There are those who claim the Tempranillo is actually a clone of the famous Pinot Noir of Burgundy, brought to Rioja by pilgrims visiting Santiago de Compostela in Rioja.)

The Pedro Ximénez and the Moscatel grapes were once much

more important in the blending of sherry than they are at present. Now, between them, they account for less than 5 percent of planted vineyards. The Moscatel is an early-ripening grape that produces a sweet wine mostly used for sweetening other sherries, although it makes an excellent dessert wine on its own. In the United States, Lustau imports a delicious Moscatel, which improves with bottle age. (Also fantastic poured over raisin ice cream!)

Pedro Ximénez makes an intensely sweet dessert wine, although it is rarely bottled as such. Most of the wine made from Pedro Ximénez goes into dessert sherry blends and brandies.

There is a Spanish legend connected with the name involving a German soldier named Pieter Siemenez who was in the army of Charles V (Charles I of Spain). The story goes that for unexplained reasons the soldier brought a vine cutting with him from the banks of the Rhine, although that seems a rather odd bit of baggage for a sixteenth-century soldier to be carrying around. This has led some to claim that the Pedro Ximénez is actually a Riesling.

The Pedro Ximénez and the Moscatel are picked earlier than the Palomino and are sometimes still dried on grass mats spread in the sun. (These days, however, the grapes are likely to be covered with plastic sheets.) This raisins the grapes, intensifying the sweetness as the water content is dried out.

Jerez is an appropriate point to enter the circular path of the Spanish vineyard season. The first Spanish wines to enter the international market originated in these seemingly whitewashed vineyards at least three thousand years ago, when Phoenician traders sold the wines of Jerez throughout the Mediterranean.

SPANISH DAYS

The harvest begins—unofficially—near the end of August or beginning of September. The fierce summer sun of Andalusia reflects back from the white soil, encoding the grapes with the same intensity that so delighted the hot-blooded Englishman Sir John Falstaff and thousands of other cold-climate creatures—before and since— who yearn for the warmth of the sun.

Centuries later the English turn to sherry as a warming, friendly drink. The drink still appeals, as Gerald Asher wrote in his thoughtful book of essays *On Wine*, to "those who lived in the shires of the south and west of England and on the wide flat farms of East Anglia, a region where I spent my entire childhood without ever once feeling warm . . . An invitation to 'come over for a glass of sherry' promises a relaxed communion of friends, comfortable shoes, an old sweater . . ."

The story is told in Jerez that the chief impulse behind Sir Francis Drake's daring sixteenth-century raid on the port of Sanlúcar (where he seized 2,900 pipes of sherry) was simply to take home enough sherry to keep Queen Elizabeth in good spirits. In fact, there was a definite upswing in the sherry trade following Drake's raid. (The pipe is a traditional measure of wine—usually sherry, port, or Madeira— little used now. The exact amount varied, but the pipe of Drake's time contained roughly 130 to 140 U.S. gallons.)

Whatever, the actual date of the picking of the grapes, the harvest celebration follows on the first or second weekend in September with the *Fiesta de la Vendimia*. The images of this festival are the pictures of Spain that most North Americans cherish. The scene could be staged by Hollywood in a lavish mood. The celebration usually outlasts the weekend and continues well into the week, with bullfights, flamenco, and the *sevillana*, a beautiful and very old dance with a more controlled grace than the fiery, emotional flamenco.

The *sevillana* is based on court dances of the eighteenth-century, probably originating hundreds of years before in La Mancha-Castile. The rhythmic ⅜-time dance was known as a *seguidilla manchega* at court and was one of several castanet dances. It was adopted with such gusto by the citizens of Sevilla—becoming a still-popular street dance—that it now takes the name of that Andalusian city.

The dance, which in the last few years has become all the thing among the trendy in Madrid, takes many forms. Traditionally, the dancers were accompanied by one or two guitars and the lyrics of the old songs that usually extolled the virtues and beauty of a woman (or a bull) or praised the wonders of the city of Sevilla. The modern dance has become a bit more energetic. There are often mariachi-like brass bands, pianos, congo drums, or even a full symphony orchestra.

And the lyrics have proved just as catholic as the music. In fact, Garvey, one of the major sherry houses of Jerez de la Frontera, has released a series of recordings of *sevillanas*, several of which sing the praises of Garvey's San Patricio sherry. The company frequently holds *sevillana* dances in the shaded courtyard of its bodega in Jerez —surely a practical linkage of wine and art.

Whatever the lyrics or the instruments, the dance music consists basically of a sequence of four usually brief songs, or *coplas*, one following the other, each with the same tempo (ranging from slow to very, very fast) and the same melody, but with different lyrics. There is really no traditional costume for the *sevillanas*. People wear whatever makes them look or feel good, so dancers in period costume can be seen sharing the floor with punk rockers and barefoot Gypsies.

It is a graceful affair with a lot of body movement, which seems to be more important than just where to put your feet. The dance feels slightly like the free-form rock dancing of the 1960s in that it does seem possible, at least after a few glasses of sherry, for novices to take part, even if you haven't the slightest idea of where your partner is leading you. You can only hope for the best.

But never mind. It's the harvest festival, and wherever your partner leads you there is sure to be good food and drink. And parades. During the festival, the parades seem endless, but the only one that really counts features the festival queen, a title that is taken very seriously in Jerez. It's a toss-up whether the horses, the women, or the men are more beautiful, perhaps depending on either an individual's inclinations or the luck of the season.

The festivities start early in the morning, virtually stepping on the heels of the dancing, eating, and drinking of the previous evening. But given enough Spanish coffee (and I will insist that there is no better coffee anywhere in the world than in Spain) one can begin to function. Don't fondly imagine that there will be time for a siesta later. Not during the festival week.

By perhaps 10 A.M., the streets of Jerez are filled. Again, Hollywood comes to mind. But if it is a movie set, it is a well-appointed movie set. The dresses of the women, the elaborate costumes of the men, the horses (everywhere the fantastic horses of Andalusia) . . . It is necessary to keep a firm grip on an easily identified reality, yet by all means follow the crowds as they move toward the Plaza de Toros, where the bullfight, the *corrida*, begins at five in the afternoon—and bullfights *always* start on time! Even if the king is expected and he is late, the bull will not wait. (The bull would not have waited for Ernest Hemingway.) The bullfights at Jerez are among the best in Spain, but during the harvest festival they are particularly outstanding. Most of the fighting bulls of Spain come from the area around Jerez, so the local fans know a good bull, and where the bulls are good, the best bullfighters follow. (The Domecq family have their own bullring on one of their farms, and members of the family occasionally take a turn in the ring themselves.) Before and after the bullfight, the bars around the Plaza de Toros are crowded with *jerezanos* drinking sherry, eating tapas, carrying on the endless conversations that beguile the Spanish hours.

The set piece of the wine festival is the blessing of the grapes on the steps of the sixteenth-century Collegiate Church of San Salvador by the Bishop of Cádiz. The harvest queen (accompanied by swirling clouds of maids of honor dressed in white with blue silk scarves) dumps a basket of grapes into an old press, where barefoot civic dignitaries and various other important folk, all with *Don* preceding their name, ritually stomp them. Then, as if to say "Hollywood, take that," huge clouds of white doves are released. The harvest has officially begun, and all the church bells in the city start ringing.

The juice from this blessed stomping is put in a wooden cask and taken to that year's bodega of choice on the traditional donkey cart. Each year the first cask is dedicated to a different country or city outside of Spain. During the following year, envoys from Jerez may take samples of the cask to various officials in the honored city.

There is also a nonstop flamenco festival, which unfortunately disappoints. Since flamenco has become so popular, many of the shows are slapdash tourist affairs where the dancers hardly work up a sweat.

Once in a while, however, lightning strikes. It is necessary to be at the right time at the right place, as we were about three o'clock one morning in a small bar near the bullring in Jerez. It seemed that the very long day was about to end with the prospect of a few hours of sleep. Suddenly, the doors burst open and a Gypsy flamenco troupe entered. These were not the costumed marvels one sees in special stage shows put on for the tourists in Sevilla or Madrid. Someone said they had just come into town from El Bosque, a small mountain village in the Sierra Ronda east of Jerez.

There was an instant revival of flagging spirits. The barman set up a long row of half-bottles of *fino* sherry, and the dancing began. The *puro* flamenco is an ancient art. Some say it goes back to the Greeks and is related to a Greek sacred dance of preclassical Athens. In this version, elements were added to the dance by the Moors and it was brought to perfection by the Gypsies. Most agree that neither the dance nor the "deep song" that accompanies flamenco originated with the Gypsies, but there is no hard evidence one way or the other.

In *puro* flamenco, the guitar often follows the lead of the dancer.

It all begins in silence. The dancer, or dancers, stand stark still, looking at nothing, usually not acknowledging the shouts or applause from the audience; that night, the music began when a tall, rather fierce-looking Gypsy woman raised her arms, castanets clicking. As the guitar rhythm cut in, her feet began driving at the floor, not moving from the space, and we were off for three hours of music, interrupted only for short breaks of *fino* and food for the dancers. At dawn, a grizzled old barefoot Gypsy man, who had been playing the guitar practically nonstop for three hours, passed through the crowd, hat in hand. Those gathered soon filled it to overflowing with pesetas.

We wandered off for a few hours' sleep before the festival continued. It is a good thing that grapes are not one of the crops that achieve three harvests a year in Andalusia. Mere humans could not endure such intense joy.

After a minimum amount of sleep, one begins to daydream of finding a small space to practice a few flamenco steps of one's own. The important thing is to stomp your feet really hard, as if trying to drown out the guitar music. A friend of ours, having just listened to a taped performance of an onstage flamenco festival, said it sounded exactly like a lot of people wearing wooden shoes moving boxes around upstairs, after having first taken up the carpet.

With all that stomping, you will be ready for another snack. There is a wonderful workingman's tapas bar, just off the Plaza Arenal, called Bar Juanito. Almost every inch of wall space is filled with pictures of bulls and bullfighters or other famous people (Ava Gardner, Frank Sinatra, and Ernest Hemingway) posing with bullfighters. The tables spill out into the narrow street (mercifully closed to cars like many streets in the older sections of Spanish towns), and everywhere there are children darting in and out, whole tides of them washing from one side of the narrow street to the other, ebbing briefly around a family table, where they quickly snatch a bite or two of food, a glass of juice or cola.

The dishes here are not refined; they have that intense gutsy quality that makes tapas such a delight to the taste buds. We ate a kind of stew called *guisado de atún* (tuna with peas) based on a *sofrito* of peas, onions, parsley, and garlic, which is utterly delicious. They also serve one of the best stuffed squid dishes we've every had. The squid was stuffed with bread, its own tentacles, veal, parsley, and onions.

Bar Juanito also has absolutely fresh *fino* sherry that is delicious.

TWO ANDALUSIAN LUNCHES

A Beach Lunch

We were meeting our sherry master, José Ignacio Domecq, Jr., at his favorite beachfront restaurant in Sanlúcar. José Ignacio is the technical director of Pedro Domecq, the oldest of the major sherry houses. It was actually founded by an Irishman, Patrick Murphy, who came to Spain in the early eighteenth century and started in the wine business in 1730. The Domecq family married into the business in the late eighteenth century. Since then the Domecqs have played a major role in Jerez, both as technical innovators and shippers. Along the way the family has established a worldwide wine and brandy empire, with huge interests in South America and Mexico.

Our simple lunch lasted about three hours, during which the only drink served was sherry. Even though much of the fare was strictly the local catch of the day and so cannot be exactly duplicated in most of the rest of the world, the approach to eating can be followed anywhere.

The restaurant Domecq had intended to take us to was closed for remodeling. He shrugged and said it didn't really matter. They were all good. Our window table at Mirador Doñana overlooked the beach and, as the name suggests, viewed the Parque Nacional de Doñana wildlife refuge across the broad, shallow estuary of the Río Guadalquivir.

Domecq, who had hunted and fished the Doñana in his younger days, gave us an excellent tableside tour. Doñana is the delta of the Guadalquivir, the "big river" of the Moors. It is the major stopover in Europe for migrating birds flying from northern Europe to Africa and back. There are also 125 species of birds that breed in the Doñana—including 17 varieties of duck—as well as 28 mammal species, including the Spanish lynx, which is found nowhere else in southern Europe.

The area was set aside as a royal hunting reserve by the kings of Castile in the thirteenth century. A few centuries later, Doña Ana de Silvay Mendoza, a duchess of Medina Sidonia, built a retreat there and the region became known as Doñana.

The national park was created in 1969. It is a huge area but is actually only a besieged remnant of the coastal marsh, or *marisma*, a vast empty area that has been slowly drained and converted to farmlands, except for the refuge of Doñana.

Domecq sipped at a glass of *manzanilla* and gazed rather dourly across the river toward Doñana. He remembered the days before the Doñana was a park, when some hunting was allowed.

"We would go in with horses and wagons and set up camp for days, even weeks at a time, going across and back by boat, for there were no roads then into the Doñana," Domecq said.

He felt, on the whole, that the Doñana had been better cared for when it was in private hands. Surprisingly enough, many conservationists would agree with Domecq.

As part of the establishment of the park, sections of the old hunting areas to the north were converted to co-op rice fields. Pesticides from those fields have now entered the ground water system of Doñana, which has caused problems with breeding birds and threatens the entire ecosystem of the park.

There is no buffer zone to protect the park boundaries from urban sprawl, and several lynxes have been run over by cars on highways that border the park. Cats and dogs have entered the park from nearby towns to play havoc with many of the ground-nesting marine birds.

Domecq feels that the Spanish government gave away too much to establish the park and that the ban on hunting has encouraged a population explosion in the wild boar and deer populations, which also threatens the ecological balance of the park.

But when the food started arriving, Domecq shrugged off his pessimistic mood over the park. The first nibbles were sea snails, baroque-looking snails, perhaps two inches long, served barely steamed in their shells, tightly spiraled affairs. We had first made the acquaintance of these snails, or their cousins, at a *xumpanyeria* in Barcelona where they were served as a tapa.

It was necessary to dig into the little beasts with a toothpick or with the pointed tip of the end of one shell to pry out the snail from another shell. The opening (in the bottom of the shell) was fairly tightly plugged by the snail's foot; but once that muscular plug was breached, there was a tiny, tasty morsel of flesh—about big enough to fill a good-sized cavity in a rear molar.

The delights just kept coming, and it was a typical *jerezano* lunch —*calamari* roe, lightly fried whole baby sole, lobster, rockfish—all accompanied by sherry. There was *manzanilla* until the fish came, then *fino*.

The theme that tied the meal together was the salsa—peppers, onions, capers, celery, and tomatoes. Domecq, an accomplished cook, remarked that he doesn't use celery in his salsa. His insistence on his own recipe for salsa is typical of Andalusia cooks, and helps explain why virtually no two dishes are ever the same. For instance, gazpacho, perhaps Andalusia's most famous culinary export after sherry, takes as many forms as there are cooks.

The lunch ended with one of the most popular desserts in Spain —a tall glass of slightly chilled, freshly squeezed orange juice. To satisfy those with a hard-core sweet tooth, the juice is served with sugar on the side. Well, and there was a glass or two of old *oloroso* sherry. And then espresso. We all agreed that a drop of Domecq brandy would be excessive. Agreed and then ordered a round.

A Country Lunch

Outside of the sherry district, the food of Andalusia takes on a kind of country richness and intensity of flavor. We remember in partic- ular a long lunch in the Hotel Juanito in Baeza, deep in the heart of the Andalusian olive country.

We drove for hours through nothing but olive groves. What an incredible experience. Forests of olives marching up the mountains, down the valleys, agromonoculture gone mad. Seemingly, no mat- ter how fast we went, at the next turn of the road there were more olive trees. Suddenly, we were very glad that the sun shone brightly, very glad there were many hours of daylight before darkness would fall on those millions of olive trees. They go back so far in Mediter- ranean culture that surely they have gathered the ghosts of long- dead civilizations in their roots; these ancient trees have absorbed so many generations of life that they appear at certain times to be more than trees, to take on an existence far beyond the merely vegetative.

We could look up statistics, the millions of gallons of olive oil exported each year, the billions of pesetas that flow out of those millions of trees. But, somehow, mere statistics appear trivial before the ancient reality of the olive trees, so characteristic of the Mediter- ranean experience, so basic to Spanish cuisine, to the entire Medi- terranean kitchen. The Roman Pliny wrote, "Except the vine, there is no plant which bears a fruit of as great importance as the olive."

Rarely, far up a hillside, we glimpsed the ruins of a castle (for this was territory the Moors and Christians fought over for generations) or perhaps an oddly modern-looking farmhouse besieged by olive trees, sunlight glinting off the television antenna.

The small towns and villages turn up like misplaced stage sets in the center of the groves, with unreal paved streets, banks, schools, churches, women gossiping on doorsteps, children playing, traffic policemen, old men with donkeys. What did they do besides watch the olives grow, pick the olives, crush the olives? We almost got scared after a while and were glad to pull the rented car into the courtyard of a hotel where we had been promised authentic Andalusian country fare by a friend in Madrid.

Besides, the drive from Valencia to Baeza had been long and hot, with the parting words of our Valencian host echoing: "You'll find nothing fit to eat in Andalusia outside the cities. Don't even bother. Drive straight through to Córdoba." The outward appearance of the Hotel Juanito did nothing to quiet the warnings.

It was away from the main part of town, across a dusty gravel street from a seedy-looking garage. A faded building of three or four stories, remarkable only for its obscurity. It could have been anything, an office building, an apartment building, even a once-grand private residence, now somewhat come down in the world.

The town of Baeza itself, ringed by olive groves, is on the way, more or less, from nowhere to elsewhere, a few miles from the headwaters of the Guadalquivir in the foothills of the Sierra Segura. There is little to recommend it, except the Hotel Juanito. But in Spain, perhaps more than anywhere else, a visitor can't judge the contents by the wrapper. Inside the hotel, we entered a different world, leaving the slightly shabby exterior miles and perhaps centuries away.

We were a bit late for lunch, but the staff took pains to make us feel welcome. Not for the first time, we wondered where the standard image of the dour, unfriendly Spaniard originated. It is true that the typical Spaniard can be a bit reserved, but there is nothing unfriendly in that reserve—just the desire to give the stranger a chance to respond, to show his or her own nature. When it became clear that we had made a rather long detour to have lunch at Juanito and that we were very interested in the local food and wine, our welcome was even warmer.

The owner-chef appeared to suggest a series of dishes, each showing off some singular aspect of the local cuisine. And there were local wines to match the dishes. The only one I had ever heard of was a Valdepeñas red wine, La Invencible, from one of the large co-ops, which was quite good. There were many other wines on the list from the Valdepeñas area. We were not that far, after all, from southern La Mancha, home of some of Spain's better inexpensive wines.

The most unusual wine on the Hotel Juanito list was a Marqués de la Sierra, a white wine from the mountains above Córdoba, roughly 100 kilometers to the west. We learned later that it was a Riesling. Riesling had been brought to the area in the sixteenth century, and is, of course, a cool-climate grape, but it has adapted well to some of the higher elevations in Andalusia. The wine had the characteristic Riesling complexity, combined with a slightly oxidized sherrylike quality. Although it was vintage-dated, we suspect it was made by the *solera* method, which would account for the oxidation.

The food was sensational, ranging from local freshwater fish to partridge, rabbit, and venison and ending in a glorious selection of fresh local fruits and cheeses. We ate and drank through the afternoon and would have willingly gone on into the evening. But we checked with the desk, and no rooms were available. Probably just as well. We might have been there yet.

The food at Hotel Juanito has taken a key leap from the simple country kitchen (which can certainly be quite good) to a more sophisticated table and is a good example of the direction in which Andalusia fare is moving. At Hotel Juanito, there is the skill and desire to take home cooking, lighten it a bit, tinker with the sauces so that they are more delicate, more complex, and turn it into an altogether more satisfying dining experience. A meal, in a sense, is theater. A one-act play, no matter how enjoyable or memorable, can never be as complex or as satisfying as a full-length production. The kitchen at Hotel Juanito has the authority of classic drama. And Juanito, located in a small backwater in Andalusia, is only one of the many superb restaurants that have sprung up all over Spain in the last decade or so.

While it is difficult to say exactly what has touched off this renaissance in the Spanish kitchen, it is everywhere, from Barcelona and San Sebastián in the north to the wilds of Andalusia. Perhaps part of it is due to the overall feeling of freedom that swept Spain after Franco's death. In the beginning this was rather tentative and took a few false starts, but as the political system has moved steadily toward democracy, we've found that the Spanish have become more confident, more certain of the work at hand, whether it was film, literature, art, or the products of the kitchen. The local young chefs of Spain, no matter what region, have kept the best of the past—

refined it, perhaps, focused it a little sharper—borrowing from other regions and other national cuisines. There is the same excitement in the better Spanish restaurants today as there was in some of the California restaurants of the mid-seventies, that wonderful sense of being there at the beginning.

At the end of the meal at Hotel Juanito, just as we thought we were finished, the waiter served tiny glasses of a cherry *aguardiente*, made by the house, not an uncommon thing anywhere in Spain. This closing flourish, this curtain call, is part of the well-developed Spanish technique of never presenting anyone with a bill until the last possible moment—so long, you see, as you have not offered money, you are a guest, and the service, the food are willingly given, as a host to a guest, not master to servant. The ugly question of the bottom line disturbs this fine balance.

Alexandre Dumas commented on this very Spanish trait in his travel memoir *From Paris to Cádiz*, first published in 1846. Dumas is describing his search for breakfast on his first hungry morning in Spain. After a long hunt, they have managed to secure chocolate and bread. Not a lot of chocolate and bread, Dumas points out, but what there was, was very good. Then the time came for settling up.

"When we wished to pay, our guide stopped us with a gesture, took a peseta from his pocket, and placed it on the edge of a chest. '*Vaya usted con Dios*,' he murmured with a gracious bow of farewell. The proprietor, without even glancing to see whether he had been correctly paid, took his cigar from his lips long enough to reply, '*Vaya usted con Dios*.' "

The beach is a circus. A swirling palate of colors, of beautiful horses, beautiful women, and handsome men. Race week at Sanlúcar de Barrameda, the oldest horse race in all of Europe. Beyond the sands of the beach at Sanlúcar, beyond the misty sunset glimmer of the Guadalquivir, the pale green of the Doñana hangs in the darkening sky. Watching from one of the bodega boxes erected at the top of the beach, we would like to imagine—and why not—an imperial eagle sweeping out of the Doñana to arrogantly observe the puny markings in the sand below.

It is the last race of the day.

Men in tuxedos with white cummerbunds at their waist dance on the sand with barefoot women in gowns that cost hundreds of thousands of pesetas, pearls like kisses on dark necks.

The steady beat of a rock band from farther down the beach where tall blonds of indefinite sex (part of that northern swarm that each August engulfs the beaches of Spain) dance topless.

The racing horses flash across the sand, nearing the finish line.

A somber man, dressed all in black, sits his white horse like an icon just beyond the racing horses. A small girl, no more than three or four, all in white save the red sash at her waist and red ribbons in her hair, sits solemnly on the saddle before him. The beautiful, pale young women next to us says he is one of the judges.

What does he judge?

She doesn't know. Perhaps riding form, perhaps the winners or losers. Perhaps the dancing that will come later. Somehow, he simply has wandered into the end of the last race of the day.

At the finish, all is confusion. From where we sit it is impossible to tell who has won, nor is there anyone nearby who knows.

At some point, some time, it will matter. Here and now it doesn't. A caterer in black and white does a "hey, presto" routine with a gleaming white cloth on the table set in the sand below us. Plates of shrimp, squid, fried fish, lobster, heaping fruit platters crowd the tabletop; gleaming glasses of chilled manzanilla sherry reflect the last light from the sun.

Someone lights the candles that line the table.

The scene repeats itself dozens of times down the beach.

The somber man and the young girl join us. Now he is laughing, exchanging toasts with our host. The young girl, his daughter, sits on his lap, smiling shyly, chewing on a huge prawn, red ribbons hanging loose down her neck. He is not a rich man. He has a very small vineyard, but for generations his family have been judges in the races at Sanlúcar. If he doesn't have any sons, he expects his daughter to be a judge one day, so she is in training.

No, he doesn't know who won. He must consult with the other judges.

What other judges?

A vague motion down the beach. They are there having dinner at other tables. Somewhere in the dusk or perhaps up on the street, watching the Gypsies from the hill towns to the east—toward Granada and Ronda—dance the puro flamenco.

They will get together later.

"You see," says the young woman who had spoken earlier, "if the judges announce the winner now, it will spoil the night for the others. Tomorrow is soon enough for that sorrow."

Yes, we understand.

The judge smiles at us and raises his glass. We raise ours. We *drink to the most beautiful women, the finest horses, and the best wine in the world.*

Tonight, we are all winners.

GUIDELINES: ANDALUSIA

Jerez de la Frontera

HOTELS

For goodness sake, find a *pensión* if you plan to spend more than a day or two in Jerez de la Frontera. The tourist hotels are all expensive, modern, and fill-in-the-blank operations that could just as well be in San Diego, Tokyo, or Honolulu. Unless you are foolish enough (as we were once) to arrive without reservations near the harvest fiesta, finding decent rooms at a moderate price should be no problem. Look for *pensiones* on the Calle Fermín Aranda or the Calle Higueras.

RESTAURANTS

Tendido 6, Calle Circo, 10. Tel. (956) 30-69-95. Right across from the bullring. Good local fare, including bull's tail. Good tapas bar, moderate.

El Bosque, Avenida Alcalde Alvaro Domecq, 26. Tel. (956) 33-33-33. A little stuffy but reliable regional. High side of moderate.

Sevilla

HOTEL

Alfonso XIII, Calle San Fernando, 2. Tel. (954) 22-28-50. A magnificent hotel, wildly expensive with extensive gardens. It's worth the price of a glass of sherry to sit in the lobby and pretend to great wealth. If you don't want to pay $5 for a sherry, you could find a garden bench and admire the flowers and birds until a guard chases you away—very politely, of course.

RESTAURANTS/BARS

See section on tapas, pages 47 to 51.

Other Places in Andalusia

HOTEL/RESTAURANTS

Parador Casa del Corregidor, Plaza de España, Arcos de la Frontera. Tel. (965) 70-05-00. One of the most spectacular settings imaginable, right at the top of the town, looking down over canyons and fields. You can cheer on the hawks hunting from above!

Hotel Juanito, Plaza del Arca del Agua, Baeza. Tel. (953) 74-00-40. A jewel of a restaurant, serving specialties of the province of Jaén, developed to an international level. Good wine list for local wines and *manchego* (La Mancha) wines.

Restaurant Alboronia, Santo Domingo, 24, Puerto de Santa María. Tel. (925) 85-16-09. A true Andalusian kitchen, with regional specialties and a good wine list, including Riojas, local table wines, and sherry, of course.

Wineries

These are only a few of the sherry bodegas in Jerez de la Frontera that offer tours and tastings. Most specify the need for appointments, but that can be as simple as a telephone call the morning you would like to visit. But it is important to note that the telephone call is *necessary*.

Gonzáles Byass, Manuel María Gonzáles, 12, Jerez de la Frontera. Tel. (956) 34-00-00. Visits by appointment, either written or by phone, Monday to Friday, 10 A.M. until 2 P.M.

Pedro Domecq, San Ildefonso, 3, Jerez de la Frontera. Tel. (956) 33-18-00. Group tours only, by appointment two months in advance.

Garvey, Guadelete, 114, Jerez de la Frontera. Tel. (956) 33-05-00. Visits Monday to Friday by appointment, either written or by phone.

John Harvey & Sons, Calle Arcos, 53-57, Jerez de la Frontera. Tel. (956) 34-60-00. Open to visitors Monday to Friday from 9 A.M. until 1 P.M.

Emilio Lustau, Plaza del Cubo, 4, Jerez de la Frontera. Tel. (956) 34-89-46. Groups tours by appointment only.

LA MANCHA

*The white road led ahead
across the red land to villages
that glittered upon the horizon.
Churches huge as fortresses
towered above the roof tiles.
These villages were all much
the same to look at; a huge
sprawling Baroque church, its
yellow plaster peeling, a bell
swinging in a tower, a stork
standing on an untidy nest; a
plaza ringed with acacia trees;
an ornate fountain where
graceful brown girls lingered
with jars poised on their hips,
and a tangle of blinding
streets.*

—A Stranger in Spain
H. V. MORTON

IN FOCUS

As you follow grapes north on E25 in mid-September, the border between Andalusia and La Mancha passes almost without notice. You are gaining on Valdepeñas and an early dinner; the fields of vines or olives don't know what region they are in, why should you?

Properly speaking, La Mancha is a part of New Castile, that picture-puzzle piece of Spain that fits snugly all around Madrid, extending to the south and east of the Spanish capital, south and west of Aragón, east of Valencia, and north of Murcia and Andalusia, fading into Extremadura in the mountainous, bleak west. Politically, Madrid-Castile-La Mancha includes the provinces of Madrid, Albacete, Cuenca, Ciudad Real, Guadalajara, and Toledo. The area is the hub of the peninsula and contains two major cities—Madrid and Toledo.

Geographically, La Mancha is a high south-tilting plain, the Meseta; the average altitude is between 1,500 and 2,000 feet, with the high mountain barriers surrounding Toledo probably raising that average several hundred feet. There are mountain ranges all around the borders, which has much to do with the lack of rain. No matter which direction the rain comes from, the mountains block it.

This is a land of castles, border battle towers, and watchtowers in that vast no-man's-land from Toledo south that existed between Christians and Moslems. This zone of conflict was ruled by several military orders owing little allegiance to any prince, only to the sword. They were granted vast sheep-grazing territory, with the sheep kept on the move much of the time, seeking fresh pasture. One can still find traces of the old sheep walks in the mountains that ring the plains of La Mancha.

There are areas of La Mancha that seem to exist almost as a museum. Cities like Toledo, for example, are filled with Roman, Visigothic, Arab, and Mudéjar art comingled with streetcorner con artists selling cheap tin swords to bewildered tourists for the cost of a good meal. (They buy them, of course, without considering how in the world they are going to get past airport security with a 42-inch sword.)

But La Mancha is less a place and more a state of mind, invented by a writer contemporary with Shakespeare—Cervantes, the creator of Don Quixote. I am convinced that one must understand Don Quixote to understand Spain. Cervantes captured the strange, bizarre spirit of the Iberian Peninsula—or most of it—in that one book, so much quoted, so little read.

Quixote was a man of great heart, great courage, great generosity, and an understanding of nothing in this life, but a perfect understanding of his ideal life, his interior life. His love, his pride, his honor knew no limits. When he enjoyed, he enjoyed hugely with no thought of the next hour, let alone tomorrow; when he suffered, his suffering knew no limits and was inconsolable, would never end.

His companion, Pancho, was his mirror image because mirrors reverse. He was not intelligent, but cunning; he couldn't read, but he understood the world; he was cynical, yet totally trusting once his confidence was won. He was willing to compromise to avoid a fight; his honor was flexible. He began thinking about where he would find his supper before his breakfast was finished. Together, Quixote and Pancho represent two sides of the complex Spanish character.

THE FOOD

But if La Mancha is a state of mind, it is a well-fed state of mind. Most guidebooks give little attention to La Mancha beyond the standard references to Don Quixote. Yet even in the deep countryside there is good food to be had. It is simple food, perhaps the simplest in Spain. For even in the north country, in the far reaches of Navarre and Aragón, the chef is likely to have at least heard about French or Catalan or Basque cuisine. He may experiment, perhaps only in a small way, with the basic peasant fare. This is not always a good thing, mind you. It could be that it is better to get the honest country stuff straight off. That is exactly the great strength of the country cooks of La Mancha.

The food of La Mancha is the soul food of Spain. For the true garlic soups, for the most *tipico* of the *cocidos*, the culinary pilgrim must search in La Mancha. It is a harsh land but with much more abundant food resources than are apparent at first sight. There are sheep and goats wherever you look, enough wheatfields to give Kansas a close run, miles of olives. And everywhere is the vine, sprawling across the ground, not tied up in neat, orderly rows as we are accustomed to seeing in California. As evidence that the cooking has a country directness, look at the dish called *galianos*—or sometimes, confusingly, *gazpachos*. (Note the s, which distinguishes it from the cold gazpacho of Andalusia.) Centuries ago, *galianos* began as a shepherd's or hunter's dish and was probably brought to Spain from North Africa by the Moors. In the traditional version, partridge and rabbit are fried with sliced onion, garlic, saffron, cinnamon, rosemary, and thyme, flavored with wine and thickened with *torta*—a flat, unleavened bread baked on a stone. Another *torta* is used as a dipping tool, and in medieval times the *galianos* was eaten directly from the pot. In the modern *manchego* kitchen, chicken and pigeon are often substituted for the game, and *torta* is rarely made these days. Instead, the dish is thickened with bread crumbs and eaten with a fork.

A similar stew is called *tojunto* or *todo juinto*, "all together," because the varied ingredients—meat, rabbit, or chicken and vegetables—are all put to cook at the same time. Sounds like a lazy cook's approach to a *galiano*.

The *pisto manchego*, the vegetable stew that is found all over Spain, is a long-running feature of the table in La Mancha. The modern versions use the New World vegetables—tomatoes, peppers, and squash—but the *pisto manchego* is based on the *alboronia* of the Moors and was originally no doubt an eggplant dish.

There are, of course, any number of lamb dishes, and a typical local salad of chopped meat—usually lamb, although sometimes kid —eggs, onion, peppers, and tomatoes, called *salpicón*, as well as many, many rice dishes and much game.

The best *churros* we've had in Spain were in La Mancha from the Plaza de Zocodover, the social heart of Toledo, a bit uphill from the cathedral. *Churros*, fried dough in twisted loops, like a light and elegant doughnut, are one of the delights of the street in Spain. They are quickly cooked in a pot of boiling fat over a wood fire on a street corner or in a plaza. You can have whatever length you want, or they are sold for take-away on willow hoops, again in various sizes. Early in the morning, crowds of children will be gathered around the *churro* maker, buying hoops of the freshly fried treats to take home for the family breakfast—*churros* and chocolate. *Churros* to feed four or five people can be bought for fifty or sixty pesetas, about fifty cents.

If there was a fiesta the night before, the *churro* maker might sleep at the stand because he or she will have been there at the end of the party. At two or three o'clock in the morning it's a marvelous treat to have a small *churro* and a cup of thick chocolate, perhaps with a touch of anise or brandy.

Perhaps the most famous product of La Mancha is *Crocus sativus*, saffron. The center of the saffron trade is the town of Consuegra, on the C400, about 70 kilometers south of Toledo.

Vegetables of all sorts run riot in La Mancha, especially vine-ripened tomatoes, peppers, beans, and herbs. Root vegetables are also excellent, as are eggplant and squashes.

The delicious breads of La Mancha are often made from locally grown wheat. There are few things better than a fresh loaf of *pan pueblo*—*pan pueblo* with some fresh *manchego*, a sheep cheese and one of the most famous in Spain. *Manchego* comes in three styles: fresh, or *fresca*, which is aged for at least sixty days; cured, *curado*, aged for thirteen weeks; and dried or aged, *añejo*, which is matured for at least seven months. The hard version can be grated like Parmesan or eaten out of hand.

Game—rabbits, pheasant, partridge, and wild boar—are often found on the tables of La Mancha, along with excellent domestic lamb, goat, pig, and chicken.

And, of course, everywhere and always, there are olives.

THE WINE

Wine grapes are the third most important product in volume in La Mancha, coming just behind wheat and olives. The vines cover an enormous amount of territory and most years produce about 40 percent of the total wine made in Spain, sometimes as high as 50 percent if the harvest is short in the north.

Of that production, a large percentage goes for distillation into brandy to feed the brandy *soleras* of Jerez; much of it is also distilled into industrial alcohol, and a considerable part of wine production is given over to vinegar. And, more recently, there has been the production of grape concentrate, which is sold all around the world for strengthening the weak wines of other areas. Much of the concentrate is sold to the United Kingdom for use in "British" wines and by home winemakers.

La Mancha has long been the supplier of cheap bulk wines to the rest of Spain and is also responsible for a good many gallons of cheap Spanish plonk that ends up on too many London dinner tables where the budget is modest and won't quite run even to an unclassified Bordeaux.

But the area is finding its way to higher quality with modern winemaking techniques and experimental plantings of international varietals such as Pinot Noir, Cabernet Sauvignon, and Chardonnay. Until the past few years, we wouldn't have given the Chardonnay much of a chance, but having seen the hotter areas of California where Chardonnay is now planted, perhaps they are on to a good thing in La Mancha.

There are four denominations of origin: La Mancha itself, the largest; Almansa; Méntrida; and the most important in terms of quality wine production, Valdepeñas.

Almansa D.O. (denomination of origin) is far to the east, mostly in the province of Albacete. Most wine from this area is sold in bulk; they are big, alcoholic red wines, although we occasionally came across a pleasant *clarete* made from Garnacha Tinta in local restaurants.

There is more wine made in the D.O. of La Mancha than any other denomination in Spain. Again, most is sold in bulk for blending. Basic production (about 90 percent) is from the Airén grape, which makes a neutral but high-alcohol white wine. Most of the wine used for distilling comes from the La Mancha D.O. As in Almansa, there are some nice rosés or *claretes*, which can be found as far afield as Toledo and Madrid, both just outside the D.O. zone, which stretches as far south as Valdepeñas.

Production costs are low because of cheap labor and very old wineries where few capital improvements have been made in the past century. With low tonnage yields and low profits, there is little incentive to invest in new equipment, which would in turn lead to better wines. However, in the past decade, some interest has been shown by outside investors, and with the introduction of stainless steel tanks and refrigeration, a number of young, fruity white wines are being made and have begun to establish a reputation for *manchego* wine quality in Madrid, but few of these wines have entered the world market.

The D. O. of Méntrida is in the north, in the provinces of Toledo and Madrid. The basic grape there is the Garnacha Tinta, which covers between 80 and 90 percent of the vineyard area. It is one of the common bar wines of both Madrid and Toledo in either a rosé or red version.

Valdepeñas is the biggest supplier of wine to Madrid, and has been since Philip II established this capital of Spain in the sixteenth century. In fact, the chief reason the railroad was pushed to completion between Madrid and Valdepeñas was to speed the wine transport. At least that is the way the *valdepeñanos* tell it. In the late nineteenth century and the early part of this century there was a daily train, the *tren del vino*, that carried an average of forty cars of wine to the thirsty folk of Madrid.

The D.O. is justly famous for light, fruity young wines made of a mixture of red and white grapes and often served from a cool jug in bars and restaurants all over Spain. The red wine grapes are Cencibel, Monastrell, and to a lesser extent, Garnacha Tinta. The white wine is the Airén, although a number of other grapes are used for both reds and whites.

The exact blend is anyone's guess, as is the exact origin. Valdepeñas has such a good reputation for wine production that grapes are brought from all the D.O.s in La Mancha and end happily as a Valdepeñas D.O. So it is usually a thankless task to try and trace the exact origin of the wine in the glass. Just drink it and enjoy!

It has been suggested that one reason for the generally high-quality wine of Valdepeñas is the existence of a local strain of yeast that does a super job of winemaking. In Valdepeñas, as almost everywhere in Spain, no yeast is added to the wine as in the United States or Australia. The enologist is content to let nature take its course.

Over centuries of winemaking, yeasts peculiar to one particular area do develop. This development is encouraged by the age-old custom of dumping the spent remains of fermentation—the lees—back into the vineyards.

Traditionally, the wines were fermented in giant earthen tanks called *tinajas*, shaped like the standard classical Greco-Roman amphorae. Each *tinaja* contains about 500 gallons. They were supported by a wooden framework. *Tinajas* are mostly decorative now (although we have been in wineries in La Mancha and Extremadura that still use them, or something very like them). They were made from clay dug in La Mancha around Villarrobledo and Toboso, authentic Quixote country.

Doubtless, the *tinaja* was a development of the amphorae, but exactly when isn't clear. We have seen them abandoned and broken up in the gardens of a Moorish fortress at Mérida in Extremadura. Perhaps they were used there for the storage of drinking water in the event of a siege.

At any rate, today's winemaking in Valdepeñas is about as modern as you can get and any *tinajas* in sight are likely to be a garden decoration, except for those on display along the Avenida del Vino.

By the way, don't sneer at co-op wines in Spain (or in France or Italy, for that matter). In the United States, co-op wines have never been very good, but the European co-ops set high standards for growers' grapes and stick to them. They often have better equipment than other wineries because they have the funds to modernize.

Typically, in La Mancha (as well as elsewhere in Spain) a grape grower will have other sources of income, say olives or fruit or a few sheep and pigs. Farming is highly diversified in Spain. Even in the more industrial parts of the country, like Catalonia, where there are huge vineyards (by Spanish standards), other crops are grown. These multisources of income give the farmers a cushion, so the co-op isn't bled dry during a bad grape year.

At one time, the world outside La Mancha viewed the native wines with a well-deserved suspicion. They were hot-climate wines with high alcohol and low acid, wines with little charm—in short, heavy, awkward, and dull on the palate. Today, thanks once more to modern methods of fermentation and refrigeration, the inexpensive wines of La Mancha can be delightful lunch or dinner companions. In the end, the most important advance in winemaking since the barrel is refrigeration, and there are many who would put the barrel even behind, in the number-two position.

The dedicated wine lover should visit La Mancha at harvest. True, the various harvest festivals are not as grand as in Jerez or La Rioja, but perhaps for that reason, we feel a little closer to the heart, the mystery of the grape.

And it should be part of the mandatory experience of La Mancha to endure the late summer heat; to at least go and stand in the vineyard while the stooped men and women move slowly down the sprawling rows of vines under that hot blue sky. The heat is baking. After a short time it becomes necessary to concentrate on usually automatic actions like placing one foot before another. After a time in such heat, the mind becomes unfocused. You become a human machine for picking grapes. (We have yet to see a mechanical harvester in La Mancha, although there are experimental vineyards near Valdepeñas that could handle them.)

The vineyards themselves look much as they must have looked five centuries ago or twenty centuries ago: a sprawling mass of vines pruned low to the ground and bent even lower at harvest under the weight of grapes. Work goes on from first light to dark, with a long lunch break in the most intense heat of the early afternoon, when nothing with any option is moving in La Mancha. There may be hotter places in Spain during the harvest than La Mancha (Sevilla comes to mind) but it is surely the hottest place anyone is picking grapes.

We once walked a vineyard near Valdepeñas at eight in the morning. The heat was already beating down from above and radiating back up from the earth. The grapes still felt cool to the touch, nestled under the heavy vine canopy that is allowed to develop in La Mancha just for that purpose, although there is little attempt to bring in cool grapes to the winery. Because of the slow handpicking system and the heat that develops in the grapes during trucking to the winery, grapes often arrive with fermentation already under way, at least at the bottom of the picking boxes.

SPANISH DAYS

Climbing from the flat heat of the vineyards toward the towers of Toledo, you finally enter a breathable zone below the walls of the city, which is instantly familiar because of El Greco's famous painting. Toledo exists, in my mind, in a curious dreamscape where museums, restaurants, and tour buses converge.

Architecturally, the city is a feast; gastronomically, it is a feast. It has only one serious fault and that is its fame. Even during the winter, Toledo is plagued with tourists, but in late summer, when the grapes are being harvested on the plains below, the city fairly swims with visitors. It is easy to see why. I'm sure that one could spend a month in Toledo and barely scratch the surface. It would take a lifetime to know the city well. (It is amusing that the Michelin green guide suggests one day for the main sights of Toledo. It takes almost that long to have lunch and book a table for dinner.)

In some other heavily touristed areas, the eating doesn't come close to matching the sights, but not so in Toledo. There are some typical local dishes, like *brocheta de ternera y butifarra*, skewers of veal and sausages cooked in a wine sauce; *sopa de almendras*, a hot milk and marzipan soup with almonds; and one of Toledo's most famous dishes, *codornices a la toledana*, braised quail served with vegetables. Of course, Toledo has its own variation of the *menestra*, or vegetable stew, found everywhere. It's called *panaché de verduras* and is made with salt pork.

A standard in the tapas bars—which are famous throughout Spain for the variety and quality of the dishes—are tiny sandwiches called *pulgas*, which means "little fleas" in the local dialect. These are bite-size treats of ham or cheese, perhaps anchovy—anything, actually, that can be put between two bits of bread.

Wander for hours (days) in the twisting, spiraling streets below the Zocodover, taking a snack here, a bit there, perhaps stopping for a time to listen to a *Tuna*, a band of musicians playing traditional music, often in medieval costume, always with a small collection of *Tuna* groupies, astonishingly beautiful young women who are given to breaking into brief dances or snatches of song.

The music of the *Tuna is* very danceable, based on the rhythm of the *sevillanas*, and soon there will be general dancing in the streets, led by the *Tuna* groups. In the old town near the cathedral, the streets are closed to auto traffic except for a few hours daily in the early morning for deliveries.

The culture and history of Toledo are incredibly rich and complex. For centuries it was one of the leading cities of Europe. It was in Toledo from the eighth to the thirteenth centuries that the cultural threads of Christian, Jewish, and Moorish thought were woven together in tolerance and mutual appreciation, each enriching the others.

The history of Toledo extends beyond the Romans. There was an Iberian village or hill fort on the easily defended site, surrounded on three sides by the Río Tajo, which the Romans seized and called Toletum. The Visigoths made Toledo their capital in 554 and Hispano-Romans, Visigoths, and Jews lived peacefully together. It was there that the Visigothic chief Recared became a Christian and maintained a rule of tolerance that didn't change even with the arrival of the Moors in 712. The city was recaptured by Christians in 1085 under Alfonso VI, who had himself crowned there as "Emperor of all the Christian and Moorish kingdoms of Spain," a title more realized in the ideal than in political reality. But at any rate, the tolerance, the cross-cultural enrichment continued until 1355, when a brutal suppression of Jewish culture began. This suppression reached a climax with the expulsion of the Jews from Spain in 1492, which proved to be a human and commercial disaster. (Perhaps a few late-twentieth-century political leaders might learn a few things about the importance of cultural tolerance by a study of life in Toledo for over six centuries.)

During that period, while most of Western Europe was sunk in a mire of dark barbarianism, Toledo shone with a brilliant light. The best scholars from the Mediterranean world gathered at its universities and royal courts.

That light can still be glimpsed today, shining in obscure corners of churches, lighting up a painting or a decorated wall down a side alley. There is so much to see in Toledo that some sort of standard tourist guide is a must. One of the most complete tours is the Toledo number in the *Passport Travel Series to Spain*, published in cooperation with the National Tourist Board of Spain.

The only guide you will need to the food is your nose. Although one evening, following a tip from friends, we set out to find the restaurant Hierbabuena—*hierba*, meaning "herb," and *buena*, "good." We had been unable to find the street, Christo de la Luz, on a map. The desk clerk at our hotel said it was somewhere "below the cathedral." That was not a comforting direction to start on, but we had plenty of time before our 10 P.M. reservations, and it couldn't be more than six blocks. The usual ploy of resorting to taxis wouldn't work because autos were not allowed in this old quarter of Toledo.

But we set off merrily enough a bit after 8 P.M., planning a few tapas stops on the way, and a visit to our rented car, the faithful *bota* patrol, parked illegally in an obscure plaza off the Zocodover.

We stopped at three tapas bars, always asking directions to the Hierbabuena and Calle Cristo de la Luz. We did seem to be moving closer and were encouraged midway through the search by actually finding our car unticketed and untowed, surrounded by several dozen other illegally parked cars. So tightly wedged in, in fact, that we couldn't have made a fast nighttime getaway from Toledo even if we had wanted to.

The streets of Toledo are an intimidating puzzle, but they are worth solving. To call them streets, even by Spanish standards, is to bend the meaning of the word. Even alleys would be too grand. Many of these are mere passageways, hardly wide enough for two people to walk side by side, and the streets (passageways) of Toledo are crowded. You must squeeze past, careful not to knock pots of blooming geraniums off the window ledges.

Except sometimes, without warning or apparent reason, you turn a corner and the narrow alley with a dim light far at the end, and only patchy, shifting darkness in between, is empty. Or is there someone standing halfway down in a doorway. You hesitate, but were told at the last bar that this was a shortcut to Calle Cristo de la Luz which would save many minutes of walking. And minutes had become critical, since we had stayed rather too long listening to the last *Tuna* band. But there was that suspicious person loitering, perhaps with intent (what *does* that mean?), and the alley was dark and deserted. Never mind, this is Spain, not New York City or East Oakland. Onward.

The suspicious person was an old lady in black, sitting peacefully on her doorstep, smoking a cigarette. She wished us a good evening and assured us that Calle Cristo de la Luz was straight ahead and to the left. Well, a bit to the left, then straight again, then to the left.

"Where are you going on Cristo de la Luz?"

"The restaurant Hierbabuena."

"Ah, yes, I know it. One moment, please."

She stepped back into her house and reappeared a moment later with a shawl over her head.

"Come, I will show you."

"But, no, señora, you mustn't do that."

She waved her hand and said, "It is nothing. I was thinking of going out for a small walk before bed anyway. It will do me good to stir my bones a bit."

There was no stopping her. We set off briskly down the alleyway, she apologizing because the streetlight had burned out weeks ago and the authorities had not replaced it. So much for our dark, suspicious alley.

Within a few minutes we were at the door of Hierbabuena, and our kind guide was off for her small walk.

We had been directed to Hierbabuena by friends in Madrid who had assured us that it was one of the best new restaurants in Spain, with a young chef-owner who was doing very exciting work in the kitchen.

However, we were forty-five minutes late (that damn *Tuna* band) and there was not a table left. The headwaiter was polite but firm at first, becoming less polite but firmer as we insisted that we must have a table. At last, we reached a compromise after pulling the old "we-are-important-journalists-from-California" routine and were seated rather grandly if grudgingly (I don't think he believed us for a moment but recognized that we needed to save face) at a table set up in the reception area, on direct display with a large pot of flowers.

The restaurant is in a magnificent setting. The building had been declared a national monument in 1870. Its exact age was not known but it had belonged (before 1870) to a painter. It was Mozarabic and had been tastefully restored where necessary but left alone where not necessary. The present owner believes it may have been a stable at one time because there is a long horse trough in the back, now the centerpiece of a small patio.

All in all, we felt rather resplendent and were ready for a wonderful feast. And so it was, from the rather spectacular beginning—a scalloped, hollowed out zucchini, with a sugar cube soaked in brandy placed inside and ignited at the table. The entire dinner was like that—fireworks all the way.

Some of the highlights included:

Crepe de puerros y gambas, folded crepe filled with béchamel, sautéed leeks, and prawns.

Grilled bread topped with avocado and anchovy cream and sprinkled with toasted cumin seeds—a very Moorish touch, that.

Cold poached bonita with anchovy mayonnaise.

Brocheta de ternera y butifarra a la salsa de tomillo, skewers of veal and sausage marinated in a wine, thyme, oregano, and lemon sage sauce—an absolutely stunning dish.

Crema de Toledo con guinda, yummy dessert of egg yolks, cream, sugar, and cherries in a cherry *aguardiente*.

There were other dishes, and the menu looked good enough to return every night for a month, but the key is the willingness to experiment, to take a bit of this and a bit of that and run with it. The mixture of anchovy and avocado on grilled bread topped with cumin is a perfect example. It seems a simple-enough idea, yet the combination of flavors had never before crossed my palate. Grilled bread is, of course, as old as Mediterranean cooking, and grilled bread with anchovy is hardly new; grilled bread with anchovy and tomato has been done, for sure, but the combination of anchovy and avocado was a superb touch. Then, to top that with a North African seasoning, cumin, was a nice wrap-up.

The veal and *butifarra* skewers draw on traditional Spanish ingredients, but are combined in an unusual and very flavorful way. The sauce and the presentation are very *manchego*, but the use of the northern meats, veal and *butifarra*, gave the sauce a new dimension.

As we were having a final espresso and brandy a young man with an Alsatian at heel came in. He heard us speaking English and asked what we were doing seated in such an unusual location. After we explained, he told us that he was from London and had been living in Toledo for more than a year, teaching English and scraping by with his dog, Geoffrey. He came in every night at closing to pick up scraps for Geoff.

"It is such a fantastic city I can't leave," he said. "I was supposed to be here for one semester to research a thesis on Judaism in medieval Spain, but I need years. Do you know how remarkable this city was? For centuries three cultures usually at war with one another lived here in peace. I simply can't learn enough about it."

We bought him a *coñac* so that we could all toast Toledo together, to the light that must never dim.

The basic table in La Mancha easily crosses some borders, so that there is some blurring, some culinary twilight zones, such as Torrecaballeros, a small village between Madrid and Segovia. Not in La Mancha at all, the mapmakers would say. Perhaps, yet well within La Mancha looking out from the kitchen.

Torrecaballeros was a pit stop, a quick dash to use the facilities into what seemed to be the only bar in town. Of course, it was our duty—and only polite—to sample a glass of the local wine. But the smells coming from the dim interior behind the bar stopped us in our tracks. We ordered a local rosé and had a closer look. The bar/

restaurant was called El Horno de la Aldeguela. An imposing plaque on the wall informed us that it had been founded in 1899 by a Cuban war hero named Zacarias Gilsanz. The bar itself seemed ordinary enough, rather plain with two windows looking out into a nondescript side yard. There was an attractive wooden bar, only about eight feet long, a couple of small tables near the back, and a narrow door.

By following our noses, we discovered that the wonderful smells were coming from the door that led into the dining room. We peeked inside. It was about one in the afternoon. We were too early for lunch on a weekend (this was Sunday), so the small dining room was empty, except for a table of waiters and waitresses having an early lunch. There were about six or eight of them, which seemed a lot for such a small place. Then we noticed another door that opened into another much larger dining room. Just inside the door was a stairway to another dining room. The room was dominated by a huge brick oven built into an exterior wall so it could be fired from outside. We had found the "horno (oven) de la Aldeguela."

There was one man working at the oven, building and shaping a wood fire. The oven itself was roughly six feet by eight feet by three feet, rounded with brick on a brick slab floor. It was an oven big enough to roast whole sheep in, which was exactly the plan. The cook worked within a three-sided box, with the fourth side being the oven. Stacked all around him were lamb carcasses. One of the three counters was a huge chopping block, the other two were serving counters.

There was already some lamb roasting, which is what had led our noses to the source. Back in the bar, we conferred briefly with our stomachs and our schedule. It didn't take long for us to decide to stay.

I asked the waiter what time lunch would be served. The first seating, he told us, was at two-thirty, and if we wanted the lamb (what else?) we should let him know right away as there were only a few left. That seemed odd, since the place was still empty, but we booked ourselves a quarter of a lamb (there were four in our party) and settled down with a pitcher of the excellent rosé.

Within fifteen minutes, the place started filling up. We took a look outside. In the parking lot there were cars from Madrid and Segovia and even a few from Toledo. By two-thirty there wasn't a vacant table in the house.

Our quarter of lamb was served with baked potatoes with *allioli* on the side, like an American restaurant would serve sour cream or butter. Before the lamb was served, there was a richly flavored *sopa de ajo*, made in the usual way, but the soup stock had been made with smoked meat. After the soup came roasted red peppers, whole grilled cloves of garlic, and sliced onions. For dessert there was a *tarta de segoviana*.

It was all utterly perfect country food. The lamb was seasoned only with what the Spanish call mountain herbs—rosemary, sage, and thyme—and even those were used sparingly. But the lamb itself was the essence of lamb. It was Plato's ideal lamb, each bite a revelation. Perfectly cooked, of course, even though the oven man was working at speed. He used a long wooden paddle, similar in appearance to the kind of paddle used by pizza makers but with a longer handle to slide the various cuts of lamb in and out of the oven. After a quick check, he would reposition the lamb in a hotter or cooler part of the oven.

There were quarters, halves, and whole lambs, which he moved quickly in and out of the oven as though he were shuffling cards; using the paddle as a serving board, he would pass a half lamb over the counter to one waiter and in the same motion turn back to the oven, slide out a quarter, and pass it over the opposite counter to another waiter, never missing a beat.

The potatoes and grilled vegetables came from the same oven, an endless cornucopia passed out along with the lamb.

It is impossible to give a recipe for the lamb. You must go there on a weekend or a holiday—it's the only time the El Horno de la Aldeguela is open. In the winter, when there is skiing in the nearby Sierra de Guadarrama, it may be necessary to book a table weeks ahead for the second lunch seating at five o'clock.

We discovered there were two other similar *hornos* in Torrecaballeros; in fact, all over both Old and New Castile and León, there are *hornos* where there is excellent garlic soup, grilled vegetables, and lamb. The Aldeguela simply happens to be the one we stumbled upon. And it is not unusual to find cars from Madrid and other large urban centers parked outside, for these country restaurants are well known and each has its following among city folk.

One is getting very close in these country places to the roots of Spanish food—simple food of absolutely first-rate quality, prepared in a way to emphasize that quality and the taste values of the food. It's an approach that would work well for the home chef.

GUIDELINES: LA MANCHA

Manzanares

RESTAURANT/INNS

El Cruce, Kilometer 173 on the N4. Tel. (926) 61-19-00. Manzanares is a charming wine-producing town, about 25 kilometers north of Valdepeñas. El Cruce serves excellent regional cuisine. For a starter, try their version of *gazpachos manchego*. Pleasant rooms, also.

Puerto Lápice

RESTAURANTS/INNS

Venta el Quijote, El Molino, 4. Tel. (926) 57-61-10. This restaurant/ inn claims to be the very place where Don Quixote first put on his homemade suit of armor. There are several other inns in La Mancha that also make that claim. Take care now before you begin debating their relative merits. Deep in the heart of La Mancha, it is difficult to remember that Don Quixote is, after all, fictional. But there is nothing fictional about the excellent country cooking and good local wines. The rooms are comfortable as well. Puerto Lápice is about 60 kilometers north of Valdepeñas on the E25.

Toledo

HOTELS

There are very few good—or even adequate—hotels outside of Toledo. See above for good country inns at Manzanares and Puerto Lápice. There are also *paradores* at Manzanares and Almagro, which should be investigated.

Hotel Residencia Alfonso VI. General Moscardó, 2. Tel. (925) 22-26-00. The hotel is just a few blocks from the cathedral and a block or so from the Plaza Zocodover. Good views of the Alcázar. Moderate.

Hostal del Cardenal, Paseo de Recaredo, 24. Tel. (925) 22-08-62. The hotel is set in a lovely garden in an eighteenth-century mansion. Good restaurant, also. Moderate.

Hotel Carlos V, Plaza Horno de Magdalena, 1. Tel. (925) 22-26-

00. A hotel between the cathedral and the Alcázar. Moderate.

Fonda Segovia, Calle Recoletos, 4. Tel. (925) 22-11-24. Quiet rooms, many with balconies, just off the Zocodover. Cheap.

Fonda Lumbreras, Calle Juan Labrador, 9. Tel. (925) 22-15-71. Near the Alcázar. Adequate, with refreshing cold showers in the summer. Not a good winter choice. Very cheap.

RESTAURANTS

There are no really first-rate, inexpensive restaurants in Toledo. It is possible to eat well on very little, however, by judicious tapas selections at several different bars. For eating outside of Toledo, stop for a glass of wine or coffee and do some deep breathing. If it smells good, give it a try.

Casa Aurelio (two locations), Sinagoga, 6 and Plaza del Ayuntamiento, 8. Tel. (925) 22-20-97 for the Sinagoga location or (925) 22-77-16 for the Plaza del Ayuntamiento. Outstanding regional dishes. The restaurant has its own vineyards and the wine is quite good. The two restaurants are on opposite sides of the cathedral, only a couple of blocks apart.

Hierbabuena, Calle Cristo de la Luz, 9. Tel. (925) 22-34-63. Difficult to find but worth the effort. Expensive.

El Abside, Calle Marques de Mendigorria, 1. Tel. (925) 21-26-50. An eclectic and exciting selection of Jewish and Arabic foods. Expensive.

La Botica, Plaza del Zocodover, 13. Tel. (925) 22--55-57. Good regional food in the upstairs restaurant, and a fine selection of tapas in the downstairs tapas bar. You can linger over a few tapas and a glass or two of wine and watch the action in the Zocodover outside. Trendy and expensive, but fun.

Wineries

"See one co-op winery, seen them all" gets very close to the truth. As noted above, most of the wine is made in co-ops and very few of those encourage visitors. If you really want to visit a stainless steel tank farm and look at a modern bottling line, try the Cooperativa del Campo Nuestro Padre Jesús del Perdón, in the Zona Industrial del Polígono in Manzanares. Tel. (926) 61-03-09. Open Monday to Friday, 9 A.M. until 2 P.M. and 4 P.M. until 7 P.M. They have some very pleasant white wines and are said to be a favorite of King Juan Carlos. The king, I am told, is not much of a drinker.

RIOJA/NAVARRE

*In Rioja we have been saved
because it is too difficult for
the tourists to find us.*

—AN OLD MAN·IN A BAR IN THE
TOWN OF LOGROÑO ON THE NIGHT
OF THE FEAST OF CORPUS CHRISTI

IN FOCUS

Most of what is now Rioja was part of the Kingdom of Old Castile, an area that swept from Madrid to the Bay of Biscay. Modern Rioja also includes parts of ancient Navarre. It makes perfect culinary and enological sense to consider them together. From that perspective, the area forms an east-tilting, rather chunky L-shaped region, extending from the high plains of Rioja Baja, south of the Río Ebro, through the foothills of the Pyrenees, into the high mountains to the border of France at the top of the L, with the foot of the L bumping into Basque territory in the Pyrenees below the Atlantic. In fact, historically, the Basque cultural movement has been extending its influence south into the heart of Rioja's famous wine country, where schooling is conducted on a bilingual basis—in the Basque language and in the Castilian.

The Pyrenees dominate the northern fringe of Rioja proper and most of Navarre, with mostly north-south running valleys between fold after fold of mountains.

The climate is described by the weather whizzes as "continental," which seems to indicate that it gets the worst of everything, from bitter winter cold, with snow and ice in the mountains, to stifling heat in the summer, especially in the flatlands of Rioja Baja, where the Río Ebro often becomes a tired, muddle trickle by summer's end.

Rioja was well known to the Romans as a wine-producing area, with ships from the Mediterranean sailing up the Ebro to Logroño, Haro, and other inland ports. The whole area was the scene of heavy fighting between the Moors and Christians in the eighth, ninth, and tenth centuries, but eventually the Moors were expelled and much of the Christian Reconquest was guided from Navarre and Rioja.

One of the most famous medieval pilgrimage routes, the Camino de Santiago de Compostela, begins at Roncesvalles on the French-Navarre border and runs through Navarre and Rioja toward its destination in the west at the Galician shrine of Santiago de Compostela.

It is difficult for us to grasp, at this far remove in time and faith from the late Middle Ages, just how important the pilgrimage was— and in fact, from a touristic point of view, still is today.

The legend of Santiago (Saint James) first came to light during the reign of the Christian king Alfonso II of Asturias (791–842), whose capital was Oviedo, in what is now Galicia. The body of the apostle James reportedly had been discovered there in a field.

There had always been a dim legend in the north of Spain that Saint James, who is the patron saint of Spain, had preached the gospel throughout the country. After his missionary work, so the legend goes, he returned to the Holy Land and was executed by Herod Agrippa in A.D. 44. His followers took his body back to Spain by sea in a marble sarcophagus.

The first of his miracles took place before he ever got back to Spain. The boat carrying his remains was off the coast of Portugal when the dead saint saved the life of a man who had been swept out to sea on a horse. Legend has it that the rider and horse rose from the sea covered with scallop shells, which later became the symbol of Saint James. (The symbol of the scallop became so well known that the shell itself or a jeweled replica of a scallop shell was often worn in France and England as a symbol that one had made the pilgrimage to Santiago. In Paris one can still see stone scallops carved above doorways of the homes of those who had made the journey to pay homage to Saint James.)

James was buried near the present town of Santiago and then largely forgotten—until he was needed, that is. In 813 Alfonso received word that the tomb of Saint James had been revealed by the presence of a bright star that stood still overhead. If the light show wasn't enough, there was also a chorus of angels on hand.

The saint had been found in time to lead the Christians in an important battle against the Moors, and the battle cry *Santiago y cierra, España* ("Saint James and close in, Spain") was sounded. The cry was raised again and again as the Christians slowly forced the Moors southward.

The saint's tomb became known as "the field of the star," and Alfonso ordered a church built on the spot. In time, a town grew up around the place and was called Santiago de Compostela (St. James of the Star Field). The original church Alfonso ordered built was made a cathedral, and in time became the goal of the pilgrims. (All this history does lead us back to the table, so be patient.)

It wasn't the Spanish, however, who promoted it, but the French Benedictine monks of Cluny who established monasteries along the route and helped spread the fame of Santiago de Compostela. For a few centuries the town and cathedral rivaled Rome and Jerusalem as a goal for pilgrims. The monks realized that Santiago would provide a nearby spiritual location for western Europe, a rallying point for the battle against the Moors that was taking place in Spain and in the Middle East.

Of course the pilgrims would need lodging, and where there were inns, there were kitchens and wine barrels, so Saint James, as we shall see, came to play a key role at table as well as on the battlefield.

Today, the political situation in both Rioja and Navarre is fluid. Both are autonomous regions, but there is pressure on them from two directions. In the north, the Basques would like to include both in an expanded Basque region, while the central government in Madrid would like them to join in a loose confederacy that would include most of the kingdom of Old Castile.

Generally, Rioja and Navarre are fairly prosperous regions, with an economy based on agriculture and to some extent—at least in Navarre—tourism. As we travel farther north, there is much more sympathy for the Basque cause, especially in the urban areas. Indeed, Pamplona almost feels like a Basque city.

THE FOOD

This is meat-and-potatoes country. The emphasis is on simple, hearty dishes, and shades into the more sophisticated Basque cuisine in the north. It is a bit odd that the French, who have had some influence over Rioja winemaking, have had very little influence in the kitchen. Taken as a whole, Riojan food is basic country fare, but as everywhere in Spain, it is country fare based on the finest and freshest ingredients.

Throughout Spain, La Rioja is well known for bean dishes. About every kind of bean imaginable and all colors are available. One of the region's most famous dishes is *congrio a la riojana*, or conger eel. How an inland region like Rioja became famous for a conger eel dish is anybody's guess. Rioja also has its own version of *pisto*, the vegetable dish that is found everywhere in Spain. In Rioja, lamb is often added to *pisto*, and sometimes chicken or partridge as well.

We have been very happy at table in Rioja and Navarre, but there are surprisingly few recipes to show for many, many hours of lovely eating. Rioja fare is perfect for summertime at the barbie. It is not food that requires a great deal of concentration, which leaves plenty of time for the wine and plenty of time for friends and lovers.

When we think of the food of Rioja, we remember the yupgour (yuppie gourmet) expression, "This is to die for!" On the contrary, the food of Rioja is to live for, and it begins with the garden. Aside from the plentiful beans, there are bushels of sweet and hot peppers overflowing at the counters at every market in the summer; dried peppers in the winter, along with supplies of fresh peppers from Huelva in Andalusia or from the Canary Islands. Leave room for potatoes, which appear on the table daily in some form.

There is trout from the rivers, often still alive at the market or in a restaurant tank. The region, like everywhere in Spain, is rich in hams and sausages, both dried and fresh. Lamb, in season, and mutton, year-round, round out the butchers' markets, with just a smattering of beef and goat.

Rabbit, quail, and partridge are all raised domestically, but also hunted, especially as you move north into the mountains. There are also deer and wild boar and ducks and geese, in season.

THE WINES

The wines of Rioja represent the world's last great wine bargains. There are world-class red wines at astonishingly low prices from Rioja Alta and fresh, fruity reds and delicious rosés from Navarre to liven up the most simple meals. The great Rioja red wines have the tremendous stamina to age well and would make an excellent foundation for anyone's wine cellar.

There have been, of course, vineyards in the Rioja area since pre-

Roman times. The Romans replanted the vineyards with vines from
Italy and exported wine from Rioja, not only to other parts of Spain
but down the Río Ebro to the Mediterranean and on to Italy.

In Navarre at Funes there are the remains of a large Roman
winery from the first century A.D. Judging from the size of the fermentation vats, perhaps 30,000 gallons of wine were produced each
year, roughly the equivalent of a medium-size California Napa Valley winery, say Cakebread Cellars. Another major winemaking center in Rioja is Cenicero, a town where the Roman legionnaires
cremated and buried their dead. In a rather grotesque linguistic
development, *cenicero* means ashtray in modern Spanish.

Winemaking declined somewhat under the Moors, although as in
other parts of Spain, the Moors didn't end winemaking altogether.
They had no objections to Christians living under their rule making
wine and selling it to one another or trading it to other areas. And,
of course, abstinence may have been the goal and ideal of true
Moslems, but like men and women everywhere, they doubtless
sometimes fell short of that goal, and Mecca was far away.

As the Moors retreated before the Christian armies, wine assumed
greater importance in the Rioja. This renaissance of Rioja winemaking came about first in monasteries at San Millan de Suso, San
Millan de Yuso, and Valvanera in the hills that lined the pilgrimage
route to Santiago. As the pilgrimage route became more important,
wine to ease the labor of the road also became more important, and
the vine thrived all along the "French road."

Until at least the seventeenth century, the basic wine of Rioja was
white by a factor of over ten to one. The vines were trained to grow
up trees or in *pergolas*, as they still are in parts of Galicia, Portugal,
and northern Italy.

As time went on, a few French merchants followed the French
monks of Cluny and the pilgrims from all over Europe along the
road to Santiago. And there are some who believe another very
important French émigré arrived at about the same time—the Pinot
Noir grape, now called Tempranillo, brought along by the monks
and others to replace the wild, high-growing and low-yielding hillside vines.

The idea that the Tempranillo grape came from France is a controversial notion to the Spanish, who are very reluctant to cite a
French origin for anything they put on their plate or in their glass,
let alone the Tempranillo, the famous red grape of Rioja, but it is a
possibility. The idea is difficult to prove or disprove botanically, as
Pinot Noir mutates more dramatically than any other wine grape.

(As one expert on Pinot Noir puts it, you could plant twenty Pinot Noir vines in a row and at the end of twenty years' growing time you could have twenty different clones of Pinot Noir.) One can imagine the changes the grape would undergo moving from the cool, sometimes harsh, growing conditions of Burgundy to the warmer, more even climate of Rioja.

It is on the palate that the Tempranillo-based wines of Rioja show such a strong resemblance to Pinot Noir. At their best, they have the same silky, velvety character, the lush forward fruitiness that is always hoped for in Burgundy but is achieved only in rare years. There is an earthy, mushroomy quality to the Tempranillo-based red wine of Rioja and the Pinot Noir of Burgundy.

Rioja (and when we talk about Rioja wines, we always mean wine made chiefly from the Tempranillo grape) has a sensual, feminine quality quite different from the harder, more closed wines of Bordeaux, which are based on the Cabernet Sauvignon and cousin grapes. And this despite more than one hundred years of effort by the French winemakers from Bordeaux to carve a Bordeaux-style wine from the Tempranillo, including the planting of Cabernet Sauvignon—now forbidden for the most part in Rioja.

The regulatory authorities believe that the addition of Cabernet Sauvignon to the red wines of Rioja would change the traditional character of the wine for the worse. There is widespread support for this belief among winemakers there, who feel there is already enough Cabernet Sauvignon in the world and that Rioja should use its own strength, not borrow from others.

There are others who note a suspected Italian influence in Rioja because of the addition of a small percentage of white wine grapes in the final blend, a common practice in northern Italy, most notably in Chianti. There were certainly Italian pilgrims on the road to Santiago, and most probably some of them were familiar with wine. On the other hand, the practice of blending a little white wine into the harsher red wine is common in most of Europe and can't be traced directly to the Italians.

As the wild hillside vines were replaced—and this is something that took centuries to happen—there was a gradual shift from white wine to red wine. There was also a shift in how the vines were grown. Rioja vineyards now are similar to the vineyards of France, with low-growing vines pruned *en vaso*, like a spreading shrub in the shape of a vase.

(The higher-trellising techniques, where the vines grow on wires four to six feet off the ground, common in California, Australia, and other modern vinegrowing areas, is gradually catching on in Spain. It has certain viticultural advantages—the grapes are more exposed to sunlight and to wind and therefore less susceptible to rot. Mechanical harvesting is also easier, a growing consideration in Spain, where labor costs are soaring as the Spanish income strives to catch up with the rest of the European Common Market.)

Rioja was an important source of wine supply for the New World, and vineyards expanded rapidly during the sixteenth and seventeenth centuries. The wine trade grew in importance, and in 1790 the Royal Society of Harvesters of the Rioja was formed for the purpose of growing better grapes, making better wine, and finding new markets—something Rioja is still busy attempting to accomplish, especially the finding of new markets.

The modern Rioja wine industry was largely the invention of the French in the nineteenth century. They were fleeing the invasion of a tiny louse from America that was devastating vineyards all over Europe.

No, the louse wasn't an American prohibitionist, but a tiny insect or root louse called phylloxera, which lives on the roots of grapevines and eventually kills the vine. Indigenous American vines have developed a tolerance for the phylloxera louse. In Europe, however —where there was no phylloxera prior to the introduction of experimental American vines in some English and French nurseries early in the nineteenth century—the pest was devastating.

Once phylloxera was established in a vineyard, it took roughly five to ten years for it to run its course and damage the vines beyond use. In desperation, the Europeans tried any number of things, including flooding the vineyards, hoping they could drown the louse, which lived in the ground. Nothing worked, and the flightless phylloxera louse moved itself rather slowly from vineyard to vineyard, area to area. Occasionally, the phylloxera would leapfrog from one place to another, carried on a vineyard worker's boots or a piece of agricultural equipment.

At any rate, by the late 1860s, the vineyards of Bordeaux (which lie only a few degrees of latitude north of Rioja) were so badly diseased that French winemakers began crossing the Pyrenees and establishing vineyards in Rioja, where there was still no phylloxera. In fact, a few French winegrowers had gone into Spain a dozen or so years before, when another vine disease, oidium, or powdery mildew, hit the vineyards of Bordeaux.

By the early 1900s, the phylloxera louse had reached Rioja, but by that time, viticulturists had learned that some American rootstocks were immune, or at least very resistant, to the louse and winegrowers were grafting the European *Vitis vinifera* vines onto American rootstock.

The arrival of the French in full force (there had been some French vintners trickling in for centuries, following the Camino de Santiago) was a mixed blessing for Rioja because of the French winemakers' passion for blending. This wave of French winemakers and vineyardists who fled phylloxera came, in the beginning, in search of wine to ship to their customers in England and the north of Europe. They bought wines wherever they could find them, blending from one district to another in an effort to approximate the shippers' wines of Bordeaux.

In Bordeaux, only the finest estates made what we call estate-grown wine—wine made from grapes grown only on the estate where the wine is made and bottled. Lesser wines were blends from various vineyards and regions both inside and outside Bordeaux. In the nineteenth century, it was common practice in Bordeaux to blend the dark red wines of Cahors and Gascony with the often light-bodied Bordeaux wines.

Rioja is still, largely, a blended wine—a blend of different vineyards, different areas, and different grapes. This historical approach to winemaking has been a handicap in the world market, where consumers believe the "great wines" to be the product of a single estate or vineyard. This is nonsense, of course, as very few vineyards can produce great wine year after year. Often there will be an element missing that can be found in another vineyard, maybe next door or perhaps 10 or 100 miles away. The art of blending is the art of winemaking at its highest degree. There are some Rioja wineries that are beginning to follow the "estate" concept, but most in Rioja still consider blending to be the key to great wines. The problem is not the wines but convincing the public that a great wine can be blended.

There are seven major—and approved—grape varieties in Rioja. For red wine there is Tempranillo, Garnacha Tinta, Graciano, and Mazuelo. Tempranillo is the most widely planted, at about 42 percent. Garnacha is next at about 32 percent.

The Tempranillo is an early-ripening grape with a very black, thick skin. The Tempranillo grape is known as the Cencibel in La

Mancha and the Ull de Llebre in Catalonia. The Garnacha Tinta is the same grape as the Grenache of the Rhône Valley, where it is a key element in the blend of Châteauneuf-du-Pape and Tavel rosés. It was probably introduced into Rioja via Aragón or by pilgrims on the road to Santiago. The Mazuelo is found in very old vineyards and is believed to be a native of the Rioja-Navarre area. The Graciano is also believed to be a native of the area, as it is found in the most ancient vineyards.

For white wines, the grapes are Viura, Malvasia, and Garnacha Blanca, with Viura the most common at about 20 percent of the vineyards. The white wines of Rioja are made almost entirely from the Viura, while the Garnacha is used for rosés.

The Viura is known in Catalonia as the Macabeo and was introduced into Rioja from Aragón. It is probably originally from the south of France. The Garnacha Blanca is another French introduction. It is a common grape throughout France and Spain. The Malvasia is also known as the Blanca-Roja. It was probably first brought to Spain by early Greek settlers, perhaps even by Phoenicians.

There has been a tremendous change in the whites and rosés of Rioja in the past decade. It didn't take the producers there long to see what a success Miguel Torres, Jr., of Bodegas Torres had made in Catalonia with his fresh, fruity white wines like Viña Sol. Torres, French-trained and with a great interest in California winemaking techniques, began making white wines using cold fermentation and stainless steel, avoiding any barrel-aging or giving only a light smack of oak. His wines emphasized the fruitiness of the grape; they were, and are, made for pure immediate drinking pleasure.

For centuries, Spanish white wines had been made in much the same way that the reds were made—hot fermentation, several years in oak casks. The results were tired, often oxidized, white wines with no hint of fruit, bogged down in oak flavors. They had a following in Spain, but nowhere else.

When Torres put his Viña Sol on the market in the 1970s, critics said it would never be a success. The Spanish, it was believed, would not take to a light, fruity white wine, and it would never get anywhere in the world market, since everyone expected Spanish white wines to be oxidized and oaky. In fact, Viña Sol was an immense success from the beginning, not only in the national Spanish market but internationally as well. It has been a huge success for Torres in the United States, where it was successfully introduced by Marimar Torres, Miguel's sister.

The Rioja winemakers quickly followed suit, as well as the larger co-op wineries of Valencia and La Mancha, so that within ten years an incredible revolution had taken place in the white wines of Spain.

The blend of Rioja reds is typically Tempranillo, Garnacha, Graciano, Mazuelo, and sometimes a little Viura. Garnacha, grown mostly in the warmer Rioja Baja, is added to raise the level of alcohol as well as to contribute a little extra fruitiness and color. The Mazuelo is a very tannic wine. Some winemakers believe that a small percentage will contribute to the aging potential of the wine. The Graciano is a very aromatic grape on its own, adding aroma and softness to the blend.

The blending of the white wine grape Viura into the red Rioja seems to surprise Americans, but it is a common practice throughout northern Italy, southern France, and most of Spain and Portugal. For example, at La Rioja Alta Winery in Haro, about 5 percent Viura is blended in each year to add a touch of acid to the blend, since the Viura, especially when picked slightly young, is a very acidic grape. This touch of Viura, the winemaker feels, adds aging potential to the wine. There are no regulations controlling the blending, so it is up to individual wineries to establish a style or a blend that meets the particular vineyard conditions of the winery.

The wine coming out of Rioja today—and not only the white wine—has changed considerably in the past twenty years. Rioja winemakers are sharply divided between those who follow the traditional methods of winemaking and those who are making lighter wines.

Briefly, the aging practice for red wines in Rioja is as follows:

Crianza is the youngest red wine. It must have at least one year in barrel and one year in bottle before release.

Reserva must have three years in a combination of barrel and bottle, of which at least one must be in barrel.

Gran Reserva must have had at least five years maturing, of which at least two years must be in barrel.

The traditionalists leave the wine in barrel much longer. For example, at Berberana, the *gran reserva* gets four years in barrel and three in bottle before release. Those wineries wanting to make a lighter, fruitier wine give the wine the minimum allowed barrel time, the rest of the time in bottle.

Of course, the entire concept of barrel aging in Rioja is very different from what it is in California or most of France. In Rioja, the barrels themselves are much older than those commonly used in California, where a barrel is generally discarded after five to eight years. At that point, the barrel has lost its oak tannins and no longer imparts oak flavor to the wine. In Rioja, barrels are used for at least thirty years and are never intended to make an "oaky" wine. The purpose of long barrel aging in the Spanish view is to allow some oxygen to penetrate the wood and soften the wine by a very slight oxidation. This is a controversial idea in California, where it is held that oxygen should not enter the barrel.

All of this, of course, means very little to most consumers. They are, rightfully, interested only in what is in the bottle on the table. And what is in that bottle has simply become better and better over the past two decades. Rioja had for centuries produced fine wines. Recently, some truly great wines are appearing.

Some of the more traditional producers—those who follow the long-barrel-aging formula—argue that the newer Rioja reds will not age as well as the wines have in the past. Perhaps. But the real answer to that is, Does it matter? Most wine is consumed within hours of purchase. What we want in our glass is a wine that tastes good right now. A wine that goes well with the food on the plate. And Rioja does that admirably.

Rioja brands to look for in the United States are Berberana, Beronia, Bilbainas, Marqués de Cáceres, Campo Viejo, Conde de Valdeman, Domecq, Faustino Martínez, R. Lopez de Heredia Viña Tondonia, Martínez Bujanda, Montecillo (excellent older vintages still available), Muga, Marqués de Murrieta, Olarra, and La Granja Remelluri (makes outstanding estate Rioja).

It can be hot in Rioja-Navarre during the harvest, but nothing like the sweltering, baking heat of the south in La Mancha or Andalusia. In fact, mornings can be chilly, and sweaters are welcome. The greatest fear at harvest is rain. In the old head-pruned vineyards, rot spreads quickly and a promising harvest can turn into a disaster in a few days.

One often hears in Rioja that it is not the variety of wine that is important but the vineyard. In fact, no one can really talk about exact percentages of grapes in Rioja blends, since only the vineyards planted in the past five to ten years are planted to a single variety. The older vineyards are a mix of both red and white wine varieties.

Since almost half of the vineyards in Rioja are more than thirty-five years old, it is obvious that the winemaker must know the vineyards from which his or her grapes come very well in order to have even an approximate understanding of what is going into the blend.

As the winter comes on, in that little lull in the vineyard year between harvest and pruning, when the wines are safely tucked into barrel or tank and the pruners have not yet entered the vineyards, it is pleasant to be inside with the wines. Even though the cellar may be colder than it is outdoors, we have the wine to keep us warm. But drinking newly made wine (or tasting, rather, this is not the time for drinking) is not a total joy. It is also the most difficult thing to learn in winemaking, this business of judging a new wine. It is really where years of experience pay off. One must be able to taste the raw young wine and compare it with the raw young wine of years past to have a clue of where it is bound in its journey through the cellar over the next several years. Is it destined to be a common everyday bottle of wine, pleasant enough but nothing special, or does it have the quality to become one of the great wines of the world? There will have been clues already, of course. The growing season before harvest is a major consideration. Was it too hot, too cool? Was there too much rain at harvest? Did rot work its way inside the bunches of grapes, often undetected until too late to do anything about it?

So we already have some sense of what to expect from the wine in the long run, again based on past experience. But when it comes right down to the wine in the barrel, there are judgments to be made, which can be based only on the taste in the mouth, not the harvest records. There is probably no winegrowing region where these first tastings are more important than in Rioja, since Rioja is essentially a blended wine. In the better houses, the wines from different areas or different vineyards are kept separate for evaluation during the blending process.

It is at this point, with fermentation finished and the wine resting in barrel or tank, that the "making" of the wine really begins. Actually, the entire notion of "making" a wine is a most un-Spanish idea in itself. All across Spain, no one is called a winemaker, except by those wineries accustomed to dealing with Americans. What we call the "winemaker" is called the "technical director" or "enologist." When the Spanish talk about winemaking (or what we would call winemaking), they use the verb *elaborar*, the first meaning of which is "to elaborate, to extend," "to make something from primary material." This is not simply an academic point of language but goes deep into the Spanish attitude toward wine. Wine is a natural, not a manufactured, product. It is something that has "made itself," and the enologist elaborates on an already created thing.

We once toured a large Spanish co-op in La Mancha with a group of American and British wine journalists. A journalist in the group spent a great of time trying to determine when a certain step in the winemaking procedure took place—we don't recall what it was—and the enologist, who spoke adequate English, was trying to tell him, but neither could follow the other's statements because of the confusion involved with making versus elaborating. The Spaniard finally threw up his hands, cut the tour short, and led them into the tasting room where they could talk about the wine in the glass, rather than how it got there.

Early one winter day, the process of "elaborating" was about to begin at Bodegas Berberana in Rioja. We were to meet Angel Yecora, an enologist at Berberana, deep in the cellars of Berberana's very modern winery in the town of Cenicero, where the ruins of an ancient Roman winery can also be found. Yecora's mission was to sample some of the tanks of new wine and talk about how he would do the blending later on.

There are no formulas to follow, he said. "The blending is in the tasting, not by recipe." Like the development of sherry, the wine determines its own future.

"The time in barrel depends on the tasting, beginning now," Yecora said. He was speaking of whether the wine would become a *crianza*, a young wine that would receive little aging, a *reserva*, or a *gran reserva*.

"It is all in the wine," Yecora repeated, as we proceeded.

We could have picked a smaller winery for our introduction to Rioja Blending 1A, but at the time we were sure we were ready to for graduate school, so no problem. Berberana had its beginnings in 1877 in the small village of Ollauri. In 1972, after decades of steady growth, they built a new winery at Cenicero with a total capacity of 25 million liters. It is one of the most modern wineries in Spain, with two huge underground storage areas containing 25,000 oak barrels, an entire forest.

But Yecora had decided to make it easy for us by tasting only five wines, a Graciano, a red Garnacha, a Tempranillo, a Viura, and a Mazuelo. What they were dealing with was the basic grape varieties without being concerned with different vineyards or growing areas. He thought that would be plenty for us to handle.

It was pretty much a given that the Garnacha was destined to be a *rosado*, and even a few months from the vine that pleasant, rather acidic fruitiness that is the mark of a *rosado* was evident. The Viura was a high-acid white wine—rather simple, but it would serve its purpose of adding some acidic backbone to the final blend. The Tempranillo was very fruity, pleasantly round on the palate. The acidity seemed low on the finish, giving the wine a flabby feeling. But that's what the Viura was for, and it wouldn't take much of it. The Garnacha, also fairly acidic, could help with that, too. The Mazuelo sample was a deep, rich red with an abundant tannic extract, which makes it a useful blending wine, especially in lighter years.

Yecora (and most other Rioja enologists) believe that with those basic five grapes (with the addition of a little Malvasia and Garnacha Blanca) they can make about anything they want in Rioja. A few growers have been urging the planting of Cabernet Sauvignon, but there is widespread opposition to that.

The idea of making a wine from a single grape varietal (as is done in California, parts of France, Italy, and Germany) is also opposed, although there have been some experiments with Tempranillo. Yecora is very much against a single variety, or even a single vineyard wine, feeling that it is in the blending that Rioja really expresses itself.

After tasting the basic five barrel samples, Yecora tapped a few more barrels, getting more and more excited about the prospects of the vintage. We were deep under the earth, going from barrel to barrel, with Yecora demonstrating the difference between Tempranillo grown at low and high elevations (more acidic at the higher elevation) and speculating on how the wines would fit into future blends or into the reserve program.

Many of the wines were surprisingly palatable for young wines only a few months old. Perhaps because the Spanish do not have the love affair with new oak barrels that California winemakers have, the young wine doesn't have the tannins picked up from new oak.

Berberana is very much a working winery, not a museum. The floors are simple concrete, the lighting is dim (to cut down on heat and energy use.) The barrel-storage area is designed for efficient use (including a central computer system for blending that looks like a set out of a *Star Wars* epic), yet there is something magical about tasting in a barrel room. It has to do with the smell of new wine, a cool earthiness coming from the casks and barrels that is very soothing, very satisfying.

RECENT RIOJA VINTAGES

1970 · Very good	1978 · Very good
1971 · A poor year	1979 · Just passable
1972 · Another bad year	1980 · Good
1973 · One of the best years in memory	1981 · Excellent year
	1982 · Another outstanding year
1974 · Fair	
1975 · Excellent year	1983 · Merely good
1976 · Very good	1984 · Good
1977 · Poor	1985 · Good

SPANISH DAYS

It was at a lunch held at the Bodegas Marqués de Murrieta that we realized we were seriously sold on Rioja. Our host, the present Marqués, asked for the year of birth of the oldest person at the lunch. There were about a dozen people present. The senior guest turned out to be Alexis Bespaloff, the New York food and wine writer. Alex was born in 1934. The Marqués asked to see his passport as proof.

Alex handed it over and the Marqués turned to one of the wine servers and called for a bottle of the '34 from the cellar. He carefully poured out a small serving for each of us. It was fantastic. Far better, we agreed, than any 1934 Bordeaux we had ever sampled. The wine still seemed young, fresh; there was definite fruitiness in the finish with only slight browning or discoloration. All in all, a remarkably lively wine for being (at the time of tasting) fifty-five years old.

Then, a few moments later, the head of the Rioja wine council stood up to give a toast to the cook whose lunch we had just enjoyed.

His words stand out as if they were graven on stone. "There is nothing more important to the Spanish than food," he said. We spend thirty-five percent of our income on food, much more than any other nation." I later verified that figure and it is substantially correct. But even at that, the modern Spaniard hasn't a patch on Don Quixote of La Mancha, who spent 75 percent of his income on food.

"At a certain village in La Mancha, which I shall not name, there lived not long ago one of those old-fashioned Gentlemen who are never without a Lance upon a Rack, an old Target, a lean Horse and a Greyhound. His Diet consisted more of Beef than Mutton; and with minc'd Meat on most Nights, Lentils on Fridays, Eggs and Bacon on Saturdays, and a Pigeon extraordinary on Saturdays, he consumed three Quarters of his Revenue."

"And not," the luncheon speaker went on to say, "because the basic foods are more expensive in Spain than in France or other countries, but because the Spaniard demands the best at his table. Just as with our fine Rioja wines, only the best will do. The best ingredients, whether it be a simple vegetable soup, such as we had here today . . ."

(How could he call the remarkable *pisto* we had that day a "simple soup"?)

". . . or the finest of seafood, it must be the best.

"And we demand variety, too, in our food . . ."

(All this was in Castilian and was much more flowery than a simple English translation.)

". . . At my house, for example, we have a different menu for dinner every day of the year. Ladies and gentleman, I give you the chef."

Indeed. A different menu for dinner every day. We wanted to rush forward and give the honorable gentleman a hug. But mostly we wanted to sign on for room and board at his house for a year. We had intended, in fact, to ask him if he allowed repetitions from one year to another, but the Marqués began sending around a *pacharán* fruit brandy from Navarre (with a touch of anise) and the question was never asked.

One bright winter day we were slated for the cellars at Bodegas Beronia, a Rioja winery with an unusual history. The name comes from the tribe of Berones, who gave the Romans a hard time in the third century B.C. The winery was founded in 1970 by a Basque gastronomic society whose members wanted to drink wine to match the food they ate. Unable to find an acceptable wine (at the price they wanted to pay, at any rate), the society started their own winery near the town of Ollauri in Rioja Alta. The winery was so successful at making the good wine desired by the Basque gastronomes that the shareholders soon realized they needed help. In 1982 they formed a partnership with González Byass of Jerez de la Frontera. The multinational Jerez firm has taken over the marketing, leaving the winemaking alone except for some capital expense in modernization. The results have been superb.

Larry must, in honesty, admit that he arrived at Beronia the worse for wear. The previous evening had been spent in Logroño, with a long dinner as a kind of rehearsal for Twelfth Night dinner, followed by a personal examination of a number of bars where one might find the best examples of that Rioja specialty, coffee caramels. At this point, he has no idea why he believed it might be possible to find the perfect coffee caramel in a bar. Or why, for that matter, Logroño has become well known for such delights. Perhaps it was simply another curious guidebook glitch.

At any rate, the host at Beronia took one look at Larry at ten the next morning and promptly led him to the dining room, calling for anise and coffee as they entered. They sat down with a bottle of Chinchón and endless cups of espresso. Larry learned considerably more about Beronia and vineyards and winemaking in Rioja over the next two hours and half bottle of Chinchón than he would have learned while walking with throbbing head through the cellars.

Larry doesn't mean this as justification for a rather more-than-moderate consumption of the best Rioja had to offer the night before, but rather as an example of the quick and gracious adaptability of the Spanish to the needs of a guest.

About vineyards:

• The location of a vineyard is more important than what is planted in it.

• Most vineyard owners in Rioja have other crops planted; they are not solely dependent on vines. Often, grapes are not even the most important source of income.

• There are only two vineyards in Rioja of more than 100 hectares.

• Because of rulings by the European Economic Community, no new plantings are now allowed in Rioja.

• One hectare of land in Rioja costs about 9 million pesetas. In other areas of Spain, a hectare of vines costs about 2 million pesetas. (One hectare is equal to 2.471 acres of land. At the time of the hangover symposium at Beronia, the peseta was about 125 to the dollar.)

• There is concern in Rioja about foreigners (French, mostly) buying vineyards.

By about the third tiny glass of Chinchón and espresso, Larry noticed that a man and woman were quietly setting a table across the room and that a hooded indoor grill had been laid with vine cuttings. Yes, that's right. He remembered that he was to be joined at lunch by a few more people, at least one of whom (Ann) had been on the unlikely search for the perfect coffee caramel the night before.

The sun was shining outside the wide windows, overlooking a bucolic hillside setting of vines and sheep. All seemed well. Chinchón, it turns out, is one of Spain's two major brands of anise-flavored liqueur, the other being Anís del Mono, which is made in Badalona, just up the Costa Brava from Barcelona. Chinchón is from the village of the same name about 50 kilometers from Madrid. Besides producing the life-restoring drink to which it lends its name, Chinchón is a charming pueblo with a particularly pleasant Plaza Mayor, where bullfights have been held since the 1500s. There are few better places to sit in the sunshine and sip the native drink at its source.

Larry was just beginning to feel guilty about neglecting the cellars when he smelled vine cuttings burning on the grill and heard the pleasant sound of a cork being pulled from a bottle. Good Lord! It was lunchtime and he had actually made it through the morning without disgracing himself.

As you might expect, anyone staffing the kitchen at a winery owned by a Basque gastronomic society would be able to serve forward a better-than-fair lunch, which was the case that day. They had, furthermore, wisely decided to keep it simple. The lunch was Rioja country food at its best. Every dish we had could be found elsewhere in Spain, yet each one had its Rioja signature.

We were introduced to Pepe and María del Valle Pascual as they were laying *chorizo* and strips of red pepper on the grill. They had been at the winery for years, handling just about any sort of entertainment from a modern but fairly straightforward working cook's kitchen. The pepper and *chorizo* were passed as a tapa before we sat down to lunch. Señor del Valle explained that the tiny, finger-size *chorizo* were a specialty of the north in Rioja, Navarre, and the Basque country. They had less filling and more meat than *chorizo* from Extremadura or parts of southern Spain. They had also been well aged and were drier, but the grilling brought out the flavor and the fat perfectly.

He was not so pleased with the peppers. It being late in the year, they had come from Huelva, in the south, most probably grown under plastic. He said that if we were to return in early summer, he could offer peppers from Rioja that would put these to shame. We found them delicious grilled, however, and he agreed, adding that he would never serve such hothouse peppers fresh.

We sat down to a heaping serving platter (which was the pan it had been made in) of *menestra de verduras*, the basic vegetable stew of all Spain. It is served year-round, with the ingredients varying with what is in season. That day it was heavy on carrots, beans, potatoes, canned peas, ham, and hard-boiled eggs (with plenty of garlic, of course). At other times of the year it would include fresh peas, green beans, spinach, artichokes, other greens in season, and perhaps beets or turnips—turnips especially in Catalonia.

There appeared a heaping platter of lamb ribs served with french fries. The ribs had been grilled over the vine cuttings to total perfection, tender, juicy, and loaded with flavor. These were, in fact, the lamb ribs that pilgrims have been traveling to Rioja to find for centuries. They were as miraculous as any saintly appearance. They were somewhat smaller than lamb ribs in the United States, and somewhat fatter, but most of the fat was left behind in the coals, leaving only the deep flavor of the meat.

We asked Señor del Valle if the vines gave the lamb its great flavor, but he shook his head. Not at all. The flavor, he said, came from the lamb itself, which had been milk-fed, not just on one ewe, but two, a specialty of the north. He used vine cuttings because the heat could be quickly raised or lowered by the fast-burning cuttings. I would like to cautiously suggest that it is not beyond question for American cooks to find vine cuttings. Grapes are grown in nearly every state now, and grown for commercial winemaking in (at last count) forty-five states. In most places, after the vines are pruned, the cuttings are simply piled at the edge of the vineyard and burned. What a waste! A Sunday drive to the nearest vineyard (whether it's a wine grape or table grape vineyard doesn't matter) anytime after mid-January should turn up enough cuttings to fill your trunk or station wagon in a few minutes.

Señor del Valle told us to forget about the knives and forks for the lamb ribs. We should eat them, he said, like we were playing the harmonica.

We had followed the ripening vines through the heart of Spain, from early September and Andalusia in the south through La Mancha,

ending finally in the lower reaches of the Pyrenees in late October
with the grape harvest finished except for a few scattered mountain
vineyards. After a quick weekend visit to English friends in San
Sebastián, we were on a weird mission, in search of the lost Basques
of Bakersfield, having read that many Basques left Spain during the
Civil War and settled in California and Nevada. This we knew to be
true. It was the next part that sent us on this odd quest, plunging
down the steep mountain road from Roncesvalles (where Charlemagne was defeated by a Basque force, and the heroic Roland lost
his life) toward the border town of Valcarlos. The article went on to
declare that many of these expatriate Basques had retired in Bakersfield, California. When Franco died they left Bakersfield and returned to Spain, settling in and around Valcarlos. There, or so it
was claimed, should the political climate once more become uncomfortable, it would be easy enough to slip across the border into
France.

It all seemed unlikely somehow. Why should émigré Basques accustomed to the mountains first of Spain, then of California, inflict
upon themselves the dry, dusty, and polluted air of Bakersfield? But
before that question, there was Roncesvalles. It hangs hawklike at
the head of the mountain pass that spills down into France, the
route of Charlemagne's retreat, the route the pilgrims took centuries
later on the way to Santiago de Compostela.

We had driven almost cross-country through the lower southern-
reaching fingers of the Pyrenees for the most of the day, having left
San Sebastián early that morning. The main roads follow the mountain valleys south-southeast toward the fertile vineyards of Navarre
or Rioja. In a small rented car dubbed the *bota* patrol, we were
cutting across those valleys, following breathtaking asphalt roads,
gravel and dirt roads.

Once, the asphalt road ended in the farmyard of a small whitewashed house, each window graced with a wooden windowbox
with blooming geraniums. Fruit trees were trained against a south
wall, the fruit already picked, only a few late leaves hanging on
against the winter, bare dark branches against the white house. A
few chickens pecked warily at the kitchen midden farther down
the hill.

Beyond the farmyard, there seemed to be a faint trace of a road,
sketched through a green, cow-dotted pasture along a hillside, disappearing into a grove of trees higher up the mountain.

A man appeared around the corner of the house. He wore the

typical Basque uniform—a baggy blue sweater over baggy colorless pants, topped off with a black beret. Was there the hint of an amused glint in his eye as he looked at the silly little red car sitting dispiritedly in the mud outside his door? Wordlessly, we offered him the *bota*. He accepted, and took a long deep squeeze of wine, which we had bought that morning in San Sebastián.

No, he said, the road was impassable except for mules and horses. We had a detailed map of Navarre, which showed the road continuing over the next pass until it reached C135, the main road to Roncesvalles.

He shook his head. *No se puede pasar, no se puede pasar!* There had been a landslide a few years before and the road had not been repaired.

Okay. We thanked him and started to get back in the car.

"Wait, wait," he said.

He went into the house. There was movement—his wife, no doubt—in one of the downstairs windows before he reached the door, and he returned with a pitcher of light red wine. He asked for our *bota*, which was nearly empty. He squeezed the last few drops into his throat, then filled the *bota* with wine from his pitcher.

"It is better. It is from my nephew's vineyard near Pamplona. Try it now."

Larry anxiously squeezed the *bota*, afraid he would spill a few drops on his shirt and disgrace himself in the old farmer's eyes. Ann, too, squeezed out some wine in a clean spinning spiral from bag to mouth. The sunlight glinted off the wine. (There is a miniature painting in the wine museum at Vilafranca del Penedés in Catalonia in which a young peasant is drinking from a *bota* at almost the same angle.)

"It is better, much better." There are wonderful light red wines, sometimes called *rosato*, sometimes *clarete*, all through Navarre. It is possible that a well-made wine from home can be better than a commercial version, because it retains its intense, fruity, forward flavor through being vinified in small batches, with no commercial shortcuts or blendings.

"Yes," he said. "Your bag is good but that wine was sour."

He topped it off again and we turned toward the car, ready to retrace a few miles before we tried the next breakthrough toward Roncesvalles. A harsh but feminine voice shouted something in Basque, and Ann turned back from the car. A small dark Basque woman appeared, and taking Ann by the elbow, led her toward the house.

While they were gone, the farmer asked Larry to spread the map on the hood of the car. He stared at it in apparent astonishment. Finally, with a grimy finger, he traced the route we should follow to Roncesvalles. Ann and the Basque woman reappeared with a quarter of a loaf of bread, some sheep cheese wrapped in newspaper, and a few parings of ham cut from near the bone.

We had one hit on the *bota* all around and were on our way.

But not for long. As soon as we were decently out of sight, we pulled to the shoulder of the road, found a dry spot in a pasture shared with dozens of suspicious sheep, and picnicked. The cheese was the typical hard sheep cheese found all over Spain but brought to perfection in the Basque mountains. Its sharp, chewy acidity was a perfect counterpoint to the young, fruity light red wine (really a rosé) squeezed from the *bota*. Lovely. For a bit we watched the hawks scour the meadows for rodents, then we got into our *bota* patrol car to follow the route the old farmer had pointed out.

After a few kilometers we reached the graveled road that he had assured me would take us over the last ridge to C135. At the corner was a small country bar. It seemed a good idea to ask directions and perhaps replenish the *bota*. There were several cars parked outside, most with Pamplona license plates—it's a sign of good food in the countryside when city dwellers drive out to the country.

A blackboard was propped behind the bar, with *hay caldo* scrawled on it. We had come to an excellent place to ask directions. *Caldo*, in Spain, can mean anything from a stock or broth to a fairly substantial soup. It can be based on anything from chicken to veal to fish, depending on where you are in Spain and what needs to be cleaned out of the kitchen. (It is not to be confused, by the way, with *cocido*, which is a different kettle of soup altogether.)

The *caldo* at that particular nameless country restaurant turned out to be a beef broth laced with pork ribs, white beans, and a dash of potatoes. Very simple soup, mostly broth, served in shallow white bowls. That particular version had some flecks of spinach or chard chopped into it, probably plants just out of the soil from a pot on a south-facing window sill, since it was too late for garden greens.

After a generous bowl of *caldo*, and reassurances that the road was open, it was time to get serious about Roncesvalles and the Bakersfield Basques of Valcarlos. First of all, Roncesvalles is mostly an act of imagination—at least historical Roncesvalles. The huddled monastery and attendant buildings draw their fame from the battle celebrated in the French epic poem *Song of Roland*. The story goes that in 778 the rear guard of Charlemagne's forces, led by the warrior

Roland, were slaughtered at the pass of Roncesvalles after Roland blew his horn in desperation for help from Charlemagne, which never arrived.

Eighth-Century Newsflashes put out the story that it was the Moors who did the dirty work at the pass, but in fact it was the Basques, infuriated because Charlemagne had destroyed the walls and poisoned the wells at Pamplona when he withdrew. At any rate, modern historians say the battle might not have taken place at Roncesvalles anyway, but in nearby Hecho.

But Roncesvalles has been a major route through the Pyrenees since prehistoric times. And when the pilgrimage route to Santiago de Compostela was established in the twelfth century, it started at Valcarlos-Roncesvalles. The route covered about 500 miles, and we had wandered that day over several dozen of those miles.

Some guidebooks say that pilgrims to Santiago can still get a free bed at the monastery chapter house, but don't count on it. The ruins have been extensively rebuilt so that little actually remains of the abbey or the original Colegiata Real, as the monastery's church was called. There is a museum, but it seems to be open on whim.

There is a *posada*, which is set on the site of a medieval inn that was inside the monastery's walls. There is another inn, Casa Sabina, which sets a very pleasant regional table. The owner, Gabriel Guerrero, is a great booster of the wines of Navarre, and while his selection is not extensive, it is quite good.

He is also very proud of an elaborate flan dessert that he claims his wife prepares "with her own hands and from her own recipe." I am prepared to believe his wife does indeed make it with her own hands, but I'll wager the recipe came from a supermarket food magazine like *Comer y Beber*, or perhaps even from a London newspaper cooking column left behind by a modern British pilgrim. The dish has a definite British "pudding" feel to it. Stick to his wine recommendations, however, and you'll be fine.

Whether his wife has anything to do with it or not, what appears on the table—other than flan—is more than passable. The Basque and Navarrese are famous throughout Spain for their appetites. Señor Guerrero seemed somewhat concerned that our lunch was not more substantial, but the food was good.

We began with a simple *trucha a la navarra*, grilled trout wrapped in ham, the trout fresh from the nearby Irati River. Because the ham gave an added dimension to the dish, we opted for a delicious *rosado* from Bodegas de Sarria, as recommended by Señor Guerrero.

The fruitiness of the wine matched well with the sweetness of the ham and fish.

Between courses, Señor Guerrero insisted on bringing a platter of the famed *chorizo* from Pamplona, which deserves its reputation. Finally, there was *cochifrito a la navarra*, a basic lamb sauté masterfully done by the Casa Sabina kitchen. With the lamb we went for a red wine from the Nuestra Señora del Romero co-op winery, made of a blend of Tempranillo, Garnacha, and a little Cabernet Sauvignon, which is a legal variety in Navarre, unlike Rioja. After Señora Guerrero's odd pudding, we finished off with a glass of the house *pacharán*.

Most of the standard guides detail the historic relics of Roncesvalles, but few pay more than a passing glance at the sheer beauty of the place. The exact site of the battlefield where Roland fell may be disputed by scholars, but no one can dispute the breathtaking road that plunges from the pass just above the monastery toward the French border and Valcarlos. On the hillsides and steep ravines stand a few remnants of the great oak forests that once covered most of Europe. It's called the Wood of Garralda and it gives a hint of what northern Navarre and the whole range of the Spanish Pyrenees must have looked like in the days of Charlemagne.

Valcarlos seems mundane after the plunge down the valley through the trees. It could be French or Swiss, even Austrian. Set in a narrow cut through the mountains, it seems to have little reason to exist. Perhaps that is the very quality that attracted the Bakersfield Basques. From one obscurity to the next.

We shot a game of pool in a small bar. A man at the bar agreed that there were Basques in Valcarlos who had once lived in California. Both he and the bartender were indifferent to the point of rudeness. Perhaps too many tourists had asked the same questions. And we were far from the Mediterranean, where people have time to answer questions.

We finished our game of pool and our beers and left. In and out of Valcarlos in twenty minutes. Back up over the pass, we raced the twilight in our *bota* patrol toward Jaca, the first capital of the kingdom of Aragón, and one of the best meals we have ever had in Spain.

In the cellars of La Rioja Alta Winery we were followed everywhere by a large white cat. Sometimes the cat would peer at us from between barrels, sometimes from atop a tall wooden upright.

There were other cats in the winery, but only the one giant white cat followed visitors, it seems.

"The cats in the winery are completely wild and no one feeds them, or very little. Sometimes they might get some lunch scraps from cellar workers, but no more. They keep us clear of rats and mice and they don't drink any of the wine, so they are no problem."

The young guide smiled. Gabriela Rezola had come in on her day off to show us around the winery, and whatever her expectations had been, she was quite enjoying the unexpected opportunity to taste some of the older wines as well as the new wine just put in barrels.

In early January the entire town of Haro in Rioja smelled of newly fermented wine, just as it did in the winery. It smelled much the same in cellars all over Spain, all over the world, no doubt, even those gleaming stainless steel pseudolaboratories that try to give the impression all wine is made by machine, that pervasive smell of just-fermented wine will out.

It is the very stuff of life, as all wise cats know.

GUIDELINES: RIOJA/NAVARRE

Haro

RESTAURANT

Terete, Calle Lucrecia Arana, 17. Tel. (941) 31-00-23. This restaurant has been serving the fine roasted meats of Rioja for over a hundred years. And they are still doing it right. Marvelous roast lamb and goat. Moderate.

HOTEL

Hostal Iturrimuri, about 1 kilometer outside Haro on the N232. Tel. (941) 31-12-13. Friendly and comfortable. Cheaper than staying in Logroño, but stay out of the restaurant.

Logroño

RESTAURANTS

Mesón de la Merced, Mayor, 109. Tel. (941) 22-11-66. Part of an old palace turned into a luxury restaurant. Very good regional dishes done with a bit of sophistication. Good Rioja wine list with some fine older vintages. Expensive.

Mesón Lorenzo, Calle Marqués de San Nicolás, 136. Tel. (941) 25-91-40. Good regional fare with a first-rate wine list. A bit cheaper than the Mesón de la Merced.

HOTELS

Los Bracos, Bretón de los Herreros, 29. Tel. (941) 24-66-08. Acceptable hotel near the center of town, only a few blocks from the river and the Catedral de Santa María de la Redonda. Moderate price. Avoid the dining room.

Pamplona

RESTAURANT

Las Pocholas, Paseo de Sarasate, 6. Tel. (948) 22-22-14. Classic Pamplonan fare, including several different dishes featuring a distinctive Pamplonan sausage called *cristorra*, which has an exterior texture much like *linguiça* but is soft and crumbly on the inside. The restaurant also features a wonderful *cordero chilindrón*, a roasted lamb dish made with lamb stew meat. If it's the bullfight season, ask for the *rabo estofado*, stewed bull's tail cooked in a red wine sauce.

Santo Domingo de la Calzada

HOTEL/RESTAURANT

Parador Nacional Santo Domingo de la Calzada, Plaza del Santo, 3. Tel. (941) 34-03-00. About 50 kilometers from Logroño, this stop on the Camino de Santiago is a charming village, well worth at least an overnight at the *parador*, one of the most pleasant and restful in Spain. The *parador* has a decent kitchen and is on the same plaza as the famous cathedral of Santo Domingo. It was in Santo Domingo that one of the most widely known miracles of the Camino de Santiago took place. It concerns a young pilgrim who was accused of robbery by the landlady's daughter when he refused her amorous advances. A woman scorned, she slipped some of the silverware into his luggage. As he and his family set off down the road, she called the cops. The young lad was sent to the gibbet and left for dead. But his parents discovered, hours later, that he was still living. They rushed to the judge, who declared that the young man was no more alive than the chickens he was about to eat. No sooner had he spoken than the roast birds started crowing and flapping about the room. Of course, the young man was spared and no doubt lived happily ever after. Ever since this medieval miracle, a live cock and a hen have been kept in a coop inside the cathedral. They have been given a place of honor, a roosting site near the main altar. If you rise early enough and walk to the plaza before the bustle of city traffic begins, it is possible to hear the cock crowing.

Tapas

The best bet is Logroño. Check the bars along the Calle Mayor or the Calle de los Laureles near the central square. There are a lot of tapas bars in Pamplona, but they seem to be filled with students whose favorite drink is beer with peach flavoring. This drink may have a lot to do with our belief that Pamplona is the most overrated city in Spain.

Wineries

The bodegas of Rioja match those of Jerez in hospitality. They often receive visitors from France, Germany, and the Scandinavian countries. In most cases, it is still a good idea to at least call in advance, as they are sometimes not comfortable with the California "open bar" attitude. The following wineries are a few that encourage visitors.

Bodegas Berberana, Cenicero. Tel. (941) 45-41-00. Open Monday to Friday, 8 A.M. until 1 P.M. and 2 P.M. until 5 P.M. Closed August.

Bodegas Campo Viejo, Calle Gustavo Becquer, 3, Logroño. Tel. (941) 23-80-00. Open Monday to Friday, 8 A.M. until 1 P.M. and 3 P.M. until 6 P.M. Closed July and August.

Bodegas La Rioja Alta, Barrio de la Estación (in the area of the railroad station), Haro. Tel. (941) 31-04-98. Open Monday to Friday, 10 A.M. until 1 P.M. and 3 P.M. until 5 P.M. Closed August.

Bodegas Marqués de Murrieta, about 3 kilometers south of the city center of Logroño on N232 southbound. Tel. (941) 25-81-00. Open Monday to Friday, 9 A.M. until 1 P.M. and 3 P.M. until 7 P.M. Closed August.

RECIPES

BASICS, TAPAS,
SOUPS, AND SALADS

HOJALDRE
Puff Pastry

The first time we visited Spain we were amazed at all the puff pastry with which we were presented: tiny puff pastry tartlets filled with crab; elegant puff pastry shells with sweetbreads and a dainty matching lid; a grand puff pastry tart of leeks and little puff pastry "fish" at the side of the plate. And all of it was delicious. Later, we came across an article by an old friend, Charles Perry, called "Puff Paste Is Spanish." Perry is an Arab scholar who for many years has researched the food of the Middle East and its many routes to Europe. His theory sounds reasonable, and certainly explains the abundance of really good puff pastry in Spain; they have had a lot of time to perfect it. We do not offer another recipe for puff pastry here because a couple of good ones already exist, and good-quality store-bought is now available. Try the versions in The Spanish Table *by Marimar Torres or* The Simple Art of Perfect Baking *by Flo Braker.*

Puff pastry makes everything seem more festive. Try one of these ideas for a special occasion. For best results, always refrigerate the puff pastry after you have formed it, before baking.

Tapas:
Using miniature tartlet pans, make small tartlet shells of puff pastry. Bake and fill with little bits of salads, vegetables, seafood, or meat.

Cut the puff pastry into rounds and fill with flavorful meats. Fold over and crimp the edges and bake. Serve as *empanadillas*.

First Course:
Make a box of the puff pastry with a lid and fill with one of the fish preparations offered in this book:

Preheat the oven to 425°F. Roll out the pastry to about ¼ inch thick and cut into any size squares. Cut twice the number of squares as people to serve. Put half the squares on an ungreased baking sheet. Moisten the edges of the squares with water. On the remaining squares with a sharp knife mark lines ½ inch from the edges but do not cut all the way through the pastry. Lay these squares on top of the other squares on the baking sheet. Bake for about 18 to 20 minutes.

Remove the boxes from the oven and cut along the marked lines and remove the "lids." Return the boxes but not the lids to the oven to dry out the insides. Pour in a hot filling, place a lid on top, and serve immediately.

Salad Course:
Make fanciful cuts of the pastry, sprinkle with grated cheese, and bake. Serve alongside the salad like toast points or croutons.

Dessert:

Crema Catalana, for example, page 306, makes a great filling paired with fresh fruit.

Make any type of container with the puff pastry, prebake, and fill just before serving with the *crema* mixed with fresh fruit.

PAN PUEBLO
Basic Spanish Bread

¡No hay pan. Dios mío!
It is inconceivable to eat in Spain without bread. Bread is essential to the enjoyment of the meal. The texture and quality of the breads vary from region to region with the quality of flour and water. And, of course, there are many different shapes. This recipe is something of a composite of the kind of bread you would find in most of Spain.

MAKES 1 LARGE LOAF.

1 tablespoon dry active yeast
(1 package or 1 cube)
5 cups all-purpose flour,
preferably unbleached bread
flour
2 teaspoons salt

3 tablespoons extra-virgin olive
oil
Cornmeal for sprinkling
baking sheet
Olive oil

Pour 1½ cups lukewarm water into a bowl. Add the yeast and let it dissolve. Stir in 1 cup of the flour. Cover the bowl and let the mixture rest for about 1 hour in a warm place.

Stir in the salt and extra-virgin olive oil and 2 cups more of the flour. Add 1 cup more of the flour and mix well. Turn the dough out onto a floured surface and gradually knead in the last cup of flour. You may not need all of the remaining cup. Shape the dough into a ball and place in an oiled bowl. Turn the dough until all sides are oiled. Cover and let rise in a warm place until doubled. This may take 2 hours.

Punch the dough down and shape into a large oval. Flatten the loaf until it is about 4 to 5 inches wide. Place the dough on a baking sheet sprinkled with cornmeal. Brush the top of the loaf with olive oil. Cover the dough and let rise until doubled.

Preheat the oven to 400°F.

Put the risen dough into the oven and bake for 15 minutes. Lower the heat to 375° and bake until puffed and golden, about another 30 minutes.

NOTE: For crusty bread, spray the loaf with water several times during baking.

CHURROS
Fried Pastries

One morning we were walking across a plaza in Toledo during a festival. The churro makers were doing a lively business. You could buy a single churro or as many as you'd like, which the churro makers would string on a long reed for you to carry along home.

A very common Spanish breakfast or afternoon snack is a cup of thick hot chocolate and a plate of churros.

SERVES 1 TO 5.

1 lemon	Oil for deep frying
1 cup all-purpose flour	Powdered sugar for dusting
1 teaspoon salt	the *churros*
1 egg	

Grate the rind of the lemon and combine with 1 cup of water in a medium saucepan. Bring to a boil and stir in the flour and salt. Cook over medium heat, stirring until the mixture pulls away from the sides of the pan. Remove from the heat and stir in the egg, mixing until smooth.

Heat oil in a deep fryer or heavy skillet until it is about 360°F.

Put the *churro* mixture into a pastry bag fitted with a medium-wide fluted tip. Hold the bag over the hot oil and force the pastry out. Cut with a sharp knife or kitchen shears into 4-inch lengths—longer if your pan will hold them. Or curl the pastry so the ends meet to create circles.

Fry until golden. Remove and drain on paper towels. Sprinkle with the powdered sugar and serve immediately.

SALSA DE ACEITUNAS
Green Olive Sauce

This sauce is quickly prepared and really adds flavor and color to grilled fish or chicken.

MAKES 2 CUPS.

1 cup pimiento-stuffed olives, finely minced
2 garlic cloves, minced
3 tomatoes, seeded and cut into small dice

3 tablespoons olive oil
1 tablespoon sherry wine vinegar
Salt and freshly ground black pepper to taste

Combine the olives, garlic, tomatoes, oil, vinegar, salt, and pepper. Allow to rest for 1 or 2 hours.

EMPANADA DE BACALAO
Salt Cod *Empanada*

Empanadas *are thin yeast dough pies filled with meat or seafood. Better known in the United States are their tiny cousins, the empanadillas. These delicious pies are found in the tapas bars of Madrid, but they are well traveled and have been exported to Mexico and Latin America, where they have become naturalized and as diversified as the countries that make them. In Galicia they are filled with meat or seafood, and this recipe filled with salt cod is a classic. It can be served as a snack, an appetizer, or a main course.*

SERVES 6.

Begin preparation 48 hours in advance.
  1 pound boneless skinless salt
    cod

DOUGH
  1 tablespoon dry active yeast
    (1 package or 1 cube)
  2 teaspoons sugar
  ½ cup yellow cornmeal

  ½ tablespoon salt
  2 tablespoons olive oil
  2½ to 3 cups all-purpose flour
    Milk for glazing the pie
    crust

FILLING:
  3 tablespoons olive oil
  2 large onions, thinly sliced
  2 large red bell peppers,
    stemmed, seeded, and cut
    into thin strips

  3 large tomatoes, chopped
  ½ teaspoon freshly ground
    black pepper
    Salt to taste, optional

Soak the cod in cold water for 48 hours, changing the water several times. Drain and squeeze dry. Shred the cod. Set aside.

To prepare the dough—Pour 1⅓ cups lukewarm water into a food processor. Add the yeast and sugar and let stand until the yeast activates. The top of the water will be foamy with yeast. Add the cornmeal, salt, and oil and 1 cup of the flour. Whirl for 30 seconds. Add 1½ cups more of the flour and whirl to form a ball. If the dough is not forming a ball or is very sticky, add more of the remaining flour until the dough is smooth and soft. Place the dough in an oiled bowl and turn to coat the top of the dough with oil. Cover with a towel and put in a warm place until doubled, about 1 hour.

To prepare the filling—Heat the oil in a skillet and add the onions. Cook over moderate heat until golden. Add the peppers and cook, stirring, for 5 minutes. Add the tomatoes and cook briskly until the sauce is thick. Stir in the prepared cod and cook over low heat for 5 minutes. Add the black pepper and taste for salt. You may need a little salt since most of the salt in the cod has been soaked out. Drain excess liquid.

Preheat the oven to 400°F.

To put it all together—Punch the dough down and divide into halves. Place half of the dough in a 12-inch pizza pan. Push and pull the dough to cover the pan, allowing a ½-inch overhang on the edge of the pan. Pour the filling into the center of the dough and spread evenly to within 1 inch of the edge. Pinch a small ball of dough off the remaining dough and set aside. On a floured surface, roll out the remaining dough so it will cover the filling. Put the dough on top of the filling to form the top crust. Pull the edges of the bottom crust up and over the top crust, rolling and pinching them together to seal in the filling. Roll the little ball of dough into a long coil and form a decoration on the top of the *empanada*. This is just for fun to break up the great expanse of dough. Something you often see on the *empanadas* of Galicia is an *E* for *empanada*.

Bake the pie for about 20 minutes. Brush the pie with milk and return to the oven until golden, another 5 to 10 minutes. Serve the *empanada* hot from the oven or at room temperature, cut into pie-shaped wedges.

FLAN DE PUERRO CON SALSA DE ESPINACAS
Leek Flan with Spinach Sauce

Alboronia, a beautifully decorated restaurant in Puerto de Santa María, near Jerez, has a delightful patio where one warm summer evening we enjoyed this flan as a first course.

SERVES 6.

2 pounds leeks, well cleaned
¼ cup (½ stick) unsalted butter
4 eggs
1 cup half-and-half
½ teaspoon salt, plus additional to taste

1 teaspoon white pepper, plus additional to taste
1 bunch spinach, washed
1 teaspoon sherry vinegar
¾ cup milk

Preheat the oven to 350°F.

Chop the white part of the leeks and a third of the green part. Heat the butter in a skillet and cook the leeks slowly, stirring occasionally, until soft and lightly golden. Reserve ½ cup of the leeks. Puree the remaining leeks in a blender or food processor with the eggs and half-and-half, ½ teaspoon salt, and 1 teaspoon white pepper.

Oil six ½-cup flan molds or ovenproof ramekins. Divide the leek mixture among the molds. Place the molds in a baking pan and pour hot water into the pan so that it comes halfway up the sides of the molds. Cover the entire pan with foil.

Bake for 30 minutes.

While the flan is cooking prepare the sauce: Place the washed spinach in a saucepan. Cover and cook until wilted. (There will be enough water adhering to the leaves to cook it properly.) Reserve 6 small, perfect leaves.

Place the cooked spinach and reserved leeks in the blender or food processor and puree with the sherry vinegar and milk and additional salt and white pepper.

Return the sauce to the pan and heat through.

Remove the flans from the oven, uncover, and remove the individual molds.

To serve, pour a puddle of the sauce in the center of 6 individual plates. Unmold the flans on top of the sauce and garnish with a small spinach leaf. Alternatively, the flan and sauce can be served cold.

PATÉ DE HIGADOS DE POLLO CON ACEITUNAS
Chicken Liver Pâté with Olives

Tapas bars are lined with fish, vegetable, and meat pâtés. Some are intricately decorated, others a simple slice on bread. A creamy chicken liver pâté studded with olives was once presented to us in a little bowl with toasted bread—one of the best.

SERVES 10 AS A TAPA.

8 tablespoons (1 stick) unsalted butter
½ cup chopped onion
2 garlic cloves, minced
½ pound chicken livers

⅓ cup dry sherry
½ teaspoon salt
Pinch of ground cloves
⅓ cup chopped green olives

Heat 2 tablespoons of the butter in a skillet and cook the onion and garlic over medium heat until softened. Add the livers and cook for 5 minutes. Pour in the sherry and cook over high heat until the liquid evaporates.

Transfer the liver mixture to a blender or food processor and blend with the remaining butter and the salt and cloves until smooth. Stir in the olives and pour into a small bowl or crock.

Refrigerate until firm.

Serve with fresh or toasted sliced baguettes directly from the bowl or unmolded on a platter and garnished with more olives.

BUÑUELOS DE PATATAS CON CHORIZO
Potato Puffs with Chorizo

We're convinced that it would be possible to collect an entire book full of potato recipes from Spain. Remember that the Spanish were the first Europeans to accept the potato as a food for human consumption.

SERVES 6 TO 8.

1 pound potatoes, peeled and cut into eighths

1 3-ounce *chorizo*, casing removed and sausage crumbled

½ cup all-purpose flour

1 teaspoon salt, plus additional to taste

½ teaspoon freshly ground black pepper

2 eggs, separated

Oil for deep frying

Bring 3 cups of salted water to a boil. Add the potatoes and cook until tender. Drain, reserving the cooking water. Put the potatoes in a bowl and mash them with the back of a fork or a potato masher. Add some of the cooking liquid to the potatoes and stir until thick and creamy.

Heat a small skillet and cook the *chorizo* over low heat until done. Drain the fat from the *chorizo*, chop coarsely, and set aside.

Combine the flour, teaspoon of salt, and pepper. Stir in the potatoes, *chorizo*, and egg yolks. Combine well. Beat the egg whites to firm peaks. Fold the egg whites into the potato mixture.

Heat oil to about 360°F. Drop the potato mixture by small teaspoonfuls into the hot oil. Cook until golden. If the potatoes cook too quickly they will be creamy in the center instead of doughy. Remove the puffs to paper towels to drain.

When all the puffs are cooked, sprinkle them with salt and serve immediately in a napkin-lined basket.

CHAMPIÑONES EN ESCABECHE
Marinated Mushrooms

These mushrooms are great as a tapa—deeply flavored, sharp, and addictive.

SERVES 6 TO 10 AS A TAPA.

Begin preparation 24 hours in advance.

2 pounds button mushrooms
¼ cup olive oil
8 garlic cloves, peeled and minced
1 teaspoon dried oregano
1 teaspoon dried thyme
3 tablespoons minced fresh parsley

1 teaspoon hot red pepper flakes
1 tablespoon paprika
½ cup red wine vinegar
1 cup dry red wine
1 teaspoon salt
½ teaspoon freshly ground black pepper

Clean the mushrooms and trim the stems even with the cap. Do not remove the stem entirely.

Heat the oil in a large sauté pan. Cook the garlic until golden. Add the oregano, thyme, parsley, and pepper flakes and cook for 2 minutes. Stir in the paprika until dissolved. Add the mushrooms and turn to coat. Stir in the vinegar, red wine, salt, and pepper and bring to a boil. Lower the heat and cook for 15 minutes. Pour into a nonmetallic bowl and cool to room temperature, then refrigerate for 24 hours before serving.

Serve in a bowl with toothpicks alongside.

ENSALADA DE BERENJENAS
Eggplant Salad

Eggplant salad is wonderful as a tapa served with toasted baguette slices. It is also good as a first course with greens or as an accompaniment to grilled meat or fish—an all-around winner.

SERVES 6.

¼ cup olive oil, plus more if
  necessary
2 pounds eggplant, unpeeled
  and cut into ½-inch dice
  Salt and freshly ground black
  pepper to taste
1 medium onion, chopped
2 red or green bell peppers,
  seeded and cut into ½-inch
  dice

3 tomatoes, peeled and
  chopped
¼ cup sugar
2 tablespoons red wine vinegar
2 tablespoons capers, drained

Heat the oil in a large nonreactive skillet. When very hot, add the eggplant and toss to coat with the oil. Lower the heat to medium. Sprinkle lightly with salt and pepper. Cook quickly until the eggplant begins to color. Remove and drain on paper towels.

Add a little more oil to the skillet if necessary and cook the onion and peppers until soft. Stir in the tomatoes and cook until most of the liquid has evaporated. Return the eggplant to the pan and stir in the sugar, vinegar, and capers. Cook over low heat until the eggplant is soft but still holds its shape. Season with additional salt and pepper if necessary.

Serve hot or at room temperature (it really is better after it cools and the flavors mingle awhile). If refrigerated, let warm to room temperature before serving.

TORTILLA ESPAÑOLA
Spanish Omelet

The best food in Spain comes to Madrid. Special overnight trains from the coast bring fresh seafood. Naturally, there are fine restaurants galore in Madrid, and it is also a wonderful city for tapas. This is a classic tapas recipe and one found all over the Spanish capital and elsewhere in Spain. It also makes a wonderful brunch dish.

SERVES 6 TO 12.

½ cup olive oil
Salt and white pepper to taste
8 medium onions, peeled and thinly sliced

5 medium Idaho potatoes, peeled, halved, and sliced ⅛ inch thick
12 eggs, lightly beaten

Heat the oil in an 8- or 10-inch skillet. Sprinkle the onions with salt and pepper, then sauté until soft.

Drain the contents of the skillet into a colander set over a bowl. Return the drained oil to the skillet and reheat. Add the potatoes and sprinkle with salt and pepper. Cook, tossing occasionally, until golden.

Drain the potatoes, reserving the oil. Combine the potatoes with the onions and eggs.

Return the oil to the skillet and reheat. Pour in the egg mixture and cook until it begins to set on the bottom. Lift the edges of the tortilla with a spatula, allowing the liquids to flow under. Cook over moderate heat until the bottom half is set and the top is still runny. Cover the top of the skillet with a large plate (or, what I find easiest, a pizza pan) and invert the skillet. Quickly slide the tortilla off the pan or plate back into the skillet and cook until the tortilla is cooked through.

Serve immediately, sliced into wedges. Tortilla Española is also delicious at room temperature.

ALCACHOFAS EN ESCABECHE
Marinated Artichokes

These are nothing like the canned marinated artichoke hearts most of us know. The fresh herbs, especially the mint, give these a really light feeling with an explosion of flavors that excite the palate. Mint is called **hierbabuena** *in Castilian, the good weed. It's a favorite home-grown herb, though it can almost always be found fresh in the market. It turns up in a lot of soups, sometimes even in gazpacho.*

SERVES 6.

Begin preparation several hours in advance.

1 tablespoon salt, plus additional to taste	⅓ cup olive oil
2 lemons	2 whole garlic cloves, peeled
6 medium artichokes	Pinch each of fresh sage, marjoram, parsley, and mint

Bring a large nonreactive pan of water to a boil with the salt. Cut 1 of the lemons in half and squeeze the juice into the water. Toss in the squeezed lemon halves, too.

Cut off and discard the stems at the base of the artichokes. Cut off and discard the top third of the artichokes. Remove any tough outer leaves.

Place the prepared artichokes in the boiling water and cook until the bottoms feel tender when pierced with a fork. Drain until cool.

When cool enough to handle, cut the artichokes into quarters with a very sharp knife. With a small knife, remove and discard the furry choke and place the cleaned artichokes in a glass bowl or pan.

Squeeze the juice from the remaining lemon and combine with the oil, garlic, and fresh herbs. Season with additional salt if necessary.

Pour over the artichokes and toss. Leave at room temperature, covered, for several hours before serving. This dish can be refrigerated, but bring to room temperature before serving.

SOPA DE BACALAO, PUERROS Y GARBANZOS
Salt Cod, Leek, and Garbanzo Soup

We first tasted this soup not in Spain but at the excellent Baywolf restaurant in Oakland, California. At the time, Carol Brendlinger was the chef, and she prepared it as part of a Spanish-week menu she was presenting. We loved the soup. Later in Spain we had it again. It offered the same great taste, but it had not been strained, and the stringiness of the cod made the soup less appealing. So here is a version of the soup inspired by Brendlinger's refinement.

SERVES 6.

Begin preparation 24 hours in advance.

½ pound boneless skinless salt cod

4 tablespoons olive oil

1 medium onion, chopped

1 pound leeks, cleaned and chopped (white part only)

2 medium carrots, chopped

1 tablespoon minced fresh parsley

1 pound can garbanzo beans, liquid drained

1 pound potatoes, peeled and quartered

4 large garlic cloves, peeled and thinly sliced crosswise

2 1-inch-thick slices white bread, crusts removed and cut into ½-inch dice

½ teaspoon white pepper

Salt to taste

Soak the cod in cold water for 24 hours, changing the water several times. Drain and squeeze dry. Cut the cod into chunks and set aside.

Heat 2 tablespoons of the oil in a large pot and sauté the onion, leeks, and carrots until they begin to color. Stir in the parsley, beans, potatoes, and salt cod and 6 cups of water. Bring to a boil, lower the heat, and cook, uncovered, until the potatoes are very tender, about 45 minutes.

Puree the soup in a blender and return to the pot through a fine sieve. Push down on the solids to obtain as much of the liquid as possible.

Heat the remaining 2 tablespoons of oil in a skillet and stir in the sliced garlic and bread cubes. Stir and cook until golden. Drain the bread and garlic on paper towels.

Heat the soup and season with the pepper and salt if necessary. Divide the soup among heated soup bowls and sprinkle with the bread cubes and garlic. Serve immediately.

GAZPACHO ANDALUZ
Cold Tomato and Vegetable Soup with Condiments

All over Spain we find gazpacho, but it is originally from Andalusia. There are as many variations as there are families who make it. It should be made at the height of the tomato-growing season, using only the best and ripest vegetables. Some places in Spain replace the tomato juice with water. Since the vegetables have such extraordinary flavor, they don't need the extra boost from the juice. If you grow your own vegetables, you might want to try it that way.

SERVES 6 TO 8.

TOMATO AND VEGETABLE SOUP

2 1-inch-thick slices good-quality white bread, crusts removed

1 large garlic clove

½ cup extra-virgin olive oil

¼ cup red wine vinegar

1 small onion, chopped

1 red or green bell pepper, stemmed, seeded, and chopped

½ cucumber, peeled, seeded, and chopped

4 large tomatoes, cored and chopped (they may be peeled and seeded for a smoother soup, but the peel adds a lot of flavor)

3 cups tomato juice
Salt and freshly ground black pepper to taste

CONDIMENTS

½ cucumber, peeled, seeded, and diced

½ large red pepper, peeled, seeded, and diced

2 firm, ripe tomatoes, cored and diced

2 tablespoons olive oil

2 1-inch-thick slices good-quality white bread, crusts removed and cut into ½-inch cubes

To prepare the soup—Soak the bread in water to cover. Place the garlic in the blender and finely mince. Squeeze the bread dry and add to the garlic and whirl. Mix together the oil and vinegar. With the motor running, gradually add to the bread. This will produce a thick white sauce. Transfer to a bowl.

Place the onion, pepper, cucumber, and tomatoes in the work bowl and blend until smooth. Pour into a large container and stir in the tomato juice and bread mixture and combine well. Season with the salt and pepper. Cover and refrigerate several hours until *very cold* and the flavors have blended.

To prepare the condiments—Arrange the vegetable condiments in rows in an oval dish. Heat the oil and cook the bread cubes until golden. Drain and put into a small dish.

Serve the cold soup in chilled soup plates, passing the condiments at the table.

ENSALADA DE POLLO EN PEPITORIA
Chicken and Vegetable Salad with
Saffron-Almond Dressing

Pollo en pepitoria, *usually presented as a chicken and vegetable stew flavored with saffron, is found on menus all over Spain, and once we saw it on a menu in Provence. We don't know what pepitoria means. We first enjoyed this version presented as a salad at a friend's house in Arcos de la Frontera, near Jerez. Try using the saffron-almond dressing for other dishes or as a dip for vegetables.*

SERVES 6.

Begin preparation several hours ahead.

DRESSING

2 eggs	Small pinch of saffron
5 large garlic cloves, unpeeled	threads
20 whole almonds	½ teaspoon salt
1 tablespoon fresh parsley leaves	1 cup extra-virgin olive oil
	Juice of 1 lemon

SALAD

1 quart chicken stock, preferably homemade, page 147	½ pound thin carrots, peeled and sliced diagonally into ¼-inch pieces
1 pound (about 12) tiny new potatoes	2 pounds boneless skinless chicken breasts
1 pound (about 12) boiling onions, skinned	

To make the dressing—Preheat the oven to 400°F. Hard-boil 1 of the eggs and set aside to cool.

Place the garlic and almonds on a baking sheet and bake until the almonds are toasted, about 10 to 12 minutes. Let cool.

Meanwhile, peel the hard-boiled egg and separate the white from the yolk. Finely chop the egg white, cover, and set aside. Cover and set aside the egg yolk.

Remove the peel from the garlic and transfer the garlic and almonds to a blender or food processor.

Turn the motor on and whirl to a paste. Add the parsley, saffron, salt, uncooked egg, and cooled yolk of the hard-boiled egg. Whirl to mix well.

Combine the oil and lemon juice. With the motor running, gradually add the mixture to the paste. Scrape down the sides of the bowl and whirl once more. The result is a creamy dressing. Pour into a bowl, cover, and refrigerate for several hours or overnight so the flavors can mingle.

(Occasionally the dressing may "break" and not thicken properly. In that case, remove the broken dressing to a container with a pouring spout. Add 1 tablespoon of tepid water to the blender or food processor and ¼ cup of the broken dressing. Whirl to blend. With the motor running, gradually add the remaining broken sauce. It should emulsify immediately. Use this same technique to fix mayonnaise or other mayonnaise-based sauces.)

To make the salad—Heat the stock in a large pot. Add the potatoes and onions and cook until tender. Remove from the stock and set aside. Add the carrots and cook until tender. Remove from the stock and set aside. Add the chicken and poach until cooked through, about 10 minutes. Remove from the stock and set aside to cool slightly. Strain the remaining stock and reserve for another use. Shred the chicken.

To serve, decoratively arrange the chicken, potatoes, onions, and carrots on a large platter. Stir and pour 1 cup of the dressing over the chicken and vegetables; sprinkle with the chopped egg white. Pass the remaining sauce separately.

FISH AND SUCH

MERO DE CANTABRIA
AL VINAGRE SIDRA
Perch in Apple Cider Vinegar Sauce with Capers

When you come upon the Landa Palace just south of Burgos, it looks like Disney has been busy at work in Spain. It is quite spectacular and gets high marks in all the hotel and restaurant guides, yet there is a surreal feeling about the place. But the genuine flavor of this perch that I had there is very real and very easy to prepare.

SERVES 6.

2 tablespoons shallots, finely minced

2 tomatoes, peeled, seeded, and pureed

¼ cup apple cider vinegar

½ cup white wine or water

1 cup Fish Stock, page 149

6 perch fillets (about 2 pounds)

Salt and white pepper to taste

¼ cup cream

2 tablespoons capers, drained

Combine the shallots, tomatoes, vinegar, and wine in a large non-reactive skillet. Cook over medium heat until most of the liquid has evaporated. Stir in the fish stock and bring to a boil. Lower the heat and add the fillets. Sprinkle with salt and pepper. Gently poach in the liquid until done, about 7 minutes, depending on the thickness of the fillets. Remove to a platter and keep warm.

Add the cream to the sauce and boil to thicken. (The sauce should be as thick as heavy cream.) Stir in the capers. Taste for seasoning, adding more salt and pepper if necessary.

Pour the sauce over the fish and serve immediately.

TRUCHAS A LA NAVARRA
Trout Navarre-Style

The river Ebro flows along the southeastern border of the Navarre region. The rich farmland that borders the river is the source of the abundant produce that forms much of the cuisine of this area. But the river itself is the source of a delicious trout, used as the inspiration for this recipe.

If you don't have a trout fisherman in your house, use the farmed trout now available in many U.S. markets.

SERVES 6.

½ pound button mushrooms, stems cut off at the base and discarded and caps sliced
1 tablespoon lemon juice
4-ounce piece prosciutto
1 large garlic clove, peeled

2 tablespoons fresh parsley leaves
2 tablespoons olive oil
6½-pound trout, cleaned
1 onion, peeled and thinly sliced
½ teaspoon salt

Toss the mushrooms with the lemon juice and set aside. Cut the prosciutto into thin strips. Finely chop the garlic and parsley together and set aside.

Heat the oil in a large skillet and sauté the trout quickly until golden but still underdone. Remove the trout and place the onion in the skillet. Sauté until soft. Add the mushrooms and cook until most of their liquid has evaporated. Stir in the prosciutto. Lay the trout on top of the mushroom mixture and sprinkle with the salt. Cover and cook for 5 minutes. Test the trout by poking it with your finger. If the flesh is firm, the fish is done.

To serve, place the trout on dinner plates, top with the vegetables and juices, and sprinkle with some of the parsley-garlic mixture.

RAPÉ EN SALSA DE CREMA
AL VAPOR DE COÑAC
Monkfish in Cognac-Flavored Cream Sauce

This is a really easy and delicious fish dish. Monkfish itself is rich and expensive, and so is the sauce, so a little will go a long way.

Somehow tomato paste has gotten a bad reputation, and indeed, much of it that is on the market is pretty tinny-tasting. Look for the imported Italian tubes that look like tubes of toothpaste. These are of good quality and easy to store after using only a tablespoon. Think of all the half-full tomato paste cans that have been dumped into the trash!

(For a real pleasure read Patience Gray's description in Honey from a Weed *of the making of sun-dried tomato paste.)*

SERVES 6 TO 8.

2 pounds monkfish fillets	¼ cup brandy
2 tablespoons olive oil	1 tablespoon tomato paste
⅓ cup minced shallots	½ cup cream
Salt and white pepper to	¼ cup finely minced fresh
taste	parsley

Remove and discard the skin from the monkfish and cut the fish crosswise into 1-inch-thick medallions.

Heat the oil in a large skillet and cook the shallots slowly until tender. Place the fish in the pan and sprinkle with salt and white pepper. Cook for 1 minute on each side.

Pour in the brandy, wait a few seconds for the fumes to settle, and carefully ignite. Combine and stir in the tomato paste and cream. Raise the heat and cook until the sauce thickens and the fish is cooked.

Serve immediately, sprinkled with the fresh parsley.

GAMBAS AL AJILLO
Prawns with Garlic

This is everybody's favorite tapa—even in California, where most of the prawns we eat come frozen. Fresh prawns in their shells and with their heads on make the dish a real treat.

The following preparation is not the traditional Spanish method, but a variation that works well with the prawns available here.

SERVES 6 AS A TAPA.

- 3 tablespoons olive oil
- 18 prawns (about ¾ pound), in their shells
- ½ teaspoon salt
- 6 garlic cloves, peeled and thinly sliced crosswise
- ½ teaspoon hot red pepper flakes
- ½ cup dry white wine
- 1 tablespoon finely minced fresh parsley

Heat the oil in a medium skillet. When the oil is really hot, add the prawns and sprinkle with the salt. Toss in the oil for 1 minute. Add the garlic and hot pepper flakes and cook until the prawns are pink. Pour in the wine and cook briskly for another minute. The sauce will thicken.

Sprinkle with the parsley and serve very hot (preferably right from the skillet), with lots of crusty bread for dipping into the sauce.

NOTE: If your guests won't enjoy licking their fingers, peel the prawns first, but be prepared to lose a lot of the flavor and some of the fun.

TORTILLITAS DE CAMARONES
Shrimp Pancakes

These shrimp-studded little pancakes are a popular tapa in the plentiful tapas bars of Sevilla.

SERVES 6 TO 8 AS A TAPA.

Begin preparation 2 hours in advance.

1 cup flour	1 teaspoon salt
1 cup garbanzo flour	½ teaspoon white pepper
1 small bunch parsley, stemmed and minced	1½ cups water
1 medium onion, peeled and minced	½ pound prawns or shrimp, peeled and coarsely chopped
	Olive oil for frying

Combine all the ingredients except the oil in a bowl and let rest, covered and refrigerated, for 2 hours.

Heat about 3 tablespoons of olive oil in a large skillet. Drop the batter by the spoonful into the oil to form 3- to 4-inch cakes. Cook until golden on both sides and drain on paper towels.

Serve immediately—the pancakes need to be eaten while they are still very hot and the edges crisp.

ALMEJAS EN SALSA VERDE
Clams in Green Sauce

*There are variations on this clam tapa all over Spain. My favorite
was in Sanlúcar de Barrameda, near Jerez, where the clams were tiny,
plump, and juicy, the manzanilla well chilled, and the night warm and
full of the earthy scent of geraniums.*

SERVES 6 AS A FIRST COURSE AND 10 AS A TAPA.

2 pounds small clams, in their
  shells
1 cup dry white wine
2 tablespoons olive oil
6 garlic cloves, minced

¼ cup minced onion
¼ cup minced fresh parsley
1 teaspoon all-purpose flour
  Salt and freshly ground black
  pepper to taste

Clean the clams thoroughly.

Bring the wine to a boil in a saucepan and add the clams. Steam
the clams and remove them from the pan as soon as they open.
Discard any that do not open. Reduce the steaming liquid to 1 cup.

Remove and discard the top shells of the clams, leaving the meat
attached to the bottom shell.

Heat the oil in a skillet and cook the garlic and onion until soft.
Stir in the parsley and cook 1 minute. Stir in the flour and cook 1
minute. Strain the reduced steaming liquid into the skillet. Cook
until the sauce begins to thicken. Season with salt and pepper if
necessary.

Add the clams to the sauce and simmer for 5 minutes.

Serve on individual plates or in a clay casserole for everyone to
share, with lots of good, crusty bread for dunking into the sauce.

MAINS

POLLO RELLENO DE ACEITUNAS
Chicken Stuffed with Olives

When you pot-roast a whole chicken, all of it stays very moist while creating its own sauce. We like this with Patatas Fritas con Allioli, page 268, even though they are usually served as a tapa.

SERVES 4 TO 6.

1 3½- to 4-pound chicken
4 tablespoons olive oil
1 medium onion, peeled and minced
2 cups day-old bread cubes
½ cup pimiento-stuffed green olives, sliced
2 tablespoons chopped fresh parsley
2 garlic cloves, minced
¼ teaspoon dried or 1 teaspoon fresh oregano
¼ teaspoon salt
½ teaspoon pepper
1 egg
1 tablespoon brandy
1 cup dry white wine

Thoroughly clean the chicken, removing and discarding or freezing the giblets for another use.

Heat 2 tablespoons of the olive oil and sauté the onion until golden.

Place the bread cubes, olives, parsley, garlic, oregano, salt, and pepper in a bowl. Add the sautéed onions and egg and toss well. Pour in the brandy and toss.

Stuff the bird with this mixture and truss.

Heat the remaining olive oil in a large pot with a cover. Place the chicken, breast side down, in the pot. Pour in the wine. Bring to a boil and lower the heat. Cover and simmer for 30 minutes. Turn the bird over. Cover and simmer for 15 minutes. Remove the lid and continue to cook for 15 minutes. Remove the chicken to a platter. Raise the heat and cook the liquid quickly to reduce to the desired consistency.

To serve, carve the chicken into serving pieces and pass the sauce separately.

POLLO CON CEBOLLITAS Y CHAMPIÑONES
Chicken with Onions and Mushrooms

Chicken, as we know it, is something fairly new in Spain. Until about thirty years ago, most Spaniards living in the country or in very small villages would rarely kill chickens until they had ceased to be good egg layers. Thus, many of the traditional chicken dishes are for what we would call stewing hens. This dish probably originally called for rabbit.

SERVES 6.

Dish may be partially prepared up to 2 hours ahead.

- 1 3½-pound chicken
- 3 tablespoons olive oil
- 1 teaspoon salt, plus additional to taste
- ½ teaspoon freshly ground black pepper, plus additional to taste
- 12 boiling onions, peeled
- 18 medium mushrooms, stems cut off at the base and discarded
- ¼ cup fresh sage leaves
- ¼ cup fresh rosemary leaves
- 1 cup dry *amontillado* or *fino* sherry

Thoroughly clean the chicken and cut into 8 pieces. Reserve the backs for stock.

Heat the oil in a large ovenproof skillet. Sprinkle the chicken pieces with 1 teaspoon of salt and ½ teaspoon of pepper and cook until they begin to color. Remove the chicken to a platter. Add the onions, cook until golden, and remove to the platter of chicken.

Cook the mushrooms in the same fat. Remove the mushrooms and set aside separately. Pour off any excess oil.

Add the sage and rosemary to the skillet and cook to wilt. Pour in the sherry and stir, scraping the bottom of the skillet. Return the chicken and onions to the pan. (At this point, the dish may be set aside, covered and unrefrigerated, for later cooking.)

Place the pan in the oven and cook for 25 minutes. Stir in the mushrooms and cook another 10 minutes. The chicken and onions should feel tender when pierced with a fork. Reduce the sauce further if desired, and season with additional salt and pepper if necessary.

To serve, place the chicken and vegetables on a serving platter and pass the sauce separately.

PATO A LA SEVILLANA
Duck with Orange Sauce

Seville oranges are slightly bitter—the preferred oranges for orange marmalade. They are also great with duck. We are certain that duck with orange sauce originated in this gorgeous city. We have added lemon juice to compensate for our sweeter oranges.

SERVES 4 AS A MAIN COURSE AND 8 AS A FIRST COURSE.

2 4-pound ducks
1 large onion, minced
  Zest and juice of 2 oranges
  Juice of 1 lemon

1 cup *amontillado* sherry
1 cup Duck Stock or Chicken
  Stock (page 147)
½ teaspoon salt
½ teaspoon white pepper

Separate the ducks into 4 breasts and 4 leg-and-thigh pieces. Remove excess fat. Reserve the backs, wings, and necks for stock (see page 147).

Heat a large, dry sauté pan until very hot. Sauté the breasts until golden. Set aside. Pour off the fat and reheat the pan. Sauté the leg-and-thigh pieces until golden on all sides and set aside.

Pour off all but 1 tablespoon of the duck fat. Sauté the onion in the fat until golden. Add the orange zest and orange and lemon juice and reduce until the liquid evaporates. Pour in the sherry and stock. Return the duck legs to the pan and cook for 30 minutes. Add the breasts to the pan and cook for 20 minutes longer. The duck breasts and legs should feel tender when pierced with a fork. Cook longer if necessary.

Remove the duck pieces to a platter and keep warm. Skim off the fat in the pan and raise the heat. Quickly cook the sauce to reduce to the desired consistency and season with the salt and pepper.

Pour the sauce over the duck pieces and serve.

STOCKS

There is nothing difficult about making meat or vegetable stocks but there is something magical about using them. A homemade stock in a recipe can turn an everyday dish into fiesta fare.

Canned stocks just don't compare, and they tend to be too salty. Occasionally, you can find frozen stocks, but at astronomical prices.

The obvious answer is to make your own and keep a supply in the freezer.

Many of our recipes call for either stock or wine. If you prefer, you can substitute stock for the wine and water for the stock but beware, the flavors will be very different. Here are three basic flavorful stock recipes.

CALDO DE PAVO, PATO, O POLLO
Turkey, Duck, or Chicken Stock

Not only is turkey healthful, but one bird provides at least three meals: the stuffed breast, page 290, Sopa de Albóndigas a la Murciana, page 276, or Pavo en Escabeche, page 152, and at least another soup from the stock.

Likewise, I rarely buy chicken or duck parts instead of whole birds. One, they are less economical and two, I wouldn't have all the backs and wing tips for stock. Just put the extra parts in a plastic bag and freeze them until there are enough to make a rich stock. (I also bag the chicken and duck livers and freeze them until I have enough for a pâté, page 127.)

Once you have prepared the stock, strain it and cool it to room temperature, refrigerate it, and then take off the fat. After the fat is removed, the stock can be boiled to reduce it. Freeze the stock in small containers or in ice trays for easy use later. If you freeze it in ice trays, empty the trays into plastic bags, close tightly, and refreeze. You can easily remove as much as needed.

1 turkey carcass, including	Onion
wings, tips, and neck, or	Carrots
several chicken or duck	Leeks
backs with additional wing	Bay leaves
tips and necks	Peppercorns

Place the bones in a large stockpot and cover with cold water. Add 1 or 2 onions (depending on the amount of bones), carrots, leeks, a couple of bay leaves, and a few peppercorns. Bring to a boil and skim off the foam that rises to the top. Lower the heat and cook over very low heat for 2 hours.

Strain the stock into a bowl. Discard the bones and vegetables. When cool, refrigerate the stock until the fat has congealed on the top. Remove the fat and cook the stock to reduce it and intensify the flavor. It may be frozen in small containers for future use or used right away.

VARIATION: Roast the bones and vegetables in the oven at 400°F. until they are browned. Put the roasted bones and vegetables into a stock pot. Deglaze the roasting pan with water or white wine and pour into the stock pot. Then continue as above. See also Veal Stock, page 148.

CALDO DE TERNERA
Veal Stock

10 pounds veal neck bones,	1 cup red wine
cracked	1 small celery stalk with
2 leeks, split and washed	leaves
2 carrots, cut into quarters	10 whole black peppercorns
1 onion, peeled and halved	2 bay leaves

Preheat the oven to 400°F.

Place the bones, leeks, carrots, and onion in a roasting pan and bake in the oven until well browned. Transfer the bones and vegetables to a stockpot. Pour off any fat. Deglaze the roasting pan with the red wine. Pour the wine over the bones and add the celery, peppercorns, and bay leaves. Cover the bones with water. Bring to a boil and remove the foam that rises to the surface. Reduce the heat to low and cook partially covered for 3 hours.

Skim the surface from time to time during simmering.

Strain the stock and discard the solids. Pour the stock into a bowl. Cool, cover, and refrigerate.

Remove the fat that covers the surface. The stock can now be reduced to intensify its flavor. It may be frozen in small containers for future use or used right away.

CALDO DE PESCADO
Fish Stock

Fish bones are available at most fish markets. Remove the gills; they are often bitter.

3 tablespoons olive oil	10 sprigs of parsley
2 medium onions, minced	2 bay leaves
3 garlic cloves, minced	10 peppercorns
3 medium-size carrots, chopped	5 pounds fish bones and scraps, rinsed
Leaves only of 2 celery stalks	

Heat the oil in a large stockpot. Cook the onions, garlic, and carrots until soft but not browned. Add the remaining ingredients. Add enough water to cover the bones by 1 inch and bring to a boil. Lower the heat and simmer for 30 minutes. Remove any scum that rises to the surface. Strain and discard the solids.

When cool, refrigerate the stock. Several hours later or the next day, remove any fat from the surface. Gently reduce the stock by a quarter over low heat.

Use the stock in any of the recipes calling for fish stock or divide among several containers, cool, and freeze for future use.

PIERNA DE PATO MOZÁRABE
Duck Leg Mozarab-Style

*We first met this duck in Córdoba. The name obviously implies an
Arab connection, and since it is found all over the south of Spain,
we're willing to believe it. This particular version, which we developed
from a couple of different Andaluz recipes, doesn't give any clue to
Arab origins, and neither did the original renditions. On the contrary,
the apples would seem to indicate a northern influence. One of those
minor culinary mysteries that would be fun, given several centuries,
to clear up.*

SERVES 6.

6 whole duck legs	2 tablespoons brandy
1 large onion, peeled and chopped	2½ cups semidry white wine
	1 teaspoon salt
1 large carrot, chopped	½ teaspoon white pepper
5 medium Granny Smith apples, peeled and cored	¼ cup sugar

Remove excess fat from the duck legs. Heat a large, dry skillet until
very hot. Place the legs, skin side down, in the pan and cook until
browned, pouring off and reserving the fat from time to time so the
legs do not stew in it.

Remove the legs to a platter and pour off all but 2 tablespoons of
the fat from the skillet. Add the onion and carrot to the skillet and
sauté until golden.

Meanwhile, coarsely chop 2 of the apples. Add to the skillet and
cook until they soften.

Stir in the brandy, 2 cups of the wine, salt, and pepper. Return
the duck legs to the pan. Cover and simmer until the legs are tender,
about 40 minutes. Remove the legs to a platter and keep warm.

Puree the sauce in a blender or food processor and pour back into
the skillet through a fine sieve. Cook gently to reduce and thicken.
Meanwhile, cut the remaining apples into ½-inch dice.

Heat 1 tablespoon of the reserved duck fat in another skillet and
sauté the diced apple until it begins to soften. Sprinkle with the sugar
and cook, stirring often, until the sugar melts and turns golden.

With a slotted spoon, remove and scatter the sugar-coated diced apple over the duck legs.

Pour the remaining ½ cup of wine into the melted sugar in the skillet. Cook rapidly to a syrup. Pour the syrup into the duck sauce and cook to reduce to the desired consistency.

Pour the sauce over the duck legs and serve immediately.

PAVO EN ESCABECHE
Marinated Turkey Legs and Wings

Marinated meats, fish, and vegetables are great to have in the refrigerator because they keep for several days to several weeks, and leftovers can be served as tapas or as additions to salads.

Escabeche differs from ceviche in that the foods for escabeche are cooked and then marinated, while ceviche preparations are only "cooked" in the marinade. Escabeche was another food-preservation method devised by those without modern refrigeration.

SERVES 6 TO 10 AS A TAPA OR PART OF A SALAD.

Begin preparation 24 hours in advance.

¼ cup olive oil	1 tablespoon fresh or 1
1 teaspoon salt	teaspoon dried thyme
1 teaspoon freshly ground	1 tablespoon fresh or 1
black pepper	teaspoon dried oregano
2 turkey drumsticks	¼ teaspoon hot red pepper
2 turkey wings, tips removed	flakes
and wings split	2 bay leaves
1 medium onion, thinly sliced	1 cup dry white wine
1 whole garlic bulb, cloves	1 cup white wine vinegar
separated and peeled	

Heat the oil in a large skillet. Salt and pepper the turkey pieces and cook until browned. Remove from the skillet and set aside.

In the same oil, brown the onion and garlic. Add the thyme, oregano, and red pepper flakes and cook for 2 minutes. Add the bay leaves, wine, and vinegar and 1 cup of water. Bring to a boil. Lower the heat and return the turkey to the skillet. Cover and cook until the turkey is tender and pulling away from the bones, about 45 minutes, depending on size.

Transfer the turkey to a glass or stainless steel pan and cover with the marinade and vegetables. Cool to room temperature, cover, and refrigerate for at least 24 hours.

To serve, remove the turkey from the marinade and shred the meat, discarding the skin and bones. Arrange the meat on a platter, strew the garlic and onions on top, and sprinkle with some of the marinade. Offer lots of good, crusty bread on the side.

PERDIZ CON MANZANAS
Partridge with Apples

Partridge is a great prize of hunters in Spain, especially in Andalusia and La Mancha. Avid British hunters often take hunting cottages during the season around Jerez de la Frontera—hunting by day, sherry by night. The birds are also grown commercially, but good restaurants will save back a few of the wild birds for their best customers.

Many U.S. restaurants are now featuring game on their menus, and game can be found in specialty butcher shops in larger cities.

SERVES 6.

6 partridge or 3 game hens
¼ pound thinly sliced pancetta
6 sprigs of fresh rosemary (3 for game hens)
12 garlic cloves, peeled (6 for game hens)
3 pippin apples, peeled, cored, and cubed

¼ cup brandy
1 cup chicken stock, preferably homemade, page 147
Salt and freshly ground black pepper to taste

Preheat the oven to 375°F.

Thoroughly clean the birds, removing and discarding or freezing the giblets for another use. Wrap the birds in the strips of pancetta and arrange them in a roasting pan. Stuff each bird with a sprig of rosemary and 2 cloves of garlic, and roast for 30 minutes. Remove the pancetta and set aside. Roast the birds another 10 minutes.

Remove the birds from the oven. (If preparing hens, cut them in half with kitchen shears.) Heat the accumulated juices in a sauté pan. Add the apples and sauté quickly. Pour in the brandy and stock and cook over high heat until the sauce begins to thicken. Add salt and pepper.

Place the birds in the pan and coat with the sauce. Chop the pancetta and sprinkle over the birds.

Serve immediately.

PERDIZ CON CHOCOLATE
Partridge in Chocolate Sauce

This dish was obviously devised post-Columbus, after chocolate was introduced from the New World. The cinnamon gives an unusual medieval taste to the birds.

SERVES 6.

6 partridge or 3 game hens
4 tablespoons olive oil
1 medium onion, peeled and minced
5 garlic cloves, peeled and minced
1 cup dry white wine
¼ cup sherry wine vinegar
1 cup chicken stock, preferably homemade, page 147

1 teaspoon salt
½ teaspoon pepper
2 whole cloves
1 teaspoon thyme
1 bay leaf
¼ teaspoon ground cinnamon
2 ounces unsweetened chocolate

Preheat the oven to 375°F.

Thoroughly clean the birds, removing and discarding or freezing the giblets for another use. Rub the birds with 2 tablespoons of the oil and put them in a roasting pan. Bake the birds for 30 minutes.

Meanwhile, heat the remaining 2 tablespoons of oil in an oven-proof sauté pan or clay casserole that later will accommodate all the birds. Sauté the onion and garlic until golden. Add the wine and cook over high heat until it evaporates.

Pour in the vinegar and stock. Add the salt, pepper, cloves, thyme, bay leaf, cinnamon, and chocolate and simmer for 30 minutes.

Remove the birds from the oven. (If preparing hens, cut them in half with kitchen shears.) Combine the birds with the sauce and bake an additional 15 minutes.

Serve the birds with the sauce spooned over them.

CHULETAS DE CORDERO A LA MADRILEÑA
Lamb Chops Madrid-Style

In this dish the lamb stays very moist inside a seasoned crust. Prepare the lamb chops for cooking early in the day, if you wish, and refriger-ate. Remember to take them out of the refrigerator and bring them back to room temperature before cooking. As the name implies, this is a classic dish of Madrid.

SERVES 6.

6 ½-inch-thick round-bone lamb chops
3 garlic cloves, minced
¼ cup minced onion
1 cup fine dry bread crumbs
4 sprigs of parsley

1 tablespoon minced fresh rosemary
1 teaspoon salt
¼ teaspoon freshly ground black pepper
2 tablespoons olive oil

Trim the chops of excess fat.

Combine the remaining ingredients except the olive oil in a food processor and whirl to a paste.

Pat the paste into both sides of each chop.

Heat the oil in a large skillet. Cook the chops over medium heat until golden on both sides and cooked inside to desired doneness.

Serve Leek Flan with Spinach Sauce, page 126, as a first course.

CORDERO AL CHILIDRÓN
Lamb with Peppers Navarre Style

Hemingway made Pamplona famous among outsiders for the running of the bulls each August. A fiesta of madness. Although we have never been there for the run, we have found very good food in Pamplona. When walking down a narrow street, look up and you are likely to see strings of peppers drying outside all the windows. This lamb stew is a specialty of both Navarre and Aragón.

SERVES 6.

3 *ancho* chilies
3 whole, large red bell peppers
2 tablespoons olive oil
  Salt and freshly ground
  black pepper to taste
2½ pounds boneless leg of
  lamb, cut into 2-inch cubes
2 medium onions, minced
3 garlic cloves, minced

¼ pound prosciutto, cut into
  strips
6 large tomatoes, peeled,
  seeded, and chopped
1½ cups dry white wine or veal
  or chicken stock, preferably
  homemade (pages 147 and
  148)

Preheat the oven to 350°F. Bring a pot of water to a boil and add the *ancho* chilies. Remove from the heat and allow to rest for 15 minutes.

Place the bell peppers on a baking sheet and bake until the skins blister and char. Remove the peppers, place them in a paper bag, and close tightly. Let them rest for 15 minutes. Remove the peppers and stem, seed, and peel them. Cut into large chunks and set aside.

As best you can, stem, seed, and peel the *ancho* chilies. Set aside.

Heat the oil in a large skillet, sprinkle the lamb cubes with salt and freshly ground black pepper, and cook in small batches until they start to color. Remove the lamb to a platter.

In the same skillet, cook the onions, garlic, and prosciutto until limp. Return the lamb to the skillet. Add the tomatoes, bell peppers, chilies, and wine. Bring to a boil and lower the heat. Cook until the lamb is tender and the sauce thick, about 45 minutes. (Ideally, the lamb is tender and the sauce is sufficiently reduced at this point. If, however, the cooking gods have not been with you, remove the lamb and vegetables to a serving dish and keep them warm. Increase the heat and reduce the sauce to the desired consistency.) Season with salt and pepper if necessary. Pour the sauce over the lamb and serve immediately.

LOMO DE CERDO CON SALSA AGRIDULCE
Grilled Pork Loin with Sweet-and-Sour Sauce

The Moors brought both oranges and sugar to Spain, and these flavors form the basis for this particular sweet-and-sour sauce. The pork is first stuffed and grilled, then served with the bittersweet sauce.

SERVES 6 TO 8.

2 1½-pound boneless pork loin roasts
Zest of 1 orange
Zest of 1 lemon
1 teaspoon minced fresh lemon sage

3 garlic cloves, minced
1 cup fresh orange juice
½ cup fresh lemon juice
½ cup sugar
Salt and freshly ground black pepper

Place the pork loins on a platter fat side down and sprinkle each with the orange zest, lemon zest, sage, and garlic. Put the pork loins together with the filling in between. Tie the roast securely at 1-inch intervals.

Pour the orange juice and lemon juice into a glass pan and marinate the pork for 1 hour at room temperature. Remove the roast to a platter and reserve the marinade.

Heat charcoal, mesquite, or your favorite wood in a covered barbecue grill. Bank the coals to one side and put a drip pan on the other side. Cover with the grill. When the coals are uniformly white, place the loin on the grill over the drip pan (opposite the coals) and cover the barbecue. Cook until the pork reaches an internal temperature of 145°F., about 45 minutes to 1 hour. It is not necessary to turn the pork during cooking.

Reserve ½ cup of the marinade and baste the pork several times during the cooking with the remaining marinade.

Remove the pork to a platter and let rest for 10 minutes.

Heat the sugar in a heavy nonreactive skillet or pan and melt and cook until the color is deep gold. Pour in the reserved marinade and any juices that have accumulated under the resting pork. (Do not use any of the drippings from the drip pan.) Cook for 5 minutes over moderate heat. Season with the salt and pepper.

To serve, slice the pork and arrange it on a platter. Pass the sauce separately at the table.

PATATAS A LA RIOJANA
Potatoes with Sausages Rioja-Style

This seems like a very robust dish to have developed in Spain's most elegant wine district, the Rioja. But we don't drink a fine vintage every night. An everyday table wine will go very well with these rustic and delicious potatoes.

SERVES 6.

2 tablespoons olive oil
3 ounces *chorizo*, cut into
   1-inch lengths
8 ounces mild *linguiça*, cut into
   1-inch lengths
1 medium onion, minced
2 garlic cloves, minced

2 bay leaves
1 cup dry white wine
2 pounds medium-size potatoes,
   peeled and quartered
   Salt and freshly ground black
   pepper to taste

Heat the oil in a heavy pot with a cover. Cook the *chorizo*, *linguiça*, onion, and garlic until softened. Add the bay leaves, wine, and potatoes and bring to a boil. Turn the heat to low and cover. Cook for about 25 minutes, uncover, and cook another 5 minutes. Season with salt and pepper.

   Serve hot.

ESTOFADO DE BUEY A LA SEVILLANA
Beef Stew Sevilla Style

There is a definite Moorish influence here, almost like a Moroccan tangine. This beef stew is exotic and at the same time comforting and homey. We like to serve this beef stew with plain boiled rice and a bottle of good Rioja red wine.

SERVES 6.

Begin preparation 24 hours in advance.

2 cups dry sherry	4 garlic cloves, sliced
3 pounds stewing beef, cut into 2-inch cubes	2 1-inch pieces cinnamon stick
	Zest of 1 orange
¼ cup olive oil	24 small green pimiento-stuffed olives
Salt and freshly ground black pepper to taste	

Combine the sherry and beef in a glass or stainless steel bowl and refrigerate overnight.

Bring the marinated beef to room temperature. Remove the beef to a large cutting board and reserve the marinade. Pat the beef dry. It is important to dry the meat so that it will brown properly.

Heat the oil in a deep skillet with a cover. Brown the beef cubes in small batches. Season with small amounts of salt and pepper as they cook. Remove when seared and set aside.

Cook the garlic in the same skillet until golden. Pour in the reserved marinade and bring to a boil. Return the beef to the skillet. Add the cinnamon stick and orange zest. Lower the heat and cover. Cook until tender, about 2 hours. Discard the cinnamon stick after the first hour of cooking.

Remove the meat with a slotted spoon to a deep serving platter and keep warm.

Raise the heat under the sauce and add the olives. Cook the sauce to reduce to the desired consistency. The sauce should be rather thin. Taste for seasoning, but additional salt may be unnecessary because the olives are fairly salty.

Pour the sauce and olives over the beef and serve at once.

CALLOS AL MAXI
Tripe Maxi's (Madrid) Style

Somehow, tripe has the reputation of being restorative. Mexican restaurants feature it every Sunday morning to help dispel the effects of the night before. The French want their tripe at the end of a market day to refresh them for the evening to come. And in Madrid, a bowl of tripe stew is just the thing to revive you before going off to the discos until dawn. Maxi's (see page 160) is an excellent place to find it.

SERVES 6 TO 8.

Begin preparation 24 hours in advance.

2 pounds tripe	5 ounces ham, cubed
2 medium onions	5 ounces *chorizo*, cut into
2 whole garlic bulbs, cloves	rounds
separated and peeled, plus 2	1 tablespoon paprika
garlic cloves	5 ounces blood sausage
2 bay leaves	2 cups cooked garbanzo beans
2 small *serrano* chilies	Salt and freshly ground black
3 tablespoons olive oil	pepper to taste

Cut the tripe into 1-inch squares.

Peel and halve 1 of the onions. Place the tripe, halved onion, 2 peeled and separated garlic bulbs, and bay leaves, and 1 of the serrano chilies, in a large pot. Cover with cold water and bring to a boil. Lower the heat, partially cover, and cook for 4 hours. Remove from the heat and allow to cool in the cooking liquid. Refrigerate overnight.

The next day, remove the tripe, reserving the liquid. Discard the onion, garlic, bay leaves, and chili.

Heat the oil in a large skillet or clay casserole.

Meanwhile, mince the remaining onion and the 2 garlic cloves. Cook in the oil until golden.

Mince the remaining *serrano* chili and add to the skillet along with the ham, *chorizo*, and blanched tripe. Stir in the paprika, blood sausage, and garbanzos. Pour enough of the reserved cooking liquid over to cover the ingredients. Season very lightly with salt and pepper. (The liquid will reduce a great deal during the cooking and the sausages will give off more of their flavor.) Cook, uncovered, for 1½ hours.

Remove the blood sausage and slice into rounds. Return to the pot. Season with salt and pepper if necessary. Add more liquid if needed or increase heat to further reduce. It should have the consistency of a thick stew.

Serve immediately, directly from the clay casserole.

RABO DE BUEY JEREZANA
Oxtails Jerez-Style

Tendida 6 is a restaurant in Jerez situated just opposite, as the name implies, Gate 6 of the bullring. There is a great tapas bar at the front of the restaurant worth a visit on its own. And the restaurant itself serves really good food—not fancy, just delicious, like this oxtail stew that is full of the flavors of vegetables, meat, and red wine that have slowly cooked together.

SERVES 6.

¼ cup olive oil
Salt and freshly ground black pepper
3 oxtails, cut into joints
2 leeks, cleaned and chopped (white part only)
1 medium onion, peeled and chopped
3 carrots, chopped

2 celery stalks, chopped
3 garlic cloves, minced
2 cups red wine
2 cups stock, preferably Veal Stock (page 148)
2 bay leaves
3 sprigs of parsley
3 sprigs of thyme or ½ teaspoon dried thyme

Heat the oil in a large skillet with cover. Sprinkle the salt and pepper over the oxtails and brown in the oil. Remove with a slotted spoon and set aside.

Cook the leeks, onion, carrots, celery, and garlic in the same skillet over medium heat until very soft. Stir in the wine, stock, bay leaves, parsley, and thyme. Bring to a boil. Lower the heat and return the oxtails to the pan. Cover and simmer until very tender, about 2 hours or more.

Remove the oxtails to a serving platter and keep warm. Pour the contents of the pan through a fine sieve into a bowl, pushing down on the solids to extract as much sauce as possible.

Serve immediately with the sauce poured over the oxtails. These are very good with Garlic Potatoes, page 385.

NOTE: The dish can be made ahead. Cool the oxtails and the sauce separately. Refrigerate for up to 2 days, then reheat the oxtails in the strained sauce.

DESSERTS

MARMELADA DE MEMBRILLO
Quince Paste

Each fall we seem to get a windfall of quinces from friends' trees. The Spanish make this quince paste into one of our favorite desserts— quince paste with white cheese and walnuts—so simple and a perfect ending.

Now our quinces are made into this quince paste for desserts in our home and as gifts for friends.

SERVES 10.

3 pounds quinces, unpeeled   3⅓ cups granulated sugar

Cut the quinces into sixths and core. Place in a heavy pot, cover with water, and cook until tender, about 1 hour.

Drain the quinces, reserving the water.

Puree the quinces and put through a fine sieve. Return to the pot and stir in the sugar and ⅓ cup of the reserved cooking liquid. Cook over medium-low heat, stirring continuously, until the mixture thickens and turns a deep amber in color.

Rinse a shallow 9- × -9-inch glass dessert mold and pour in the paste. Spread evenly. Cool, then cover tightly and refrigerate. Allow to set until firm.

Cut into thin slices at serving time.

PERA AL VINO
Pears Poached in Wine

This is a favorite dessert in Spain. The addition of the star anise was a specialty of Café Tango. We served a whole pear in a pool of syrup with a few pink peppercorns sprinkled over the top and a sprig of mint on the side.

SERVES 6.

2 cups wine (port, red wine, or, my favorite, muscat)
1 cup sugar
2 2-inch pieces cinnamon stick
6 star anise
6 ripe pears (Bosc, Comice, or Anjou, depending on the season)

In a large nonreactive pan combine the wine, sugar, cinnamon, and star anise. Bring to a boil and lower the heat. Cook for 20 minutes.

Peel the pears, leaving the stems attached. Core the pears from the bottom. Add the pears to the cooking liquid for about 30 minutes, turning the pears from time to time so all sides have absorbed color and flavor from the liquid.

Remove the pears when they feel tender when pierced with a fork. Reserve the cooking liquid. Arrange the pears on a deep serving platter. It may be necessary to cut a slice from the bottom of each pear so it will sit upright.

Remove and reserve the cinnamon and star anise. Boil the sauce to thicken—careful not to burn it.

To serve, pour the syrup over the pears and garnish with the cinnamon and star anise. These may be eaten hot or cooled to room temperature.

NOTE: The pears can be refrigerated and served later, but they must be brought to room temperature before serving.

ARROZ CON LECHE
Rice Pudding

One unusually wet June evening we trudged several blocks through the streets of Madrid, propelled by some new friends who had appointed themselves our special guides. We moved toward what they insisted was the best rice pudding in Madrid and all of Spain. Alas, there were far too many little bars to slip into for other research and we arrived after the restaurant had closed. The next day we returned to Bar Neru and tasted the arroz con leche, and it was indeed excellent. Rice pudding is a very nurturing kind of dish in any language.

SERVES 4 TO 6.

1 cup short-grain rice	½ cup sugar
1 2-inch piece cinnamon stick	Pinch of salt
Peel of 1 lemon, in 1 long strip, more or less	6 cups milk
	Ground cinnamon

Place the rice, ⅔ cup of water, cinnamon stick, lemon peel, sugar and salt in a pan and bring to a boil. Cover and simmer over low heat until most of the water has been absorbed, about 10 minutes. Add the milk and continue to cook over low heat, stirring occasionally, until most of the milk is absorbed and the rice is very tender. This should take about 1 hour. Remove and discard the cinnamon stick and lemon peel.

Pour into a glass bowl, cool to room temperature, and refrigerate.

To serve, place in pretty bowls and lightly sprinkle with the ground cinnamon. Too much cinnamon on the top of the pudding dulls it.

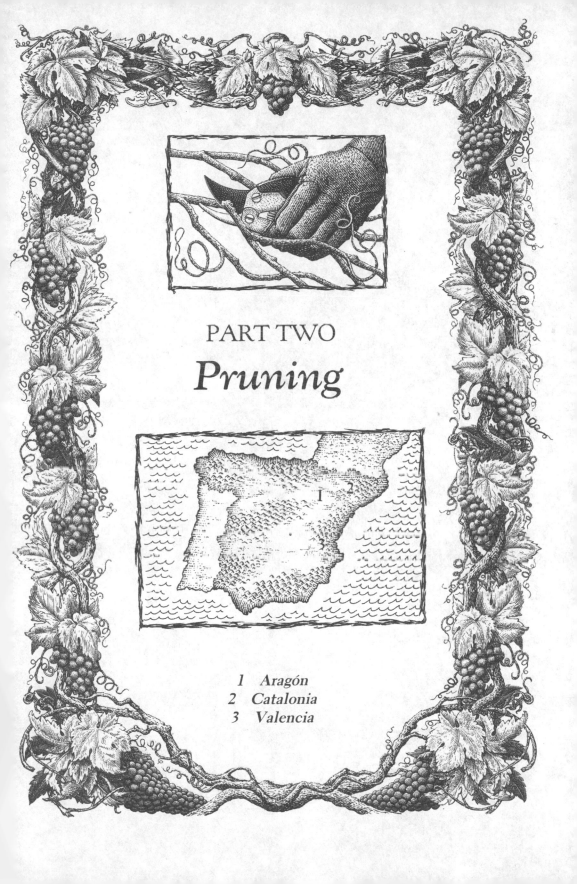

PART TWO

Pruning

1 Aragón
2 Catalonia
3 Valencia

By the end of January the wine is resting in barrels or tanks. All traces of fermentation should be finished. The first of the preliminary tastings and decisions as to the wine's future are under way.

In the vineyards, pruning crews are at work—in the bitter cold of the north and the milder climate of the south. Pruning is as essential to wine as the harvest, for without proper pruning, the vine would bear only a small crop and little wine could be made. Each year in midwinter, the old growth must be cut away from the vines. The vine cuttings are usually gathered for burning, sometimes by locals who depend for much of their winter firewood on these cuttings, other times by the winery.

The traditional method of pruning in most of Spain is called *vaso* because the bare, pruned vine is shaped like a glass or vase, with a bulge in the center. The vines, like those in France, are cut back low to the ground, only 18 to 24 inches high.

In much of Catalonia, parts of Rioja, and some of Jerez, recently planted vineyards are trained to grow on wires strung tightly between posts at the end of the vine row and evenly spaced down the row. There are various systems of pruning for vine growth, but whether by *vaso* or wire trellis, the point is to leave only a limited number of nodules—tiny swollen knobs—on the old vine. From these knobs new vines will burst forth to carry the fruit of the next harvest.

Casual laborers are hired for the picking during harvest, but pruning is a different matter and a good pruner is highly prized. He must be able to look at a vine and quickly assess where to make the first cut, for the dormant vine in January will be a tangle of branches. Although women may be hired for harvest or leaf pulling, they are rarely pruners. Often, with the closely planted rows it is even difficult to tell where one begins and the other ends. So into this puzzle of branches the pruner must boldly strike and begin cutting.

At midwinter the vines are bare, often under a light dusting of snow in the Pyrenees zone and whipped by cold winds in the plains of the south. Pruning is a bleak job in all zones; workers rise before the light to go to the fields. If you are up early enough, you can see them stopping at some of the early-opening bars for a quick *carijillo*, or *café con leche* (sometimes with a small tumbler of anise on the side), stepping out onto the sidewalk to look at the sky (they do not prune in the rain), stepping back in for one more espresso before going out to the campo.

It's a long day, and often biting cold. The vineyards are usually muddy and the cold from the mud seems to get right inside even the best-shod foot. (I once met an old farmer in Arboc in Catalonia who wore only sandals, even on the coldest winter mornings. He was from northern Aragón in the Somontano area, where it gets quite bitter in the winter. This man was in his sixties and swore he never had worn shoes and socks, even on his wedding day. His feet were like hooves.)

About midmorning a fire of vine clippings is built at the edge of the field and the first meal of the day is brought out—usually *bocadillos*, little sandwiches made of bread and ham and cheese, washed down with wine and brandy. At about one, following a short break at noon, the workers take a lunch break of one and a half to two hours. If the weather is good, it may be taken in the field; if not, there is usually some kind of shelter available. Lunch will be a bit more elaborate, perhaps a jar of soup or stew, often heated in some kind of camp kit over the outdoor fire or the indoor stove. There will certainly be bread. (Remember there is no meal without bread in Spain.) Many employers furnish the wine, especially if the vineyards are owned by a winery. It is usually available in five-gallon carboys at the foreman's shed. Each worker bring his own bottle and no one minds he refills it at least once during the day, meaning that it isn't at all unusual for a vineyard pruner to drink two liter bottles of wine during the work day. Mind you, they are engaged in hard physical labor and are never the worse for drink at the end of the day. They usually come off work at about five o'clock during the winter.

This routine is followed in vineyards everywhere in Spain, with only slight variations for changes in climate and weather. Everywhere the vineyard crews are made up chiefly of men over fifty, often much older. There is the occasional young man, but few are willing to put in the hours for the pay, which ranges from four to six dollars an hour, often paid under the table, which means the worker doesn't have to pay any taxes, but also he is not covered by any of the Spanish government's unemployment or other insurance plans.

There is some concern about who will work in the vineyards when the old men are gone. Very few of the vineyards are planted to accommodate mechanical harvesting or pruning, and many vineyard owners do not have the capital to invest in such equipment. In the meantime, casual vineyard work is the surest way for an undocumented worker to earn a few pesetas in Spain.

The foods of the pruning season are winter foods—rich stews, roasted game, sausages, and dried beans in dozens of variations. The table at pruning time is heavy and designed to keep away the cold and lift the gray spirits of winter.

ARAGÓN

*The brutes certainly knew how
to fight.*

—THE NAPOLEONIC MARSHAL
LANNE'S COMMENT AFTER THE
FRENCH SIEGE OF ZARAGOZA IN
1808–9, WHICH LEFT 54,000
ARAGONESE DEAD

IN FOCUS

Aragón terrain ranges from the near-wilderness area of Ordesa in
the Pyrenees (one of the few places in Europe where there are still
wolves and bears) to Zaragoza, one of Spain's most pleasant, most
thoroughly civilized cities. The entire region is one of those great
unexpected pleasures that travelers often meet in Spain.

Except for Zaragoza, Aragón is a land of small towns, villages, and
rugged—often harsh—countryside, a bit reminiscent of the Bad-
lands of West Texas and northeastern New Mexico. Aragón runs
south from the French border in the north to the Sistema Ibérico
mountain range, which separates it from Castile and Valencia. It
borders La Rioja and Navarre on the west, Catalonia on the east.
The Río Ebro runs through the center of Aragón, winding pleasantly
through Zaragoza and on toward the Mediterranean. The river
drains a large central valley, which is very fertile when properly
irrigated.

The climate ranges from desert heat in the south to alpine cold in
the north, with all shades and variations in between.

In most guidebooks Aragón is called the ancient kingdom but
rarely is this explained. The reference is to a ninth-century revolt in
the foothills of the Pyrenees by a local Christian baron against the
Moors. A few years later, in 1035, Ramiro I turned the tiny fiefdom
into a kingdom, with his capital at Jaca in the north. In the early
1100s, the Christians broke through the Moorish defenses and captured Zaragoza, which then became the capital of Aragón. The
hilltop towers where the Moors lit huge fires at night to warn against
Christian advances are still visible.

In 1154 a marriage united the kingdom with the counts of Barcelona, and the combined states became a major power for the following two centuries in the western Mediterranean, its fiat extending south into Valencia, into southern France as far as Toulouse inland and to Nice on the coast, east to Rioja, and including the Balearic islands and Sicily. This was the height of Catalan power in the Mediterranean, with Catalan merchant princes playing a major role in the commerce of the entire region. Although the Aragonese were not Catalan speakers, Catalan was the commercial language of the kingdom.

Aragón's power went into decline after 1476, when Ferdinand II of Aragón married Isabella the Catholic of Castile, uniting the two kingdoms into the core of what is now modern Spain. Aragón's independence was gradually stripped away. With the opening of the Americas, the interest of the central government in Madrid turned away from the Mediterranean toward the Atlantic and the west.

There was another, more subtle, but perhaps more telling, casualty of the marriage: Isabella had no tolerance for Moors. They were expelled from Aragón, and that unique Spanish culture known as Mudéjar collapsed. The Moriscos, Moors who had converted to Christianity, made up almost 20 percent of Aragón's population, including many of the artisan class—when they left, the economy collapsed. The Moors had also kept a complex irrigation system in operation around the Río Ebro in the great central valley of Aragón, and that too fell into disrepair. The arid, semidesert of southern Aragón replaced the rich agricultural fields the Moors had tended for centuries. The Christians paid a heavy price for their religious purity.

THE FOOD

Aragón shares some of its table with Catalonia, some with Navarre, and some, even, with the French. The food has been described as uninteresting, but that is a hasty judgment. The ingredients are simple, yet they are combined in rich and complex ways. An example would be *chilindrón*, probably the most famous dish of Aragón. It's made with lamb or chicken—though lamb is preferred—braised with tomatoes and peppers, garnished with strips of sweet red pepper. Simple ingredients found, let's say, in any peasant kitchen, yet combined in such a way as to create a marvelous dish.

Another treatment of lamb—*ternasco*—is completely simple. It's baby lamb cooked (ideally) over a wood fire with only salt, garlic, and bacon fat for seasoning. In fact, the list of lamb dishes that figure prominently in Aragonese cooking is quite long and includes lamb testicles, lamb head, and lamb tails, which are called *espárragos montañés*, or mountain asparagus.

Aragón is well known for charcuterie, especially *morcilla*, black pudding, which is made with rice, cinnamon, and either pine nuts or hazelnuts. The hams of Teruel are well known throughout Spain and featured in the tapas bars of Zaragoza.

Soups, especially winter soups, are excellent in Aragón. A favorite is a shepherd's soup with garlic, potatoes, bread, and egg, as served at La Rinconada de Lorenzo in Zaragoza. At the same restaurant, we had an upscale *migas* dish, with ham and grapes added to the typical *migas* base of dried bread fried in pork fat. (It's a solidly winter dish almost anywhere in rural Spain.) There is a wonderful soup called *presa de predicador*, or preacher's game, made with beef, mutton, pork, chicken, and sausage. There is a delicious garlic soup, *sopa de ajo*, made with almonds and eggs, and a kind of bread soup, *sopa de pan*, made very thick with tomato, pepper, and *chorizo*. Other winter meals include a variety of bean and sausage dishes that approach the consistency of soups or stews.

WINE

The best-known wines of Aragón are from the Cariñena denomination of origin (D.O.), which covers a large area (22,000 hectares) south of the city of Zaragoza. Until very recently, the wines of Cariñena have been strong, dark, and high in alcohol, made from the Garnacha. They often reached 17 or 18 percent alcohol and were much in demand for blending, especially in those regions of France not so blessed (if that is the word) with scorching summer temperatures. The trend in the past decade has been toward making lighter wines by picking grapes earlier, and using new temperature-controlled fermentation equipment. By holding down the temperature of the fermenting must, it is possible to emphasize the fruity flavors.

But the biggest change taking place in Cariñena is the replacement of the all-purpose Garnacha with the Tempranillo grape from Rioja and the Macabeo grape from Catalonia. There is also more white wine being made here than ever before, mostly from the

Viura, another Rioja variety. This white wine quality has also been made possible also by the introduction of cool-temperature fermentation and chilled stainless steel tanks.

The D.O. of Campo de Borja, west of Cariñena, produces a short list of fruity reds and rosé wines. The tiny region of Somontano, in the foothills of the Pyrenees, was only given D.O. status in 1982. It is small, about 3,000 hectares, with only 1,000 now planted. With the cool foothill climate, vineyards there may very well have the potential to produce the best wine in Aragón. In fact, they may already be doing just that. It is possible to find some Somontano wines in good wine shops around the United States. Look particularly for those from the Bodega Cooperativa Somontano.

Wines have been made in the Somontano region for thousands of years, but a real boom came when the phylloxera-stricken French were looking for places to replant in the late nineteenth century. Most of them went to Rioja, but a few crossed the Pyrenees into northern Aragón and found Somontano. They replanted the typical Garnacha with Cabernet Sauvignon and Cabernet Franc and blended them with the local Moristrel (the Monastrell of Catalonia.) Although these wines flourished for a time, they were hurt by the drying up of the local labor market in the early 1960s. But in the past few years, some of the old vineyards have been replanted and there is an air of excitement there. There are some commercial plantings of Sauvignon Blanc, Chardonnay, and Pinot Gris.

THE VINEYARDS

There are about 33,000 hectares of vines in Aragón, yet a visit to the important Cariñena region in the blazing heat of midsummer or the bitter cold of midwinter would lead one to believe that nothing could survive there, let alone a delicate-looking wine grape. As usual, wine grapes turn out to be tougher than expected, as the Romans knew, since they were making wine there when Cariñena was called Carae.

There are also records from the third century B.C. of wine made by Iberians from grapes and honey, so despite the climate, Cariñena has excellent references as a winemaking area. In fact, as early as the seventeenth century, laws were passed regulating the kind of grapes planted there and new plantings were forbidden without a license.

As mentioned above, older vineyards with traditional varieties are being replaced all over Aragón by vines that produce wines more appealing to the modern palate. This practice, in combination with winemaking techniques yielding fruitier, lighter wines, is rapidly changing the image of Aragón as a producer of big, alcoholic wines.

SPANISH DAYS

We had the good luck to arrive for one of our first visits to Aragón in the early winter, driving from the northern Navarre to Jaca. We say it was good luck because Aragón is winter country. Even in the dry dusty plains south of Zaragoza we think of winter. Perhaps it's the food, the rich stews and soups, the hearty meat dishes, the dozens of treatments of mutton and pig; or perhaps it has something to do with Aragón's place in our history of Europe. Aragón is medieval, remote, somehow edged in ice, and a bit stern. It is fantasy, kings and queens in fine robes, drinking rich red wine from jeweled chalices, plotting the next campaign against the Moors or the French. And the landscape of fantasy is so often a winter journey.

Jaca fits that image well. Carved out of a hillside terrace above the Río Aragón valley, with the mountains to the north and south, it could be a sepia drawing on a chill winter day from a book of fairy tales. It was the first capital of Aragón and the center of resistance to the Moors.

Jaca was also a jumping-off point for the pilgrims bound for Compostela in the Middle Ages. It is said that pilgrims going to and from Santiago de Compostela in Galicia filled the town, giving it an unusually international cast for the time.

Jaca, with a population of under fifteen thousand, still has that feeling, although now the pilgrims are more likely to be en route to skiing in the Pyrenees or birdwatching in the Ordesa park to the north. Or perhaps, as we were one dark and bleak evening in early January, en route to the Hotel Conde Aznar, or more exactly, the restaurant in the hotel, La Cocina Aragonesa. As the name suggests, it offers a typical Aragonese menu and has the reputation of doing that quite well.

We thought we had surely been sent astray when we arrived at the hotel. It seemed, as best we could make out in the darkness, a commonplace, rather modern establishment, with a television lounge opening just off the office/entryway.

But we had been driving for hours in a fine rain that kept threatening to turn to snow. We were packed like tourists into the notorious *bota* patrol car, and it was Saturday night. There was no point in being too picky. In fact, the room was comfortable, the water was hot, there was really no reason to complain. And within the hour, we discovered that the Aragonese table was a splendid place to be seated. And more surprising and gratifying, it was a bit the way I would image a medieval fantasy feast to be, only without the cold drafts, the dogs, and the fleas—but magnificent food.

Begin with the dining room. It was all dark wood, on two levels and divided by railings into several separate areas, with each area guarded or watched over by a ghostly knight in armor. There was a working fireplace and the light was dim, but bright enough to see what was on the plate—very important in unknown restaurants.

There were no oppressive, hovering waiters, too often encountered in hotel restaurants in Spain. (Although the Argonesa's relationship with the hotel was vague. There is a separate street entrance but the telephone number is the same and the check can be charged to one's room number.) There was a comfortable, motherly-looking woman who knew the menu thoroughly, and even more surprising, knew the wine list thoroughly. And what a wine list! Not only the selection, but the pricing was so exceptional that we wanted to change all travel plans and simply last out the month, drinking up all that lovely wine. The wines offered are a good example of what one can commonly find in Spanish restaurants—good restaurants, at any rate.

For openers there was a Bodegas San Marcos 1973 Rosato from the wine town of Barbastro. At the time, that was a seventeen-year-old rosé. "Much too old to be drinkable," says common wisdom. Good thing we didn't listen, because the common wisdom would have been wrong again. Although the color was a bit faded and dull to the eye, the flavor was rich and nutty with chocolate tones on the finish. It was about ten dollars a bottle. We had it as an apéritif. Followed by a bottle of Señorío de Lazán Reserva Montesierra 1984, a glorious red wine from the co-op of Somontano. The waitress suggested it, as it had just been released and was not yet on the wine list. It was still young, but what deep, rich flavors! Mark it up at about five dollars a bottle.

We stuck with it through the next few courses. First we had a *mousee de aiernos y cigales*—a green sauce layered with prawns and very delicately flavored, just a touch of garlic—and *hojaldre de puerros*, a thin layer of housemade puff pastry baked with a custard of leek, cheese, and eggs. Then there was *pan crujiente*, another pastry filled with a *morisco* of crab, clams, and prawns with a deep-green asparagus sauce.

Another bottle of the '84 greeted a half pheasant in a sweet Madeira sauce with pureed vegetables—utterly lovely. The use of Madeira in the sauce was a slight Aragonese curtsey to other kitchens. No doubt, the dish originally was in a red wine sauce.

We carried on with the '84 right through a sea bass, roasted with sautéed garlic served in a *caldo* with clams in the shell—the sauce had just a slight hint of vinegar, which gave it a piquant twist that echoed nicely against the sweetness of the fish, both matching well with the fruitiness and depth of the wine.

With the final dish, medallions of venison stewed with whole shallots in a rich brown sauce, we switched to a 1964 Campo Viejo (younger versions are available in some U.S. markets) from Rioja. It was a mark of the waitress's true appreciation of wine that when asked what she thought was the best older wine on the list, she went outside Aragón for her choice. Yet she didn't go for the most expensive or the best-known, for there were wines from Muga, La Rioja Alta, and other much better-known Rioja bodegas on the list. The Campo Viejo turned out to be a super choice, especially with the venison. The wine had mellowed to a soft, velvety texture in the bottle, which went well with the rich flavor of the venison. For a twenty-five-year-old wine of the quality of the Campo Viejo, I would have expected to pay well over one hundred dollars at almost any U.S. restaurant—only, of course, it would not be available. In Jaca, it was a bit under thirty dollars.

The dessert that night was the perfect finish, somehow reflecting the flavors of the dinner while adding a final brushstroke of perfection. We had a fig mousse, made with dried figs and served with a hot custard sauce covered by chopped walnuts. Our pleasure truly knew no limits.

We finished off with a glass or so of the house *aguardiente*, flavored with plums. It left a warm, glowing, fairy-tale feeling in the mouth, as we went off to bed with happy thoughts and sweet dreams before our drive south to Zaragoza next morning.

An old black-shawled woman goes up and down the sidewalk of the shops of the Vía César Agusto in Zaragoza, with bent back and frayed straw broom, spending the gray morning sweeping away the dried mud and dust. The street is being torn up to build an under-

ground parking garage, only a block from the mercado. *By noon it has started to rain and there is nothing she can do against the new mud slowly building up. She stands motionless in the doorway of the Hotel Marisol, where no matter how thoroughly we clean our feet on the mat, we track mud up the carpeted stairs to the gleaming tile floor of our room.*

Later that afternoon, the rain had become a fine mist drifting down without any seeming possibility of change from the single-clouded sky. The old woman was gone from the doorway, but as we stepped out onto the sidewalk, we saw her a few doors away in front of a small bar sweeping the fine, sandy wet mud steadily back toward the broken street.

The history of Zaragoza goes back to an Iberian river-crossing settlement of uncertain age called Salduba. It was (and still is), from its position on the Río Ebro, a key to travel routes through north and central Spain, from Tarragona and the Catalan coast to Rioja and the Basque country, and from France, through the pass at Jaca to the south and Madrid, Toledo, and Córdoba.

The Romans took Salduba in 25 B.C. and renamed it Caesaraugusta. Later, the Moors seized the city and changed the name to Sarakusta. After its recapture by the Christians it became, as Saragosa, one of the most prosperous cities in Spain, an important commercial and cultural capital. The ruling body—*the fueros*—was for several centuries the most liberal in Spain. Zaragoza (now beginning with Z) offered full protection to the Moors, so there are excellent examples of the Mudéjar style through the churches and those houses still standing in the old town that were not destroyed by the French in the nineteenth century.

The city's commercial fortunes have been up and down (they seem to be up just at present) over the centuries, but there has been one constant—the fame of the Virgin of Pilar. The story goes that on the second day of January in the year A.D. 40, the Virgin Mary appeared in a vision to the apostle James—then, as the story goes, a resident of the city. As proof, she left a pillar. A basilica was later built around the pillar (the present church is the third on the site) and the Virgin of Pilar's fame spread throughout Spain. It is pretty much a toss-up whether more girl babies in Spain are named Montserrat (from the Catalonia Virgin) or Pilar. We once met a woman in Barcelona named Pilar Montserrat—all bases covered.

October twelfth is the Virgin's festival day, with fireworks, torchlight parades, giant cardboard figures, and, so we are told, the usual madness that accompanies major fiestas in Spain. We have never been lucky enough to be on hand for that particular party, but have often created our own fiestas in Zaragoza.

Zaragoza, in our memory, is a city of winter. It has always been raining in Zaragoza and it has always been Christmas, or just before or just after. Lights gleam on concrete and brick, crowds of people jam the Corte Inglés, shopping on a scale that no American, however well trained in suburban malls, could possibly deal with.

Shopping, like most other things in Spain, is a family experience —Mom, Dad, the kids, Grandma, Grandpa, and probably a few cousins. And you don't go shopping in Spain in Spandex workout clothes. In any of the big cities, shopping is a dress-up experience, and the Spanish probably dress "up" better than anyone in the world. Personal image is important in Spain—think of the bullfighter's "suit of lights"—and it starts early.

In Spain, it starts with the smallest children. Babes in arms wear outfits that must have set the family back a day's wages. There are high-fashion childrens' clothing stores on any serious shopping street. And I'm not talking about a stack of jeans and T-shirts, but designer-label threads.

Most of Zaragoza was rebuilt, following the wars with France in the early nineteenth century, with broad, graceful streets that seem to invite leisurely strolls and keep beckoning the shopper on to the next window and then the next.

After the mixed-generation shopping spree (or maybe as a quick break between stores) a Zaragoza family can pick and choose from some of the best tapas bars in Spain. There are several good areas for tapas. Any of the streets leading away from the Plaza de Aragón toward the Puerta del Carmen or the Plaza San Sebastián are good. Closer to the river there are good tapas bars a few blocks from the cathedral, known in Zaragoza as La Seo, and another cluster of good bars in the university section.

Two of my favorites near the Plaza de Aragón are San Siro on Calle de Costa and the Bar Cochera on Calle de Casa Jiménez. The specialty at the latter is *pinchos*, a small skewer of meat—it can be veal, lamb, goat, or beef—sautéed with garlic and served on a piece of toasted bread, with a glass of the full-bodied red wine from Cariñena. Just the fuel needed to get you back into the shops.

There is an outstanding seafood tapas bar near the cathedral called the Bar Casa Amachio on the Calle del Captún. It's a favorite hangout of Galicians, since most of the shellfish there comes from the Galician coast. There are lovely fresh oysters, clams, crabs, all sorts of prawns, and fresh fish. They are shipped by fast train or reefers from the Galician coast and have not been out of the Atlantic more than ten to fifteen hours. (This is a fairly typical experience, even in inland Spain, where much energy is devoted to seeing that absolutely fresh food is available in even fairly remote areas. It is ironic that other Europeans consider the Spanish to be inefficient and backward. But when it comes to dealing with things they consider important, they can be as efficient as any northerner.

There are very good restaurants around the wide, pleasant streets bordering the Plaza de Aragón. Some, like the Mesón del Carmen, have achieved landmark status as typical Aragonese restaurants, while serving indifferent food. Every visitor to Zaragoza (or any other large Spanish city) should make the tourist office the first stop. You don't lose any points by admitting that you are a tourist, and you could come out way ahead. Sometimes, I'm afraid, the gastronomical guides get a bit lazy and simply repeat with a few variations what has been in every edition since the beginning of tourism. Things do change. Restaurants are sold to new owners, chefs come and go. Reviewing a restaurant isn't like reviewing a monument, after all. It requires some real updating. And that's what tourist offices do.

At one time Méson del Carmen might have been worth a visit, but no more, at least not for dinner. There is a pleasant-enough tapas bar there, with good *pinchos*, although it does try a bit too hard to look *típico*. Mesón del Carmen isn't even listed in the *Gastronomic Guide to Aragón*, published by the Turismo de Aragón. Yet it is one of the three recommended restaurants for Zaragoza in the usually reliable *American Express Pocket Guide to Spain*. At any rate, another example to affirm our oft-repeated warning: beware of foreign guides or at least try to get on-the-ground local confirmation before booking a table or hotel room.

Just around the corner from Mesón del Carmen, however, is the previously mentioned Rinconada de Lorenzo (translated, "Larry in the corner," so how could we resist?). It offers outstanding Aragonese cuisine in a bistrolike setting with a friendly staff who actually know the food and wine and like to talk about it. They'll even give it a try in English. It's worth having a closer look at Lorenzo, if for no other reason than simply because all the richness of Aragonese cuisine can be found on one table.

A particular triumph is an upscale version of *migas*, a basic country dish that, if you are not careful, will be offered to you all over Spain. In general, it consists of unmentionables preserved in pork fat, served with crumbled, stale bread. And one must be trying hard to be authentic or had a bit too much *vino tinto* to have more than one spoonful.

But at Lorenzo it is served as a tapa. The unmentionables have been replaced with thin slices of excellent ham, the stale bread has been replaced with dry but still tasty crumbs of bread. Instead of pork fat, lamb suet is used in the preparation, and fresh grapes are put in at the last minute. It is served just slightly above room temperature, and it is delicious.

We were served an Aragón *cava*, a 1985 Blanc de Blanc Brut Nature from Hinzón, which was delicious, absolutely dry, tasting faintly of apples and pears. If *cava* such as that were put in the world export markets, there would be a much better appreciation of Spanish *cava*.

Another typical Aragonese dish was the soup, a *sopa pastor*, or shepherd's soup, served in a *cazuela*. It has a bit of everything— garlic, potatoes, bread—topped with an egg that has been fried with slivers of garlic in olive oil. This is a catchall soup, and the cook's imagination and/or supplies at hand are the only things that might limit the ingredients. (Topping off with a fried egg is an Aragonese trademark. *Huevos al salmarejo* is a ham, sausage, *lomo*, asparagus, and pea stew, also served with a fried egg on top.)

A specialty of the house was blood pudding, or *morcilla*—house-made with rice, cinnamon, and hazelnuts, one of the endless variations on *morcilla* to be found throughout Spain. Practically every area, almost every city has a *típico morcilla*. In Asturias, for example, the traditional *morcilla* is made from bacon fat and onions and the blood of pig and cow. A version of *morcilla blanca* (white sausage) is found all over Spain and is the famous *butifarra* of Catalonia. In Jaén, in Andalusia, it is made with sherry, dried fruits, and nuts. In several areas rice is used and sometimes sugar is added. In fact, almost anything in the way of fruit or cereal can be added to blood pudding. In Galicia, I have had *morcilla* with apples, in Extremadura, with potatoes.

Blood sausages come out of the fall hog-butchering ritual, when blood is abundantly available. Hog blood is most commonly used in Spain. In the United States it is next to impossible to find hog blood, but a good butcher may be able to get cow blood. The blood should not be frozen, as freezing spoils the flavor. And *morcilla* does taste very good when properly made, although I have found the name blood sausage does turn off some modern American cooks. Perhaps if you think of it by the French term *boudin noir* it will be more acceptable. . . .

As we drive east out of Zaragoza there is a promise of sunshine up toward the Pyrenees. The streets are still damp after a night of gentle rains, which stopped before dawn. Early traffic is light enough that we can stop the car for a few moments on the Puenta de Santiago and look back down the Ebro toward the cathedral, or La Seo, and the Nuestra Señora del Pilar. A light mist rises from the water and a few birds—impossible to identify at this distance—are working the rising currents of warm air, looking for insects a few hundred yards downsteam. There is enough light to reflect the tower of the cathedral in the water. Suddenly, a single narrow beam of sunshine like a heavenly spotlight hits the very top of the eighteenth-century tower, reflecting from the glass windows of the observation platform at the top in a blaze of white light.

GUIDELINES: ARAGÓN

Jaca

HOTEL

Hotel Conde Aznar, General Franco, 3. Tel. (974) 36-10-50. Perfectly fine sleeping, reasonable.

RESTAURANT

La Cocina Aragonese, Calle Cervantes, 5. Tel. (974) 36-10-50. Superb restaurant. Worth a long detour.

Zaragoza

HOTELS

Hotels in Zaragoza are overpriced (as they are in much of Spain). Again, look for *pensiones*. My favorite is the Marisol at César Agusto, 72. Cheap and comfortable. Try not to track mud in, though.

RESTAURANT

La Rinconada de Lorenzo, Calle La Salle, 3. Tel. (976) 45-51-08. Fine regional food, very knowledgeable staff with some English.

Wineries

Bodegas Fábregas, Calle Graus, 14, Barbastro. Tel. (974) 31-04-98. Open Monday to Friday, 9 A.M. until 1:30 P.M. and from 4 P.M. until 7:30 P.M. Open on Saturday from 9:30 A.M. until 1:30 P.M. Visitors are welcomed at this small, family-owned winery in the Somontano area, but as elsewhere in Spain, a call ahead will be appreciated.

Heredad Balbino Lacosta, Hermana Matilde, 31–33, Cariñena. Tel. (976) 62-03-89. Open daily, 8 A.M. until 3 P.M. Closed in August. This is a family-owned estate winery, producing excellent wines.

Bodegas Cavas Lopez Pelayo, Almonacid de la Sierra, about 10 kilometers from Cariñena. Tel. (976) 62-70-15. Open Monday to Saturday, 3 P.M. until 8 P.M. Closed July 23 until August 15. A charming winery, with centuries-old cellars dug out of the rock.

CATALONIA

IN FOCUS

Catalonia has enough geography to be a continent in itself. The terrain ranges from the spectacular Costa Brava on the Mediterranean in the east (very much like the Big Sur coast in California), to the peaks of the Pyrenees in the north, to the flat plains of Aragón in the west, down to the rugged back country of Tarragona in the south. From sea resorts to ski resorts, the land is remarkable in its beauty and diversity.

The coast is one of the most celebrated in the world. The Costa Brava between Barcelona and the French border is too crowded to contemplate in the summer season, stuffed to the surf line with the British, Germans, and Scandinavians, but in the fall and winter its truly spectacular beauty can be appreciated. There are good restaurants all along the coast, and many places to rent sailboats—another way to beat the crowds. The coast south of Barcelona toward Tarragona and Valencia is a little less spectacular and less developed, but the coastal superhighway has opened it up for even the most casual day trip.

Along the coast the climate is Mediterranean and mild in winter; however, summers can be a bit muggy, especially in Barcelona, which seems to have been built in a swamp. But the smaller coastal resort towns are quite pleasant, even in the peak of summer's heat. Inland the climate is more extreme, with snow at fairly low elevations in the winter and intense summer heat.

Catalans have always been the only real Europeans of Spain. You are in Spain, there is no doubt of that, but it is a far different Spain from Castile or the south. The centuries-old Catalan drive for independence from Madrid is not so much an attempt by the Catalans to wreck Spanish unity (almost a mythical concept in any event) but to assert the authority of the Catalan consciousness and to reestablish the former independence of Catalonia.

Barcelona, the chief city of Catalonia, was the most powerful city in the Kingdom of Aragón while Madrid was still a muddy river crossing, baking on the plains of La Mancha. For much of the thirteenth century, Catalan naval power was supreme in the Mediterranean, and Catalan princes ruled the Mediterranean coast from Valencia to Nice. The combined kingdom of Catalonia and Aragón, with Catalonia the dominant partner, held the island of Sicily and exercised tremendous influence in Athens and northern Italy.

Through the centuries, the rivalry between Catalonia and Castile has been constant. Some of the bloodiest and most bitter battles of the Spanish Civil War were fought in Catalonia. Today that competition is largely fought out in the commercial arena (or on the soccer field), but it is still there.

Catalans are fiercely proud of their language, which on the printed page looks like a mélange of French and Castilian but on the tongue has a harshness, a bit like a French speaker using German. The first written Catalan dates from the ninth century; it was doubtless developed as a spoken language as early as the seventh century. Catalan is spoken by about 6.5 million people and it is a major social blunder to refer to it as a "dialect" of Spanish or Castilian. Besides Catalonia, the language is spoken in about two-thirds of Valencia, a wide strip of western Aragón, the Balearic Islands, the Republic of Andorra, parts of the Italian island of Sardinia, and the area of Roussillon in France.

But it is more than language that separates Catalonia from the rest of Spain. Historically, Catalonia was the most Romanized of any area of Spain. There was minimal contact with the Moors, and it has always had closer contacts with the French and northern Europe than the rest of Spain. In the nineteenth century, Castilians referred to Catalans as Francos. Today, new ideas in social thought, art, or literature usually make their way into Spain through Barcelona.

The social customs are also quite different. There are more self-service stand-up bars in Barcelona than elsewhere in Spain, more people look at their watches, the trains run on time, and lunch and dinner go a bit faster.

Catalonia is Europe with a Spanish accent.

THE FOOD

The cuisine of Catalonia is rich and sophisticated, with roots in the ancient Mediterranean tradition reaching back to Rome and Athens, and shooting forward to the Moors and the New World. It is distinct from the rest of Spain, indeed from the rest of Europe. It is a unique and complex cuisine and is worth a great deal of attention.

One of Spain's first cookbooks was written in Catalan in 1477 by Ruperto de Nola. Its subject, oddly enough, was Italian food. By the nineteenth century, Barcelona was known for its fine hotels and restaurants, many of which were Italian or French. The native Catalan chefs were not shy about taking a foreign dish and making it their own. And anyone who has ever tasted *canelones* from Barcelona will never again think of them as an exclusively Italian dish.

The twelfth to fourteenth centuries were a time when rice and other foods of the East were being introduced into France and Italy, quite possibly by Catalan seafarers. This turning outward to northern Europe and to the sea has expanded the Catalan table tremendously and has made Catalan cuisine the dominant cuisine of Spain. Bear in mind that Catalan cuisine should not be tied in a narrow sense to Barcelona and the immediate area, but should embrace coastal Spain to Valencia. Remember that like the region, the cuisine sprawls north into present-day France as far as the city of Toulouse and into the interior of Spain at least as far west as Aragón, where it meets the other major Spanish cuisine, Basque, lapping over the Pyrenees into Rioja and Navarre.

Considered in this larger sense, Catalan cooking is clearly a major European cuisine. The Catalan cook uses the resources of the Mediterranean, the interior valleys of the Pyrenees, the rich pasture land of Aragón, the rice fields of Valencia, and the culinary heritage of Provence to create a unique food style that is still growing and developing. In short, Catalan chefs have reached beyond the culinary borders of Catalonia, taking what they like and adapting it to the Catalan kitchen.

A major culinary influence in the past twenty years has been the influx of workers fleeing the farms of Andalucia, Murcia, and Extremadura. These people (although many chic Catalans would never admit it) have enriched the Catalan table with a tasty injection of the vigorous peasant cuisines of those areas. Younger Catalan chefs have also reintroduced Catalan dishes from the south of France and from the Balearic islands.

Out of this have emerged five Catalan kitchen "basics":

• *Allioli*. A garlic, olive oil, and egg sauce served with grilled fish, lamb chops, snails, fowl, rabbit, prawns, bread—just about anything. It is surely the most important Catalan sauce, found on almost every table. It's simply a mayonnaise-like mixture of olive oil, pounded garlic, and sometimes egg yolk, although purists reject the egg. The sauce is traditionally made in a mortar and pestle.

• *Picada*. A ground mixture of garlic, almonds or hazelnuts, sometimes bread, less often saffron.

• *Romesco*. The secret sauce of Catalonia. It probaly originated in the ancient city of Tarragona as a humble fishermen's stew. Fishermen at sea would make it using the trash fish they knew couldn't be sold on land. Gradually, the ingredients of the sauce—almonds, red peppers, garlic, onions, tomatoes, and olive oil—became more important than the fish, although in Catalonia it is still usually served with fish. Now every cook in Catalonia has his or her favorite recipe, which is jealously guarded.

• *Samfaina*. A blend of onions, tomatoes, peppers, eggplants, and zucchini sautéed in olive oil.

• *Sofrito*. Onions and tomatoes sautéed in olive oil, occasionally with garlic or peppers. Sofrito is not so much a sauce by itself as a base for other sauces.

There are two major food festivals in Catalonia. The first is the fiesta of La Calçotada, which is held every year in the neighborhood of Valls, a few kilometers north of Tarragona. It is held when the almond trees first break into bloom. *Calçot* is a Catalan word which means "green onion." But there is much more to it than that, as there usually is in Catalonia.

To understand La Calçotada, it is necessary to know how these simple-looking green onion shoots are grown. And that gives some insight into the Catalan attitude toward food. It all starts about eighteen months before the festival itself, when onion seeds are planted in late September or early October at the waning of the moon. The seedlings are set out in January and grown until midsummer, when they are pulled from the ground and laid out to dry in bunches under the shade of a tree. In a few months the dried bunches begin to sprout again and they are then put out in trenches and earthed up, like Belgian endive. (It is this "earthing up" that actually gives *calçot* its name, since the word comes from *calcar*, which means to "pull on one's shoes or boots" in Catalan. In other words, the young onion shoots are covered, as if they were wearing boots.) By January they are ready to eat.

The entire *calçot* season could be regarded as a long-running festival, since the original Valls celebration (which began on a very small scale) has worked its way around to many of the neighboring towns. The actual *calçot* season usually lasts into March or perhaps April. The onions are grilled, ideally over a fire of vine cuttings. At the more upscale *calçot* feasts, they are served in curved tiles (like roofing tiles), which look quite nice but are actually a bit heavy and awkward as serving platters. More informally, they are served wrapped in newspapers.

However they are served, the important thing about eating a *calçot* is that it is necessary to get very messy. Eating a *calçot* is a learned technique that requires years, perhaps decades of practice. Colman Andrews, in his book *Catalan Cuisine*, describes it well.

"A *calçot* is grasped in the left hand by its blackened base and in the right hand by the inner green leaves at its top, then the black part is slipped off and discarded. The glistening white end of the *calçot* is next dipped into the aforementioned spicy nut sauce— formerly called *salvitjada* and now known mostly just as *salsa per calçots*—then lowered into the mouth with one's head thrown back jauntily, and bitten off about where the green part starts. As might be imagined, this is messy work, and everyone wears bibs at a proper *calçotada* and retires frequently to a nearby sink or pump to rinse off the soot."

Colman's *salsa per calçots* is simply *romesco* in a specialized version, which leads rather neatly to the next great Catalan food fiesta, the annual Romescada held at Cambrils near Tarragona in April. The contest draws thousands of people, and many of the cooks are fishermen, since *romesco* began as a fisherman's sauce. There is much dispute about just when it began, but in its modern form it could only date from the discovery of America, since the capsicum (from America) is one of the major ingredients. So whatever the beginnings of *romesco*, it did not take its present form until the sixteenth century, when that pepper was first grown in Catalonia.

Whatever its origins, the word *romesco* has three different meanings in Catalan. First it is the pepper itself, called *nyora* in Catalan, *nora* in Castilian; it is also a sauce and a seafood dish. In some respects it is the most interesting of all Catalan seafood stews or soups.

In any recipe calling for peppers, there is always some debate over exactly which particular pepper is meant, since peppers are legion, both in popular and scientific terminology. The *ancho* pepper is a good "universal" pepper.

> *There are six primary ingredients in Catalan*
> *cooking: olive oil, garlic, onions, tomatoes,*
> *nuts (almonds, hazelnuts, and pine nuts), and*
> *dried fruits, particularly raisins and prunes. In*
> *addition, the four traditional herbs are*
> *oregano, rosemary, thyme, and bay leaves.*
>
> —MARIMAR TORRES
> *THE SPANISH TABLE*

Marimar has it about right. Beyond the primaries, there is seafood of all sorts from the Mediterranean, rice from Tarragona, poultry from Gerona—chickens, ducks, geese, and turkeys. Much of the fowl is free-range. In much of Spain, chicken is a poor man's dish and often disregarded. But Gerona pays attention to chicken—and it shows. There are also snails, both sea and land, outstanding lamb from Gerona and Lérida and, of course, game, including venison, rabbit, and wild duck. There is pork and sausage from Lérida and Gerona, exotic mushrooms from Gerona and the foothills of the Pyrenees, and a wide selection of garden vegetables. And you can end the meal with a selection of good local goat cheeses from Lérida, known generically as *queso de cabra*.

THE WINE

> *For more than two thousand years the peoples*
> *living along the coast of the Mediterranean*
> *have drunk wine to quench their thirst, to*
> *accompany food, and for simple enjoyment.*
> *Their art, history and literature are closely*
> *linked with wine; and their poets have sung*
> *its virtues. Its red and golds have inspired our*
> *most famous painters; and in cathedrals and*
> *palaces, sculptors and architects have used the*
> *vine as a symbol.*
>
> *Roman civilization has been called the*
> *civilization of wine; and its production and*
> *consumption were central to the life of those*
> *early Mediterranean settlements whose*
> *culture was to spread throughout the world.*

> *Today our society stands more than ever in*
> *need of wine: honest, sincere wine, which*
> *brings men together and helps them surmount*
> *the barriers of prejudice. . . . Those tight*
> *clusters of grapes contain within them the*
> *essence and mystery of life, of the earth, the*
> *rain, the sun and man's labour.*
>
> —MIGUEL A. TORRES
> *WINES AND VINEYARDS OF SPAIN*

This lovely homage to the grape is a fitting way to walk into the Catalan landscape. Since the opening of trade between Spain and the rest of the Mediterranean centuries before the birth of Christ, wine has been one of the most important products of the area.

Phoenician and later Greek traders established outposts on the wild Spanish shores from the eighth to the sixth centuries B.C. One of the first things they did was plant vines, typical eastern Mediterranean varieties, and one of the first items of trade was wine.

Catalan food, culture, even land laws and usages have grown up around the vine. It grows at the very heart of Catalan culture. It is in Catalonia that the most thought and care is given to the matching of food and wine. It is this slightly self-conscious approach to the table and the wine vat that distinguishes Catalonia. Yet I must quickly add that it never reaches the point of unconscious parody that it sometimes does in the United States.

Without doubt, Catalonian wine deserves an entire book to itself, and in fact, there have been several, one of the best by the thoughtful gentleman quoted above, Miguel A. Torres, the talented and internationally famous winemaker at Bodegas Torres in Vilafranca del Penedés. Unfortunately, his book *The Distinctive Wines of Catalonia* has not been published in the United States. It is available in English, but to my knowledge only at the winery. I don't believe there is another book in English about the wine of Catalonia at present.

Catalonia produces a greater range and variety of wine than any other region in Spain. There are red and white table wines, the sparkling wine called *cava*, which is made according to the *méthode champenoise*, dessert wines, and brandies. At their best, the red wines of Rioja may be better than any single Catalan wine, but the overall quality of Catalan wines is higher than anywhere in Spain.

There are six denominations of origin in Catalonia: Alella, Ampurdán-Costa Brava, the Penedés, the Priorato, Tarragona, and Terra Alta. Conca de Barberá has been granted a provisional denomination, and the Costers de Segre in Lérida will probably be granted its own denomination soon. The autonomous government of Catalonia has also granted a denomination for Brandy de Catalonia, but that has not yet been recognized by either Madrid or the European Economic Community in Brussels.

The wines of Alella were famous in Roman times, and it is one of the oldest winegrowing regions in Catalonia. The area of Alella is on the highly developed coastal strip north of Barcelona. Like many wine-producing regions in the world, it is struggling for survival against a sea of concrete. In 1967, when the coastal highway running from Barcelona (now from south of Valencia) to the French border was completed, the number of hectares planted to vines was 1,400. Today, there are only 380 hectares left, and the pressure is still on.

It seems that it is more profitable to grow condos to sell or rent to the British, Germans, and Swedish than to maintain vineyards that have been in existence for over two thousand years. There have been some encouraging signs recently. The local councils have stopped (well, at least almost stopped) issuing building permits for sites on vineyard land. There has also been some investment in the wineries, particularly in stainless steel fermentation equipment, enabling producers to make the lighter, fruitier wines that tourists (and increasingly the Spanish) prefer. This is especially important for Alella, since most of the production there is white wine, which benefits the most from a cool, controlled fermentation.

Grape varieties are the Garnacha Blanca (the same we have met all over Spain), Pansa Blanca, Pansa Rosada, and Xarel-lo (*charel-o*). There aren't too many red wines made, but the Tempranillo (called Ull de Llebre in Catalonia) is widely planted.

There is some *cava* made in Alella and also some very pleasant sweet dessert wine, which is made by adding sweet must to a dry white wine (see pages 194–95).

The district of Ampurdán-Costa Brava stretches from the French border, high in the Pyrenees, to the Costa Brava—with a total of 5,800 hectares of vines. The area is best known for rosés, which account for over 70 percent of the wines. They are made from the ever-present Garnacha and Cariñena (from which a few red wines are also made). There are some white wines made from Xarel-lo and Macabeo.

The Penedés district is one of the most important in Spain, not only for the *cava*-filled ships that take that product all over the world, but also for a handful of excellent table wines that have established the Penedés as one of the world's finest wine-producing areas. There are about 45,000 hectares of vines. Table wine and brandy production are centered in the town of Vilafranca del Penedés with the *cava* capital a few kilometers away in San Sadurní de Noya.

Penedés is an old winegrowing area. It is believed that the Phoenicians were the first to plant grapes there, although it is possible that Celt-Iberian vintages may have been harvested in the Penedés before the coming of the Phoenicians. But without doubt, *cava* has had the greatest influence in the Penedés area, taking up the vast majority of the region's grape production. Traditional Penedés reds are made from the Ull de Llebre, Garnacha Tinta, Monastrell, Cariñena, and a handful of other local varieties that are being phased out.

There is a very special dessert wine made in the Penedés region from a few vineyards near the beach resort of Sitges. The wine is made from the Malvasia grape, probably first planted on the coast by Greek traders in the seventh and eighth centuries B C. There is very little of it to be found—at least very little of the true Malvasia. There are sweet wines on the market that manage to represent themselves as Malvasia but in fact they are not made from Sitges grapes at all but from much cheaper and more abundant Moscatel grapes.

There is a great deal of experimentation going forward in the Penedés with plots of Cabernet Sauvignon, Chardonnay, Merlot, Riesling, Pinot Noir, and Cabernet Franc planted by Torres, Jean León, and a few other wineries. The innovations in the vineyard were preceded by changes in the winery that have had a profound effect on Spanish wine, both at home and in the export market.

The Torres' Viña Sol, first introduced on the Spanish market in the 1970s, was a revolutionary wine. As mentioned before, it completely overturned the belief that Spaniards would drink only wood-aged partially oxidized white wines. Miguel Torres, using stainless steel cold fermentation, retained the intense perfumed fruitiness of the Parellada grape. Bottled young with only a touch of oak, it was on the market less than a year after the harvest. Torres was told, "This will never sell in Spain." Now the wine can be found in almost every bar in Spain and is exported to dozens of countries.

Cabernet Sauvignon was first officially planted in the Penedés by Jean León in the early sixties. His hunch that the varietal would do well in the Mediterranean climate was right. León's plantings were followed by plantings of Cabernet, Chardonnay, Merlot, and Pinot Noir at various Torres vineyards. Torres has a vineyard at Pachs, outside of Vilafranca, with dozens of experimental vines, including California Zinfandel.

It is this kind of research, a willingness to experiment and look beyond the traditional methods, that has brought the wines of Catalonia and especially the Penedés so far in such a short time.

The district of Priorato is quite distinctive. Much of the 3,700 hectares of vines are planted in a wild, scenic landscape of steep hills and valleys; grapes are taken from vineyards where mechanical harvesting is impossible. Grapes are carried down the steep hillsides in fifty-kilo bags and often taken to the winery in mule-drawn carts.

Yield is very low (even by Spanish standards) on the decomposed slate and volcanic soils of the region. Because of this low production and the ever-increasing costs of labor, many of Priorato's vineyards have been abandoned in the past ten years.

The red table wines of Priorato are well known in Spain for deep, rich colors and great concentration of flavor. They respond very well to barrel aging, becoming richer and more intense as time goes on.

Because of the intense color and high alcohol content of the Priorato wines, the unbottled wine is often sold to producers in the Penedés for blending. This is a pity. Obviously, the producers could make a greater income selling bottled, aged wines on the Spanish and international market, thus enabling them to keep the low-yielding, expensive vineyards planted. Luckily, a few firms have understood this and are making an effort to produce slightly lighter but still quite intense wines that would be more accessible for short-range consumption by a wine-drinking public that has grown increasingly uninterested in aging wines.

Some of these wines can be found in the restaurants of Tarragona and Barcelona. Look for De Muller, Masía Barril, Cellers de Scala Dei, Bodegas Vi del Raco, and three co-op wineries—Agrícola de Bellmunt del Priorato, Agrícola Gratallops, and Vinícola del Priorato.

Also, look for an unusual dessert wine from Priorato called *rancio*. This is not a grape name or a wine growing district, but a style of winemaking in which a sweet white, sometimes fortified, wine is aged in wood with exposure to air. It is not uncommon to find such wines all over the Mediterranean, but they are particularly good from this area, perhaps because they begin with such a high alcohol content, which tends to retain certain flavor properties in the wine.

Unlike those dessert wines of the world that have followed fashion and gone upscale, *rancio* is still fairly inexpensive. In the area around Tarragona, it can often be found in local bars for as little as twenty to twenty-five cents a glass.

Rancio wines have been compared to Madeiras, dessert sherries, even the Banyuls wines from the south of France, but they are much more intense, more distinctive, so rich that a very small glass can be quite satisfying. Because of the intensity of concentrated flavor, *rancios* often leave an impression of sweetness on the palate, but a true *rancio* is a dry wine. Sweet *rancios* are made by the addition of a sweet must to a dry *rancio* that then undergoes additional aging. This is the same method used in Jerez to produce the dessert sherries. When *rancios* are bottled they age very slowly, and the rare bottle of aged rancio is a great treasure.

One of the most incredible winetasting experiences we've ever had was after a memorable Christmas-season dinner, tasting down a row of a half dozen or so barrels of *rancio* wine maintained by the Celler del Penedés, a very good country restaurant just outside Vilafranca del Penedés. At Celler del Penedés, they maintain a *rancio solera* according to the age-old methods found until recently in most Catalan *masías* (farmhouses.) A barrel of wine was kept in the darkest corner of the cellar and was called *la bota raco*, the butt in the corner. The barrel would never be completely filled—nor completely emptied—and it was renewed each year by the addition of young wine. Occasionally, those barrels were wheeled out into the open air and exposed to the sun for a time. In some modern farmhouses, the *rancio* is stored in glass or clay carboys, called *bombonas* (perhaps because of the container's shape), and spends most of its time on the farmhouse roof or in the courtyard.

Whatever the method of production, the evaporation causes a concentration of alcohol and flavor that is remarkable.

Tarragona, at 25,000 hectares, is the largest winegrowing district in Catalonia. Like most of Catalonia, Tarragona's vintages were famous throughout the Roman empire. Now much of Tarragona's table wine production could be classed as elbow benders, easy-drinking wines of good quality and low price. Tarragona is divided into three sub-denominations. The Campo de Tarragona is a coastal strip near the wine center of Reus. Mostly white wines are made there of the standard Catalan varietals—Macabeo, Xarel-lo, and Parellada. There are also a few red wines made, from Ull de Llebre (Tempranillo) and Cariñena. The sub-denomination of Comarca de Falset is inland and runs alongside the Priorato zone; it makes very similar wines. Finally, there is the Ribera de l'Ebre area, which produces uninteresting reds, whites, and rosés, commonly met with as the house wine in local bars.

Tarra Alta is the southernmost district in Catalonia and the second largest, with about 16,000 hectares of vines under cultivation. As far as quality wines go, Terra Alta is relatively unimportant, with most wines of fairly high alcohol.

The Conca de Barberá, which has gained a provisional appellation status, is about midway between Barcelona and Lérida, near the ancient town of Poblet in the province of Tarragona.

Until very recently, most of the wine made from the 9,000-plus hectares of vineyards in the Conca have gone into bulk wine or to the *cava* houses of Sadurní de Noya. Now there are plantings of Chardonnay, Cabernet Sauvignon, and Pinot Noir, which grow well there. Local growers believe the area has a great future for those wines because of climatic conditions that encourage the growth of quality grapes.

Cava, the Spanish sparkling wine, is not, strictly speaking, exclusively Catalan. Until the mid-1980s, any sparkling wine made anywhere in Spain that followed the French *méthode champenoise* regulations was entitled to be called *cava*. Now *cava* can be made only in the Catalan provinces of Gerona, Barcelona, Tarragona, and Lérida, or in Zaragoza, Navarre, and a small area of Rioja. However, over 99 percent of all *cava* is made in Catalonia. *Cava* is made from the white varietals Parellada, Xarel-lo, and Macabeo. Parellada (which is also the basis of a fresh, fruity white wine, best known on the world market in the Torres's Viña Sol version) adds crispness and ageability, the Xarel-lo adds body and color, and the Macabeo gives acidity to the finished *cava*.

Spain, like other areas that make sparkling wine, has adopted the regulations concerning production in force in the Champagne province of France. These regulations, taken as a whole, are known as *méthode champenoise*. In fact, in many cases, the Spanish rules go beyond the French regulations, although that is a matter of the individual winery. *Méthode champenoise* describes minimal rules for aging (both in barrel previous to bottling and in bottle) but sets no top-of-the-line standards. The key to *méthode champenoise* is that the secondary fermentation takes place in the bottle, the same bottle that you buy at the wine shop. There are a number of other technical details of champagne production that really need not concern us here. The main point is that the rules are followed in Spain.

A further note on champagne or sparkling wine nomenclature: The French have won legal disputes in most of Europe and South America regarding the use of the term "champagne." They naturally insist that usage should be confined to those sparkling wines made in the Champagne region of France. In the United States and Australia, courts have ruled that champagne has become a generic term (like venetian blinds or Cuban heels). The French view has a strong following in California (perhaps because a number of California sparkling-wine producers are owned by French companies?). But one of the best sparkling-wine producers in California, Schramsberg Vineyards, uses the term *champagne* on its label.

The French recently won another important legal battle. Now the term *méthode champenoise* itself will be banned from labels sold in the European Community. This does seem a bit much, since *méthode champenoise* simply describes how the sparkling wine is made, not where it is made.

I asked Juan Juvé, the owner of Juvé y Camps, perhaps the best *cava* in Spain, how he felt about this. Without missing a beat, he replied: "It is my goal to make *cava* that is so good the world will soon forget about champagne."

The history of *cava* is curious. It is so dominant in Catalonia— between 60 and 70 percent of all the wine grapes grown there go into *cava*—that it seems almost built into the landscape. In fact, the first bottle of *cava* wasn't made in Spain until 1872, and then in sincere imitation of champagne. It was made by José Raventós, who traveled widely in France and was especially dazzled by the wine he found in Champagne—the old bubbly got to him in a big way. Back in Spain he experimented with the techniques he had observed in France (the *méthode champenoise*) and produced his own sparkling wine.

The family had been in the wine business since at least 1551, when a will by Jaime Codorníu left wine presses, barrels, and vats to his heir. In 1659, María Anna Codorníu married Miguel Raventós. Codorníu is still completely owned by the Raventós family, making them one of the world's oldest wine dynasties.

There is great dispute over whether Codorníu is (as it claims) the world's largest producer of *méthode champenoise* sparkling wine. Another giant Spanish *cava* house, Freixenet (which was founded in 1889 by the Ferrer family, still the owners), also claims to be the largest. We suppose the only way to know for sure would be to go around and count each bottle. It certainly doesn't make any difference in the bottle on the table tonight, so let's not worry about it. (It is of some interest that these two rival Spanish *cava* goliaths have also opened wineries in California within a few miles of each other in the Carneros region, just north of San Francisco Bay.

What is astonishing is that despite the huge production, the quality level is so high in both companies. Certainly, the inexpensive lines of Freixenet, Codorníu, and other *cavas* are not a match for most champagnes, but they really aren't intended to be. What the Catalans have managed to do with *cava* in the past twenty years (for it has only been since the death of Franco that the explosive export growth in *cava* has taken place) is something the French were unable to do in centuries. They have brought sparkling wine within the reach of the everyday wine drinker. And remarkably, wine of fair quality as well.

Companies like Freixenet, through various promotional efforts and television ads, have posited *cava* as a fun, anytime drink. One of the most successful promotions is Freixenet's creation of the "little cellar boy." A charming, pre-teen lad is used in posters and commercials and featured in a children's book, explaining in color cartoons the history of *cava*, how it is made, and what a wonderful thing it is.

(This use of a child to promote *cava* would, of course, create a frenzy in the antialcohol movement in the United States, where alcohol in any form is untouchable until the mystical age of twenty-one. But it might be worth noting that around the Mediterranean, where you are judged old enough to drink when you are tall enough to get your nose over the top of the bar, there are far fewer problem drinkers than in the United States, Scandinavia, Russia, and other countries where alcohol is restricted from minors. Children of the Mediterranean grow up with wine at the table. When they are very small, they probably get a thimbleful of wine in a glass of water. As they grow older and their noses approach bar level, the ratio of wine to water increases. Children in Spain grow up aware of both the pleasures and dangers of alcohol. Remember that wine is closely associated with food. In fact, wine is hardly ever taken without food, either in public or at home, and it is as much a part of the meal as bread or olive oil.)

The Spanish *cavas* have created an entirely new taste range for sparkling wine. Although *cava* was more or less invented in Catalonia as a painstaking experimental re-creation of champagne, it has become an entirely different creature. Where champagne is austere, aloof, *cava* is embracing, friendly. Champagne demands attention, *cava* is willing to be taken for granted.

In the mouth, *cava* has a distinct earthiness combined with a forward, fruity freshness; the acid level is generally lower than that of champagne, which makes it easier to drink.

Mind you, these are the less-expensive *cavas*. At a higher level of more-limited-production *cavas*, there are some wines that will challenge any in the world. *Cava* producers like Juvé y Camps, Cavas Hill, and Rovellats (all in the Penedés) and some of the top-of-the-line Freixenet and Codorníu make outstanding sparkling wine, which could be served at any table in the world.

Yet even at the top, *cava* is a distinctive wine. It has more in common with California sparkling wine than with French. There is a fullness of flavor that is unmistakable. Part of this is simply that the grapes used in *cava* production are different from those in champagne, where Chardonnay, Pinot Meunier, and Pinot Noir form the base cuvées. But it is also a question of climate. As in California, the grapes used for sparkling wine in Spain are riper than those in the colder climate of France. The riper grapes, of course, produce more flavor.

Unfortunately, because there is so much very drinkable cheap *cava* on the market, it has made it difficult for the more expensive and better *cavas* to gain acceptance. Eventually, one hopes, the wine drinkers of the world will learn that *cava* is not just a cheap substitute for champagne or sparkling wine and will pay the price that good wine demands.

The huge Spanish appetite for *cava* has led to a wonderful institution called the *xampanyería*, or champagne bar, in Catalonia. These are, in effect, tapas bars where the chief drink is *cava*. They often feature forty or fifty different *cavas*, most of them available by the glass. Some *xampanyerías* are upscale operations that could be in San Francisco, Paris, or London. This is the usual approach in Barcelona, where there is likely to be British or American rock or jazz playing on tape.

But the more traditional *xampanyería* often has that slightly raffish air that is common to the best Spanish bars. There is that momentary hesitation at the door that most Americans feel when they see a floor filled with tossed paper napkins, cigarette butts, and obscure scraps of this and that. For that is the usual way of disposing of debris when you have a drink and a bit of food at the bar—simply drop it underfoot. Someone will be along later to sweep it up. (I know a bar cleaner in Barcelona who has quite a nice collection of foreign coins that somehow got dropped at the bar. She once found a small plastic bag of cocaine and occasionally runs across, quite inexplicably, used condoms.) It is simply necessary to ignore the debris. Once you smell the delicious scents coming from the kitchen, you'll be hooked.

As Cabernet Sauvignon, Chardonnay, Pinot Noir, and other non-Spanish vines are planted, the look of the Catalan vineyard is changing. These varietals are staked on wires and pruned in an arching cordon, rather than cut low in the traditional *vaso* shape. This new shape requires more skilled workers, driving the labor costs higher.

The traditional red wine grapes in Catalonia are Ull de Llebre, which is the Tempranillo of Rioja, Garnacha Tinta, Monastrell, Cariñena, Samsó, and Sumoll. The last two are very old varietals, quickly disappearing from vineyards. The Ull de Llebre is used in most red table wines; it has good acidity and a perfumed nose; the Garnacha adds color and fruit and the Cariñena adds body.

For white wines, the traditional grapes are Parellada, Macabeo (called Viura in the Rioja), Xarel-lo, and the Subirat-Parent, or Malvasia. Except for the Malvasia, they are all used in *cava* production, but the Parellada is often made as a white table wine as well.

As much as we admire the wines made from these varietals at Raimat and other parts of Catalonia, we have a great deal of misgivings about the planting of Cabernet Sauvignon, Chardonnay, and Pinot Noir there. There is enough Chardonnay and Cabernet in the world. The strength, it seems to us, of the wines of Catalonia comes from the indigenous grape varieties.

No doubt great Cabernet Sauvignon has been and will be made in Catalonia. But haven't we lost something by this internationalization of the wines of Catalonia? It seems that when all the wine in the world is either Cabernet Sauvignon or Chardonnay, no matter how good it might be, the table will be a duller place.

However, in reply to this kind of criticism, Miguel Torres wrote:

Certain French experts have commented that our viticultural policy could mean the loss of identity of our traditional wines. They argue that the important thing is to keep the character of the wines that were made here one or two hundred years ago. . . .

That point of view can be very respectable, although naturally we do not agree with it. In the first place, it could be said that this consideration should be extended to areas like California, Chile, South Africa, etc., which have also introduced lately high-quality European vines with great success!

On the other hand, Cabernet Sauvignon wines, for instance, made in Bordeaux, in California, or in Catalonia, will always be easily identified due to the differences of soil, climate, and, also, as a consequence of the criteria followed in each country, as regards vine cultivation as well as vintification and aging of the wines.

Possibly, that new Catalan viticulture should be classified, despite so many years of history, with the relatively new wine countries: here, we have had to start from scratch.

Certainly, there is much truth in what Miguel Torres has written, but we believe it is important for Catalan wines to maintain their identity. By planting the same grapes used in France, there is a natural tendency to accept the French standards regarding what is and isn't a good wine from those grapes. As close observers of California winemaking, we know that for many years California struggled to find its own image, always comparing what was made in California with what was made in France, struggled always to achieve a "French" quality and thus blurred even the geographical distinctions mentioned by Torres.

Clearly, the decisions to plant the classic French varietals has as much to do with marketing as with wine quality. For example, in 1982, at a famous wine judging in France, the Torres Gran Coronas (or Black Label) was awarded top prize over a number of first-growth French Bordeaux red wines. This was the event that really pushed Torres into the international spotlight. That wine contained no Cabernet Sauvignon; it was made of Garnacha, Ull de Llebre, and Cariñena. Today, the Torres Gran Coronas is 100 percent Cabernet Sauvignon, and it is a completely different wine.

On the other hand, Catalans have always been innovators and experimenters, in food and wine as in other areas. Certainly, much of the excitement surrounding the new Catalan kitchen can be laid to that bold, experimental approach.

It was a pleasant Sunday morning in May. In front of the cathedral in Barcelona, hundreds of people were moving gracefully through the intricate, balanced steps of the sardana, *that most Catalan of dances, controlled, precise, nothing left to chance or the aching strum of the guitar. The* sardana *is one of the many ways that Catalans like to proclaim that Catalonia* No es español, *in the words of the spray-painted graffiti.*

Tourists from all over Europe crowded the edge of the dancers, spilling off the steps of the cathedral, cameras at ready, wanting to understand.

Two Gypsy women, barefoot, wearing that constant, slightly arrogant, aloof Gypsy face, watched the crowd watching the dancers. The older woman had a baby at her breast. Occasionally she turned to the tourists leaving the church, one hand clutching the baby, the other extended like a claw, mocking the universal gesture for alms.

From time to time the younger woman, perhaps fourteen or fifteen, darted into the crowd. She looked her prey in the face, backing them against the wall of the church or the unmoving curtain of tourists. There was danger in her eyes. They were old. She moved like a dancer, alert to the crowd before her, staring down her victims like the prima dancer of a flamenco troupe. She spoke rapidly, harshly, switching from Castilian to Catalan to French to English to German. Never bothering with Calais, her native tongue. She didn't ask. She demanded. The pockets of her dress were filled with silver.

SPANISH DAYS

I once met a man who had supported himself for several years teaching English to the whores in the Barrio Chino in Barcelona. As he described it, he would stand at the mirror and write English words in lipstick while the women sat on the bed behind him and repeated the word or phrase. The Barrio Chino is a former working-class district near the foot of Barcelona's famed Ramblas. It's now given over to gaudy nightclubs, sex clubs, and other places you wouldn't want to take Aunt Sandy from Chicago.

But don't worry. There are plenty of places in Barcelona to take sweet aunts. Barcelona is one of the more exciting cities in Europe and is the cultural heartbeat of Catalonia. It's been a world-class port since the days of the Carthaginians.

Barcelona is a wonderful walking city—being mostly on the flat.

The chief walk is, of course, down the Ramblas, that marvelous street fair/flea market that runs for about three or four kilometers from the Plaça de Catalunya to the port. Many cities and towns in Spain have a *ramblas* (the word is derived from a word meaning watercourse or stream), but nothing anywhere matches the Ramblas in Barcelona.

The accompanying sights range from the simply silly to the utterly bizarre, from whores of all sexes (the two major, plus several vague indeterminate) to religious fanatics who stand all day draped on an imaginary cross, arms extended, tears on cheek. There are sidewalk painters, bird sellers, book sellers, and sellers of items that even in liberal Barcelona could get you locked up. The rule seems to be, If you don't lean on people too heavily, the cops will let you play. That's on the Ramblas. Wander off into one of the areas close to the port, like the Barrio Chino or the Barrio Gótico, and the rules change, especially after dark. Although you are not really likely to be physically damaged, you could certainly be financially inconvenienced. Take care.

We're always a bit cynical about the touristy bits, but we recall a moving late-night visit to the Sagrada Familia, architect Antonio Gaudí's unfinished testimonial to spiritual fantasy. It had been raining lightly earlier, but at midnight the clouds were starting to break up as a cold north wind that felt straight off the Pyrenees began to blow. Suddenly a full moon broke through and fell like a visual chorus of angels on the fantastic spires of the cathedral.

Earlier in the day, we had been for our first look at the famous cathedral that anchors the city in the Barrio Gótico, with those massive gothic towers, thrusting toward God, the entire great church like a fortress, massive and magnificent, full of the importance of the men who had designed and built it. In front of us by moonlight was Gaudí's incredible modern creation, hanging against the sky like a burst of obscure Catalan laughter from a dark room. The contrast was remarkable.

On another night of light rains (without moon) Larry discovered La Barcelona de Vin & Spirits. This gleaming, very modern *xampanyería* has wood walls lined with single malt scotches and over two hundred different wines including perhaps sixty *cavas*. He was trying to walk off a miserable San Francisco–New York–Madrid–Barcelona flight and a rather disappointing afternoon. Alone and feeling sorry for himself, he was inclined to view life with misgivings.

Lunch had been at Los Caracoles, a well-known Barcelona tourist restaurant in the Barrio Gótico, where the food is actually passable to good. Our lunch companions had all seemed charming, witty, wise, and well dressed, whereas Larry had felt unkempt, surly, and difficult. On the way to lunch he had bought a rose from a Gypsy girl in the nearby Cathedral close and, trying to strike a pose of whimsey, had stuck it in his buttonhole. It had promptly wilted.

After lunch (by the way, the grilled rabbit was excellent, as was the Torres Gran Coronas that accompanied it) he went to one of the first bullfights of the season—almost like a spring training game. Predictably enough, it was terrible. Catalonia isn't really bullfight territory, anyway. Two of the bulls were actually sent back. One of his companions, Eunice Fried—the New York wine and food writer and an old bullfight hand going back to her days in southern France —was thoroughly disgusted with the spectacle.

At any rate, Larry was prepared for La Barcelona de Vin & Spirits to be a disaster, but instead, the place rescued his day. Beginning with the welcoming glass of Jaume Serra Brut Reserva and a plate of excellent *jamón serrano*, his spirits began to rise. He consulted with the barman about the prawns, which were small and taken from the Mediterranean. He was assured that they were absolutely fresh and so tasty they were served without sauce. He was right. They had been quickly boiled (with the heads on) and the flavor was creamy and rich. They needed nothing but perhaps another glass of Jaume Serra.

Things were looking up.

The barman and Larry discussed the bullfight for a bit. The barman had not been there, but his girlfriend had. She had told him it was not good. "But," he said, shrugging, "it is only to be expected, so early in the season."

Larry agreed and ordered a plate of *caracoles del mar*. The barman recommended a glass of an unusual wine called Can Feixes, a Penedés blend of Parellada and Macabeo. It combined the characteristics of those two grapes perfectly, the intense perfumy quality of the Parellada a perfect foil for the fresh acidity of the Macabeo. The sea snails were a little on the chewy side, but by that time balance and order had been restored in Larry's soul. He was back in Barcelona, back in Spain.

We were walking the vines in the mountain vineyard of Pontons, about 40 kilometers from Barcelona, deep in the winegrowing heart of Catalonia. These low hills, worn and ancient outriders of the Pyrenees, bear a passing likeness to the coastal ranges of California; there is the same extravagant rush of green in the spring, the same slow fade to brown by fall.

As one looks down from about half a mile up, the perspective becomes temporal as well as spatial. There is a scattering of small farmsteads, and it is impossible, at a slight distance, to know whether they are still living farms or throwaway husks of Spain's rapid post-Franco urbanization. There are traces of terraces, there are sight-lines of abandoned roads intersecting still-used dirt tracks, all winding toward the paved road we had driven up on. The landscape had a used look to it, like an old shirt, worn and comfortable with the years, thrown in the corner of the closet now, but still there when one wanted it.

Yet there is wildness in Spain. There are still wolves in Spain, in the mountains, and in bad winters in the lower valleys; those last lonely symbols of a wilderness world far removed from vineyards, far from the undoubtedly smug hyperactivity of international food trends. This is what makes Spain so unexpected, so un-European. In a single field, perhaps first cultivated by a Greek slave, we see the traces of the neolithic in a footpath curving against the opposite hillside. Faint outlines break and cast new perspectives on the merely human landscape we find in so much of Europe—and increasingly in the United States.

We were in the second-highest vineyard in Europe. (The other is in Switzerland.) It is planted to white wine varieties—Parellada and Riesling. The man with us was Alberto Fornos, who is a man-of-all-trades for Bodegas Torres.

He is a dark, intense man, a native of Catalonia. He takes his work seriously but also knows how to enjoy it. One of the burdens of his job is to put up with visitors from England and the United States, because his English is perfect (as are his French and German). At that time, he was just learning Russian. "In case I should want to surrender," he said.

We are doing a leisurely auto tour of the Torres vineyards, from the home vineyards near Vilafranca del Penedés to these high mountain vines. There was a pale early February sun, which had just dipped below the row of pines at the southern edge of the vineyard; heavy sweaters felt comfortable.

As we walked along, Fornos kicked at the clods of dirt, occasionally reaching down to pick up something, then tossing it. We had known each other for some time, having met on previous trips to Spain. Fornos was relaxed. He had laid aside his "public relations" face.

We weren't really doing anything in particular. Larry was trying to stay away from the Torres winery until 5 P.M., when he had a tasting scheduled with Miguel Torres, Jr. We were just on a break from the car really, just appreciating the mountain air, the view back down the valley with the small whitewashed stone house framed between pines at the foot of the vineyard. This was a new vineyard, and the vines, which were trained to wires, had not yet been pruned. They were a bare, brown tangle; it was impossible to imagine where to start cutting to shape the season's growth. Fornos stared thoughtfully at what looked like a flat, oblong stone he had picked up. He wet his finger and rubbed it a bit.

"You remember me telling you that I worked for an American company for a few years, in communications?" He was vague, as always, about that particular job.

"CIA, right?" Half-joking.

He smiled. It was an old game with us.

"Doesn't matter. I made a lot of money. But I had to quit."

"Why?"

He shook his head, still rubbing at what we thought was a stone in his hand.

"They wanted me to take forty-five-minute lunch breaks. Be there at eight, lunch at twelve, back at twelve-forty-five, home at five. Couldn't do it. Now I work longer hours, but I have time to go home for lunch, couple of hours. I take coffee, a glass of wine when I want. Have a talk with a friend," he said, smiling across the vines at us.

"Now, I get more work done in a day than I did with the American company, and I have time to think about what I am doing. My daughter is fifteen. She comes home from school for lunch and I can have lunch with her. That's important." He nodded; he had convinced himself long ago. But his argument is still running in Spain, where many believe they must act like Americans to become Europeans; become some sort of super-European to compensate, perhaps, for all those centuries when Spain turned its back on Europe. They feel they must give up those long, inviting lunches, the comfortable siestas, taken in sleep or other refreshing activity, and bond themselves to the "heart-attack machines" of modern business.

"Look," he said, handing Larry the "stone" over the row of vines.

It was a rectangular shard of blue and white pottery, perhaps two

inches wide by three inches long. "My daughter has been taking a
class in Catalan history. For her project she is collecting bits of
pottery, so every time I go into the fields, I am on the lookout, you
see. I've been helping her label things and I think this is fourteenth-
century. You can see a bit of the zigzag pattern that was typical
then, and the crinkled white finish is typical, too."

"That will be a good find for her collection," Larry said, handing
it back.

Fornos shook his head. "No, you keep it. She has plenty. They
are common here, many much older than that. We Catalans have
been here a long while."

We still have that bit of pottery. We can look at it, touch it, feel
the ancient Mediterranean culture living thickly in the few ounces
of dried clay, the flecks of paint.

We looked from the pottery toward the stone farmhouse.

Fornos, seeing our glance, said, "Yes, it could have come from
there. The house is at least that old. See, there are no wires leading
to it. No electricity yet."

"Someone lives there?"

"A local man and his family. They work in the vineyards. That is
their orchard, there beyond the pines. They keep a few sheep."

As if on cue, a tall woman wearing a black shawl appeared around
the corner of an outbuilding. A dozen or so sheep trotted along
behind her, like odd woolly dogs. When she saw us, she stopped.
Fornos waved, shouted something in Catalan. She shouted back,
walked on through the garden, leading the sheep a brisk pace.

"The sheep follow her. Why?"

"She is taking them to pasture," Fornos replied. "They've probably been penned up all day while she was doing other work. Now
they get a few hours grazing in the new grass and they are glad of
that."

As we drove back down the narrow road toward Vilafranca, Fornos tried to explain the unique historical landholding system of Catalonia called *rabassa morta*, a system which developed as early as
the ninth century. Whatever the reason for it, it worked for several
hundred years to virtually put the small peasant farmer in thrall to
the vine and greatly influenced the cultural history of Catalonia.

Fornos explained it like this: The landed proprietor would lease
land to a farmer but stipulate that it must be planted in vines. After
the vines were established and producing, the owner would share
the produce with the farmer, the percentage going to each party
determined by terms of the particular contract. The farmer could

continue to operate the vineyard until the vines died, which could be more than a century.

This arrangement seemed to work fairly well, except that the advent of a number of vine diseases—including phylloxera and black rot—during the nineteenth century forced growers to graft vines onto native American vine roots. These roots have a much shorter life span than *vinifera*, the traditional European wine grape. Of course, the grafting led to all sorts of disputes and legal tangles, some of which are still being sorted out.

Once, we had to slow and creep along the edge of the road while a few dozen sheep took the middle. This time the sheep were in the lead, followed by another woman in a black shawl. She could have been the sister of the woman at the vineyards. The same angular, dark good looks laid on a somewhat sullen expression. It was impossible to tell her age—somewhere between twenty-five and fifty. As we drew even, Fornos spoke to her in Catalan. She answered briefly and shook her head, frowning furiously.

Fornos chuckled. "I was asking her if they would like a ride. I don't think she has a sense of humor." He drove thoughtfully for a few minutes.

"I really shouldn't have teased her," he said. "It is a very hard life out here in the country. And lonely, too. You know, in the fifties and sixties a lot of people left the country, went to live in Madrid and Barcelona. Until very recently, the big cities were ringed with shantytowns. Little houses made of cardboard, cast-off lumber. The government started building houses, and now most people have homes. But it left the country almost depopulated."

He looked briefly in the rearview mirror, as if to be certain the sheep weren't catching up. "At first it was a disaster. The country people had no money, so they would rip out the appliances, the pipes, the sinks to sell. But it got better when the government started schemes that allowed people to buy the apartments."

We were only about 60 or 70 kilometers from Barcelona, yet it could have been the timeless landscape of the Middle Ages: the black-shawled shepherdess and her sheep, a straggle of vines below the road, brown upland pasture above. There were still plain signs of old terraces cut into most of the hillsides, but they were slowly eroding, fading back into the brown undergrowth. It was odd to hear talk of housing projects in such landscape. I didn't want to think about housing conditions in modern Spain, which seemed to have much in common with housing conditions in modern St. Louis or San Francisco.

I asked Fornos about the terraces.

"God knows how old they are. Some may go back to the Romans. This was great wheat country then. But they are cut only wide enough for horses or oxen to work. Nobody farms the terraces any more."

We stopped on a bare hillside where a rutted dirt road—little more than a path, really—led down into a thickly wooded canyon. Through the trees, there were glimpses of a small rapidly moving stream.

"If we had time, we could walk down there and I'd show you some caves back up in the limestone cliffs on the other side of the river where people lived fifty thousand years ago."

We stood for a moment listening to the wind in the trees, the sound of water drifting up from below. We walked a few yards down the dirt road and looked hard into the canyon, waiting for a wolf to break through the underbrush, to disrupt the pattern of the "new Spain." Back up on the road, the baaing sheep were drawing closer.

"Look, we'd better go," Fornos said, "before she gets here. She may have changed her mind and decided to accept a ride—sheep and all."

Some of the best sheer countryside in Spain can be found while wandering the Catalan backroads of the interior, perhaps taking a wayward route toward the great Monastery of Poblet, about 50 kilometers from Tarragona and Lérida and over 100 kilometers from Barcelona. The fortified Monastery of Poblet was founded in 1150 by Count Ramón Berenguer IV in thanksgiving for a victory over the Moors. It became an important symbol of Catalonia's power in the Middle Ages and was also the burial ground of a long line of the counts of Catalonia.

The monastery was sacked and burned in 1835, during one of Spain's innumerable nineteenth-century civil wars. The greatest loss was the destruction of the twenty-thousand-volume library, which must have contained books that were utterly irreplaceable. The monastery lands were sold off after that and restoration didn't begin until after the civil war in 1940. Even though little remains of the original building, it is still an impressive site, looming over the surrounding vineyards like a ponderous stone ship.

The Monastery at Poblet was of great importance to Spanish viticulture in the period of Catalan expansion in the twelfth and thirteenth centuries. New varieties of grapes from Italy, Sicily, and the

Middle East were planted there. The cellars at Poblet have been extensively restored and are a good guide to what winemaking in the Middle Ages was like.

The village of Montblanc, about 15 kilometers from the monastery, is lovely. It is a walled town, well preserved, and giving some of the feeling of the Middle Ages. It's a good village for walking about, because it is fairly flat. And you will find good country cooking at the Fonda Colom.

There were also cellars and vineyards at the Monastery of Santa Creus in the village of Santa Creus only about 30 kilometers from Tarragona. Santa Creus has also been restored and is open to visitors.

The Monastery of Our Lady of Montserrat, about 50 kilometers from Barcelona, is set in a splendid site at about 1,000 meters in the Sierra de Montserrat, looking out over the Penedés. It's a pity that it has been turned into another roadside attraction, with seemingly nonstop tour buses belching diesel fumes as they labor up the narrow, winding road to the monastery, there to join dozens of other buses parked with engines running, while tourists from all over Europe scramble for a quick look at La Moreneta, the Dusky One, the twelfth-century wooden statue of a black virgin. That is, the scholars say it dates from the twelfth century. Any loyal Catalan knows the legend that it was first brought to Montserrat by St. Peter, later lost, then rediscovered in the ninth century.

The Montserrat legend, the presence of the Black Virgin, brooding for centuries atop the jagged, dramatic range of peaks, permeate the Catalan consciousness. Before meeting someone for an early-morning coffee or blinking out into the sunshine after lunch, look toward the sierra and somehow the day will feel better if those black peaks are in view. Then you know that Montserrat is watching over you.

The Dusky One exercises her power in other ways as well. Every other woman in Catalonia is named Montserrat, shortened usually to the everyday Montse. One way or another, Montserrat is ever in the thoughts of most Catalans.

If Montserrat is the spiritual face of Catalonia, Sitges represents the secular, the frankly carnal. Sitges is an improbable place. A beautiful, gently arcing white-sand beach backed by a half amphitheater of wooded hills, with twisting, narrow streets fitting so snugly into

the canyons and hillsides that they are almost impossible to spot
from the very Victorian nineteenth-century beach promenade.
About 40 kilometers from Barcelona and 50 from Tarragona, it's an
ancient town, dominated by the Baroque church of San Bartolomé
and Santa Tecia, standing on a high rocky promontory thrusting out
into the Mediterranean.

With its sheltered bay, it has been a haven for fishermen for thousands of years. These seafaring folk must have been surprised, perhaps even terrified, about the turn of the century when a Catalan
cultural maven named Santiago Rusiñol formed a group of artists
and literati who made Sitges their summer home. Rusiñol would
probably have been surprised, in his turn, to find that modern-day
Sitges is one of the capitals of the European homosexual community.

Sitges itself is—after all these centuries—still a wonderful place
for a visit, from a few hours to several days. With a room rented in
one of the *pensiones* in the old town, it is easy to fall into the rhythm
of Spanish days. And there are miles of beaches, with the ones
nearest the town center naturally being the most crowded. There
are many nudist beaches, as is usual on the Mediterranean coast of
Spain.

The high point of the year in Sitges is the carnival just before
Lent, although Corpus Christi is also an important fiesta, with many
streets carpeted with flowers and bright fabric hung from the windows and balconies.

We have never been in Sitges at carnival time, but have it from a
hardworking spy that total madness reigns: "It is very, very bizarre,"
the spy wrote after the carnival of 1990. "There is a quality to the
celebrations that carries a certain edge of Spanish menace without
actually being threatening. It actually adds to the pleasure, that hint
of danger. It must be why people climb sheer rock cliffs without rope
supports.

"But you asked me about the food. I couldn't find anything special, and I did look, since I was starving. I had hitched straight in
from Valencia in the morning and got stuck for hours in L'Arboc.
Do you know it? It's a small farming town about 10 klicks south of
Vilafranca. Not a bad place to get stuck, but I shouldn't have been
there anyway. I wasn't paying enough attention to where the driver
was going. Before retracing my steps to El Vendrell to get on the
road to Sitges, I had a quick beer at a weird bar there called the
Agricol. Why? I swear to God it was like being in a bar in a college

town in Iowa or Oklahoma (and I've been in both) that is pretending to be an English pub. There were dart games and a pool table, and some Brit twit was playing acoustic guitar and singing Peter, Paul, and Mary songs. Come on! But the owner was nice. When I told him I was hitching to Sitges for carnival, he bought me a beer on the house.

"Anyway, I was hungry by the time I got to Sitges. I headed straight for the roast chicken booth, got a half and a bottle of cold beer, and went to the beach. It was still daylight, but I could see things were weirding up pretty good.

"As I chewed on my chicken bones, a whole troupe of lovely 'ladies' passed dressed in stylish-looking *sevillana* dresses, looking like they just stepped out of a travel film. Except these ladies had hairy legs. Or would have if they hadn't shaved. But they sure looked pretty.

"Back on the street, I found a bar, El Xatet, where the barman remembered me from the summer before and let me stash my backpack in the storeroom. Just to fortify myself for the night, I had a *ración* of *xato*—you know, that *romesco*-like salad with a glass (or was it three?) of *cava*—and I was ready!

"It was dark by this time and the streets were full of people. Sitges is the last major carnival in Catalonia before Lent, so there were people from everywhere more or less running around getting ripped out of their skulls, going off two by two down little alleyways, up to God knows what.

"I bought a little black domino mask from a street vendor and slipped into one of the trendy bars on the Calle Dos de Mayo, which the locals call the Calle del Pecado, or Sin Street. I spotted a girl from Barcelona whom I knew slightly and attached myself to her group, all the better to get my drinks bought. There were about a dozen of them with Montse [of course her name was Montse] and they were all a few years younger than me. When they found that I was from California, was hitchhiking around Spain with nothing but a backpack and a happy smile, I became a kind of instant cultural hero.

"It was one of those bars that I call early white concrete. All the rage, you may remember, in Catalonia. The seats were poured concrete benches against the walls, covered with pillows. There were low concrete tables before the benches and the walls were stressed concrete. Not that you could see much of anything that night. The place was totally jammed, shoulder to shoulder, thigh to thigh with people. There were hundreds of balloons bobbing around the walls and ceilings and occasionally one would pop and this would set the 'ladies' to screeching.

"Bottle after bottle of *cava* kept coming to our table and I was almost high on just sniffing the pot smoke in the bar—that was before the pre-Olympic crackdown on smoking weed in bars.

"Anyway, I bailed out to the streets, where 'most everything was happening. Gays were dancing with gays, straights with straights, straights with gays, but mostly you couldn't tell one from the other and mostly no one seemed to care. It was Carnaval."

Lérida ("Lleida," in Catalan) is one of Spain's lost cities. Our definition of a lost city (sometimes even of a lost region) is any place the standard guidebooks somehow overlook or vastly underrate. Spain is simply not as well known to travelers as France or Italy, so many places that are worth a visit are passed by with a sentence or two.

But Lérida is only one of many Spanish cities or towns that receive brief notice in the tourist guides but that repay a little closer attention. Not that the guidebooks get it wrong, certainly cities like Córdoba or Cádiz or Sevilla have much to offer the visitor. Yet as the tourist pressure increases on those cities, which are touted in every guide and travel magazine, the experience becomes less than a spontaneous reaction between the visitor and the territory; a certain element of self-consciousness comes into play. One is aware of being a tourist in a special place.

In the smaller, unsung towns —such as Lérida, Vilafranca del Penedés, Zaragoza, Logroño, the villages of Extremadura and Andalusia, the rainy byways of the Basque or Celtic north —the unexpected is found at every turn. One is once again involved in simply living life as it comes, not in watching oneself be a tourist.

The same applies perhaps in even stronger terms to food and wine. Anyone with an adequate supply of funds and the right guidebooks can go to the great restaurants, can seek out the great wines. And to some degree that's a good game to play, because naturally those restaurants and those wines that are great receive a lot of attention. They are proclaimed far and wide, and more often than not with good reason.

But it is possible to worship too seriously at both the table and the wine barrel. There is also the added danger that as a restaurant such as Reno in Barcelona, or Zalacaín in Madrid, takes on an international reputation, it subtly shapes itself to that international clientele, in the process losing the very thing that drew the international clientele in the beginning.

Meanwhile, Lérida remains a lost city. The *American Express Pocket Guide* to Spain gives it a grudging two inches, commenting that there is "little of ancient origin or artistic accomplishment to see." Well, we don't travel by "ancient origins" or "artistic accomplishment."

Lérida is in fact a vibrant, welcoming city, the center of a rich agricultural zone that ships garden produce and fruit all over Spain. The irrigation system that keeps the orchards and gardens so productive was first put in place by the Moors. Even after the Moors were officially driven out, the Moriscos (Moors who converted to Christianity) who stayed on helped establish one of the country's most prestigious universities, which by the fourteenth century was known all over Europe. But by the sixteenth century, Lérida had begun to decline, at least in part because of the expulsion of the Moriscos by Isabella the Catholic.

Lérida was the site of an ancient Iberian hill fort with beginnings going back, no doubt, into ancient times. The two local Iberian heroes—Indibil and Mandonius—carried on successful guerilla warfare against both the Carthaginians and the Romans. They were finally overwhelmed by the Romans. The Moors held the hilltop citadel from the eighth century until the twelfth century. The Counts of Catalonia seized the fort, which is high atop a stone outcropping, in the thirteenth century. It was partially destroyed by the French in the nineteenth century, and what the French left was finished off in the Spanish Civil War in 1936.

But more important to our purpose than a fort are the surprising number of good restaurants, including one of the best restaurants in Spain, Pati de Noguerola. Although it may seem a bit out of the way, a determined eater can easily rise well past dawn, have a walkabout and an espresso in Zaragoza, and cover the 150 kilometers to Lérida for lunch, then be in Barcelona, just under 150 kilometers, in time for tapas, if you find a parking place in Barcelona.

Pati de Noguerola is, first of all, visually lovely. There are attractive dining rooms scattered throughout an old house, creating a feeling of dining in a private home. Each room contains only a few well-spaced tables, adding to the air of intimacy and privacy.

The food is an imaginative blend of Catalan country cooking and the latest trends from Barcelona, but there are no rough edges showing where the graft takes place. A thoughtful menu or recipe should be like a well-balanced wine—one should simply be aware of the pleasures of eating or drinking, not of how it is put together.

Pati de Noguerola serves some of the best *arroz negro* we have had. We always have that for openers, which is how the dish is meant to be served. A specialty of the house is *col rellenado*, small cabbage rolls filled with pork, veal, and egg and cooked in a casserole with vegetables.

Take eggplant flan as an example of Pati's creative yet playful approach to food. The dish is more or less standard repertoire in Catalonia. It's made like a charlotte (with custard), often with bits of meat inside. At Pati there is no custard, and instead of meat the eggplant is filled with sautéed, minced mushrooms, then turned out of the mold and served on a base of tomato sauce.

The treatment of *perdiz* (partridge) at Pati appears to be strictly traditional Catalan. Half a bird is served roasted, then sauced in a typical highly reduced dark-brown sauce of red wine and stock, but at the finish the sauce is flavored with black currants or whatever wild berries are in season. It surprises the palate with piquant, unexpected flavor.

Pati also prepares the traditional Catalan dishes splendidly, like the *lenguado con almendras*, a whole small sole, scaled and topped with toasted almond slices, or the *javali de cevet* (wild boar), which has been marinated for two days in red wine, then roasted on a bed of vegetables and served in a brown sauce thickened with the pureed vegetables. *Bacalao Lérida* is, as you might guess from the name, a specialty of the area. It's a dish of chunks of salt cod in a *sofrito* sauce, topped with diced apples and carrots with toasted pine nuts scattered on top.

In truth, after a late lunch at Pati, we were not inclined to push on to the coast. Even though we had been to the restaurant on at least two other occasions, we had simply exited the freeway, driven straight to the restaurant—along the Río Segre and near the rail station—then driven straight back to the freeway.

That particular day, we agreed that we had had enough of the road. We found a comfortable if unremarkable hotel just across from the river, near the old city, which sprawls up the hill toward the cathedral and the fortress site.

It worked out well. Lérida is another marvelous city for walking, and if there is nothing "old" to see (there is, actually, especially given what Americans define as old), there is a very inviting pedestrian mall that rambles for several blocks behind the hotels and shops that line the riverfront. The mall opens up at the top into a quite attrac-

tive plaza, where there is a tourist office. Just before that is a cluster
of small bakeries where some truly delicious treats can be found.
One Lérida specialty is the light, fluffy, anise-flavored roll called the
ensimada, which is shaped like a snail and is undoubtedly connected
to the great snail-eating feast held each year in early May, the Aplec
del Caragol.

Snail lovers come from all over Spain for the event, which takes
place along the banks of the Segre. Snails are roasted by the thousands for this strange festival. Some people speculate that the origin
of the snail feast goes back to an obscure point in history when
Lérida was under siege and the only thing to eat was snails. It is
worth considering that the spring festival of snails could be related
to the earth opening up with new growth in the spring, just as a snail
becomes more active and moves around in warmer weather.

Vilafranca del Penedés is the Napa of Catalonia, one of the most
important wine cities in Spain, yet again it is completely ignored by
our handy *American Express Pocket Guide to Spain.* We can't really
find fault with the editors for ignoring this commercial but on the
surface rather charmless city. Yet, there are some very good restaurants in Vilafranca del Penedés, as there should be in a major wine-
producing center. The touristic veteran of California's wine country, however, will look in vain for the expense-account restaurants,
the countrified shopping malls crowded with antique shops, and the
T-shirt emporiums. There will be no cute little bed-and-breakfasts,
so filled with antiques that you are afraid to move. In fact, there may
not even be a vacant room. This is also true of other major wine
areas like Logroño and Haro in the Rioja. Even Jerez de la Frontera
—where the British taught the Spanish to capitalize on sherry as an
incentive to tourism—has a severe shortage of hotel rooms during
the international horse show *(feria)* in May and the vintage festival
in September.

You may end up staying in a bare-bones truckstop motel. But you
will eat well, as we did one cold January night at the Celler del
Penedés just outside Vilafranca. (There had been a light dusting of
snow on the vineyards that afternoon, which had chased the pruners
out of the field.) Dinner was long and extraordinary, opening with
escudella d'anec, a winter soup with duck, potatoes, garbanzos,
leeks, and sausage. It was incredibly warm and inviting and would
certainly have been enough by itself. But of course we didn't stop
there.

The season was right, so we followed with *rovellons* (wild mushrooms) grilled in olive oil and sprinkled with extra-virgin olive oil, garlic, and parsley. But hold on, to call *rovellons* wild mushrooms is like calling Will Clark a baseball player. We are dealing here with another dimension. The mushroom has an orange-red cast and grows in the foothills in scrubby underbrush. It is the object of many freezing tramps into the hills in late autumn and early winter. The best of these autumn treasures appear after the first rains and during the time of *scirocco*, the drying winds from North Africa.

The next course was a *cazuela de conejo con caracoles*, a wonderful casserole dish of rabbit and snails based on a *picada* of almonds, garlic, and chilies. The almonds give it away as an old dish, as does the combination of snails and rabbit. Finally, there was *perdiz dessosada en col*, which was presented in the *cazuela*—boned partridge with shredded cabbage stuffed into a huge softball-size cabbage leaf.

Contentment was spreading fast. We were seriously discussing skipping dessert, even talking of a fast drive over to Sitges for a walk on the beach and perhaps a coffee and brandy to end the evening, although we were reluctant to leave the restaurant. It's a huge rambling building, divided into a number of cozy rooms, each containing perhaps a half dozen tables—overall, probably seating about two hundred people.

It looks like a tourist trap but it is quite the opposite, and the favorite of the locals. And from the first night we were taken there by Marimar Torres, Miguel Torres' sister (who has her own winery in California), it has been one of our favorite Spanish restaurants. The ceilings in the bar are thick with dozens of hams from all regions of Spain; there are old farm and vineyard tools hanging on the walls, along with painted tiles, old plates, and enough Catalan memorabilia to send antique dealers reaching for their checkbook. A couple of the rooms have fireplaces, but all have the feeling of being candle-lit and warmed by an open hearth.

At any rate, there we sat, contemplating a turn of virtue by skipping dessert, when the waiter appeared with a fresh bucket of ice (we had opened with a half bottle of Cavas Hill Brut de Brut, a magnificent Penedés sparkling wine) and another half bottle of Cava Hill, this one a rosado.

"It is from the two gentleman across the room," he said, pointing to two men at a corner table, who gave every appearance of being well fed and contented, puffing on cigars with coffee and brandy before them.

It wasn't too clear why we were being treated, but I told the waiter we would be delighted if the gentleman would come over and have a glass of *cava* with us. They came to our table and explained that they were surprised at how well we had ordered. We were obviously foreigners, so how did we know Catalan food?

After introductions all around we learned that they were Catalonia's biggest dealers in mushrooms and truffles, specializing in the giant *rovellons* and the rare Catalan black truffles, the *tofonas negras*, which the French and Italians will cheerfully tell you don't exist in Spain. At any rate, the glass of *cava* led to another bottle and that led to a simple dish of *mel i mato*, a dish of honey and soft white cheese. Probably one of the oldest desserts in the world, and one of the most satisfying.

It was served with a glass of *rancio* from the small village of L'Arboc, only a few kilometers away. Larry mentioned that he believed the wine to be quite good and one of the men nodded. "Yes, to be sure. But have you tasted the other *rancios* in the cellar here?"

Larry admitted that he had not and the waiter sent for Señor Pere Clave, the owner of Celler del Penedés, who appeared from somewhere in the depths of the kitchen, looking a bit shopworn, like a working cook is apt to look following a twelve-hour shift. It was now about two in the morning—only a few tables were left and he could come out of the kitchen.

This of course demanded another bottle of *cava* and an extensive exchange of compliments regarding the restaurant, the quality of the *rovellons*, and what splendid Americans we were. In time, we got around to the cellar and the tastings of *rancios*. In all honesty, I must report that the wines were superb. And the only place they can be tasted is at the Celler del Penedés in Catalonia.

It was past three when the last barrel had been sampled. It was suggested that we should top off with a brandy. We pled an early appointment the next day and we parted, but only after Señor Clave had pressed into our not-unwilling hands a small jar of black truffles packed in brandy and a huge bag of *rovellons*, still smelling of the fresh earth.

We slept well.

Down a dirt road outside Vilafranca del Penedés to the tiny village of La Bleyda and a rambling indoor-outdoor sort of place, called El Merendero.

The root meaning of *merenda* goes back to the Latin *merum*, which means "pure." In fact, there is a modern Italian word, *mero*, for unadulterated wine. But as we've noted, around the Mediterranean basin, wine is rarely taken neat. There is usually a bit of food at hand, perhaps only bread and olives, but something. So in Spain, *merenda* has come to have the meaning of a snack or a meal of simple food. Not snack in the American sense. The snack, to Americans, means food taken on the run, but in Spain, *merenda* involves food shared with friends.

And there were plenty of friends that night. There were, in fact, two cars of us; yet that isn't as many as it sounds, since we were traveling in Seats, the subcompact Spanish automobile patterned on the Fiat of Italy. Still, we managed to make quite a noisy time of it. There was never quite an accurate crowd count. Friends of friends kept showing up and joining our table; others hopped away to the nearby tables. Although there is not the equivalent of "doing tapas" in the north of Spain as there is in Madrid and the south, there is still a lot of friendly tablehopping. The conversation was an arcane mix of English, Castilian, and Catalan, with a smattering of French now and then—the *lingua franca*, as it were.

Even during the Franco years, the Catalans hung on to their language, although Franco tried to establish Castilian as *the* language of Spain. Today there are at least two daily newspapers published in Catalan, and one of the major Spanish television networks broadcasts in Catalan. Catalan is also the language of the vineyards and wine cellars.

It is an indication of the fierce regional pride of the Spanish that the repressed languages sprang up in full bloom as soon as Franco's linguistic rules were relaxed. They had all been spoken at home, right through the Franco years, when those guilty of speaking Catalan (or Basque or Galician) in public could easily end up in jail.

While waiting in the small bar of the restaurant for a large-enough table to clear, we were crowded into a corner near the open brick oven built into the wall. Everything El Merendero served came out of that oven, grilled over or roasted in the coals of vine clippings.

Cooks knelt on the floor in front of the oven feeding food in and out. The heat was intense, which is probably why we kept ordering a delicious chilled white wine made a few kilometers down the coast at Tarragona. If we had asked for the vintage date, we probably would have been shown the door. It was a simple *vino blanco* with no pretensions at all, but a charming willingness to please.

The air was filled with smoke from the oven and, of course, from cigarettes. If you are not prepared to put up with a little tobacco smoke from time to time, best to steer clear of Spain—or most of the Mediterranean region for that matter. The idea of a no-smoking section in a Spanish restaurant is laughable. Yet somehow the smoke was not as offensive at La Bleyda as it might have been in Berkeley or Carmel.

Across the room a swarm of small children clustered around two ancient pinball machines. Larry kept trying to get close enough to see if the devices on the machines were in Spanish or English. Above the clang of the machines a television set blared but no one seemed to be watching. The Catalans are a noisy lot. The common noise—beyond pinball machines and television sets—was the human voice, raised constantly (and loudly) in argument.

We recognized two vine pruners we had met the week before. They were in a holiday mood because that day, despite some light rains, they had just finished their last pruning job. We kept passing the bottle around followed by a plate of spiced olives. The talk turned, as it still often does in Spain, to the Civil War of the 1930s. My Catalan friends were poking perhaps not such gentle fun at us for spending part of the afternoon riding around in a Jaguar with a winery executive from San Sadurní de Noya, where about 95 percent of that cheap and delicious Spanish *cava* comes from. We told them his sad story. The family—as many wealthy Catalans—had been pro-Franco. When the regime began to become more liberalized they had fled to Portugal into the welcoming arms of the dictator Salazar and had only returned to Catalonia when Salazar had been overthrown.

Now they were back in Spain, thriving and getting even richer under a centrist Socialist regime but still not feeling quite comfortable with it all. After all, hadn't the name of the Avenida Franco in Barcelona just been changed to El Diagonal? What kind of name was that for a street?

This got one of the more radical members of the party—a young woman just out of school—started on a list of problems the workers of Catalonia still faced. Oddly enough, two of the most urgent being the U.S. military bases in Spain (of which there are none in Catalonia) and the Spanish presence in NATO.

But never mind. In the nick of time we were called to table. After demanding more wine, switching now to red, of course, plus plenty of bread, *allioli* and *romesco*, we began the feast.

At El Merendero the *romesco* was made to order, as was the pungent *allioli*. We opened with *cebollots*, a delicacy available only a few weeks each year. *Cebollot, or calçot* in Catalan, means onion shoots. In fact, there is a festival held near the Catalan town of Valls each year that celebrates the *cebollot* (see page 188). At places like El Merendero they are commonly served wrapped in newspaper (rather like fish and chips). The *cebollots* are eaten out of hand, dipped in a *romesco*-type sauce.

The *cebollots* were followed by a salad of *bacalao*, dried, salted codfish, ubiquitous in the Iberian Peninsula. It is one of the foods shared by Spain and Portugal, but it is not found anywhere else in Spain served as a cold, uncooked salad. Salt cod is a northern dish and was perhaps first brought to Spain by the Basques, who ranged right across the Atlantic and were fishing off Newfoundland before Columbus was even born—by a few centuries, in fact.

The meal went on, of course, as Spanish meals have a way of doing. But by midnight we were through with the main dishes, which were absolutely delicious grilled pork and rabbit—cooked so simply that the chef had hardly touched them. They had been drizzled with olive oil, scattered with a handful of herbs as they grilled, and sprinkled with a bit of salt and pepper—superb. The rabbit was served either in half—split from stem to stern, as it were, with head left on—or whole, on a trencher of bread.

After lively discussion, our party split. One car of celebrants left for Sitges to paddle in the Mediterranean—one of the first beach parties of the early spring—and drink brandy. The rest of us stayed behind for a few *porrones* of Malvasia and *postre de músico*.

We love drinking from the *porrón*. It is a bit tricky, but once you get the hang of it, quite fun. We'll try to describe what happens. A *porrón* is a glass vessel with a long, tapered spout—that you drink from—and a large upright spout that receives the wine and is used later as a hand grip. The *porrón* is raised above the head and (for beginners) held a few inches from the mouth. That's important. The mouth must never actually touch the *porrón*. Very bad form, that. A thin stream of wine—about the diameter of a pencil—is released when the *porrón* is tilted. This is, obviously, directed toward the mouth. As the drinker becomes more confident, the *porrón* is extended to full arm's length so that a stream of wine perhaps 20 to 25 inches long is pouring into the mouth. You can drink an amazing amount of wine that way as well as run up some staggering laundry bills.

Malvasia is a local dessert wine made from the grape of the same

name, probably first brought to Spain by the Greeks or the Phoenicians at least four thousand years ago. It's now grown all over Spain
and is added to ordinary table wines in the Rioja area. But in Catalonia a very sweet dessert wine is made from the grape, with the
principal vineyards only a few kilometers from our table. It has a
ripe, golden color. In fact, one of the brands imported into the
United States is called Malvasia de Oro.

Músico is a simple dessert made of dried fruit and nuts. It is said
that the dish goes back to the Middle Ages, when groups of musicians wandered the countryside singing for food and maybe a bed.
The Spanish hold music in such reverence that even the poorest
household would try to give something to the players, even if it was
only a handful of nuts and dried fruit.

It was well past two by the time the last *porrón* was emptied, the
last plate taken away. We were not the last to leave, however; several
tables of locals were still there drinking coffee and brandy, talking
quietly. The Spanish, as someone said, are nocturnal. But the oven
had been banked and closed, and a young boy was mopping the bar
area.

We took our last coffees outside and sat at a table under the deep
black sky. There was a full moon, low in the sky, but no electric
lights to be seen. A small hill blocked the few lights of Vilafranca. It
could have been a thousand years ago.

And surely there were wolves just in the next ravine, sniffing the
rabbit-thick air of the well-fed Catalonia night.

*He had been preparing himself for days, he told Larry years later,
over a glass of* cava *in a very upscale Madrid restaurant called Cabo
Mayor.*

*"I was ten years old, but nothing that I have ever done has been
as exciting, as concentrated, if you know what I mean."*

*He was now in his forties, a very successful attorney toying with
the idea of running for national political office. His beautiful wife, a
leading actress on Spanish television, smiled by his side, although
what he had just said must have been painful for her, if she was
even listening.*

*"I was told a few weeks ahead of time that I would be the top of
the tower in the main plaza during Semana Santa in Vilafranca del
Penedés. You know how they build those towers of men?"*

I nodded. The castels *are built in a rough square of four or eight
men. The biggest, strongest men in the town formed the foundations, then the next row of slightly smaller men scrambled on their*

shoulders, and so forth, up to a height of nine men, with the very top of the castle being a small boy. A small boy for two reasons: He was lighter, of course, and less a burden for those under him; also, if he fell, he could be more easily caught.

"The biggest towers, as you know, are made during Semana Santa. All the eyes of the town would be on me. It was incredible. I have talked to bullfighters who say they feel that same concentration, that same sense of withdrawal from ordinary life that I felt for those few days. But you see, I am not a good person to describe it for you. Because I was so inside myself that although I remember each second, climbing up the shoulders of the men, reaching the top, and standing for a few glorious moments in the sun, looking face to face at my mother standing on the first-floor balcony a few feet away, I cannot really say what happened that day. I could describe other fiestas, the crowds, the dancing, watching the tower grow like a living thing—as it is, I suppose—but not the one I was involved in."

"Did you fall?"

"Never. Never. I stood for a few moments, then leaped into the arms of my older brothers standing below. Our tower came down perfectly, injuring no one."

There was still intense pride in his voice as he looked back on his role in the building of a perfect castel.

No one really knows the origins of the living towers that are built during fiestas throughout most of present and past Catalan territory. All sorts of ingenious theories have been advanced to explain them. Some believe the towers were invented as military lookout towers if an armed force was moving on a treeless plain. That seems a little far-fetched. Others have tried to relate the towers to relics of some religious ritual. None of the explanations seem to account well enough for the sheer joyful madness, the incredible tension of the event.

As each step of the tower is completed, the tension grows, the swirling crowd clapping and shouting until near the finish, when the crowd becomes quieter, almost anxious, as the small boy climbs to the top, usually carrying a Catalan flag or something with the Catalan colors.

Some towers are carefully planned, with each person's role as a building block known in advance. These are for the major festivals, but tower building can also be spontaneous. One never knows when it will happen or exactly why.

While we were sitting quietly once in the ramblas at Vilafranca *del Penedés, having a single expresso, writing postcards—being complete tourists, in fact—when a group of young men ranging perhaps from early to midteens came running into the ramblas at the upper end, from the old part of town. It was late afternoon of a perfectly ordinary day in early spring. There were no official fiestas going on or contemplated, but these young men had obviously been holding their own fiesta, no doubt with good cause.*

When they reached the center of the ramblas (it is only about two blocks long), jackets and shoes were discarded amid much laughter and shouting. They were beginning to draw a crowd already— housewives shopping for dinner at some of the stalls that were open, even though it was not market day, men from nearby bars coming out, drinks in hand, to see what all the shouting was about.

Four of the largest teens linked arms, forming a small hollow square; quickly, three more levels formed but the impromptu tower was already leaning worse than Pisa. As the next "level" started up the tower, the whole rickety structure suddenly began to stagger sideways, almost doing a circle dance as the foundation struggled to maintain balance and keep the whole thing upright, but it was hope-less. In a few seconds, the tower crashed into a leafless plane tree at the edge of the Ramblas and the structure collapsed, with some of the upper floors caught in the branches of the tree.

Even before it was clear that no one was hurt, the crowd was helpless with laughter. The whole episode had taken about three minutes, start to finish, and now the broken bits of the tower lay about on the concrete giggling and gasping.

A barman came rushing out with a tray of glasses and several bottles of cava, which one of the onlookers had ordered. The true origin of the tower building then became obvious. It's never a good idea to pass up a glass of cava. The teenage boys were joking and laughing.

"Why did you do it?"

He looked puzzled. How could anyone not know? "Because it was fun."

BRIEF SITINGS IN CATALONIA

The Picasso Museum in Barcelona. Near the old cathedral. Check any tourist guide for hours, address. Go when it's raining and look out the windows at the pots of geraniums on the balconies of nearby apartments. Imagine yourself in a movie about Picasso. Two young boys in blue pants are sitting on a bench in the Blue Room. They are very still. Looking at the pictures, they become the pictures. On another bench an old woman knits lace, watching the blue boys on the bench watch the pictures.

The Mercado San José in Barcelona. There is a light late-morning rain. A crew of street workers have built a fire from wood scraps in a cut-down barrel. They are grilling their lunch. Fish from the *mercado*.

Olives. There are twenty-two different kinds of olives for sale in the *mercado* at Vilanova.

Cats. One lazy afternoon we counted twenty-nine cats from the back balcony of our son David's apartment in Vilafranca. It was the day the hot water failed and we showered cold. The corner of the bed was propped up with a volume of *Lord of the Rings*.

Gaudí. An astounding architect. Roots in the Gothic and science fiction. Look for Gaudí designs in buildings along the Ramblas in Barcelona before you see the church.

George Orwell. Keep *Homage to Catalonia* on your bedside table or in your backpack. Don't read it. Jot down the telephone numbers of strangers you meet in bars on the inside front cover. Lose it at the airport.

GUIDELINES: CATALONIA

Restaurants

Barcelona, Sitges, Tarragona, and the Costa Brava are very well covered in the guides, especially those published by the Spanish Tourism Board. If you read Spanish, pick up a copy of *Guía Gastronómica y Turística de España* for the current year. Most large newsstands carry it.

There are world-class restaurants in Barcelona (with world-class prices to match.) Everyone goes to Eldorado Petit, which is Spanish nouvelle cuisine, as is Jaume de Provença. There are a lot of frankly out-and-out tourist restaurants in Barcelona, of course. The surprising thing is that many of them are quite good, like Los Caracoles in the Barrio Gótico. Some guides are still writing about Agut d'Avignon as if it were an outstanding restaurant. It isn't.

In Tarragona, try Sol Ric on the Vía Augusta or La Galería on the Rambla Nova. Outstanding seafood in both places.

On the Costa Brava, try to find places where Spanish, French, or Italian families are eating. There are very good seafood restaurants all along the coast. Don't go near a place with British or Germans in it. They are there for "good value."

HOTELS

Hotels in this area are very expensive. If possible, stay in a small town and take the local buses or trains into Barcelona. It's a maddening city to drive in under the best of conditions. If you want to stay in Barcelona, look for a *pensione*. There are a lot of them in the streets around the Plaça de Catalunya, which is near the university at the head of the Ramblas, where perfectly good rooms, many with bath, can be had for under $50 a night.

Wining and Dining Off the Tourist Track

Lérida

El Pati de Noguerola, Plaza Noguerola, 5. Tel. (973) 23-74-32. Outstanding regional dishes in a very pleasant setting.

Also, when in Lérida, sample the bakeries and pastry shops. Be sure to include Prats, with two locations at Doctor Fleming, 23, and Paseo Ronda, 88.

San Sadurní de Noya

Mirador de les Caves. Tel. (93) 899-31-78. Call for directions. High on a hill overlooking San Sadurní de Noya, Vilafranca, and miles of rolling vineyards. Very upscale renditions of traditional Catalan cuisine. Outstanding wine list.

Sitges

La Masia, Paseo Vilanova, 164. Tel. (93) 894-10-76. This informal country restaurant, on the road between Vilanova and L'Arboc, is famous for its grilled meats and *allioli*.

Vilafranca del Penedés and nearby area

Cal l'anna, outside of Vilfranca, in a country setting amid vineyards. Don't try to find it in the dark. Tel. (93) 899-14-08. First-rate restaurant. In France, it would probably have a star or two.

Cal Ton, Carrer del Casal, 8. Tel. (93) 890-37-41. Very good regional specialties; great care and attention given to food, and an outstanding wine list. A few blocks from the old quarter.

Before dinner at Cal Ton, be sure to visit the Museo del Vino in Vilafranca. It's on the lovely Plaza Jaime I in the older part of town. The building itself is worth a visit. It was a royal castle belonging to the kings of Aragón in the twelfth century. It's open daily except Sunday.

Celler del Penedés. Tel. (93) 890-20-01. A few kilometers outside of Vilafranca in a tiny village called Sant Miquel d'Olérdola on the Sitges-Vilafranca road. Great regional food with a country accent.

El Merendero. No street address, no listed telephone. From Vilafranca, take the road toward La Bleyda-Pachs. You will soon cross over a bridge. Just before the village of La Bleyda, watch to the right for a gravel-and-dirt road that cuts uphill toward what looks from a distance like an abandoned barn in Texas. That's El Merendero. Open Friday, Saturday, and Sunday night only.

Wineries

Barcelona

Raimat Estate. Tel. (93) 301-46-00. To visit this fantastic estate north of Lérida, it is necessary to call the winery offices in Barcelona for an appointment and for directions.

San Sadurní de Noya (no street address needed here—it's a small town.)

Codorníu. Tel. (93) 891-01-25. Open Monday to Friday, 8 A.M. until 1 P.M. and 3 P.M. until 7 P.M. Closed, July 30 to August 15.

Freixenet. Tel. (93) 891-07-00. Open Monday to Friday, 9 A.M. until noon, and 3 P.M. until 6 P.M. Closed August.

Tarragona

De Muller, Calle Real, 38. (977) 21-07-20. Open Monday to Friday, 9 A.M. until 1 P.M. and 4 P.M. until 6 P.M. A lovely winery in the heart of Tarragona.

Vilafranca del Penedés

Bodegas Miguel Torres, Calle Comercio, 22. Tel. (93) 890-01-00. Open Monday to Friday, 9 A.M. until noon and 3 P.M. until 6 P.M. Closed August. Also a brandy distillery.

RAIMAT

Those tourists who are interested in wine should plan a long detour to one of the most remarkable wineries in Spain, the Raimat Estate, established by Codorníu on the barren plains north of the city of Lérida, about 200 kilometers west of Barcelona. The 8,000-acre estate was purchased by the Raventós family (the owners of Codorníu) in 1914. In Catalan, *raim* means "a bunch of grapes" and *mat* means "hand." Thus, combined, Raimat means something like "the hand that picks the grapes."

Although grapes had been grown there since at least the thirteenth century, much of the farmland had been abandoned. The area had always been dry, with low production. A cynical person might wonder if Don Manuel Raventos might have had advance word in 1914 about the Catalonia and Aragón canal that was built a few years later, bringing water from the Pyrenees to irrigate the once-dry plains. But if the family had an advance tip, they have made it pay off to the benefit of all concerned.

It is an incredible estate, with over 2,000 acres of vines and thousands of acres of fruit and cereal crops. Codorníu has built a model village for the estate workers, a school, a railway station, and sporting grounds.

But, for our purposes, the grapes are what counts, and there the future looks bright. In many respects, Raimat is perfect grape country, especially the weather. The well-balanced wine grape should have just the right ratio of sugar to acid. Too much sugar and the wine will taste flat and flabby, no zip. Too much acid and the wine will be sharp, unpleasant on the palate. The hot days at the Raimat Estate push up the sugar levels in the grapes, and the cool nights help hold the acid level high. The result, happy grapes and good wine.

But there's more than well-balanced grapes to see at Raimat. The last time we were there, there were no grapes to see at all. It was early winter and had been raining for days. The bare vines huddled against the red, raw earth. It was an enormous contrast to an earlier visit, when the vines had been lush and green, rippling like a vast carpet in the wind.

The first winery on the estate was built by Don Manuel shortly after he bought the estate in 1914. It was designed by Rubio Bellver, a pupil of Antonio Gaudí's. There is nothing quite like it in northern Spain. You would have to go to the great sherry bodegas of Jerez to find the same cathedral-like atmosphere, accented here by the small stained-glass windows in the roof, throwing shafts of rainbow-tinted light over the barrels below. This old winery is now used as barrel storage only, with the real work of winemaking taking place in the bodega, which was finished in 1988.

The entire building (which contains a reception center for visitors, a working winery, and more barrel storage) is a bit like a pyramid with a flat top that has been sunk into the hillside and then earthed over. One of the believe-it-or-not aspects of Raimat is that vines actually grow on top of the winery. Cabernet Sauvignon is planted there.

The first plantings at Raimat were the traditional Penedés grapes —Macabeo, Parellada, and Monastrell—which Codorníu used in its *cava* production. But since it seemed a waste to grow grapes at Raimat that would grow perfectly well elsewhere in the Penedés, Codorníu turned to the New World, California, for advice. And California, of course, was quick to give it. After visits by experts from the University of California at Davis and the University of California at Fresno, Chardonnay, Cabernet Sauvignon, Merlot, and Pinot Noir were planted. Now those grapes dominate the vineyards at Raimat.

VALENCIA

In Focus

Of the three chief cities of Spain, Valencia has more in common with Barcelona than with Madrid, yet there is a strong rivalry between the two Mediterranean ports. If you gain the confidence of a *valenciano*, he or she will almost certainly let you know that Valencia is far superior to Barcelona. The *valenciano* will bristle if you suggest that the local language is a subset of Catalan, as spoken in Barcelona, and will insist that it is a separate language (although related to Catalan) owing nothing to Barcelona.

The strong regional ill will between the two cities seems to go deeper than the usual Spanish regionalism. *Valencianos* feel that Barcelona has unfairly gained a certain historical stature by its resistance to Franco's forces in the Civil War, while few outsiders are aware that Valencia was the last major city to fall to Franco.

If Barcelona is the New York of Spain, then Valencia is a curious blend of Chicago and New Orleans. There is an unexpected bustle to Valencia that must come naturally, since it has been a major trading port from before Roman times, with wine and food being shipped throughout the Mediterranean. The modern Valencian port of Grao is the largest port in Spain in terms of volume shipped. Valencia is also an auto-manufacturing center and makes and exports goods such as jeans, shoes, carpets, textiles, and computers.

But none of these industrial exports is as important as food and wine. A seemingly endless supply of rice, fresh vegetables, and citrus fruits are shipped from Valencia (with the famous Valencia oranges only the tip of the market basket).

Valencia gives its name to a long strip of the Mediterranean coast as well as an inland area reaching up into the mountains, where it joins New Castile-La Mancha in the west. The entire district, south along the coast through the province of Murcia, is known as the Garden of Spain. Included in the "garden" is a coastal strip called the Levante, an ancient name for the area, which, politically, includes the provinces of Castellón, Valencia, and Alicante as well as the northern parts of the province of Murcia.

Valencia itself is an ancient city. The Phoenicians and Greeks traded and planted grapes—at least the Greeks planted grapes—all along the Mediterranean coast, but it was the Romans who established Valencia as a major city in the second century B.C., after kicking the Carthaginians out. The Moors came early in the eighth century and loved the Valencian coast, with its seemingly eternal spring and the streams that flow down from the mountain lakes in the rainy season. They lost it briefly to the legendary hero El Cid in 1094 but won it back only six years later, holding it rather late, resisting the Christian Reconquest until 1238, when the Aragón-Catalan expansionist tide rolled over them.

Valencia's rich history of craftsmanship in metal work and ceramics owes a great deal to the Moors. Many Moorish craftsmen remained in the city after the Christian Reconquest, but they were finally expelled in 1609 by Philip III, and Valencia suffered a cultural decline that lasted several centuries, perhaps until the popularization of paella (which, to the casual eye, is easily Valencia's major industry). And if the Arabs hadn't introduced rice, there would be no paella (nor, a bit to the north and east, risotto, for that matter.)

Valencia had been part of the enlightened Al-Andaluz caliph—governed from Sevilla—and great advances were made in agriculture under Arab rule. The Arabs took an irrigation system that had been first used by the Romans and expanded and perfected it into a water-delivery network that is still in use today. Water use was so important that the Arabs established a special court to settle disputes over water. That court, now called the Tribunal de la Aguas, still meets every Thursday at noon on the steps of the cathedral. It has the final word on all water rights arising out of the Valencian irrigation system.

The thirteenth-century conquest by Aragón-Catalan forces left *valencianos* speaking the Catalan language and acquiring some of the bustling work ethic of the Catalans, but nicely tempered by more southern attitudes.

As elsewhere in Spain, mountains are never far. Occasionally, they break through the coastal plain, forming high rocky cliffs above the Mediterranean, but mostly they parallel the coast a few miles inland. Summers are relatively cool once you are far enough up from the humid coastal plain. It is becoming fashionable in both Madrid and Valencia to spend a few weeks in these mountains to escape the heat of the city. Most of the wine grapes grow in the mountains. They like the same kind of weather that people like, so the cooler summers are good for them, too.

One of the most prominent geographic features is Lake Albufera, a large freshwater lake just outside the city of Valencia. Although large, it is being steadily nibbled away by rice paddies and other less-scenic developments. When the rice fields were established by the Arabs in the eighth century, the lake was twice as large as it is now, a wilderness of fish and birds.

Today, the rice paddies have to share the marshy lake shore with automobile plants and housing developments. Somewhat surprisingly, the lake itself has remained fairly unpolluted. There are a number of good restaurants around the lake that specialize in fish, freshwater shellfish, eels, and snails from the lake's waters.

On a sunny day it is a pleasant-enough outing from the city—only a ten- or twenty-minute drive, but in bad weather it takes on a gloomier appearance, with the kind of flat, pearly light associated with the low countries or northern France. One can brood over a glass of wine and imagine century upon century of men—Romans and Arabs and their attendant slaves, no doubt—diking, draining, digging to chip away at the vast, marshy lake to put rice on the tables of the world. The cooks and eaters of the world would no doubt agree that it was a good thing. But probably not the sandpiper, busy on a mudflat just outside the restaurant window.

The sandpiper and his kin have seen the marshy shoreline of Valencia (and other areas of Spain) disappear at a faster and faster rate. The drainage projects the Romans began almost two thousand years ago to grow food are being completed by faceless international businessmen who are planting only resorts. Perhaps it would be more bearable (for the intelligent traveler, if not the sandpiper) if the resorts were not so damnably (and boringly) alike.

The hydrographics of Lake Albufera are complex and date back to Arab times. The name itself is Arabic; Albufera means "small sea." It is divided from the Mediterranean by a fairly narrow sandbar called the Dehesa, which is cut by three drainage channels; two are natural, one is manmade. The drainage channels can be opened or closed to allow water to flow into the Mediterranean. Although Albufera is the largest freshwater lake in Spain (about 7,000 acres), it is very shallow, ranging from 3 to 8 feet in depth.

The rice paddies are one of the things that threaten the existence of Albufera, but they are also one of the things that attract enormous numbers of birds and their camp followers, birdwatchers, to the lake. About 250 species of birds, 90 regular breeders in the area, have been recorded at Albufera.

But a far-greater threat than the rice paddies (which, after all, depend on the waters of the lake for annual flooding) is the growing contamination of the water by industrial poisons and domestic and agricultural sewage washed into the lake each year. Albufera has long been a battleground, with conservation groups and duck hunters usually ranged against local authorities who too often go for the quick peseta fix despite the threat of long-range disaster.

Finally, in the early 1980s, Albufera became a *parque natural*, with very stringent protective measures imposed by the government of Valencia. At the moment, conservationists rate it an area "in stress."

But like the sandpiper, one must eat, putting one's global conscience to the side. It's a very good idea to follow the sandpiper's lead in the case of Albufera and go for the local cuisine. A famous local dish is *all i pebre*, eels fried in garlic and pepper sauce. The sandpiper has to settle for just the eels solo.

THE FOOD

It is a pity that most people think of Valencia only in terms of oranges. If they are a bit more sophisticated about Spanish food, they will know that paella is a Valencian dish. But if they stop there, they will have missed the richness and abundance of Valencian cuisine, from the mountains to the sea.

Paella—the basic ingredients are rice, saffron, and olive oil—has certainly come a long way from its peasant origins (perhaps over a shepherd's campfire in the mountains behind Valencia) to its present international icon status for Spain, much as pizza is for Italy.

The name itself comes from the *paellera*, the pan in which it is cooked. Probably most people are familiar with the shape, a round, shallow flat-bottomed pan, about two to three inches deep. The dish called paella is only one of the many prepared in the *paellera*. The dishes are customarily those in which the liquid stock is all absorbed by the rice.

Much of this rice cookery originated during earlier times, when Lent was strictly observed. No doubt paella owes some of its origin to early Lenten dishes of dried cod and rice. But as the dish became popular it took on a livelier aspect. Americans are most familiar with the seafood paellas loaded with shrimp, fish, perhaps even lobster. In Valencia, one is more likely to meet with a country paella—

chicken, rabbit, garden vegetables, perhaps snails, fresh rosemary, and white beans.

In Valencia, preparing and cooking a paella has become "man's work," very much like the weekend stint at the barbecue in many American families. In the same way, there is infinite secret lore exchanged on the best way to go about cooking a paella. Great numbers of tireless angels dance on a great many pinheads over whether the paella should be finished in the oven or brought to perfection on top of the stove—or best yet, many insist, on an outdoor fire. And if a fire is used, should it be a fire of vine prunings or orangewood? There are great debates over the precise ratio of water to rice and when to add the water and even how to add it.

For food beyond paella, there is a whole galaxy of rice dishes on the Valencian coast—at least two hundred in all. Then there is the seafood (both fish and shellfish), meat pies, grilled lamb, rabbit, chicken, plump and tasty snails, and many, many vegetable dishes, including the ever-present *menestra*, the rich vegetable stew that has been described as an entire garden in one pot.

But don't forget the orchards. Begin with the oranges, which, depending on variety, are harvested nine months a year. There are very few Valencia oranges grown in Valencia, by the way. The actual Valencia orange makes up only about 2 percent of the crop. There are any number of different varieties grown, with harvesting beginning with the Clementina in September.

What most people mean when they talk or write of Valencia oranges is the sweet orange, which is a mutant of the bitter orange and was introduced into the west by Portugal in the fifteenth century. In fact, the Elizabethans called the sweet orange the Portyngale. The navel orange is a further mutant of the sweet orange, as are the mandarin and the tangerine, which many believe to be simply another name for the mandarin.

The orange, which looms so large in the image of Valencia, is a native of south China—both the bitter and the sweet varieties. By the first century A.D. it was in India and from there spread via Arab sea-trade routes to North Africa and (the bitter varieties) to Rome.

There may have been oranges in Spain during Roman times, but the first certain records date to the ninth century, when the Moors began planting huge groves of bitter oranges between Sevilla and Granada. The bitter orange was originally grown for its ornamental uses and the aromatics of the fruit and blossom, but the juice was also used as seasoning in several fish and meat dishes, including the famous *pato sevillana*, duck Seville, which is by all odds the origin of the French duck à l'orange. This bitter orange is also the orange used in orange marmalade.

The Arabs also gave the general word for oranges to the Spanish, *naranja,* which is very close to the Sanskrit, *narranga.* The Spanish call the sweet oranges *chinas* and the bitter oranges *cachorenas.*

One of the first records of orange exports from Spain is a shipment to the port of Southampton for Eleanor of Castile in 1290, who must have been yearning for a taste of the sunny south in the bitter fogs of London. The most famous orange merchant in England was, of course, Nell Gwyn, Charles II's very well-known "protestant whore." Her oranges were of the sweet variety; Gwyn and the other "Orange Girls" were notorious in the theater district. Louise de Keroualle, the Duchess of Portsmouth, who shared the king's favors with Nell, said of her: "Anybody may know she has been an orange wench by her swearing." One assumes that the duchess was not implying that oranges had anything to do with Nell's use of language.

The orange reached the New World quite early. Columbus, on his second voyage, in 1493, planted them on the island of Hispaniola. They were first planted in Florida in 1539 by Hernando de Soto. According to Waverley Root, the Seminole Indians took to the fruit (it must have still been the bitter orange) and served red snapper steamed with fresh oranges to the naturalist William Bartram when he visited the Florida tribe in 1791. There is a Spanish dish much like this.

Oranges (Valencia's biggest cash crop by far, dwarfing the wine business by a factor of twenty) are just the beginning of the Valencian orchard and garden. There are apricots, apples, asparagus, anise, peaches, melons, grapes, grapefruit, plums, pears, cherries, olives, garlic, capers, saffron, onions, mushrooms, peas, broad beans, green beans, tomatoes, lettuce, cucumbers, and on through an entire shopping cart of vegetables and fruits.

Out of the garden and into the mountains, there is lamb, rabbit, dove, partridge, beef, and pork; from the sea, a staggering variety of fish and shellfish.

But whatever the eating occasion, it is rice that remains at the heart of Valencian cuisine. Valencian cooks are so famous for their rice dishes that in recent years Japanese chefs have been spending time working in Valencian restaurants in order to learn the techniques of proper short-grain rice cookery.

The Moors first planted rice in Andalusia in the eighth century, then in Valencia a short time later. From Valencia, rice culture spread to Italy, perhaps as early as the tenth century, although there is no hard evidence for that fact. But it is certain that rice was extensively cultivated in the Po river valley of Italy by the fourteenth century at the latest. Rice was not grown in France until early in the seventeenth century, and the French are still not great consumers of rice.

There are at least a couple of reasons that rice cultivation leap-frogged from the Mediterranean coast of Spain to northern Italy. Spain had long been active—militarily and politically—in several parts of Italy, beginning with the conquest of Sicily by Peter III of Aragón in 1282. At various times over the next few centuries, Sicily and the Kingdom of Naples were controlled by the Spanish.

I believe it is possible to see a clear Spanish influence on one certain dish that is normally thought of as "Italian." The techniques for preparing risotto and the Valencian dish *arroz abanda* are almost identical. But there is an even more direct link between the Moor-ish-Spanish rice cuisine and the famous risotto of Italy, and that is risotto alla milanese. Risotto alla milanese contains saffron, which is rarely used in Italy, except in some Italian fish soups, and is not considered an important spice. Yet there it is in risotto alla milanese, which in some forms can look very much like a paella. Especially with the addition of "chickens, duck, game, lobster, mussels, oys-ters, prawns, mushrooms, truffles, goose or chicken livers, artichoke hearts, peas, aubergines, almost anything you like," as Elizabeth David suggests.

There is a pretty story concerning the invention of risotto alla milanese, which is repeated in Anna del Conte's book *Gastronomy of Italy*.

"In 1574, the daughter of the craftsman in charge of making stained glass for the windows of the Duomo was getting married. One of the apprentices, who had a passion for adding saffron to the molten glass, hit on the idea of making the plain risotto for the wedding dinner turn gold like his windows. He gave some saffron to the host of the inn where the dinner was to take place and asked him to mix it into the risotto. The result was a most beautiful golden risotto."

Although Del Conti calls this a pretty legend, she suggests that other food historians are probably a bit closer to the mark in sug-gesting that the origins of the dish "lie in the East, and it reached Italy via Sicily."

It seems quite possible that it did, indeed, reach Italy via Sicily.

But it reached Sicily not from the East but rather from Valencia, where the technique of slowly adding liquid to the rice may have originated, as well as the inspiration of adding saffron. It is quite possible that the Moors brought both the cooking technique and the use of saffron with them to Spain, but it is also possible that it was developed in Spain.

THE WINE

The vines here bud out early, at least at the lower elevations. By mid-March, there are many places in which you can walk up through the lush scents of an orange grove into already-green vineyards. Most of the vines are still pruned in the old style, close to the ground, but in an attempt to keep the wine industry in Valencia up to date, some of the growers are training the vines on wire trellises off the ground. In the mountains, pruning is likely to be still going forward when the lower-elevation vines are in bud.

Valencia and other ports of the Levante were shipping wine long before anyone around the Mediterranean had ever seen an orange. The Phoenicians traded in Valencia wine by the sixth century B.C. Now, roughly half of all Spanish wine exports are from Valencia, a number that even most Spaniards are astonished to learn. In a national survey taken in 1985, only 2.4 percent of Spanish wine drinkers knew anything of Valencia wines. The ever-positive *valencianos* take this as a good sign. At least, they note with an optimistic smile, the wines don't have a bad image. Simply no image at all. Even in Valencia itself the wines are often neglected, with 90 percent of total Valencian production going to the export market. One is more likely to find the wines of Rioja or La Mancha or the Penedés on Spanish restaurant wine lists than Valencia wines, and this lack of demand has held down the price of Valencia wines. Quite good wines can be purchased in bottle for under two hundred pesetas, or less than two dollars in the local markets and shops. Yet in 1988 Valencia shipped 1.25 million cases of wine to the United Kingdom; Rioja shipped half a million.

Perhaps part of the reason for the invisible image of Valencia wines is that the vineyards are hidden away, with only the obvious farms in sight—orange groves and rice paddies. But oranges do not grow above the 400-meter level, so that's where the vineyards begin.

And since the usual tourists never get above sea level, they never see the vineyards. Therefore, no Valencia wine.

It must be very frustrating to the winemakers, who have made tremendous technical gains in the past decade. Probably no area of Spain, except possibly the Penedés, has a more modern winemaking technology than Valencia. And it shows in the wines, which are fresh, fruity, and delightful, perfect tablemates with the garden-seashore freshness of Valencian cuisine.

There are five denominations of origin in the Levante: Alicante, Jumilla, Utiel-Requena, Valencia, and Yecla. The five together produce more wine than any other region of Spain except La Mancha.

The region of Alicante, closer to Murcia than to the city of Valencia, is best known for a wine that rarely stands alone. The *vino de doble pasta* is not a wine to order with a double serving of spaghetti, but a deeply colored blending wine, shipped in concentrated form all over the world to beef up local vintages. It needn't overly concern us unless we happen to be in Norway and wonder where the red wine on the table comes from. Probably Alicante. But there is a delightful rosé—it goes well with local seafood—made from the free-run juice of the *doble pasta*. There are also some quite good red wines (some bottled as *reservas*) and an unusual and rather hard-to-find dessert wine called Fonchillon, which has a startling copper color. Grape varieties in Alicante are the Monastrell, the Garnacha, and the Bobal.

The Valencian wine most likely to be found in the United States is from the area of Jumilla, a mountainous inland region in the northern part of the province of Murcia. In the past, big, high-alcohol red wines from Jumilla (made mostly from the Monastrell grape) were popular in Spain, especially in the south. In the last few decades, Jumilla winemakers have been producing wines of higher acid. As a result, they are fresher and not so heavy and alcoholic on the palate, qualities that are meeting with favor in the United Kingdom and the United States, especially for those bargain hunters who can recognize a good wine for under five dollars a bottle. Jumilla wines to look for include the Bodegas Señorío del Condestable, the Jumilla Union Vinícola, and the Cooperativa de San Isidro.

Yecla—the smallest denomination in the Levante, lying inland from the city of Alicante—produces wines quite similar to those of Jumilla.

At the moment, the region with the potential for the best-quality wines is Utiel-Requena, in the mountains at the extreme western edge of the province of Valencia. In fact, the area has more in common with New Castile and La Mancha than the coastal province, and there is a strong political movement to split away from Valencia and join the province of New Castile.

There are those who believe that Utiel-Requena could produce outstanding wines if the right varietals were planted. This accounts for some of the experimentation going forward in the vineyards. Utiel-Requena produces some white wines, but most of the production is reds and rosés. The rosés particularly have an excellent reputation. Recently there has been some experimentation with Chardonnay, Carbernet Sauvignon, Tempranillo, and Garnacha. Tempranillo (the red grape of Rioja) looks very promising. Other growers have planted a few rows of Syrah, the great red grape from the Rhône valley of France. It, too, looks to be doing well.

There is a move under way to combine the Utiel-Requena wine district with that of Valencia, which would probably be a great mistake for Utiel-Requena. Whatever possibility exists there for the production of quality table wine would be swallowed up in the vast, almost industrial production of Valencia, where wine is made in gigantic wineries that strip the product of every shred of romance. And, it should be noted, often of individual character.

Having said that, one must admit, that the wines that set out from these plants are quite drinkable in an honest, anonymous kind of way. They make their way all over the world, from Africa to Scandinavia to the Far East and Eastern Europe. Over 90 percent of the wines shipped from Valencia are sold in bulk—that is, sent to another nation and bottled there, often without any Spanish identity at all.

In a technical sense they are well made, very easy to drink. What you might call friendly wines. An English writer called them "working man's wines," and that seems fair enough. It seems, in fact, to fit well with the rough but friendly and bustling egalitarianism in Valencia.

SPANISH DAYS

There is a certain attractive seediness about the city of Valencia. It seems, on first impression, to have more in common with a Mediterranean port city in France, or perhaps North Africa, than in Spain. There is a tropical core to Valencia, in mood if not always in climate, that is utterly lacking in Barcelona. Perhaps it is that Valencia is a

bit theatrical; even the modern buildings look as if they were designed more as backdrops to some human drama than as places of
business, department stores, or banks.

We expect to see Peter Lorre brooding over a glass of wine at a
sidewalk café while mysterious men in trench coats appear briefly
on the sidewalk behind us only to disappear down a narrow alley
when we look back.

Once, we were slightly lost in the older part of town near the
mercado. We knew, in a general sense, where we were and where we
were going, but in the tangle of narrow streets, it is easy to become
confused. It was just dusk, on the first day of the Fallas, the week-
long carnival held every year in mid-March. The celebration goes
back to the Middle Ages when Valencia was a city of craftsmen. It
springs from the custom of the carpenter's brotherhood burning
accumulated wood shavings on St. Joseph's (the carpenter's) Day.
The term *fallas* comes from the Latin *facula*, or torch.

Over the centuries the craftsmen began making objects just to
burn. Often, unpopular political figures were created, only to go up
in flames. Finally, the wooden figures were replaced by pasteboard
or plaster floats made by artisans or merchants from different sections of the town. Over time the floats have become more and more
elaborate, even bizarre, and the entire thing has taken on an air of
fantasy. The streets are filled with grotesque, gigantic figures; there
is much wandering to and fro. There is a fine madness in the air,
punctuated by the sights and sounds of fireworks, all building toward
the incredible fiery climax of the evening of March 19, when the
floats and figures go up in flames.

It is during the week of the Fallas that the heart and roots of
Valencia become evident—it is a Spanish city through and through.
No one approaches fun with more seriousness yet with a greater
sense of style than the Spaniard.

But that night, whatever street we turned in to, seemed to lead to
an even narrower street. Rationally, we knew the people around us
were perfectly friendly, but shadowy figures in doorways took an
unexpected threatening air. A trio of whores standing outside a bar
drinking beer and laughing were suddenly laughing *at* us.

It was all nonsense, of course; in a few minutes, we had come out
into the Plaza de Zaragoza, and the sinister-looking man who had
been following us turned out to be an Englishman, a fellow guest in
the hotel who was trying to catch up with us to ask directions back
to the hotel. But the feeling persists that in Valencia anything is

possible. And good heavens, it *is* Peter Lorre. And he *is* getting up, smiling that delightful elfin smile, eager to meet you. But no, sorry. It isn't Peter Lorre after all. It is only a local *rodríguez* rising to meet another half a dozen *rodríguez.*

Rodríguez is what the *valencianos* call the phenomenon of clusters of slightly bewildered middle-class, middle-aged men on their own for the week or weekend because their wives and children have gone to the mountains or down the coast to a beach cottage to escape the heat. It all seems harmless enough. As one *rodríguez* described it, the action seems to consist of various groups of *rodríguez* meeting to drink wine or coffee, have dinner, share a good gossip (probably much the same things their wives are up to), and get home to bed early, because while the family plays at the beach or in the mountains, the wandering *rodríguez* must be back at the office the next day. Perhaps the custom is left over from Arab days, when the males gathered in the streets to talk while the women stayed safely behind the walls of their houses. If it is, it should be added to the long list of foods and customs that Valencia owes to the Moors.

Valencianos, in general, love cooking over a firepit and eating outdoors. The local version of the chamber of commerce reports that there are 320 days of sunshine a year in the area—many of those days quite warm—so holidays and weekends become occasions for great bursts of festive outdoor partying that may last until dawn in the warm summer months, with all hands snatching a few hours' sleep before the next day's alfresco lunch, which may be held at a fashionable cottage at Lake Albufera.

The whole area around the lake (on the higher ground above the rice paddies) was once market gardens, or *huertas*, as gardens are called in Valencia. As the gardens were slowly eaten by urban expansion, the growing Valencian middle class bought the old cottages, or *barracas*, and remodeled them for weekend or year-round homes. The cottages are simple A-frame structures with whitewashed walls and thatched roofs of marsh rushes or rice straw.

The rich, sandy soil around the lake yields two vegetable crops a year in the mild Valencian climate, and at one time the owners of the cottages supplied vegetables for the tables of Valencia. Only a few decades ago, they would set out long before dawn in horse- or donkey-drawn carts for the *mercado central* in the city.

The market is one of those marvelous iron and glass buildings that look as if they might have been designed as a railway station somewhere in southern Germany or northern England sometime around the turn of the century. Its vastness—almost 10,000 square yards—is filled with such splendid goodies, especially in the spring, that it's worth getting out of bed before dawn, just to catch the market at its peak.

There are entire aisles devoted to hams and sausages, including the famous *morcilla*, or blood sausage, sometimes stuffed with onions and *piñones*. There are huge *alonganiva de aragón*, which is a sausage made in a U-shaped loop. There are *choricitos*, little round sausages in a long loop, tied off every two inches.

At the next aisle, there are whole oceans, beaches, bays, and estuaries filled with shellfish (tiny little blood red shrimp called *quis-quilla* gathered from the city's beach and served in tapas bars, traditionally with a glass of cold beer), various sorts of sea snails, *langostino*, and *cigala*, which looks like a seagoing crayfish. Endless fish, large, small, and of virtually every shape and color. Fish that are untranslatable but supremely edible.

There are half a dozen different kinds of salted or smoked tuna, each tasting a bit different because of a different smoking technique. There is the delicious *mojama*, a dried tuna ham that is a favorite tapa in Valencia served alongside a glass of the steely local rosé or *fino*.

There are cheeses from the mountains made of sheep and goat milk, booths filled with garlic crowded next to peppers, potatoes, and every kind of leafy green imaginable. In the spring, there are the crisp, little, pencil-thin asparagus, which the Spanish call *espár-rago trigo*, or wild asparagus, because it often grows on the margins of wheat (*trigo*) fields. There is wild asparagus in Spain, but that seen in the city markets is garden-grown.

The peppers can be especially dangerous. There is a pepper called the *padrón*, which is often grilled and served as a tapa. The particular mystery of this pepper is that after grilling, it is impossible to tell from the shape, color, and size whether it will be a sweet pepper or a hot pepper.

There is booth after booth filled with tomatoes that actually taste like tomatoes, an agreeable sensation that one frequently meets in Spain. There are dangerous signs, however. Spanish farmers have learned that the northern Europeans will pay the same price for tomatoes picked green as for ripe red tomatoes. Green tomatoes are easier to pack and ship better. They also can be grown faster and will take on a reddish cast while held in warehouses before sale. But still, for the home market, most tomatoes are picked ripe.

If it is early in the day, one can easily get stuck in the pastry section. Valencian pastry chefs and bakers are famous for delights such as *tarta cristina* or *pan quemada*.

Once one is past the sweet delights, there is an amazing selection of *empanadas* of all sizes and stuffings. One particular knockout is a stewed artichoke *empanada* made with a whole-wheat crust. Another yummy is a red pepper and *bacalao empanada* with a crust like a very short pie crust.

Once, in a midmorning fit of hunger after several hours' wandering through the market, we loaded a bag with pastries and *empanadas* to take back to the hotel. We should have been satisfied with the free samples the ladies at the pastry booths kept pressing on us, but greed won out and the bag was filled.

Wisely, we also got a bottle of a local Valencia sparkling wine. It was not so sweet that it competed with the pastries but only slightly sweet—just enough to blend perfectly with them. We sat in the middle of the slightly oversized single bed the Spanish call a *matrimonial* and ate pastries and *empanadas* and drank bubbly.

Pedro de Arechavaleta de Peña is very much a modern Valencian businessman. He has been involved globally selling everything from irrigation equipment to wine. Yet Pedro, one of the people who first introduced us to the wonders of Valencia, thinks nothing of whizzing 60 or 80 kilometers down the *autopista* for a lunch that might last three hours.

One brilliant summer day we drove south from Albufera, where the coast arcs out toward Denia and Cabo de la Nao in a lovely sweep of sand, rocks, and palm trees, with groves of oranges clinging to steeply terraced hillsides. Pedro noted that it is a good thing oranges make such a fine cash crop, else the hillsides would most likely be growing cut-from-a-pattern retirement villas for northern Europeans. The silver-lining side of the tourist rush is that this particular stretch of coastline has more good seafood restaurants per kilometer than any place else on earth. The variety is amazing, as is the quality almost everywhere. But Pedro was heading for a particular restaurant in Denia called La Pegola.

"It is very hard to get a table," he explained, "and they were not answering the telephone this morning, so I couldn't try for reservations."

As we moved at a steady 160 kilometers an hour down the *autopista*, Pedro discussed how the Spanish do business.

"Car telephones will not happen here. Why should I want to talk business when I am out of the office? Going to lunch is to get away from business—yes, even if it is a business lunch. Perhaps some business gets done, but it isn't why we get together."

(Pedro might have added that another reason cellular phones may not have a future in Spain is the Spanish driving style. The Spanish are quite good drivers, actually, even courteous, but they are also very aggressive, very bold drivers. It is really scary to think of someone dialing a number while doing the auto shuck-and-jive through the streets of Madrid, where reports of gridlock are frequent. Yet what looks like gridlock to an American is simply a challenge to a Spaniard.)

When we reached La Pegola, Pedro directed us to wait in the car. He would have lost face if seen in the company of *dos americanos*. He disappeared inside the resturant for about five minutes. This was maybe twelve-thirty in the afternoon. No one, of course, would dream of arriving for lunch before one or one-thirty. Pedro was not trying to get us in on the spot but to make reservations for later in the afternoon. Finally, he emerged, beaming.

"I did it. He pretended he didn't remember me even though I was here only two weeks ago and bought him a *coñac* after lunch. But when I mentioned my wife's family, he said we could come at two."

It had made his day. He had been a victor in a peculiarly Spanish hustle. Pedro is not *valenciano* but Basque and therefore begins any sensitive local negotiation with a strike against him. His wife, however, comes from generations of *valencianos*, going back, perhaps, to El Cid himself. Her family name is like a talisman, finding tables in restaurants where there were no tables.

And it was worth it. La Pegola is right on the Mediterranean, with a sweeping view toward Ibiza, but the food is so good there was little thought for the view. There is no menu. The waiter simply begins to bring food. First, there is a salad with lettuce, tomatoes, peppers, pickled fish, radishes, and grated carrots. Enough of a salad to satisfy most any salad-craving American. On the day we were first there, it was followed by *gambas*, served Spanish-style with heads on. After eating the body of the shrimp, we would pick up the head and suck out the nutty-tasting substance inside.

Then came the *arroz abanda*, which La Pegola is famous for. The name *arroz abanda* originally meant simply "rice on the side." In *arroz abanda*, fish stock replaces water in cooking the rice. Originally, this stock-cooked rice was served to the side of the same fish that went into the stock, with saffron added. Now if there is fish served, it is usually freshly grilled.

La Pegola's *arroz abanda* was beyond wonderful. It was rich and crunchy, outrageously good. The crunch came from the *quemada*, the slightly burned rice at the bottom of the pan that is scraped loose and mixed with the rest of the rice. The rice was the Valencian short-grain, the only kind that should be used in *arroz abanda* (or paella).

The chef had not spared the olive oil in the *sofrito*, and *calamares* and *merzola* (a local Mediterranean fish) were sparingly mixed into the whole.

Wonderful! And with a little planning, most people can get a table without knowing Pedro's inlaws.

It was late spring, high in the mountains about 100 kilometers east of Valencia, near the small town of La Portera—10 more klicks off the main highway between Valencia and Madrid. The map reads local road number 330, which leaves the main highway at Requena. You should get there in time for lunch. That particular windy day of high blue skies, lunch was lamb chops and local sausages grilled over an open fire with only sprigs of fresh rosemary as garnish. The romero (rosemary) had been gathered by the vineyard jefe's four-year-old boy and some of it was thrown over the white coals of the vine cuttings just before the chops were removed from the grill.

There was a huge platter of chops and sausages for four of us. And a huge bowl of salad, fresh from the garden, and bread. That was all.

There were several kinds of garden greens in the salad, and some freshly gathered wild greens that the jefe's wife—who looked as if she had just stepped out of a painting by Goya—could find no Castilian words for. Her husband, the jefe, was a small, spare man who, surprisingly, talked about his latest experiments in the vineyard as if we were at a seminar at the viticultural school of the University of California at Davis.

"And how do you think Chardonnay will do at this altitude?" he asked. "I believe it could have a good future here. The microclimate is right for it, according to some reports I've seen. I've planted a few rows. I'm going to put it on a high wire and open up the center, pull the leaves, to let plenty of air circulate, because sometimes we get rain near the harvest and the Chardonnay is very thin-skinned, right? It rots easily. It should do well on the English market, too, a Valencia Chardonnay, don't you agree?"

And there, just there, we were at the heart of modern Spain. A man who moments before had been grilling freshly butchered lamb chops very much as they had been grilled in these mountains for thousands of years was easily up to date on viticulture and wine marketing.

We were so deep in the country that in the conversational silences you could hear the thin, high scream of a hawk hundreds of yards away. The jefe's little boy sat on his lap and gnawed at a chop bone and his wife poured fresh glasses of a fruity, slightly chilled red wine that danced a delicious duet with the lamb across the palate.

The boy slid off his father's lap and dashed out the door, waving his arms furiously at half a dozen magpies who had gathered around the remains of the open fire, picking at the scraps of lamb. He threw his bone at an urraca *and watched in amazement as another of the birds seized the bone and flew away. He ran crying to his mother, who laughed and gave him a crust of bread dipped in red wine.*

GUIDELINES: VALENCIA

The city of Valencia is so well represented in tourist guides that it would be a waste of space here to mention specific hotels. Valencia is worth an extended stay, so you should look for a *pensión*. There are several good ones near the Plaza del País Valencia. Our favorite is the **Hostal-Residencia Universo,** Calle Vilaragu, 5. Tel. (96)351-94-36, which on some rooms has pleasant balconies where you can watch the street go by.

Enrique Gran is the chef at **La Catedral del Jamón** at Mosén Fermades, 7. Gran is locally famous for making giant paellas in huge pans up to twenty feet in diameter. You can also order several different kinds of paella there, and if you express a keen interest, he will probably invite you upstairs to watch a video of his trip to Italy, when he made paella for hundreds of amazed Italians.

There are several good tapas bars and restaurants all along Mosén Fermades, which is closed to auto traffic except for early morning deliveries. It's a good place to wander and is not far from the cathedral.

There are a number of restaurants on the shores of La Albufera in the area called La Dehesa del Saler, between the shore of the Mediterranean and the lake. They are quite pleasant on hot summer days because most have outdoor tables. Quality is generally good, especially for seafood and specialties from the lake.

Wineries

Vinival, Avenida Blasco Ibañez, 44, Alboraya, Valencia. Tel.
(95)371-01-11, open Monday to Friday 9 A.M. until 1:30 P.M. and 4
P.M. until 6:30 P.M. Closed August. A huge, high-tech winery that
will give you a good idea how the wine business operates in Valencia.

Bodegas Asencio Carcelén, Baron del Solar, 1 and 3, Jumilla. Tel.
(968)78-04-18. Open Monday to Friday, 9 A.M. until 2 P.M. and 5
P.M. until 7 P.M. Jumilla is the interior, south of the city of Valencia
and inland from Alicante. It's a lovely little town, worth a visit. The
Bodegas Carcelén is a charming winery with a tasting room in a
small wine museum.

RECIPES

BASICS, TAPAS, SOUPS, AND SALADS

ALLIOLI
Catalan Garlic Sauce

All-i-oli, garlic and oil, that's it. The original sauce was no more than the two ingredients. Now, more often, you will find an egg added to make it easier to hold the sauce together.

Of the two methods presented here we prefer the handmade. The consistency is much nicer and it really is very easy to make. One of our sons even demonstrated making allioli in front of his speech class.

The sauce is delicious with rice, grilled meats, and fish, as a dip for vegetables, and a spread for bread. Just put it on the table and guests will find a way of using it, we assure you.

MAKES 2 CUPS.

HANDMADE
4 medium-large garlic cloves, peeled
2 egg yolks

1½ cups olive oil
Salt to taste

Place the garlic in the mortar and mash it with the pestle until a rough paste is formed. Stir in the egg yolks. Always stir in the same direction so that the surface tension of the forming emulsion is not broken. Continue stirring with the pestle while very gradually adding the oil—a drop at a time at first—until a thick sauce is formed. This is called the emulsion. Sprinkle in a little salt and check for seasoning. Add more salt if desired.

VARIATIONS: A handful or a pinch of fresh herbs or a pinch of saffron can be pounded with the garlic for a flavored *allioli*.

MAKES 2 CUPS

MACHINE MADE

6 medium-large garlic cloves, peeled	1 egg yolk
	2 cups olive oil
1 egg	Salt to taste

Place the garlic, egg, and egg yolk in a blender or food processor and whirl until the garlic is well minced with the egg. With the motor running, very slowly add the oil in a thin stream. Sprinkle in a little salt and check for seasoning. Add more salt if desired. The allioli should be the consistency of a homemade mayonnaise.

VARIATION: Add 1 cup of basil leaves and 1 teaspoon of lemon juice with the garlic, egg, and egg yolk. Proceed as directed.

NOTE: We prefer to use a very good olive oil, not an extra-virgin olive oil for the sauce. The extra-virgin oil gives a much stronger flavor and too much "bite" for our taste.

COCA DE LÉRIDA
Flatbread with Assorted Toppings

We visited a bakery in Lérida that produced no fewer than twenty-eight cocas. Different ones kept coming out of the giant ovens about every fifteen minutes. The toppings are limited only by your imagination. Avoid putting to much stuff on top, though. The idea is something between focaccia and a pizza, but the dish is entirely Spanish.

You will also find sweet cocas topped with candied fruits and drizzled with sugar syrup. The dough for these types of cocas usually contains sugar, some grated orange and lemon peel, and perhaps anise liqueur.

You needn't bake all four cocas the same day. Half of the dough can be punched down after the first rising and put in a plastic bag and refrigerated until the next day. Simply bring the dough to room temperature, form into cocas or a small loaf of bread, let rise, and bake.

MAKES 4 11-BY-6-INCH COCAS, SERVING 4 TO 12, MORE OR LESS, DEPENDING ON HOW HUNGRY THEY ARE.

DOUGH
1 tablespoon yeast
2 tablespoons olive oil
1½ teaspoons salt
4 cups flour

Cornmeal for sprinkling the baking sheet

Place 1½ cups of warm water in the food processor bowl and add the yeast. After about 5 minutes the yeast will dissolve and begin to foam. Add the oil and salt and 1 cup of the flour. Whirl for 1 minute.

Add the remaining cups of flour and whirl until a ball forms. The dough may be a little sticky. Do not add more flour.

Turn the dough out into an oiled bowl. Roll the dough over so it is covered with oil. Cover the bowl, put in a warm place, and let the dough rise to double its size. Punch the dough down and divide into quarters.

Preheat the oven to 450°F.

Have ready 4 baking sheets lightly sprinkled with cornmeal.

Roll the dough out into long oval shapes, place on the baking sheets, and top with any of the following toppings, or make up your

own. Let rest 10 minutes, then bake until the *coca* is golden underneath and cooked through, about 15 minutes.

Serve immediately or at room temperature.

ASSORTED TOPPINGS

TOPPING 1

4 tablespoons extra-virgin olive oil	Salt and freshly ground black pepper to taste
1 pound eggplant, cut into small cubes	½ cup pitted black olives, such as Kalamata

Heat the oil in a medium skillet. Cook the eggplant until very tender,
sprinkling with salt and pepper as it cooks. Cover one of the *cocas*
with some of this topping. Sprinkle with the additional tablespoon of
oil. Let rest and bake as directed above.

TOPPING 2

2 tablespoons olive oil	6 anchovy fillets, drained of excess oil and cut in half lengthwise
2 medium onions, peeled and thinly sliced	
Salt and freshly ground black pepper to taste	Extra-virgin olive oil
2 large, ripe tomatoes, thinly sliced	Paprika

Heat the oil in a medium skillet. Cook the onions until soft and
golden, sprinkling with salt and pepper as they cook.

Arrange the tomato slices over the surface of the *coca*. Strew the
onions over the tomatoes and arrange the anchovy strips in a pattern
over the onions. Let rest and bake as directed above. Remove from
the oven, sprinkle with the extra-virgin oil, and top with a light
dusting of paprika.

ASSORTED TOPPINGS (CONTINUED)

TOPPING 3

1 tablespoon olive oil
1 red bell pepper, stemmed,
  seeded, and sliced into thin
  strips
3 ounces firm *chorizo*, sliced
  into thin rounds

2 large, ripe tomatoes, thinly
  sliced
Extra-virgin olive oil, optional

Heat the oil in a medium skillet. Cook the peppers until soft but not browned. Add the *chorizo* and cook for 2 minutes. Drain the excess oil.

Arrange the tomato slices over the surface of the *coca*. Scatter the pepper and *chorizo* over the tomatoes. Let rest and bake as directed above.

Can be sprinkled with extra-virgin olive oil after baking, if desired.

SALSA DE ROMESCO
Sweet Red Pepper and Almond Sauce

*Romesco is one of the great Catalan sauces that can be served along-
side grilled meats, fish, and vegetables, can be a component of a wonderful fish stew (see Romesco de Peix, page 278), or can be an
indispensable accompaniment to Calçots, page 386. This recipe makes
a lot but keeps well refrigerated for 2 weeks. It can also be easily cut
in half, but you will find so many uses for it that you'll want to make
the full amount.*

MAKES 5 CUPS.

1 cup whole almonds
3 1-inch-thick slices white
bread
6 garlic cloves, unpeeled
2 red bell peppers, stemmed,
seeded, and chopped
6 tomatoes, quartered
3 tablespoons paprika

1 teaspoon salt
1 teaspoon freshly ground black
pepper
1 tablespoon hot red pepper
flakes
2 cups olive oil
1 cup red wine vinegar

Preheat the oven to 400°F.

Place the almonds, bread, and garlic on a baking sheet and bake
until the almonds and bread are toasted, about 15 minutes. Cut the
bread into cubes and place along with the almonds in a food processor. Whirl until very finely ground.

Peel the garlic and add to the processor along with the bell peppers, tomatoes, paprika, salt, black pepper, and pepper flakes. Whirl
until the mixture is smooth. With the motor running, gradually add
the oil and then the vinegar until the sauce is thick and smooth.

TORTILLA BANDERA
Triple-Layered Vegetable Omelet

This tortilla is a real architectural feast. Don't be overwhelmed by all the instruction. It is not that difficult to make and it is so delicious and beautiful that you will want to add it to your kitchen.

We had known this tortilla before as three separate omelets stacked one on top of the other. Antonio Buendía, the talented Catalan chef who came to Café Tango in California from Montse Gillian's Spanish restaurant in New York, introduced us to this version and it is so wonderfully interesting. The colors are supposed to represent the flag of Spain, by the way.

SERVES 8 TO 12

3 small heads broccoli   Salt and white pepper
1 large head cauliflower   12 eggs
   Olive oil
3 large red peppers, stemmed,
   seeded, and cut into 1-inch
   squares

Separate the florets from the broccoli and cauliflower and cook separately in lightly salted boiling water. Cook only until just tender. Drain and keep the vegetables separate.

Heat 1 tablespoon of oil in a skillet. Cook the peppers until soft, lightly sprinkling with salt and white pepper to taste as they cook. Remove from the heat.

Heat 1 tablespoon of oil in a 10-inch heavy skillet, over low to moderate heat. For best results, use a well-tempered cast-iron skillet.

Meanwhile, beat 4 of the eggs with salt and white pepper to taste. Combine the peppers with the eggs and pour into the hot oil. Cook until set on the bottom. Put a plate or pizza pan over the top of the skillet and turn the omelet out onto the pan and then slide it back into the skillet. Use a spatula to tuck the edges under. Cook until set.

Beat 4 more of the eggs and combine with the broccoli. It will seem as if there are not enough eggs, but don't worry. Season with salt and white pepper to taste. Arrange the egg-coated broccoli on top of the red pepper omelet, leveling it with the back of the spatula. Cook for about 8 minutes. Turn the whole omelet over using the pizza-pan method again.

Combine the cauliflower with the remaining 4 eggs, adding salt and white pepper to taste. Again there will not seem to be enough eggs. Pour the cauliflower mixture over the omelet and flatten it with the back of the spatula. Cook for abut 10 minutes, occasionally running a spatula around the edge of the omelet. Turn the whole tortilla over using the pizza pan again. Cook until the tortilla is firm. It may be necessary to turn it over again. It will be golden and beautiful.

Serve immediately, cut into wedges. Also good at room temperature.

XATO
Escarole Salad with Tuna and Almond Sauce

*A salad, a festival, and a sauce. The festival, in Vilanova i la Geltrú,
takes its name and purpose from this simple salad with an incredibly
delicious sauce of the same name. Indeed the sauce is another type of
romesco sauce, so, of course, the Catalans would take an opportunity
to celebrate as they do many other romesco-related dishes. This salad
is usually made with chicory, which the Catalans call escarole.*

SERVES 6 TO 8.

SALAD

1 head escarole, washed and drained

1 head chicory, washed and drained

1 12½-ounce can of albacore tuna, flaked

½ medium onion, cut into rings

12 good-quality black olives

2 ripe tomatoes, quartered

Tear the cleaned escarole and chicory into pieces and arrange on a
platter. Scatter the tuna, onion, olives, and tomatoes over the
greens. Half an hour before serving toss with the dressing and rear-
range attractively. Let stand at room temperature. The greens
should wilt a little from the dressing before serving.

SAUCE

1 *ancho* chili

¼ cup hazelnuts

¼ cup almonds

6 garlic cloves, unpeeled

2 small tomatoes, quartered

8 sprigs of parsley

⅓ cup olive oil

2 tablespoons red wine vinegar

¾ teaspoon salt

½ teaspoon freshly ground black pepper

Preheat oven to 400°F.

Bring a small pot of water to a boil. Add the chili pepper and
remove from the heat. Let stand until needed.

Place the nuts and garlic cloves on a baking sheet and bake until
the nuts are toasted, about 12 to 15 minutes.

Transfer the nuts to a food processor or blender and finely chop.

Slip the skins off the garlic and combine with the nuts. Add the tomatoes and parsley to the nuts and whirl to form a paste. Drain the chili pepper. Stem and seed it and add to the food processor. Puree. With the motor running add the oil, vinegar, salt, and pepper. Proceed as directed above.

ESPINACAS CATALANAS
Spinach with Pine Nuts, Raisins, and Apricots

This spinach dish was a main draw at Café Tango because it is simple, colorful, and bursting with flavors. The combination of the vegetable with the pine nuts and raisins make this a Catalan classic.

SERVES 6

3 bunches spinach
2 tablespoons salted butter
⅓ cup pine nuts

⅓ cup raisins
⅓ cup dried apricots, cut into pine nut–size pieces

Clean the spinach very well. It is not necessary to remove the stems. Place the cleaned spinach in a large pan. Cover and cook until wilted, about 5 minutes. (There is enough water clinging to the leaves to cook the spinach without any additional liquid.)

Drain the spinach. When cool enough to handle, squeeze dry with your hands. Chop the spinach and set aside. This can be done early in the day.

Heat the butter in a skillet. Add the pine nuts, raisins, and apricots and cook over medium heat until the pine nuts and apricots are golden and the raisins plumped. Stir in the spinach and toss to combine. Cook until it is heated through.

Serve immediately.

NOTE: We do not usually add any salt or pepper, but we do use salted butter.

ESQUEIXADA DE BACALAO
Codfish Salad

Bacalao—dried, salted codfish—appears in the cuisine of both Spain and Portugal. This dish, however, is found only in Catalonia and is often served as a first course.

SERVES 6

Begin preparation 24 hours in advance.

1 pound boneless skinless salt cod

1 red or green bell pepper, stemmed, seeded, and cut into strips

1 medium red onion, peeled and thinly sliced

1 ripe tomato, cut into quarters

½ to ¾ cup extra-virgin olive oil

¼ cup red wine vinegar

4 large garlic cloves, chopped
Salt and freshly ground black pepper to taste

12 black olives

2 hard-boiled eggs, quartered

Soak the cod in cold water for at least 24 hours (longer is better), changing the water several times. Drain and shred the cod by hand. (Do not use a knife, as that will cause the flesh to compact and stick together.)

Toss the cod with the bell pepper, onion, and tomato.

Combine the oil, vinegar, and garlic in a bowl, blend well, and pour over the cod. Toss the mixture and season with salt and pepper. Garnish with the olives and hard-boiled eggs.

Serve with Tortilla Bandera, page 254, as a complete lunch or light supper.

FLAN DE BACALAO Y COLIFLOR
Salt Cod and Cauliflower Flan with Red Pepper Sauce

Combining salt cod and cauliflower intensifies the flavors of both, and the resulting flan is creamy with very distinct character. This is really one of the best flans we have ever tasted. The spectacular view from Le Mirador de les Caves, the lovely restaurant perched high above San Sadurní de Noya, sparkling-wine capital of Spain, was just an added bonus when we first had this dish.

SERVES 8.

Begin preparation 24 hours in advance.

½ pound boneless skinless salt cod	1 teaspoon salt
1 1-pound head cauliflower	½ teaspoon white pepper
2 cups cold milk	Grating of nutmeg
2 tablespoons butter	4 eggs
1 tablespoon all-purpose flour	2 red bell peppers
	⅓ cup cream

Soak the cod in cold water for 24 hours, changing the water several times. Drain the cod, squeeze dry, and cut into chunks.

Preheat the oven to 350°F.

Separate the cauliflower into florets and steam over boiling water until very tender.

Heat 1 cup of the milk in a small pan and poach the cod in the milk for about 5 minutes. Do not let the milk boil. Remove pan from heat and let cool.

Heat the butter in a small saucepan. Stir in the flour and cook for 1 minute. Add the remaining cup of cold milk all at once and cook over medium heat, stirring constantly until it thickens. Season with the salt, white pepper, and nutmeg. Remove from heat and let cool.

Whirl the cauliflower in the blender or food processor with the cod, poaching milk, white sauce, and eggs. Taste for seasoning. Set aside 1 cup.

Pour the flan into a buttered glass baking pan or other 5-cup mold. Place the baking pan in a larger container with boiling water coming halfway up the sides of the baking pan. Bake until a knife inserted in the center comes out clean, about 35 minutes.

Meanwhile, place the peppers on a baking sheet and roast for 30 minutes in the oven until they blister and begin to char. You can do this while the flan is cooking. Remove the peppers and place them in a paper bag. Close the bag and let the peppers steam for 15 minutes. Take the peppers out of the bag and stem, seed, and peel them. Whirl the peppers with the reserved flan mixture and cream. Warm in a small pan. Taste for seasoning, adding more salt and pepper if desired.

To serve, unmold and slice the flan while it is hot. Arrange the slices on a platter with the sauce poured down the center of the row of slices or serve on individual plates in a pool of the sauce. Serve immediately. Can also be sliced cold and reheated in the oven or microwave.

TARTA DE ESCALIVADA
Eggplant, Pepper, and Tomato Tart

Escalivada refers to vegetables that have been cooked in hot ashes, but today in Spain the vegetables are more often cooked over a wood fire or in the oven. Cooking the vegetables over wood gives them a wonderful smoky flavor. If you want, you can cook the vegetables for this tart that way. Nowadays, stylish Catalan cooks like to play around with their basic Catalan preparations, and this vegetable tart is an excellent example of that approach.

SERVES 6 TO 8.

TART SHELL
- 1 cup all-purpose flour
- ½ cup butter

FILLING
- 1 pound eggplant, sliced into ½-inch-thick pieces (unpeeled)
- 4 medium tomatoes
- 2 medium onions, peeled and sliced into ½-inch-thick pieces

- 3 tablespoons ice water

- 1 red bell pepper
- Olive oil
- Salt and freshly ground black pepper
- 4 eggs, beaten
- ⅔ cup cream
- ¼ teaspoon salt

To prepare the tart shell—In the food processor pulse the flour with the butter. Gradually add the ice water, pulsing until the dough is well dampened. Gather the dough into a ball, wrap in plastic wrap, and refrigerate for 30 minutes.

Remove the dough and flatten and roll out on a floured board into a 12-inch circle. Place the dough in a 9-inch tart pan, folding the edges under and pressing them against the sides of the pan. Refrigerate for 30 minutes. Ten minutes before the tart shell is ready to come out of the refrigerator, preheat the oven to 400°F. The oven will stay on until the filled tart is baked.

Line the shell with waxed paper and fill it with dried beans or pie weights. Bake for 10 minutes. Remove the beans and paper and cook the shell another 8 minutes.

Meanwhile, prepare the filling—Place the sliced eggplant, whole tomatoes, sliced onion, and whole bell pepper on 1 or 2 baking sheets. Sprinkle with olive oil, salt, and pepper to taste and place in the oven.

After 10 minutes remove the tomatoes. Peel and seed them and set aside.

Roast the eggplant and onions until golden and turn to cook on the other side. Remove the eggplant and onions and coarsely chop.

Continue to cook the red pepper until the skin blisters. Remove it and place it in a paper bag. Close the bag and let steam 15 minutes. Peel, stem, and seed the pepper. Chop coarsely.

Combine all the vegetables in a bowl. Stir in the eggs and cream, ¼ teaspoon salt, and ¼ teaspoon pepper. Taste for seasoning. Pour into the prepared tart shell and bake in the oven for 20 minutes.

Serve hot or at room temperature.

NOTE: Milk can be substituted for cream. If so, cook about 20 minutes longer.

ARROZ NEGRO SIN TINTA
Black Rice

This is a variation on a well-known Catalan dish of rice that is tinted black with squid ink. We kept hearing of a black rice made without the ink and finally tasted it at the home of a wonderful waiter we met at Lérida. We had such a good time talking about all the foods at the restaurant that he invited us to his home to taste his arroz. *It was delicious, and while not quite black, at least a decent dark gray.*

We use a 12-inch paella pan to prepare and serve this dish. It can also be done in a nonreactive skillet.

SERVES 6

⅓ cup olive oil
1 large onion, minced
3 garlic cloves, minced
2 medium artichokes, bottoms only, cleaned and finely minced
1 pound cleaned squid, cut into ¼-inch rings

7 cups boiling Fish Stock, page 149, or water
3 cups short-grain rice, preferably Arborio
2 teaspoons salt
1 recipe hand- or machine-made Allioli (page 248) optional

Heat the oil in a 12-inch skillet. Add the onion, garlic, and artichokes and sauté over medium heat, stirring often, for 10 minutes.

Add the squid and cook 5 minutes.

Pour in 1 cup of the boiling stock or water and cook over medium heat until dry.

Stir in the rice and salt.

Pour in the remaining 6 cups of boiling stock or water. Bring to a boil, lower the heat, and cook for 20 minutes. Do not stir. (You can slide the pan around on the burner so the heat source reaches all areas of the pan.) Remove the pan from the stove and cover with a cloth. Let rest for 10 minutes or longer.

The Spanish, in general, don't care if a rice dish is piping hot when served. It certainly makes it easier to assemble the rest of the menu if you can have done the rice a bit in advance. We love the rice with a couple of spoonfuls of *allioli*, so you can stir some of it right into the rice.

VARIATION: If you want your rice really black, follow the recipe above but eliminate the artichokes. You can add ¼ cup slivered prosciutto if you wish. Dissolve two packages of squid ink (available in specialty stores and many Latin markets) in ½ cup hot water. Substitute this ½ cup for ½ cup of the stock.

NOTE: In uncleaned squid you will find a little ink pouch under the tentacles when you pull them from the body tube. It's an awfully little bit of ink and it takes a lot of squid to get enough of it, but it is possible to get ink this way.

ARROZ ABANDA
Rice Cooked in Fish Stock

This version is billed as "the best arroz abanda *in all of Spain" at the restaurant La Pegola in Denia, on the coast south of Valencia. We must agree. The rice glistened in the pan golden brown from the sofrito and the fish stock. We dug our forks into the rice and found the* quemada—*the crusty bottom of the pan, the sign of a perfectly done rice dish. Each grain of rice was distinct and full of flavor.*

Equally famous is fideuà abanda, *the same recipe and preparation but with short pieces of thin* fideos *(noodles) substituted for the rice. It's quite delicious with a unique melting texture.*

SERVES 4 TO 6.

4 tablespoons olive oil
1 medium onion, minced
3 garlic cloves, minced
2 pounds tomatoes, chopped
8 cups homemade Fish Stock,
   page 149

½ teaspoon saffron threads
3 cups short-grain rice
1 tablespoon salt
2 cups hand- or machine-made
   Allioli, page 248

Heat 2 tablespoons of the oil in a large nonreactive skillet. Cook the onion and garlic over medium heat until soft. Stir in the tomatoes and cook slowly to a paste. Pour in the stock and cook until reduced to about 6 cups. Strain the stock into another pan, discarding the solids, and bring to the boiling point.

Heat a paella pan or other flat skillet and toast the saffron, crushing it with the back of a spoon. Do not let it burn. Add the remaining 2 tablespoons of oil to the saffron and stir in the rice. Stir and cook until the rice is coated with the oil and begins to color. Add the salt. Gradually add the stock—without stirring the rice—one cup at a time, adding more stock only when the rice has absorbed all of the previous stock. Ideally, a nice crust, called a *quemada*, will have formed on the bottom of the pan and the rice will be tender but not mushy. Allow the rice to rest, covered with a towel, for 5 minutes before presenting it at the table. Pass the *allioli* for guests to stir into the rice if they wish.

NOTE: Some purists say that the *allioli* should only be served with the rice if you are serving the fish that went into the stock as well. Since at this point the fish would have given all its flavor to the stock, it would need some *allioli* for taste. We find that the *allioli* stirred into the rice punctuates the already-creamy texture and makes it even more appealing.

PATATAS FRITAS CON ALLIOLI
Deep-Fried New Potatoes with Allioli

Hot and crisp on the outside with creamy essence of potato on the inside, and topped with a dollop of cool garlic mayonnaise, these potatoes are one of our favorite tapas. And from the numbers of orders of these that we served at Café Tango, we are not alone.

SERVES 4 TO 8.

2 pounds red new potatoes
  Olive oil for deep frying (not
  extra-virgin)
  Salt

1 recipe hand- or machine-made
  Allioli, page 248

Bring a large pot of salted water to a boil and cook the potatoes, whole, until they feel tender when pierced with a fork. Drain the potatoes. When cool enough to handle, cut into quarters or eighths, depending on their size. (The potatoes can be precooked and fried much later, but do not cut them until it is time to fry.)

Heat the oil, preferably in a deep-fat fryer, to 365°F. If using a regular frying pan, check the temperature with a deep-fat thermometer and carefully maintain the temperature, because olive oil will burn if its gets hotter than that.

Fry the potatoes until golden. Drain on paper towels. Toss with salt and heap on a platter.

Serve immediately with the *allioli* on the side or put a big dollop on the top.

CARACOLES CON SALCHICHÓN Y VINAGRETA
Snails and Sausages in Vinaigrette

Snails are a favorite treat in Spain at Easter. The snails have been sealed in their shells for the winter and poke out their heads in the spring to feed on all the new little shoots. They are at their tastiest then. There is a famous spring festival in Lérida in Catalonia, where snails are the center of the feast. This recipe is from nearby.

SERVES 6 TO 8

DRESSING

1 tablespoon balsamic vinegar

2 teaspoons red wine vinegar

1 garlic clove, peeled

1 teaspoon mustard

2 tablespoons olive oil

Salt and freshly ground black pepper

SNAILS AND SAUSAGES

1 tablespoon olive oil

1 pound breakfast sausage links, cut into ¾-inch pieces

3 garlic cloves

1 large onion, minced

24–30 snails (if canned, refresh under cold running water. If fresh, see headnote at Rabbit with Snails, page 294)

To prepare the dressing— Combine all the ingredients and let rest while the snails and sausages cook.

To prepare the snails and sausages—Heat the oil in a nonreactive skillet, and cook the sausages until done. Remove and set aside.

In the same pan cook the garlic and onion slowly until the onion begins to caramelize. Pour in ¼ cup hot water and stir. Return the sausages to the pan along with the snails. Cook until heated through and the pan is dry.

Stir in the dressing and toss well.

Serve hot from the same pan or a small, preheated casserole, with small plates and tiny forks or toothpicks. Spear a piece of sausage and a snail for each bite.

SAMFAINA
Vegetable Stew

Samfaina is one of the basics of Catalan cuisine, related to the rata-
touille of France and the caponata of Italy. The Catalans do a lot
more with their version, though, making it into a sauce by pureeing it
(sometimes adding cream), using it as a base for other dishes such as
Pollo en Samfaina, page 286, and serving it as a vegetable side dish.

SERVES 6 TO 8

¼ cup olive oil
2 medium onions, thinly sliced
2 garlic cloves, sliced
2 red bell peppers, seeded and
cut into ½-inch cubes
1 pound eggplant, peeled and
cut into ½-inch cubes
5 ounces zucchini, cut into
½-inch cubes

½ pound tomatoes, peeled,
seeded, and chopped
1 teaspoon salt
1 teaspoon freshly ground
black pepper
2 sprigs of fresh parsley
1 sprig of fresh thyme

Heat the oil in a large skillet. Cook the onions and garlic over low
heat until very soft, about 20 minutes. Add the bell peppers and
cook for another 10 minutes. Add the eggplant and zucchini and stir
to coat with the oil. Cover and cook for 15 minutes. Uncover and
stir in the tomatoes, salt, pepper, parsley, and thyme. Cook, uncovered, over low heat until the eggplant is soft. Taste for seasoning.

VARIATION: Do not peel the eggplant, and do not cover the pan at
any time. Increase the amount of tomato by ½ pound.

This method produces a vegetable stew that lets you still be aware
of the individual vegetables.

SOPA DE PELOTAS
Meatball and Pasta Soup

This soup, accompanied by a salad, is really substantial enough to serve as the main course for a lunch or light supper. In that case, count on only four servings.

SERVES 4 TO 6

2 1-inch-thick slices bread
½ medium onion, peeled
3 garlic cloves, peeled
3 tablespoons fresh mint
   Salt and freshly ground black pepper
⅛ teaspoon cinnamon
1 egg

¼ pound ground veal or beef
¼ pound ground pork
⅓ cup all-purpose flour
8 cups good-quality chicken broth, preferably homemade (page 147)
3 ounces vermicelli, broken into small pieces
   White pepper

Puree the bread, onion, garlic, mint, ½ teaspoon salt, ¼ teaspoon pepper, cinnamon, and egg in a food processor. Pour into a large bowl and mix thoroughly with the ground meats. Form into 18 to 24 meatballs. Dredge with the flour, shaking off excess flour. Discard any leftover flour.

Bring the broth to a boil. Drop the meatballs into the boiling broth, lower the heat to medium, and cook for 10 minutes. Add the vermicelli and cook another 10 minutes. Season with salt and white pepper to taste. Serve hot.

CHÍCHAROS CON CEBOLLA CARMELIZADA
Black-Eyed Peas with Caramelized Onion and Anchovies

Black-eyed peas, a favorite in the southern United States and a dish Ann's mother served every New Year's day to ensure a lucky, prosperous, and healthy year, are very popular in Spain, especially in Catalonia. Neither of us was particularly fond of this legume until we tasted it at L'Olivé in Barcelona. Absolutely do not leave out the anchovies.

SERVES 6

Begin preparation 24 hours in advance.

1 pound dried black-eyed peas	2½ teaspoons salt
1 whole, small onion, plus 3 medium onions, peeled and sliced into ¼-inch-thick rings	2 tablespoons butter
	½ teaspoon freshly ground black pepper
6 whole cloves	1 cup dry white wine
1 bay leaf	2 2-ounce cans anchovy fillets

Clean the beans, removing any stones. Rinse under cold running water, then soak overnight in 3 to 4 cups of cold water.

Drain and rinse the beans. Combine with the whole, small onion studded with the cloves and bay leaf in the stockpot. Pour in cold water to cover by 2 inches. Bring to a boil, lower the heat, and cook for 40 minutes. Add 2 teaspoons of the salt. Continue to cook until the peas are tender, about another 10 minutes. Drain and discard the clove-studded onion, bay leaf, and cooking liquid.

Meanwhile, heat the butter in a skillet. Cook the onion rings slowly for 15 minutes, sprinkling them with the remaining ½ teaspoon salt and pepper as they cook. Pour in the wine and cook over moderate heat until the pan is dry and the onions have begun to caramelize. Remove from the heat.

To serve, arrange the black-eyed peas at one end of a large platter. Heap the onion rings beside the peas. Drain the anchovy fillets of excess oil and arrange at the end of the platter beside the onions. Encourage your guests to take some of each and mix each biteful.

BERENJENAS RELLENAS CON ANCHOAS L'EMPORDÁ
Baked Eggplant with Tomatoes and Anchovies

Ampurdán, an excellent restaurant in Figueres, has a rather institutional decor but lots of light. The foods they serve are a wonderful mix of classic dishes from the L'Empordá region and some modern adaptations.

The very satisfying flavors of these eggplants can stand alone as a first course or can accompany a simple grilled fish or meat course.

SERVES 4 TO 8.

2 1-pound eggplants
3 tablespoons olive oil
5 anchovy fillets

3 large tomatoes, peeled and
   seeded

Preheat the oven to 375°F.

Do not peel the eggplants. Cut the eggplants into quarters lengthwise, place on a baking sheet, and sprinkle with 2 tablespoons of the oil. Place in the oven and bake for 20 minutes.

Meanwhile, heat the remaining tablespoon of oil in a small sauté pan. Mince the anchovies and sauté them in the oil until they dissolve. Chop the tomato pulp and slowly cook with the anchovies until it is dry and thick.

Remove the eggplant from the oven. With a thin-bladed knife, split open their tops lengthwise and divide the tomato sauce among them. Return to the oven and bake until the eggplant is tender, about 20 minutes.

Served immediately with the accumulated juices.

PATÉ DE MONTAÑA CON SALSA DEL MAR
Chicken Liver Flans with Prawn Sauce

The Spanish enjoy their many montaña *creations. This one may sound odd but tastes delicious. The smooth richness of the pâté is balanced by the texture, color, and sharper flavors of the sauce.*

It is a very dramatic first course. Don't be daunted by the length of this recipe. Much can be prepared ahead, which makes it simpler than it looks. These flans make a fantastic party dish.

SERVES 8

PÂTÉ

1 garlic clove	¾ cup milk
½ pound chicken livers	½ teaspoon salt
4 eggs	⅛ teaspoon white pepper
¼ cup cream	Grating of nutmeg

SAUCE

3 tablespoons unsalted butter	½ cup dry white wine
1 small onion, minced	½ cup cream
2 garlic cloves, minced	¼ teaspoon salt
1 pound tomatoes, chopped	⅛ teaspoon white pepper
½ pound prawns in their shells	

Preheat the oven to 350°F.

To prepare the pâté—Mince the garlic in a food processor or blender. Add the remaining pâté ingredients and puree. Pour into 8 well-buttered ½-cup molds. Place the molds in a flat-bottomed glass baking dish. Pour boiling water into the dish so that it comes halfway up the sides of the molds. Bake until the flans are firm to the touch, about 20 minutes. Remove from the oven and remove the flan molds from the water. (All of this can be done ahead and reheated in the oven or microwave before serving.)

To prepare the sauce—Heat 2 tablespoons of the butter and cook the onion and garlic until soft. Add the tomatoes and cook to a dry paste.

Meanwhile, peel the prawns and reserve the shells. Cut the

prawns into small pieces and set aside. (Refrigerate the prawns if preparing the sauce ahead.)

Heat the remaining tablespoon of butter in a small skillet. Add the prawn shells and cook briskly for 5 minutes. Add the wine and cook for 2 minutes. Strain the liquid into the tomato mixture.

Puree the tomato mixture in the blender with the cream. Pour through a fine sieve into a saucepan. Push down on the solids to extract as much sauce as possible. Season with the salt and pepper. (The sauce can be prepared ahead to here.)

To serve, reheat the sauce and add the prawns. Cook until the prawns are done—about 5 minutes. Immediately divide the sauce among 8 warmed plates, and unmold the hot flans onto each plate.

MAINS

SOPA DE ALBÓNDIGAS A LA MURCIANA
Meatball and Vegetable Stew

Sometimes you will find this dish served as a stew rather than a soup. Whole pieces of turkey leg will be cooked with vegetables and the meatballs added last.

In Catalonia you meet people from many parts of Spain, especially from Andalusia and Murcia. An old woman who now lives in a small village just south of Barcelona but who still holds tightly to the ways of her youth gave us this recipe. We enjoyed bowlfuls in her home on a cold, wet January Sunday.

SERVES 6.

1 pound raw, skinless turkey meat cut from the thighs
½ pound lightly smoked bacon or pancetta
4 garlic cloves, minced
1 tablespoon toasted pine nuts
2 tablespoons minced fresh parsley
1½ teaspoons salt
½ teaspoon white pepper
½ pound fresh bread crumbs

1 egg
8 cups Turkey Stock, page 147
¼ teaspoon freshly ground black pepper
1½ pound potatoes (red new potatoes or Finnish potatoes), peeled and cut into 1-inch cubes
2 celery stalks, tops removed, cut into ½-inch pieces

Combine the turkey, bacon, and garlic in the food processor and whirl to a medium grind (or use a meat grinder). Mix the ground meats with the pine nuts, parsley, 1 teaspoon salt, white pepper, bread crumbs, and egg. Mix well, using your hands, and form into 1-inch meatballs.

Bring the stock to a boil and add the meatballs. Lower the heat and cook for 15 minutes. Remove the meatballs. (The stew can be done ahead to this point. Allow everything to come to room temperature, then refrigerate.)

Taste the stock and add the remaining ½ teaspoon salt and black pepper. Season with more salt and pepper if necessary. Add the potatoes and celery to the stock and cook until tender. Return the meatballs to the pan and heat through.

Serve immediately, preferably in flat soup plates.

ROMESCO DE PEIX
Fishermen's Fish and Shellfish Stew

Romesco, romesco de peix. *The first a sauce, or many sauces; the second a fish stew. A son and grandson of Catalan fishermen once explained to us that fishermen would take the sauce romesco out on the boats to be eaten as an accompaniment to their fish dinner. And sometimes the sauce, which contains spices and vinegar, would be poured over raw fish to preserve it for a future meal on land—a stew —and thus* romesco *the stew was born.*

Whatever its origin, it's one of the best fish stews we've ever eaten.

SERVES 6 TO 8.

2 *ancho* chilies
6 tablespoons olive oil
26 prawns (about 1 pound), in their shells
  Salt
6 garlic cloves
2 1-inch-thick slices good-quality white bread
½ cup almonds or hazelnuts or a combination of the two
1 medium whole tomato
1 sprig of parsley
1 teaspoon paprika

3 cups Fish Stock, page 149
1 medium onion, peeled and minced
½ pound small clams, in their shells and scrubbed clean
½ pound mussels in their shells, beards removed and scrubbed cleaned
2 pounds mixed firm fish, monkfish, snapper, and sea bass, cut into 2- to 3-inch pieces

Place the chilies in a bowl and cover with boiling water. Leave in the water for 15 minutes. Drain and discard the water. Remove the stems and seeds. Chop the chilies and set aside.

Heat 3 tablespoons of the oil in a clay casserole or wide skillet about 3 inches deep. Add the prawns and sprinkle lightly with salt. Sauté 1 minute and remove. The prawns should not be fully cooked.

Add 2 tablespoons more oil to the pan and sauté the garlic, bread, and nuts until golden. Add the whole tomato and the chilies and cook 2 minutes more over medium-high heat.

Put this mixture, the *picada*, into the food processor; add the parsley, paprika, and black pepper and whirl to form a paste. Pour in 1 cup of the fish stock and continue to whirl until smooth.

Heat the remaining tablespoon of oil in the pan and sauté the onion until soft.

Stir in the puree. Pour in the remaining 2 cups of fish stock and add ½ teaspoon salt. Cook to reduce by half. (The dish can be prepared ahead to this point. Allow to come to room temperature, then refrigerate. Reheat before continuing.)

Taste the sauce for salt and add some if needed—keep in mind that the fish and shellfish will add a certain amount of salt. Arrange the clams, mussels, and fish in the sauce and cook for 5 minutes. Scatter the prawns over the fish and shellfish and cook until the clams and mussels have opened and the fish is cooked, about another 5 minutes.

Serve the stew on large dinner plates or in flat soup plates with plenty of bread for soaking up the sauce.

SALMÓN EN SALSA DE AZAFRÁN
Salmon in Saffron Sauce

Usually a recipe with saffron sauce has a rich cream base. This recipe from north of Barcelona is really different and really delicious. The saffron is part of a paste that is put on top of the salmon fillets and then the salmon is baked. This recipe is very easy and a perfect party dish served as a main course or first course.

SERVES 8 TO 10 AS A FIRST COURSE AND 6 AS A MAIN COURSE.

6 salmon fillets, 3 to 4 ounces
   each
2 tablespoons olive oil
   1-inch-thick slice white
   bread, crusts removed
2 garlic cloves

1 medium onion, chopped
½ teaspoon saffron threads
2 teaspoons fresh parsley
   leaves
½ teaspoon salt
½ cup dry white wine or fish
   stock

Preheat the oven to 400°F.

Check the salmon for any obvious bones, pulling them out with pliers if necessary.

Heat the oil in a skillet and cook the bread until golden. Remove the bread to a blender or food processor. Sauté the garlic and onion in the remaining oil. Add to the bread along with the saffron, parsley, and salt. Whirl.

Spread the paste on top of the salmon fillets and place them in a single layer in a baking pan. Pour in the wine or stock. Bake for 10 minutes, or until the salmon is cooked to your liking.

Serve immediately with some of the liquid poured over the fillet.

FILETE DE SALMÓN CON ANCHOAS
Salmon Fillets with Anchovies

Rich, flavorful salmon is not overwhelmed by this sauce, just given another dimension.

SERVES 6.

6 4-ounce salmon fillets
2 tablespoons olive oil
3 garlic cloves, minced
3 large or 6 small anchovy
   fillets
3 red bell peppers, stemmed,
   seeded, and cut into thin
   strips

12 black olives, pitted and
    chopped
⅔ cup dry white wine

Check the salmon for any obvious bones, pulling them out with pliers if necessary.

Heat the oil in a 12-inch skillet with a cover. Cook the garlic and anchovies until the anchovies dissolve and the garlic turns golden. Add the pepper strips and olives and cook until soft. Add the wine and cook quickly to reduce by half.

Place the salmon fillets on top of the anchovy mixture. Cover the pan and steam until the salmon is done, about 8 to 10 minutes.

Serve immediately.

PEZ DE SAN PEDRO A LA PARRILLA CON SALSA DE ACEITUNAS Y PIMIENTO DULCE
Grilled Fish with Olive and Sweet Red Pepper Sauce

We first tasted grilled fish with olive sauce in Andalusia. There the olive sauce was served like a Mexican salsa, cold on the side of the fish. You can find that olive sauce on page 123.

This particular grilled fish and warm olive sauce we had at Ampurdán, an outstanding restaurant in Figueres, home of the Dalí museum. It's about an hour north of Barcelona.

If you can, grill the fish over a fire. The smoky flavor of the fish is really wonderful with the sauce.

SERVES 6 TO 8.

3 pounds sea bass fillets or
  other firm white fish fillets
2 tablespoons olive oil
  Salt
½ teaspoon white pepper
1 onion, minced
6 garlic cloves, minced

½ pound tomatoes, chopped
2 red bell peppers, roasted,
  stemmed, seeded, peeled, and
  chopped
½ cup minced green olives
  Freshly ground black pepper
  to taste

Prepare a charcoal fire and allow it to burn until the coals are evenly white, or preheat the broiler.

Place the fish fillets on a platter and rub with 1 tablespoon of the oil, ½ teaspoon salt, and the white pepper. Set aside and let come to room temperature before cooking.

Heat the remaining tablespoon of oil in a pan. Add the onion and garlic and cook until they begin to color. Stir in the tomatoes and red peppers and cook until thick and dry. Puree the tomatoes and peppers and stir in the minced olives. Taste for seasoning. Keep warm or reheat before serving.

Place the fish on an oiled grill over the fire or cook under the broiler until done.

Serve the grilled fish topped with the warm olive and red pepper sauce.

LUBINA CON PIÑONES Y PASAS
Sea Bass with Pine Nuts and Raisins

L'Olivé, a bustling restaurant in Barcelona, is always full. The food there is very good and not overly sophisticated. This sea bass, with its Catalan combination of fruit and nuts, is a good example.

SERVES 6 AS A FIRST COURSE AND 4 AS A MAIN COURSE.

3 tablespoons olive oil
½ cup minced onion
⅓ cup pine nuts
⅓ cup raisins, preferably golden
2 pounds sea bass fillets, cut into 4 or 6 pieces
¼ teaspoon salt

¼ teaspoon white pepper
2 teaspoons fresh rosemary leaves
¾ cup dry white wine
3 tablespoons cold unsalted butter, cut into pieces

Heat 2 tablespoons of the oil in a large, nonreactive skillet and cook the onion until it begins to color. Add the pine nuts and raisins and cook until the nuts are golden. Remove the onions, pine nuts, and raisins and set aside.

Add the remaining tablespoon of oil to the skillet if it is dry. Cook the fish fillets until they begin to color, sprinkling them with the salt, pepper, and rosemary as they cook. Add the wine and bring to a boil. Lower the heat to medium and add the raisin mixture. Cook until the fish is tender, about 5 minutes, depending on the thickness of the fillets.

Remove the fish to a platter and keep warm. Raise the heat and boil the liquid in the skillet for 2 minutes. Gradually stir in the cold butter until a thick sauce is formed.

Pour the sauce over the fish and serve immediately.

MAR Y MONTAÑA
Chicken with Prawns

*The Costa Brava, north of Barcelona, is spectacular seaside country
with the mountains dropping dramatically into the Mediterranean.
The area along the sea harbors many delightful resorts and several
splendid restaurants—a combination not often found. Chicken and
prawns are another unusual combination but one that is very popular
in L'Empordà region. You will also find combinations of rabbit and
various shellfish.*

SERVES 6.

¼ cup whole almonds
21 prawns (about 1 pound)
1 bay leaf
¼ cup all-purpose flour
  Salt and freshly ground
  black pepper
½ teaspoon cinnamon
6 boneless skinless chicken
  breasts
1 tablespoon unsalted butter
3 tablespoons olive oil
1 medium onion, minced
¾ pound tomatoes, peeled,
  seeded, and chopped

2 tablespoons anise-flavored
  brandy
1 cup dry white wine
1 ounce unsweetened
  chocolate, minced or grated
3 garlic cloves, peeled and
  chopped
1 tablespoon fresh parsley
  leaves
  Pinch each of fresh thyme
  and oregano

Preheat the oven to 400°F. Toast the almonds on a baking sheet for
12 to 15 minutes.

Peel the prawns and set them aside. Place the shells in a small
saucepan with the bay leaf and cover with 5 cups of water. Bring to
a boil, lower the heat, and cook for 15 minutes. Drain, reserving the
stock and discarding the shells.

Place the flour, 1 teaspoon salt, ½ teaspoon pepper, and cinnamon in a bowl. Dip the chicken breasts into the flour mixture, coat-
ing the breasts on both sides.

Heat the butter and 1 tablespoon of the oil in a clay casserole or
skillet. Cook the chicken until golden on both sides and remove to a

platter. Add the prawns to the skillet, cook half a minute on each side, and remove to a platter.

Heat the remaining 2 tablespoons of oil in the skillet and cook the onion until golden. Add the tomatoes and cook until dry. Stir in the brandy, wine, and reserved stock, and cook until reduced by half.

Meanwhile, in a mortar, grind together the chocolate, garlic, toasted almonds, parsley, thyme, and oregano. Add a little of the reduced stock and grind the mixture to a paste.

Return the chicken to the sauce and cook for 5 minutes. Add the prawns and stir in the paste. Taste for salt and pepper, adding more if necessary. Cook until the chicken and prawns are cooked through and the sauce has thickened, about another 5 minutes.

Serve immediately, directly from the skillet or casserole.

POLLO EN SAMFAINA
Chicken with Mixed Vegetables Catalan Style

This is almost not a recipe, just a map leading to a very enjoyable dish. Ideally, this dish takes one full recipe of Samfaina, but if you have less it will work, too. Add a little broth or wine and some herbs, too, if you like.

SERVES 4 TO 6.

2 tablespoons olive oil
1 3½-pound chicken, cut into
  serving pieces
  Salt and freshly ground black
  pepper to taste

1 recipe *Samfaina* variation,
  page 270

Heat the oil (preferably in a clay casserole). Add the chicken, sprinkle with salt and pepper, and cook until golden on the outside but about half-cooked on the inside. Remove to a platter.

Pour off the excess oil in the casserole and stir in the *samfaina*. Return the chicken to the casserole and cook, stirring several times so it does not scorch, until just done, about another 30 minutes. Correct the seasoning, adding more salt and pepper if necessary.

Serve immediately, directly from the casserole.

POLLO A LA CATALANA
Chicken Catalan-Style (with Dried Fruits and Nuts)

The combination of the dried fruits, nuts, and meat and the use of the picada makes this a very Catalan recipe.

SERVES 6.

4 tablespoons olive oil
1 3½-pound chicken, cut
  into 8 pieces
6 ounces pitted prunes
⅓ cup black raisins
⅓ cup pine nuts
1 medium onion, minced
2 tomatoes, chopped

1 cup Chicken Stock, page 147
¼ cup whole almonds
1 1-inch-thick slice good-
  quality white bread
½ teaspoon salt
¼ teaspoon freshly ground
  black pepper

Preheat the oven to 350°F.

Heat 2 tablespoons of the oil in a skillet and sauté the chicken until golden. With a slotted spoon, remove the chicken to a platter. In the same skillet, sauté the prunes, raisins, and 2 tablespoons of the pine nuts until the fruit is plump and the nuts are golden. (With a slotted spoon, remove the fruits and nuts to the platter of chicken. Brown the onion in the skillet and add the tomatoes. Cook rapidly until all the liquid has evaporated. Pour in the stock, return the chicken, fruits, and pine nuts, and cook, uncovered, for 20 minutes.

Meanwhile, toast the almonds on a baking sheet in the oven for 12 minutes. Heat the remaining 2 tablespoons oil in a small skillet and sauté the bread until golden.

In a food processor, grind the almonds, bread, and remaining pine nuts to create the *picada*. Stir into the cooking liquid in the skillet along with the salt and pepper. Cook another 10 minutes and taste for seasoning, adding more salt and pepper if necessary.

Serve immediately, directly from the casserole.

PATO CON PERAS
Duck with Pears

Meat combined with fruit and nuts indicates a Catalan dish. This recipe is a variation on a Catalan classic that is more of a stew with the pears cut into cubes.

This is a perfect party dish. So much of the preparation can be done ahead and the presentation is really spectacular. The individual plates can be arranged in the kitchen, each with a leg, a breast, and an upright pear—definitely hearty fall or winter fare.

If you prefer smaller portions, cut the pears into halves and arrange a pear half and one piece of duck on each of eight plates.

SERVES 4 TO 8.

Begin preparation 24 hours in advance.

2 4-pound ducks	1 cup dry white or red wine
1 carrot, cut into 1-inch pieces	
1 medium onion, peeled and quartered	

PEAR SAUCE

6 pears, *small* Bosc or other, peeled, leaving stem attached	¼ cup brandy or pear brandy
1 carrot, minced	1 teaspoon salt
1 medium onion, minced	½ teaspoon white pepper
3 garlic cloves, peeled and minced	

Preheat the oven to 400°F.

Day one—Cut the ducks into 4 whole legs and 4 breasts. Cover and refrigerate. Reserve the backs, wings, and necks for the stock. Freeze the livers for a later pâté or a *picada*.

Place the duck backs, wings, and necks in a baking pan with the vegetables and brown in the oven for 1 hour.

Remove the duck parts and vegetables to a stock pot. Pour off any grease from the baking pan and add the wine to the pan. Scrape to loosen any particles and pour into the stock pot. Cover with cold water and bring to a boil.

Lower the heat and cook, partially covered, for 2 to 3 hours.

Strain the broth, discarding the bones and vegetables. Let cool to room temperature, then refrigerate overnight.

Next day—Remove the fat from the stock. Bring the stock to a boil and lower the heat to medium-high. Poach the pears in the stock until tender, about 20 minutes. Remove the pears and slice a piece from the bottom of each one so they will stand upright.

Cook the stock rapidly to reduce to 3 cups.

Preheat the oven to 400°F.

Heat a dry sauté pan until it is very hot. Place the duck legs in the pan, skin side down, and cook until golden. Remove the legs to a large baking pan or clay casserole. Pour off the fat from the sauté pan and reserve for cooking another time.

Reheat the pan and place the breasts in the pan, skin side down. Cook until golden. Remove the breasts and arrange around the legs.

Pour off all but 1 tablespoon of the fat. Add the carrot, onion, and garlic and sauté until golden, about 10 minutes. Add the brandy and cook until evaporated. Pour in the reduced duck stock and season with the salt and pepper.

Pour the sauce over the duck legs and breasts. Place in the oven and bake until the duck is tender, about 1 hour.

Near the end of the cooking time, reheat the pears in an oven or microwave.

Remove the legs and breasts to a platter, scraping off any sauce, surround with the pears, and keep warm. Cook the sauce quickly to reduce to the desired consistency and puree in a blender or food processor.

Serve immediately, with the sauce strained over the duck and pears.

PECHUGA DE PAVO RELLENO
A LA CATALANA
Stuffed Breast of Turkey Catalan Style

Turkey stuffed with dried fruits and nuts is a traditional Catalan
Christmas dish. Stuffing and braising only the breast is becoming
more popular, since the breast meat stays more moist cooked this way
and it is also very easy to carve and serve.

SERVES 6.

1 10½-pound turkey
2 tablespoons olive oil
½ pound mild Italian sausage,
    casing removed
½ cup pine nuts
1 Granny Smith apple, cored
    and finely chopped
½ pound assorted dried
    apricots, raisins, and pitted
    prunes

2½ cups Turkey Stock, page
    147
½ cup dry sherry
    Salt and freshly ground
    black pepper to taste

After disjointing the turkey as you would a chicken, place the breast, skin side down, on a cutting board and set the remaining pieces aside to be used in other recipes. (They may, of course, be frozen. I've found that it is a good idea to write what they are on the outside of the freezer package.) Using a thin-bladed boning knife, remove the breast bone first, then the rib bones, leaving the breast whole and the skin intact. This is relatively simple, just keep the knife close to the bone at all times. Reserve the bones for a stock.

Lay the breast out, skin side down.

Heat 1 tablespoon of the oil in a medium skillet and cook the sausage. Add the pine nuts and cook until golden. Stir in the apple and dried fruits and cook for 2 minutes. Add ½ cup of the stock and the sherry. Season lightly with salt and pepper and cook over medium heat until the fruits have absorbed the liquid. Cool slightly for easier handling.

There will be a natural trough between the breasts. Place the filling in the trough and bring up the sides and ends to encase the filling. Hold the sides together with long skewers. Tie the breast at

1-inch intervals and around from end to end, twice; then again a couple of times around to keep the two lengthwise strings in place.

Heat the remaining tablespoon of olive oil in a large pot with a cover and brown the breast all over. Pour in the remaining 2 cups of stock and bring to a boil. Lower the heat, cover, and cook until the internal temperature is 165°F., about 1 hour.

Remove the breast to a cutting board and let rest for 10 minutes. Skim the fat from the sauce and keep the sauce warm.

To serve, slice the breast and arrange on a platter, passing the sauce separately at the table.

PERDIZ EN COL
Partridge in Cabbage Rolls

We love cabbage. There is something homey and nurturing in the smell as it cooks and the way that it tastes. Cabbage can lend itself to fairly sophisticated cuisine, however, as in this dish. We first encountered this variation on the classic Catalan dish perdiu amb farcellets de col at Celler del Penedés, just outside of Vilafranca del Penedés. The original dish is partridge served with little fritters of cabbage. At first glance, there seem to be a lot of steps in the preparation, but just break them up and it really becomes a do-ahead party dish.

SERVES 6.

2 partridges or game hens, or 1 duckling
3 tablespoons olive oil
¼ pound pancetta, chopped
2 leeks, cleaned and chopped (white part only)
3 carrots, coarsely chopped
1 medium onion, coarsely chopped

3 garlic cloves, minced
Salt and freshly ground black pepper to taste
3 cups Chicken Stock, page 147
1 large head savoy cabbage

Preheat the oven to 450°F.

Thoroughly clean the birds, removing and discarding the giblets or freezing them for another use. Rub them with 1 tablespoon of the oil. Put the birds in the oven and immediately reduce the heat to 350°F. Begin to test them after 45 minutes of cooking by jiggling the leg. The leg hould move freely, and when pricked with a fork, the juices should run clear. When done, remove the birds from the oven and allow to cool before handling.

Reduce oven temperature to 350°F.

Heat the remaining 2 tablespoons of oil in a large ovenproof pan or casserole and sauté the pancetta until golden. Add the leeks, carrots, onion, and garlic and cook slowly over medium-low heat until tender. Season with salt and pepper. Remove half of the vegetables and set aside. Pour in the chicken stock and continue to cook the remaining vegetables slowly for 30 minutes.

Meanwhile, bring a large pot of salted water to a boil. Core the cabbage and gently separate the leaves, leaving them whole. Cook the leaves briefly until tender in the boiling water. Remove the leaves and drain and dry them.

Lay out 6 large leaves, patching any holes with smaller leaves. Reserve the remaining leaves. Remove the skin and bones from the birds, leaving the meat in fairly large chunks. Combine the meat with the reserved vegetables.

Divide the meat and vegetables among the 6 large leaves. Top with the remaining leaves and roll into 6 large bundles.

Puree the remaining vegetables and broth. If you wish, put it through a fine sieve. Return the puree to the pan or casserole. Place the rolls on top of the sauce, spooning some of the sauce over them. Cook in the oven until heated through and the sauce has thickened.

Serve directly from the pan or, more formally, arrange on individual plates with the sauce, and garnish with steamed baby carrots and steamed leek curls.

FRITADA DE CONEJO O POLLO CON CARACOLES
Rabbit or Chicken with Snails

This seems an unlikely combination but makes a delicious contrast of flavors and textures. It's found in Catalonia and other areas of the north—Aragón, Navarre, and Rioja. In Spain the snails are small and available at the market in their shells. Here, you can use canned snails without shells. Or better, get real revenge on the garden snails that have been nibbling on your herbs and eat them—they will be nicely preseasoned. Snails from the garden will need special handling. We refer you to Joy of Cooking, which contains complete information on the processing of garden snails.

SERVES 4 TO 6.

3 tablespoons olive oil
1 rabbit, cut into 6 pieces, or 1 3½-pound chicken, cut into 8 pieces
Salt and freshly ground black pepper
24 to 30 snails
6 garlic cloves, peeled and thinly sliced
¾ pound onions, peeled and minced
2 small red bell peppers, stemmed, seeded, and chopped
1 pound tomatoes, peeled, seeded, and pureed
2 sprigs fresh thyme or ½ teaspoon dried thyme
1 cup Chicken Stock, page 147

Preheat the oven to 350°F.

Heat the oil in a skillet. Add the rabbit or chicken and cook until golden, lightly sprinkling with salt and pepper as it cooks.

If using canned snails, refresh them under cold running water, removing any grit. Set aside.

Remove the rabbit or chicken from the skillet and set aside.

Add the garlic to the skillet and cook over moderate heat until browned. Add the onions and cook until soft. Stir in the peppers and cook 1 minute. Add the tomatoes and cook to a paste. Add the thyme and stock and cook until the liquid is reduced to ½ cup. Mix with the meat in an ovenproof casserole. Add the snails. Bake for 30 minutes.

Serve immediately, directly from the casserole.

CONEJO CON PERAS Y NABOS
Rabbit with Turnips and Pears

Turnips were a popular vegetable in the Middle Ages (before the potato came to Europe), so this recipe could go back several centuries. It is also typical of medieval cooking to mix fruit and game. Many dishes from the Middle Ages can still be found in the Catalan kitchen.

SERVES 6.

2 tablespoons olive oil
1 2½-pound rabbit, cut into 6 serving pieces
1 medium onion, peeled and minced
2 leeks, cleaned and finely chopped (white part only)
2 garlic cloves, peeled and minced
1 carrot, peeled and chopped
1 tomato, peeled, seeded, and chopped

1 bay leaf
Sprig each of fresh thyme, marjoram, and oregano
Salt and freshly ground black pepper
6 small pears, peeled and uncored
2 cups Chicken Stock, page 147
1 cup dry white wine
2 pounds turnips, peeled and cut into 3½-inch strips

Heat the oil in a large skillet and sauté the rabbit until golden. Remove the rabbit pieces. Add more oil if necessary and sauté the onion, leeks, garlic, and carrot until soft. Add the tomatoes, herbs, 1 teaspoon salt, and ½ teaspoon pepper and cook over high heat until reduced to a paste.

Return the rabbit to the sauce and arrange the pears around the rabbit. Pour 1 cup of the stock and the wine over all and cook, covered, over medium-low heat until the rabbit feels tender when pierced with a fork, about 30 to 45 minutes.

Meanwhile, bring the remaining cup of stock to a boil in a saucepan and add the turnips. Cook, covered, until tender but not falling apart. Drain, reserving the stock and setting aside the turnips on a heated platter.

Remove the rabbit and pears from the skillet to the heated platter of turnips and keep warm. Puree the sauce in a blender or food processor, pour it through a fine sieve into the skillet, and add the reserved turnip stock. Cook over high heat to reduce and thicken the sauce. Taste for seasoning, adding more salt and pepper if necessary. Pour the sauce over the dish and serve immediately.

CONEJO AL SALMOREJO
Rabbit Cooked in Wine and Vinegar with Herbs

This recipe involves a lot of steps, none of which takes much time. Once you start making and using picadas to flavor and thicken, you'll find the process very simple and rewarding.

SERVES 4 TO 6

Begin preparation 24 hours in advance.

1 2½-pound rabbit, cut into 6 serving pieces, liver reserved	3 cups dry white wine
	¼ cup olive oil
1 bay leaf	¼ cup whole almonds
1 sprig of fresh oregano	1 1-inch-thick slice white
1 sprig of fresh thyme	bread, crust removed
6 whole black peppercorns	1 teaspoon salt
8 garlic cloves, peeled	½ teaspoon freshly ground
⅓ cup wine vinegar	black pepper

Preheat the oven to 350°F.

Place the rabbit in a nonmetallic bowl. Add the bay leaf, oregano, thyme, peppercorns, garlic, vinegar, and wine. Cover the bowl and marinate the rabbit, refrigerated, overnight.

Remove the rabbit from the marinade and pat dry. Reserve the marinade.

Heat the oil in a large ovenproof skillet or clay casserole. Add the rabbit pieces and cook until golden. Remove the rabbit and set aside.

Remove the garlic from the marinade. In the oil remaining in the skillet, sauté the garlic until golden. Remove the garlic to a blender or food processor. In the remaining oil sauté the almonds, bread, and rabbit liver until golden. Remove the liver as soon as it is firm. Add the almonds, bread, and liver to the garlic and blend to a paste. Reserve.

Pour off any remaining oil from the skillet. Strain the marinade into the skillet and bring to a boil. Add the rabbit. Place the skillet in the oven and bake for 30 minutes.

With a slotted spoon, remove the rabbit pieces to a platter and keep warm. Place the skillet over a burner set to high and bring to a boil. Cook quickly to thicken. As it starts to thicken add the garlic paste, the *picada*. This will thicken the sauce more. Season with the salt and pepper. Cook to the desired consistency. Return the rabbit to the sauce and turn it to coat with the sauce.

Serve the rabbit at the table in the casserole.

CONEJO EN SALSA DE ALMENDRAS
Rabbit in Almond Sauce

At first glance this recipe and the recipe for Conejo al Salmorejo *seem to be very alike. They both use* picadas *to thicken and flavor, but the* picada *is used differently in each and the resulting flavors are unique to each dish. These two dishes demonstrate the variety of styles that can be achieved using a* picada.

SERVES 4 TO 6

¼ cup olive oil	1 tablespoon chopped parsley
1 medium onion, chopped	10 black peppercorns
6 garlic cloves	2 whole cloves
20 whole almonds	Pinch of saffron
1 2½-pound rabbit, cut into 6	1 teaspoon salt
serving pieces, liver reserved	2 cups dry white wine
½ teaspoon cinnamon	2 bay leaves

Heat 2 tablespoons of the oil in a skillet or clay casserole. Cook the onion, garlic, and almonds until the onion is limp and begins to color. Add the rabbit liver and cook until firm.

Place these ingredients in the blender or food processor with the cinnamon, parsley, peppercorns, cloves, saffron, and salt. Puree with ½ cup of the wine to a paste.

Heat the remaining oil in the pan and cook the rabbit pieces until golden. Stir in the paste, remaining wine, and bay leaves. Bring to a boil and cook until the rabbit is tender and the sauce has reduced and thickened, about 30 minutes. Discard the bay leaf.

Serve immediately, directly from the skillet or clay casserole.

TERNERA ASADA A LA ARAGONESA
Veal Shanks Aragón-Style

Veal is eaten more often than beef in Spain. Spanish veal is larger and tastier than most American veal. These braised veal shanks are economical but fancy enough for any dinner party.

SERVES 6.

All-purpose flour
3 whole veal shanks (have butcher cut each into several pieces)
½ cup olive oil
Salt and freshly ground black pepper to taste

1 medium onion, minced
3 garlic cloves, minced
2 celery stalks, chopped
¼ cup fresh rosemary leaves
2 cups dry white wine

Lightly flour the veal shanks. Heat the oil in a large skillet with a cover and cook the veal until golden, sprinkling lightly with salt and pepper as it cooks. Remove the shanks.

Add more oil to the skillet if necessary. Cook the onion, garlic, and celery until they begin to color. Add the rosemary and wine. Bring the wine to a boil and return the veal shanks to the skillet. Cover the skillet and cook the veal over low heat until tender, about 2 hours.

Remove the veal to a deep platter. If necessary, boil the sauce to reduce. Season with salt and pepper if necessary.

To serve, pour the sauce over the veal. This dish is delicious served with rice to soak up some of the wonderful juices.

BUTIFARRA AMB MONGETES
Sausage and Beans

Although we are using Castilian for the names of recipes throughout this book—except, of course, for such things as escalivada, which have no equivalent in Castilian—we make an exception here. This is not just butifarra con judías, sausages and beans, it is a very special Catalan eating experience. It was a real favorite at Café Tango, striking a chord as real comfort food with zip. We served ours with a generous dollop of allioli and recommend it that way. Butifarra are hard to come by in the United States, so we suggest you use a mild Italian sausage.

SERVES 6 TO 8.

6¼ pounds mild Italian
    sausages
2 tablespoons olive oil
6 cups Great Northern white
    beans, cooked and partially
    drained (see Lamb Shanks
    with White Beans, page
    406)

Salt and freshly ground
    black pepper to taste
1 cup Allioli, page 248
2 tablespoons finely minced
    fresh parsley

Prick the sausages in several places and grill or panfry until done.

Meanwhile, heat the oil and sauté the beans, seasoning with salt and pepper.

To serve, divide the beans among 6 plates and place a sausage on the side and a dollop of *allioli* on the top. Sprinkle with the parsley.

CIERVO CON SALSA DE ESCALOÑAS
Venison Steaks with Shallot Sauce

Venison, wild boar, hare, and other game are often found on Spanish menus in the fall and winter. Preparations range from simple grills to warming stews. These steaks, with their delicious sauce, are a wonderful match with one of the great red wines from Rioja or one of the older Torres Gran Coronas.

SERVES 6.

Begin preparation 24 hours in advance.

6 5-ounce venison steaks	Salt
1 bottle good-quality dry red wine	1 pound shallots, peeled and finely chopped
2 bay leaves	2 cups Veal Stock, page 148
6 juniper berries	8 ounces (2 sticks) cold
1 teaspoon coarsely ground black pepper, plus additional to taste	unsalted butter

Place the venison in a flat, nonreactive pan and add the wine, bay leaves, juniper berries, and coarsely ground black pepper. Cover and refrigerate for 24 hours.

Bring the steaks to room temperature. Remove the steaks from the marinade and pat dry. Strain the marinade and reserve the liquid. Discard the bay leaves and juniper berries.

Heat a dry skillet until it is very hot and sprinkle with a very little salt. Cook the steaks 2 minutes on each side and remove from the pan.

Add the shallots to the pan and pour in the reserved marinade and veal stock. Bring to a boil and cook over high heat until the liquid is reduced to 1½ cups. Return the steaks to the skillet and cook for 2 minutes on each side. Remove and keep warm.

Keep the butter in the refrigerator until just before using. When ready to use, cut it into small pieces. Turn the heat under the skillet to medium and gradually whisk in the butter, a piece at a time. You don't want the butter to melt too quickly or it will not combine with the sauce to thicken it. Season with salt and pepper if necessary.

To serve, place the steaks on individual plates with the sauce poured over. Delicious with a simple potato dish and seasonal vegetable.

SWEETS

CATANIAS
Chocolate-Covered Caramelized Almond Candies

Catanias are a specialty of Vilafranca del Penedés, just south of Barcelona. There you will find them as individual almonds, caramelized and coated in white chocolate and then rolled in ground chocolate. They are so good! If you don't have the patience to hand-dip each of the almonds, use this idea. They taste the same, just easier to achieve.

MAKES ABOUT 1½ POUNDS.

½ pound whole almonds with
  skins
½ pound sugar
½ pound white chocolate, in
  small pieces

2 tablespoons sweetened
  ground chocolate

Have ready a buttered 12-inch pizza pan.

Heat a heavy skillet. Add the almonds and cook for 1 minute. Pour in the sugar. Stir and cook the almonds in the sugar as it melts. The almonds will start to pop and crack. Keep stirring and cooking over medium heat for about 3 to 5 minutes. You don't want the caramel to burn, but it should get to be a very deep amber color.

Pour the almonds and caramel onto the prepared pizza pan and spread evenly. Allow to rest 5 minutes.

Sprinkle the white chocolate over the almonds. As the pieces melt, spread smoothly with a spatula.

When the white chocolate has set, dust the top with the ground chocolate. Break into pieces to serve. Keep tightly covered in a tin.

NOTE: This makes an attractive gift. Wrap the whole circle of candy in clear or colored cellophane and tie it with a big bow.

MONJA
Easter Bread

Monja *means "nun" in Spanish. Perhaps this Easter bread is so named in reference to the women who went to the tomb of Jesus and found it empty. Pure speculation. However, Easter breads with red-dyed eggs are popular throughout the Mediterranean.*

This one is baked in a circle and topped with a cross, with the eggs at the four corners of the cross. It makes a spectacular decoration for your Easter table and tastes great, too.

SERVES UP TO 20.

1¼ cups milk	Zest of 1 orange
⅓ cup sugar	4 eggs
1 tablespoon yeast	4½ cups all-purpose flour
¼ cup (½ stick) unsalted butter, softened	4 hard-boiled eggs, dyed bright red with food
2 teaspoons salt	coloring

Gently warm the milk in a saucepan. Remove from the heat and check the temperature—it should feel comfortably warm to the wrist. Stir in the sugar and yeast. After about 5 minutes the yeast will have dissolved and activated. Stir in the butter and salt.

In the food processor, whirl the orange zest, 3 of the raw eggs, and 1 cup of the flour. Add the remaining 3½ cups of flour. With the motor running, pour the milk mixture through the feed tube. Whirl for a minute. The dough will not necessarily pull together.

Remove from the processor and gather the dough into a ball; place the dough in an oiled bowl, turning the dough to oil all sides. Cover and let rise in a warm place until doubled in size.

Punch the dough down. Pull off a small handful of dough and set it aside. Flatten the large piece of dough into about a 10-inch circle and place on an oiled baking sheet. Make 4 indentations in the dough—at the top, bottom, and both sides.

Beat the remaining raw egg with a little water. Brush the dough with the beaten egg. Put one of the dyed eggs into each hole. Divide the reserved dough in half. Roll each half into a long rope of about 12 inches. Put one of these ropes over the dough, covering the tops of 2 of the eggs at opposite points of the "cross." Put the other rope over the first rope to cover the remaining 2 eggs. You will have formed a cross with an egg at the top of each point of the cross. Tuck the ends of the ropes under the loaf.

Preheat the oven to 370°F.

Let the dough rise for 30 minutes. Bake until the top and bottom of the bread are golden, about 35 minutes.

TOFFE DE CHOCOLATE CON CREMA DE MENTA
Chocolate Flan with Mint Sauce

A dense combination of chocolate that is part creamy custard, part rich chocolate cake, and part the best chocolate candy you've ever tasted, this specialty of restaurant Ampurdán in Figueres is a chocolate lover's dream.

SERVES 8 TO 10.

Begin preparations several hours in advance.

FLAN

12 ounces bittersweet chocolate, melted	6 eggs
1 cup sugar	1 teaspoon cinnamon
12 ounces (3 sticks) unsalted butter)	2 tablespoons dark rum

SAUCE

2 tablespoons sugar	1 cup crème fraîche
¼ cup crème de menthe	

Preheat the oven to 375°F.

To prepare the flan—Melt the chocolate in a double boiler and cool slightly.

Cream together the sugar and butter. Add the eggs and mix well. Stir in the chocolate, cinnamon, and rum.

Line a 9-inch pan with a removable rim with buttered paper and cover the outside bottom and sides of the pan with foil so that there is no chance of the water from the water bath seeping into it. Pour in the chocolate mixture. Cover the top of the pan lightly with foil.

Place the mold in a larger ovenproof container and pour boiling water halfway up the sides of the mold. Bake for 30 minutes. Remove the foil top and bake until the top of the cake is fairly firm, about 10 minutes longer. (The top should not poof up, however.)

Remove from the oven and take the mold from the water. Set aside. When cool, refrigerate for several hours or overnight.

To prepare the sauce—Dissolve the sugar in the crème de menthe and then stir into the crème fraîche. Allow the flavors to mingle several hours or overnight.

To serve, unmold the flan and slice ½ inch thick. Put a slice on each plate and pour a little of the sauce over or around the flan.

CREMA CATALANA
Soft Egg Custard with Burnt Sugar Topping

Each time we served this at Café Tango the aroma of burning sugar wafted through the restaurant, enticing other diners to order this simple custard dessert with its crust of burnt sugar. It is so much fun to use your spoon to break through the crust into the creaminess below.

SERVES 4 TO 6.

Rind of 1 lemon	½ cup sugar
1 2-inch piece cinnamon stick	2 tablespoons cornstarch
4 cups milk	Granulated sugar
8 egg yolks	

To prepare the custard—Combine the lemon rind, cinnamon, and milk in a heavy-bottomed saucepan and bring to a boil. Remove from the heat and let rest for 30 minutes.

Meanwhile, beat together the egg yolks, sugar, and cornstarch. Strain the milk, discarding the lemon peel and cinnamon, and add one cup to the eggs and beat. Return the rest of the milk to the saucepan. Add the egg mixture to the milk in the saucepan and cook over low heat, stirring until thickened. The custard should coat a spoon. Pour into a bowl and allow to cool. Refrigerate.

To caramelize the top—In Spain there is a special branding iron for this purpose—a round disk with a long handle. Sometimes these are available in kitchenware shops in the United States. If you don't have one of these irons, here are a few options.

Pour the custard into individual heatproof bowls and sprinkle the tops generously and evenly with granulated sugar, then:

Option 1: Place the bowl close under the broiler to brown the tops.

Option 2: Heat a small cast-iron-skillet on a burner until red hot and use it to scorch the surface of the custard.

Option 3: Use a small acetylene torch *carefully!*

Option 4: Do not sprinkle the sugar over the custards. Cover a baking sheet with wax paper. Measure the inside top of the bowls and draw this onto the paper. Heat 1 cup of sugar with 1 tablespoon water in a heavy pan and cook until a medium-dark caramel is formed. Using a fork, lift the caramel from the pan and quickly make a delicate latticework of the caramel within the circles on the paper. When this has cooled, peel away the paper and place the caramel on top of the custard just before serving.

BRAZO DE GITANO
Gypsy's Arm

The top of this rolled cake is sometimes covered with cream and then put under the salamander or broiler to brown the top, creating the browned arm of the Gypsy. Fillings vary from thick pastry creams to flavored whipped creams.

SERVES 8.

CAKE

5 eggs, separated
¾ cup sugar
 Grated zest of 1 lemon
½ teaspoon baking powder
 Salt

¾ cup cake flour
 Powdered sugar
1 tablespoon cocoa

FILLING

1⅓ cups cream
1 cup semi-sweet chocolate
 chips

1 tablespoon brandy
1 tablespoon sweet anise
 brandy

Preheat the oven to 375°F.

To prepare the cake—Beat the egg whites until they form stiff peaks. Set aside.

Beat the egg yolks with the sugar, lemon zest, baking powder, and a small pinch of salt until thick and lemon-colored.

Fold the egg whites gently into the yolks. Fold in the flour a third at a time. Do not overmix or you will lose the volume you have created in the eggs.

Pour into an ungreased paper-lined 10-by-15-inch jelly roll pan with a 1-inch lip. Bake until the cake is golden and has begun to pull away from the sides of the pan, about 10 to 12 minutes.

Have ready a clean towel lightly sprinkled with powdered sugar. Immediately after taking the cake from the oven, turn it out onto the towel and remove the paper. Roll the cake in the towel long sides toward each other. Cool in the towel.

Meanwhile, prepare the filling—Warm ⅓ cup of the cream in a small pan. Gently melt the chocolate in the cream. Pour in the brandy and anise and let cool.

Whip the remaining cream until stiff. Fold the cooled chocolate into the cream. Refrigerate for 30 minutes until the mixture begins to firm.

To assemble the cake—Unroll the cake and spread the chocolate cream over the surface, keeping a 1-inch border free all around. Carefully roll the cake and place on a platter. Combine 2 tablespoons of powdered sugar with the tablespoon of cocoa powder and sprinkle over the cake. Chill, covered, until serving. (The cake is firm enough to cut after one hour.)

TARTA DE MÚSICO
Musicians' Tart

The Spanish love music and recognize the worth of musicians. In the past, if a household was very poor, they might not be able to give the musicians any money or much food, but there were usually some dried fruits and nuts around and the musicians would be served a bowl to share. In time, this became an informal dessert for casual meals and was known as postre de músico, *or musicians' dessert. This tart is a modern development using the ingredients of the traditional* músico. *It is proper to eat it with your fingers just as you would the original* postre de músico.

SERVES 8.

PASTRY

1½ cups all-purpose flour	1 egg, separated
2 tablespoons sugar	3 tablespoons ice water
½ cup (1 stick) unsalted butter, cut into pieces	

FILLING

1 cup sugar	¼ cup minced pitted prunes
½ cup (1 stick) unsalted butter	½ cup raisins
½ cup whipping cream	1 tablespoon brandy
½ cup pine nuts	1 teaspoon almond extract
½ cup sliced almonds	
¼ cup minced dried mission figs	

To prepare the pastry—Combine the flour and sugar in the food processor. With the motor running, cut the butter into the flour with a few pulses. Add the egg yolk and quickly mix. Add the water, 1 tablespoon at a time, pulsing, until the mixture holds together.

Turn the pastry out onto a flat surface and gather into a ball. Flatten and roll into a circle to fit a 9-inch tart pan with a removable rim. Place the rolled dough in the pan. Turn the edges under to form a double rim.

Refrigerate the pastry for 30 minutes.

Preheat the oven to 350°F.

Line the tart shell with waxed paper and fill it with dried beans or pie weights. Bake for 15 minutes. Remove the paper and beans.

Beat the remaining egg white. Brush the crust with the beaten egg white and bake for 10 minutes more. Remove from the oven and set aside.

Raise the heat to 375°F.

To prepare the filling—Cook the sugar and butter in a heavy-bottomed pan, stirring until the sugar dissolves and begins to caramelize. Cook to a dark golden color. Pour in the cream and mix well. Stir in the nuts, fruits, brandy, and almond extract. Remove from the heat.

Pour into the tart shell and smooth the top. Place in the oven and bake for 20 minutes. Remove from the oven and allow the tart to rest until firm, about 2 hours.

Remove the rim and serve.

TARTA DE PERAS, NUECES Y QUESO
Pear Tart with Walnuts and Cheese

The best pears in Spain come from Lérida, we were told. This rustic, not-too-sweet pear-and-cheese tart covered with walnuts convinced me.

SERVES 8.

CRUST

2 cups all-purpose flour
1 cup (2 sticks) unsalted butter
Pinch of salt

3 to 5 tablespoons ice water
1 tablespoon granulated sugar

FILLING

5 large pears (about 3 pounds), peeled, cored, and cut into ½-inch cubes
1 cup walnut pieces, coarsely chopped

½ cup sugar
½ cup grated sharp cheese (aged *manchego*, Asiago, or Parmesan)
Grated zest of 1 lemon

Place the flour in the processor work bowl. Cut the butter into pieces. Add to the flour with the salt and pulse a few times to distribute and cut the butter finer. Add the cold water a tablespoon at a time, pulsing, until the butter is in very tiny pieces and the dough is dampened.

Gather the dough into 2 balls and wrap in plastic wrap. Flatten the balls. Refrigerate for 1 hour.

Uncover one of the dough halves and roll out on a floured surface. Roll into a 12-inch circle. Carefully transfer the dough to a 10-inch tart pan with a removable rim.

Preheat the oven to 400°F.

Combine all the ingredients for the filling and pour into the prepared shell.

Roll out the remaining dough half into a 12-inch circle. Cover the filling with the dough. Pinch the bottom and top dough overhangs together and tuck under attractively. Slit the top of the tart with a sharp knife in 2 or 3 places. Sprinkle the top of the tart with the tablespoon of sugar.

Place the tart on a pizza pan so any juices that run over won't go all over the oven. Bake for 15 minutes. Lower the heat to 350°F. and bake until the tart is golden and the fruit is tender, about 45 minutes more.

We like this tart served warm, no cream.

ZUMO DE NARANJA CON FRUTAS FRESCAS
Freshly Squeezed Orange Juice with Fruit

A big balloon glass half-filled with sliced fresh kiwi or tiny wild straw-berries or dead-ripe raspberries floating in freshly squeezed orange juice is one of the most welcome and refreshing desserts you can offer. A dramatic presentation makes it even more inviting.

Sliced kiwi, sliced strawberries, fresh raspberries, sliced figs, blueberries, or any good combination of fruits	Freshly squeezed orange juice

Slice or otherwise prepare the fruits and divide among 6 glasses or bowls. Cover with the orange juice and serve immediately.

NOTE: Don't let the fruit stand in the juice any length of time or it will begin to wilt. In Spain a bowl of granulated sugar is served with the dessert for each guest to add to his or her taste. We prefer it without.

HELADO DE CREMA CATALANA
Crema Catalana Ice Cream

This is an example of what some of the newer restaurants are doing to keep alive the classic recipes while inventing a new variation. We think this concept is so exciting because it is real—rooted in the authentic cuisine.

SERVES 6.

ICE CREAM
1 recipe Crema Catalana
(custard only), page 306

CARAMEL SAUCE
¾ cup sugar   ½ teaspoon vanilla
1 cup whipping cream

To prepare the ice cream—Cool the custard and refrigerate until cold.

Make the custard into ice cream according to your ice-cream machine's directions.

To prepare the caramel sauce—Heat a dry, heavy-bottomed skillet until it is very hot. Add the sugar and stir until a medium-dark caramel is formed. Pour in the cream and cook until there is a glistening surface of tiny bubbles. Add the vanilla and stir.

We prefer to serve this dish with the hot sauce poured over the cold ice cream, but the sauce can also be cooled to room temperature. If you make it ahead and want to serve it warm, heat it in a double boiler over warm water or warm in the microwave.

PART THREE
Budbreak

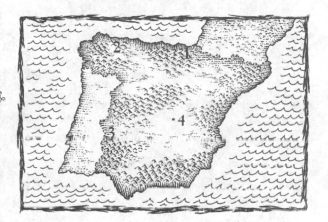

Budbreak. Where it all begins. Well, qualify that. Remember, in the circle of the vine's season there is truly no beginning, no end. Step into the circle at any point, but budbreak is traditionally thought of as the beginning of the vineyard year. The word defines itself. It is when the "force that through the green fuse drives the flower," as Dylan Thomas puts it, reaches the tip of the vine stem, swells, and bursts through.

After several weeks the first true leaves appear, then more weeks until flowering, which, in most vinegrowing districts happens mid-to late May. The flowers themselves seem insignificant, yet the fruit that makes the vintage is contained within the minuscule blossoms.

(For reasons that we don't understand—but that are, no doubt, perfectly clear to the more botanically minded—vines that produce large crops one year are likely to produce small crops the next year, and the other way around. Somehow, the vine carries within itself a diagram of the past to match against the future. Even the vine learns from history.)

The vine is most vulnerable during these first stages of growth. A sudden chill can kill the tender new growth; heavy rains, hail, or prolonged damp weather can shatter the budding flowers, so that little fruit will be set. All growing plants are particularly vulnerable during these early stages of life. It is a critical time, when the fruits of the season hang in balance. One could construct a fable using the vine as a metaphor, depicting modern Spanish culture as being in the flowering stage. It is also very vulnerable. The growing tips of the vine contain Spain's future, yet the country cannot escape the past.

PAÍS VASCA

I abandoned myself to shameless gluttony in San Sebastián, and went from little restaurant to little restaurant in the old city as one might move from picture to picture in the Prado. The Basques are perhaps the greatest eaters in Spain and no one, even in France, knows better how to cook the finest and most varied fish in the world.

—H. V. MORTON
A STRANGER IN SPAIN

IN FOCUS

The País Vasca (Basque country) as a state of mind is larger than the political entity. Politically, the three Basque provinces are Gipuzkoa, Bizkaia and Alaba or, in Castilian, Guipúzcoa, Vizcaya and Alava. But the Basque cultural influence extends south into Navarre and La Rioja. The Basque culinary influence, however, reaches around the world.

Language is the first item that separates País Vasca from the rest of Spain. The other languages of Spain—Castilian, Catalan, Galician, Andaluz—are all linked through the common mother language of Latin. Basque is completely different and is not related to any other European language. It does have certain vocabulary in common with some Berber languages of North Africa and some languages still spoken in the Causcasus. Recent research, based on bloodtypes and skull shapes has revealed the fascinating fact that the Basques may be the descendants of Cro-Magnon man, the original Europeans.

The Basques were already isolated in the steep valleys and mountains of the Pyrenees when the Romans arrived. Although nominally under Roman rule, the Basques were in fact in a fairly constant state of rebellion for centuries. From then until now, they have continued to resist any government imposed from outside their mountain territory.

The land itself is beautiful. País Vasca (along with the rest of the northwest) gets plentiful rain off the Atlantic. The brown, bare hillsides typical of Spain are replaced by a landscape as green as Wales or Ireland. At low altitudes the winters are mild, the summers balmy.

During the summer, the coastal cities and towns are shoulder to thigh with northern folk from all directions who come to bake winter from their pale bodies and sweat the ice from their souls. Avoid those cities. There is no point in going to the Costa Vasca for the beaches. There are better beaches in Spain anyway. Go to the Basque coast in the late spring when the vines and other plants are in flower; take an umbrella and wander the old section of San Sebastián, sniffing carefully at the door of each bar. Find one that smells good, order a tapa *caliente* and a glass of *txakoli*, and watch the rain fall. Rain is good for the vines and keeps the northerners away.

THE FOOD

Basque cooking really forms two separate cuisines, one from the sea and the other from the mountains. Americans are probably the most familiar with the "Basque" restaurants of the American west, where many Basques went in the late nineteenth and early twentieth centuries to work on sheep ranches. This hybrid cuisine is remotely related to the simple Basque mountain fare of the homeland, which is quite similar to that of La Rioja, Navarre, and Aragón.

The coastal table, on the other hand, has been developed into one of the world's great cuisines by emphasizing the tremendous selection of seafood and fresh vegetables available. This style has been called *cocina nueva vasca*, as if it were a version of nouvelle cuisine; that is a handy label, but doesn't quite get at what this "new" Basque cuisine actually is. Perhaps the influence of Paul Bocuse, among others, helped the Basque chefs to break away from the old-style restaurant dishes, but the basis of the "new" cuisine has always been inherent in the flavors and raw material of the region. It is a cuisine that respects the older traditions, uses them, and builds on them—a pattern that we have seen all over Spain. Modern Basque chefs, like

Juan Marí Arzak at his Arzak restaurant in San Sebastián, have simply lightened dishes by using traditional ingredients in unexpected ways. And they have had the good sense to emphasize the incredible Basque garden produce and fresh seafood, as mentioned above.

One of the surprises of the Basque kitchen is mayonnaise, which the Basques have transformed from its role in humble home kitchens to a marvelous restaurant sauce. Mayonnaise is so basic in the Spanish kitchen that it is usually considered beneath the notice of restaurant chefs, except as a dressing for the ubiquitous Salade Russe. (Mayonnaise shares this fate with chicken dishes. Chicken—hen, actually—is so basic to the Spanish home diet that hardly anyone would think of ordering it in a restaurant.) There is no ready explanation of why mayonnaise should suddenly appear on all sides in San Sebastián and elsewhere in País Vasca. Perhaps it's the weather. In most of Spain it is too warm to risk using mayonnaise in dishes that might not be consumed for several hours. Or perhaps it's simply that the Basque have a lot of eggs, and mayonnaise is one way to use them up. (That isn't quite as silly as it sounds. The Basque kitchen prides itself on the freshness of its produce, dairy products, and eggs.)

Mayonnaise is, in fact, so common in Spain that the Spanish claim to have invented the sauce doesn't seem entirely out of the question. There are those who say that mayonnaise sauce was taken to France by the Duke of Richelieu, the leader of the French invasion force that seized the port of Mahón on the island of Menorca in 1756. As the Spanish tell the tale, the duke was very taken by a certain Menorca lady who tempted his palate with a special sauce—as well as certain other nonculinary temptations. The Duke, so the story goes, later popularized the lady's sauce in Paris, calling it sauce mahonnaise.

A pretty story, but mahonnaise or mayonnaise most probably goes back to the Romans or possibly the Greeks, though we can't find any evidence of it in Greece. The Italian versions of mayonnaise are very much like the Spanish, and it is only the French who add mustard or white pepper to mayonnaise or use any oil other than olive oil.

One of the most famous Basque dishes is *elvers*, or young eel, called *al pil-pil*. Frankly, we can't stomach it, even though there are few foods or dishes we have ever turned away from. These young European eels are spawned in the Saragoso Sea and almost immediately start back across the Atlantic to their "home" river, where mom and dad eel originated. It takes three years to complete the journey. They enter the rivers in the fall and are netted and trapped in great numbers to be converted—often a very laborious preparation, mind you—into a dish that looks a great deal like a bunch of earthworms and tastes like rubber bands. The great virtue of the *al pip-pil* recipe is that the flavor (or rather lack of flavor) is enhanced by garlic, oil, and hot red pepper.

True aficionados claim to be able to tell which river the young eels were caught in. Perhaps. But since the odds of finding fresh *elvers* at your local fish market are slim to nil, we'll skip the recipe.

But we have never really missed our plate of eels. There are so many other seafood delights—crab, hake, all sorts of shellfish, tuna, squid, bream, clams, mussels, oysters, lobsters, barnacles, and, of course, *bacalao*—that we can be fairly cavalier about dismissing the eels. And there's always beef, lamb, goat, pork, all sorts of fowl, and an abundance of small game should thoughts turn inland from the sea. Also, because of the relatively mild maritime winters, fresh local produce is available throughout most of the year.

In the past corn flour or cornmeal was an important item in the Basque diet, though its use has faded except in the country areas. For some reasons the Basques took to corn earlier than other Europeans, who thought of it as pig food. Corn grows fairly well in the mild coastal valleys and is not so subject to rot from damp weather as is wheat. A kind of corn mush or porridge called *morokil* is still served to Basque children. In the deep countryside a corn bread called *talo* is still made. It is exactly like the Mexican tortilla, prepared and used in the same way. It is even crumbled into milk as a kind of instant soup as is done in the countryside of Mexico.

Basque bakers are proud of the local wheat flours, especially that from the Bardenas Reales region of Navarre, which is in great demand by pastry bakers all over Spain. But they also import the hard durum wheat from Canada, especially to use in breads.

The local eggs are quite good, perhaps because egg production has not yet reached the factory stage achieved in the United States. Most chickens are still fed on corn, which does produce tastier eggs with a bright yellow yolk.

There are also outstanding local hard and semisoft cheeses, most made from ewe's milk—look for the Idiazábal cheeses from Doncal or the delicious Arauh cheeses. Many of the cheeses are unbranded and sold in bulk at the farm door or the local market.

THE WINE

Most of the wines drunk at the Basque table—at least on the coast —are white wines from the province of Alava, which pokes down into Rioja. They are fairly simple, straightforward wines that go well with seafood. In the mountains, the hearty red wines of Navarre are likely to be the drink of choice. There is one wine that is truly *típico* Basque and that is *chacolí* in Castilian, or *txakoli* in Basque. This highly acidic wine very much like the Portuguese *vinho verde* is a delicious staple in the tapas bars of San Sebastián. Again, like the *vinho verde*, *chacolí* is low in alcohol (8 or 9 percent), so a lot can be consumed with little effect. The taste is a bit odd. Someone described *chacolí* as tasting like flat beer, and that isn't far off, although with food the wine tastes better than it sounds.

In País Vasca the vineyards are a sea of mud in the spring. During a normal winter the vines stand with their feet in water for weeks at a time. This does them no harm at all. In fact, it does one very good thing: The constant wetness disrupts the breeding cycle of the phylloxera root louse. Because the louse has never really established itself in the wet, mountainous vineyards, the vines can be grown on their own roots.

Rain squalls sweep into the Pyrenees all through the summer but rarely break over the high peaks into the more famous vineyards of Rioja and Navarre, where the vines are often stressed by drought by the end of the summer. There is seldom such stress for Basque wines.

The *chacolí* is made from Ondarrubi Zuria or Ondarrubi Beltza, white and red versions of the same grape. *Chacolí* is usually made as a rosé, a blend of the red and white.

And that's about all there is to say about Basque wines. The real "wine" of the area is apple cider, delicious with many of the local cheese and egg dishes. Cider, or *sidra* in Spanish, can be 8 or 9 percent in alcohol and is made from the fermented juice of pressed apples; usually in Spain the fermentation is from wild yeasts. Cider can be either dry or sweet, depending on the fermentation process. In Spain it is far more often finished dry and very often sparkling. The Spanish call this "champagne" cider, and it is made by adding a small amount of sugar syrup. The sugar syrup produces a secondary fermentation that in turn produces carbon dioxide, which is then captured in the bottle or barrel. Cider from the Basque country or from Galicia is a very popular summer drink in the heat of Madrid. Served slightly chilled with a bite of cheese or with fried sardines, it refreshes the spirit as well as the palate with a mouthful of the cool north.

SPANISH DAYS

There is a subtle shift in Spain north of Logroño and Haro, at the frontier of the Basque region in northern Rioja. The land falls away in a series of deeply eroded red-sand canyons that could be west Texas or eastern New Mexico. Ahead are the intensely green mountains of the Pyrenees, deep in Basque country. By the time we reach Pamplona in Navarre, we have left the Mediterranean life behind. The change in the people, in the rhythm of life is evident. (Even in Rioja- -climatically and geographically in the Atlantic-Continental zone—the spirit is still Mediterranean, perhaps carried up the Río Ebro from the Mediterranean coast.)

North of Pamplona, there is a rush, an awareness of the passage of time that is very familiar to an American or Northern European. Clocks become more important, as in Catalonia. Appointments are set for two-fifteen, rather than "around two."

The largest Basque city, San Sebastián, has a very French feeling. It could almost be in one of the minor regional capitals of France—perhaps Toulouse or Bordeaux.

Sevilla, we remember, is regarded as the tapas capital of Spain, and the reputation is deserved. But if the tapas lover has an overwhelming urge for a nibble while in Basque country, there is plenty to satisfy. There are a few surprises. The first, as noted earlier, is mayonnaise, a substance rarely seen around a tapas bar or anywhere else in Spain outside of the home. On the Basque coast, from San Sebastián to Bilbao, we find shrimp with mayonnaise, tuna with mayonnaise, vegetables with mayonnaise, vegetable pâté, fish pâté, many different egg dishes—all with mayonnaise.

Mind you, the Basque approach to mayonnaise is a far cry from the jellylike substance available in a supermarket jar. We sat once in the Bar Asador Gambara in the Old Quarter of San Sebastián watching the mayonnaise maker at work. He must have made gallons of the stuff. The Asador is one of the best tapas bars we've ever been in. There is also a restaurant there that we have intended to try on every visit to San Sebastián. Somehow, we can't get past the bar.

It's an attractive space, with an almost California look of light wood and tiles. During certain hours of the day it fairly hums, moving toward critical customer mass, with people lined up two to three deep at the tiny bar and spilling out in San Jerónimo street. The bar itself is staffed by three to four very fast-moving young men (including the man on the mayonnaise machine), but the kitchen is filled with women who all look like fashion models.

As is common everywhere in Spain, the cold tapas are displayed on top of the bar, where you can help yourself if you wish. Don't be afraid to grab whatever looks good, especially if the barman in your section is busy. Just try to keep track of what you have so you can settle your score in an honest fashion. Hot tapas come from the kitchen.

A specialty in San Sebastián is a tiny croissant, about the size of a baby's hand, with a piece of ham or cheese or sausage wedged inside. It is finger food, of course, and a delicious two bites, max. At the Bar Asador (and everywhere else in town) they claim to have baked the croissants on the premises. That's doubtful. They are probably from one of the excellent bakeries in San Sebastián, perhaps the Bollería Reciente just around the corner on the Calle Mayor in the Old Quarter. This bakery looks like a simple storefront bread/cake shop, but underneath there is a huge basement filled with ovens that go twenty-four hours a day. The Bollería Reciente turns out a marvelous *turrón* called *vasco pasas* (Basque *turrón* with raisins) with a thin sugar glaze on top. They also do various wholegrain breads and health breads that are gaining some popularity in Spain, especially in those areas where northern Europeans travel.

The "homemade" bread at the Bar Asador probably comes from Bollería Reciente as well. But they do marvelous things with it, offering a range of *bocas* (finger sandwiches) of ham, cheese, and green or red peppers, served with a teaspoon of mayonnaise on top. Or try something with eggs. The Basque are mad about eggs and serve them with just about anything imaginable—shrimp, sausage, and, of course, mayonnaise.

Encouraged by the fare at the Bar Asador, we abandoned plans for dinner and set out on a tapas crawl. Our base was the Pensióne Amaiur, next to the church of Santa María and just off the Plaza de

la Trinidad, which in turn backs up to Mount Urgull—a San Sebastián landmark.

The steps of the church of Santa María make a good starting point
for a walk around the Old Quarter. All through the late afternoon
and far into the evening, people come together there to meet
friends, to make plans, to set out for the night.

At about 8 o'clock we zigzagged around the corner to the Zirika,
on Fermín. (We picked the tapas bar by the number of people inside. If we had trouble getting up to the bar to order, it seemed like
a good place to be. The bar at the Zirika was so filled with tapas
plates that there was hardly room to set a glass of wine down.) We
began with a puff pastry tartlet—about the size of a silver dollar—
stuffed with finely chopped *bacalao*, red pepper, and garlic. It's
called *bacalao al ajo arriero*, or salt cod mule-driver style. The name
comes from the days when mule drivers carried fresh seafood over
the mountains from the coast. Like today's truckers on the interstate
highways, they insisted on eating well—and usually simply—and
this is one of the dishes from that era.

We could easily have spent the evening at Zirika, but that would
be in violation of basic tapa rules, which mandate forward movement. But before moving, we succumbed to a few other tapas, notably, *mejillones rellenos*, a mussel dish common on the Basque
coast.

Next stop was several doors down at the Bar Eibartarra, where we
sampled a thin potato tortilla served on a slice of bread with strips of
red pepper across the top. This style of tapa is called a *montadito*,
which means literally "to mount." The Eibartarra served a superior
txakoli, which had been made just for them.

The specialty at the Bar Txiki, on Calle de Lorenzo, is the *bocas*,
lots and lots of little sandwiches, including one that is shaped like a
swan. Very campy, but fun to eat and it tasted good so no harm
done. It consisted of a small piece of bread, covered with a slice of
hard-boiled egg, then mayonnaise, then a shrimp, vertically
mounted on the mayonnaise in the shape of a swan. Really. Very
nice *rosado* at Bar Txiki; it came from Navarre.

There are several tapas bars on the Plaza Constitución, a block
away from Calle de Lorenzo, and most of the standard guides say it
is the best place for tapas in San Sebastián. It is a good area for
tapas, but also the most expensive. One excellent bar there is called
Tamboril (a kind of Basque drum). They serve an especially wonderful tapa—a finger-size pickle stuffed with fresh tuna, with an an-

chovy held in place on top with a toothpick. Yummy and bizarre. Tamboril also had some excellent puff pastry, little tartlet shells stuffed with various bites, and a fine hot tapa of whole tiny mushrooms on bread.

We ended at the Casa Igara, a very old-fashioned bar that looks out on the steps of Santa María. The people in the bar were older, not so stylish-looking. The language of the bar was Basque. The tapas were plain, unassuming, more like something from a country bar in Extremadura or Andalusia. There were hams hanging from the ceiling, jars of olives and pickles sitting on the bar. Not a drop of mayonnaise in sight. Coming straight from the glitter of the trendier bars, it seemed dull, uninteresting. We ordered a plate of ham and olives, a glass of *txakoli* and settled a bit on a couple of stools. Outside we could look straight across at a shop called Trips, which looked very Californian—full of rather pricey things that no one could really need made by people who didn't care. It was profoundly depressing. We were sitting in old Spain looking out the window at the new Europe.

Turning back into the bar, we discovered we were literally in a kind of museum. A small back room had a few tables—perhaps they served lunch there. The room was lined with shelves and cabinets displaying everything from religious relics to old winemaking equipment and odds and ends from ancient Basque kitchens. True, it was a small place, perhaps 20 by 30 feet, but well worth a look. And it is rare that we have had a chance to tour a museum with glasses of wine in hand.

There was a kitchen, closed for the night, at the back of the museum and a group of women seated around a table. Bread, ham, cheese, and wine. One of the women was nursing a baby, a bright-eyed black-haired girl. When she has her own baby, will the Casa Igara be a souvenir headquarters for the trendy of the next century?

Just to shake the gloom, we decided on one glass of wine and then an early evening. We settled on a small bar-restaurant in the Plaza Trinidad, next door to our *pensión*, and had a small glass of *rosado*, which went down well for only forty pesetas (about twenty-five cents).

We had started at about eight and finished off around eleven. We visited ten different tapas bars and had at least one tapa and one glass of wine each (small glasses, don't forget) in every bar. Total cost for the evening: just under thirty dollars.

There is a delightful Baroque whimsey to be seen in some of the decorative effects of the tapas in San Sebastián. I'm thinking now of the prawn posed as a swan gliding in a mayonnaise lake. We are one step away from food as nourishment here, balanced on the edge of a culinary fantasy that bears, after all, a very Spanish accent.

A long taxi ride from the Old Quarter of San Sebastián is the ancient fishing port of Pasajes de San Juan on Spain's Costa Vasca. We despaired of ever reaching it. There are interminable miles, or so it seems, of decayed factories. There is a gray dreariness of row houses (some mad scheme of one of Franco's ministers, no doubt intended to appease the sometimes surly Basques) giving way to shipyards that seem somewhat cheery, as there is at least some visible activity.

At last, the taxi pokes cautiously onto a narrow, twisting street off the main road, leaving behind all the signs with arrows pointing toward Francia.

It had been a dry winter, but now there was an early spring rain falling, making the narrow street we turned into seem almost like a carwash rain tunnel. The sides of the taxi barely cleared the buildings. There was a long stoplight. We waited while a few cars and Vespas emerged from a street even more dark and narrow. Finally, the light changed and we edged into the dark opening. We also began to have doubts about the Restaurant Txulotxo, which we had been assured—by a taxi driver the evening before—had the best and the most *típico* Basque food in the entire sea area of San Sebastián.

And he hadn't been just any taxi driver. He belonged to a *confradia*, or dining society. These societies are usually open only to men, although recently a few have agreed to admit women. They originated in the nineteenth century and each has its own kitchen and dining room. Members are called *tripasais*, which means someone who looks after his belly. We were his last fare the previous day and he was anxious to get to his club, where a special feast was on for that night.

"Ah, but it will not compare with the feast we held on King's Night this year," he said. "That night, the wine flowed so freely that we had to wear rubber boots to keep our feet dry."

Suddenly the current taxi burst into the light. It was fairy rain, a fine light rain falling through bright rays of sunshine. Before us lay a narrow finger of bay (the Passage of St. John—perhaps a hundred yards wide) with a few streets of stone cottages wandering up the hill on either side of the water. Sunlight broke through the rain, and the

factories, shipyards, and dull row houses were out of sight behind a
wooded ridge and centuries away. But for our taxi and a few other
cars, we could be deep in the past. Basque fishermen sailed from the
Pasajes de San Juan to fish for cod off the Banks of Labador in
the thirteenth and fourteenth centuries, hundreds of years before
the wily Columbus sold Isabella the Catholic his passage-to-India-
get-rich-quick scheme.

These fisherman probably introduced salt cod (*bacalao*) into Europe, although now much of it comes from Scandinavian fishermen.

We were early for lunch at Txulotxo—just past one—so were able
to get a table by the window overlooking the bay. There are only a
dozen or so tables in the restaurant, which is operated by a Basque
family with the help of a Portuguese daughter-in-law who is an expert on witches. We learned this at the end of the lunch—a meal
that goes by the impossible Basque name of *apalaurreaudiak*—when
she told how the Portuguese witches of her hometown had once put
a curse on her husband's shirts during a visit. When her husband
opened his suitcase, he discovered that all his shirts were filled with
holes.

We had got on to witches because her accent in speaking Castilian
(none of our party can manage Basque, which she spoke fluently)
sounded Galician. We weren't far off, because Galician, that language spoken in the far northwest corner of Spain, is very similar to
Portuguese. And witches are very important in Galicia.

The lunch, as served by our student of witches, was incredible!
From the elegant *txangurro* (crab steamed in a yummy sauce, then
put back in its shell) to *cigalas*, like a Spanish crawfish taken directly
from the bay outside the window and so fresh it tasted of the sea,
the flavors and sauces were superb.

There was a delicious *sopa de pescado*, which was an entirely
different kettle of fish from the Mediterranean version. Here it becomes more like a fish stew rather than the lighter *sopa de pescado*
one finds in Catalonia or Valencia. This preparation could be duplicated anywhere there is access to fresh or even fresh frozen fish and
fresh clams or mussels. Don't be afraid to experiment with local
seafood. Aim for rich, thick stewlike soup with strong fish flavors to
match the abundant onions and garlic. After all, this is a fisherman's
stew, it should be hearty and filling—the kind of fish dish that invites
a light red wine alongside.

There isn't much you can do about getting the next two dishes on
your table in the United States or England, since the raw ingredients

are not available. But if you find yourself hungry for the sea on the Basque coast, two dishes you must try are *chipirones en su tinta* and *cigalas*. The first is squid cooked in its own ink. At the Restaurant Txulotxo they serve a whole squid (about the size of a baseball and just taken fresh from the bay outside the window) perfectly cooked in its own ink. Squid, done properly, has an almost sweet feeling on the palate, simply bursting with flavor. It's true that it is possible to get squid and the accompanying squid ink in other parts of the world, but rarely such a large one and rarely so fresh. But it's worth a try.

Cigalas, I'm afraid, are impossible to duplicate elsewhere. They are like a seagoing crawfish, only a bit bigger. They are found on both the Atlantic and Mediterranean coasts of Spain and are absolutely delicious.

Our main dish was *merluza a la vasca*, hake Basque style. *Merluza* is found all over Spain. In fact, it is quite likely to be Spain's favorite fish and can be done in a number of ways, even something as simple as a Spanish version of fish and chips. But the Basque do it exceptionally well. Any good Basque cook can come up with half a dozen recipes for *merluza* without a second's hesitation. It's a white, firm-fleshed fish. Substitute cod, haddock, or whiting for *merluza* in most recipes.

The Englishman Jan Read, the dean of Spanish wine writers, has turned up a nice story concerning *merluza a la vascas* in his book *The Wine and Food of Spain*. Read cites a letter written in 1723 by Doña Placida de Larrea of Bilbao to a friend living in Navarra: "Doña Placida specifies that the fish must be caught from a small boat by hook and line and describes how she stewed it in an earthenware *cazuela* and served it with cockles and crabs in a green sauce from parsley and with a garnish of asparagus, a present from friends in Tudela."

Read gives this as evidence of the origin and date of the dish, but I suspect its origin reaches much further back than the eighteenth century. The parsley green sauce also identifies it with a dish called *kokotxas en salsa verde*, which is a specialty of San Sebastián. The *kokotxas* is the tiny bit of delicate, very perishable flesh from the fish's throat. This use of a green sauce with hake is found nowhere else in Spain. In Andalusia, there is a hake dish that uses parsley, but the parsley is simply chopped and added to a sauce of tomatoes, nuts, and white wine—quite a different dish altogether.

After a lunch lasting more than three hours, our apprentice witch of a waitress realized that she was dealing with serious eaters. We had watched the sun move across the bay and had finally even changed tables in order to get the last few rays of light as the early spring sun ducked low above the ridge toward San Sebastián.

We were ready to pass on dessert. Having gone through several bottles of an excellent Rosado Viña Ecoyen from Señorío de Sarria (a Navarre wine), it seemed more like siesta time than sweets time. But we were thwarted. We were presented with a kind of *menú de gustación* of desserts and a bottle of *aguardiente* from Galicia, which is used in the famous Galician witches' brew called *quemada*. Although the drink is said to have originated in Galicia, it is found all over northern Spain and down into Murcia. At its simplest, the *aguardiente* is poured into white china wine bowls and a match is put to it to burn off some of the alcohol. Oddly enough, when the flame dies out, the *aguardiente* is still cold.

We have had more elaborate versions in Catalonia, where a bottle or so of *aguardiente* is poured into a large *cazuela* with sliced lemon, roasted coffee beans, and perhaps other fruit as well, then a match is put to the whole thing. It looks quite spectacular and warming on a cold day and the procedure doesn't actually do any damage to the spirit under the flames.

It was past five and the Pasajes de San Juan was in shade by the time we finished. Four hours at table, each better than the last. Especially since we learned that we didn't have to take that long dreary taxi ride back to the old section of San Sebastián. There was a water taxi just below the restaurant that cut the journey back in half with a five-minute run across the bay, where another taxi (called by our waitresses) would be waiting. And so to siesta.

It was a small café in the very industrial outskirts of San Sebastián, catering to taxi drivers, truck drivers, local day laborers. We had stopped to ask directions and once there decided on a cup of espresso and a small brandy. The waitress was flirting with one of the two drivers at the next table. When he left to go to the toilet, she grabbed his jacket and took it behind the bar.

"Tell him the witches took it," the young girl giggled to his mate.

The man frowned. Suddenly, the fun was gone.

"Don't joke about witches. You young girls know nothing about witches." He looked around the Formica and stainless steel café as if an old hag on a broomstick might pop out from behind a curtain.

Ann, sensing a story and recognizing his accent as Galician, said

*she had heard there were many witches in his homeland, but surely
there were no witches in a big city like San Sebastián?*

He looked glumly at her.

"You are American?" he finally asked.

"Californian," Ann corrected, being stubbornly provincial.

"You don't have witches in California?"

*"Well, I'm not sure," she answered. "At least, I don't know of
any."*

*He nodded, "Yes, one does not know of witches until you meet
them."*

*He leaned forward and nodded his head briskly, as if he had just
made up his mind.*

*"I could tell you about witches—or at least one witch, right here
in this city."*

*"We would like to know," Ann said. "Please tell us." She ordered
another brandy all around, as the other driver had just returned.
The girl meekly handed over his jacket without a fuss.*

*"It was when I first left Galicia for San Sebastián, almost fifteen
years ago. I was looking for a job then and took a room in a boarding
house. There was a young woman there, a cousin of the manager, I
believe, who kept flirting with me, but I had no money and no time
then for women. Besides, I had a girlfriend back home. And on top
of that, she was as ugly as the devil, with a big wart right on the end
of her nose. Can you imagine?"*

He took a sip of brandy, as if to ward off her ugliness.

*"Anyway, I must have made her angry. One morning at breakfast
I noticed that she was gone. When I asked, the manager said she
had gone back to her home in the mountains. When I went upstairs
to dress for a job interview I went to the closet for a freshly ironed
shirt. Now you will never believe what I found."*

*Again, he looked over his shoulder and all around the café. The
young waitress had given up any pretense of waiting on other customers and was standing wide-eyed beside the table, listening.*

*"I had four shirts hanging in the closet, all just laundered, you
understand. The buttons had been cut from all of them. Neatly cut
away as if by a small knife. I saw at once it was witches' work and
called the manager. He knew what I was thinking because without
even being asked, he said his young cousin had left at noon. My
shirts had not been returned to me until about six o'clock, several
hours after the girl had left."*

He paused, as if his point were proven.

His mate nodded, "Yes," he said. "That was the work of a witch for sure. They can do things like that at a distance. You are lucky she didn't do worse."

The man nodded. "I think so. Later, I found the buttons in an ashtray in the hallway. The manager had them sewn back on at his expense. He knew it was his cousin. I tell you, I got out of there in a hurry, the next day. I didn't want her thinking of more mischief."

The two truckers finished their brandy and left. Ann asked the waitresses if she believed the story.

"But it must be true," she said. "Only a witch could have done that."

GUIDELINES: PAÍS VASCA

San Sebastián

HOTELS

Hotels are as usual vastly overpriced. You'll want to stay in the Old Quarter anyway, so it might as well be a *pensión*, cheap and convenient.

Pensión Amaiur, Calle 31 de Agosto. Tel (943) 42-96-54. Quiet rooms at the back, a little noisy at the front, but wonderful wrought-iron balcony overlooking the street. Cheap.

Pensión San Lorenzo. Calle de San Lorenzo, 2. Tel. (943) 42-55-16. A lively, friendly place in the heart of the Old Quarter. If the San Lorenzo is filled, they will call around the Quarter and find a room for you.

RESTAURANTS

These two restaurants are must stops in San Sebastián:

Akelarre, Barrio Igueldo. Tel. (943) 21-20-52. Great view of the bay from Monte Igueldo. A showplace restaurant but the food is sensational. Great seasonal menu.

Arzak, Alto de Miracruz, 21. Tel. (943) 27-84-65. One of the best restaurants in Spain. The chef, Juan Marí Arzak is famous throughout Europe and was one of the inventors of the new Spanish cuisine.

TAPAS BARS

The following bars are all in the Old Quarter of the city.
Zikika, Fermín, 46.
Bar Eibartarra, Fermín, 24.
Bar Txiki, Calle de Lorenzo, 9.

CANTABRIA, ASTURIAS, GALICIA: CELTIC SPAIN

IN FOCUS

The three regions of the Celtic north are Cantabria, Asturias, and Galicia. They stretch west from País Vasca along the Atlantic coast. Galicia is the largest of the three, with a long Atlantic coastline running south to Portugal. Driving east along the coast from San Sebastián, through Santander and on toward Oviedo, we plunge into fairyland—Celtic territory. A landscape of intense green hills and craggy mountains, tiny hamlets tucked up under the shadow of rocky cliffs. Spain, at least the Spain of Hollywood films and travel posters, is left behind. Also, part of historical Spain is left as well. The Moors never penetrated these Celtic hills and it was from this area that the resistance to the Moors was first mounted.

The Cordillera Cantabrica, a jumbled mountain range that stretches from the Pyrenees to Portugal, forms the southern border of Asturias and Cantabria, with Castile-León to the south. The range, one of the largest wild areas in Europe, runs more or less parallel to the Atlantic Costa Verde, from Galicia to Bilbao and on south to the edge of the Meseta, that high upland plateau that dominates Central Spain. There are wave after wave of hills covering over eight million acres. There are bears and wolves there, one of the few places in Europe where both these creatures are found in the wild.

For centuries the Cordillera has formed a barrier, a natural frontier that has not only made it difficult for national governments in Madrid to extend complete control over this wild, Celtic northeast, but stopped the Moors as well.

A small Moorish force did make one brief excursion into the mountains and was defeated in a skirmish at Covadonga in modern Asturias in 722 by Pelayo, an Asturian chieftain who later became the first king of Asturias. After that defeat—which is recalled in local folklore and history as a major battle but was most probably a skirmish between an advance guard of Moorish calvary and local mountain folk—the Moors fell back south of the mountains. This gave Christian forces the opportunity to regroup and begin the centuries-long war of conquest.

In modern times the region has not prospered, and Galicia is the second poorest area in Spain, next to Extremadura.

THE FOOD

The lack of Arab influence is evident at the table, and the cuisine depends heavily on the sea for basic ingredients. It is, in some respects, a rich food, but most dishes are more closely related to the peasant fare of other parts of Europe than what is usually considered Spanish food.

There is no winter growing season here, except perhaps for a few greens. Instead, there are beans, corn and other grains, and legumes, such as lentils. The food is hearty, not subtle but very satisfying—it keeps away the winter cold. There are wonderful fish stews of all sorts and an unusual turnip stew from Asturias called *estofado de buey*, which includes calf's feet in the list of ingredients. One of the most famous Spanish dishes from this region is *fabada*, a ham-and-bean dish that is also made in Galicia with beef. Many of the typical dishes of Spain's Celtic area feature local ciders, as with *lubina a la asturiana*, which is prepared with clams and cider. Also, the area produces wonderful blue cheese, and subsequently a sauce is made from it called *salsa de cabrales*. It appears as a dip for vegetables for starters, as a salad dressing, as a steak sauce, or all by itself as a dessert course. Surely, *salsa de cabrales* is one of the most versatile sauces in the world.

They eat a lot of mussels in the coastal areas of Celtic Spain. Mussels fresh from the sea are a sentimental favorite of ours, since we practically lived on a version of *mejillones a la marinera* during the mid-sixties in Monterey, California. There are few things in life (maybe two or three) more wonderful than a mussel only minutes out of the water.

There are superb dishes made from the pig, including the *empanada de loma a la gallega*, the famous Galician pork pie, which is delicious served hot or cold. The Galicians were great travelers in the nineteenth century. Galicia was a poor area even then. Galicians were often found in Central or South America, where in some areas the word for an immigrant from Spain was *gallego*, regardless of what part of Spain the new arrival was from. This *empanada* dish was a lasting Galician import to Latin America, where most countries have some version of it. Christina Franjetic, a partner in Café Tango, was an Argentine and her *empanadas* were a local favorite.

There is also a version of the Galician *empanada* in the Canary Islands, this one brought back from Venezuela, where many Galicians went in the nineteenth century. After World War II, many Canarians went to Venezuela to find work. Those who were successful returned to the Canaries, bringing with them still another variation on the original Galician *empanada*.

The Celtic kitchen benefits from a wide range of raw materials—such as cool-season vegetables like turnips, carrots, and cabbages—seldom seen in the rest of Spain. There are also a number of different beans and lentils. Wheat, rye, and oats are all grown in Galicia and used for local breads. There are 250 varieties of apples grown in the region, many used exclusively in cider production.

Like their Basque neighbors, the Spanish Celts have a rich selection of seafood, including hake, tuna, salmon, squid, sardines, scallops, oysters, clams, and other local shellfish. There is also good freshwater fish, including trout. The pig is easily the most popular domestic food animal, with many tasty variations played on the theme of bacon, sausage, ham, and salt pork.

There's plenty of game in the northeast, with long stretches of forest and mountains harboring partridge, pheasant, duck, quail, rabbit, deer, and wild boar.

We've left the olive far to the south and are well into butter country here. There are also a number of local cheeses, including *pasiego*, a wonderful blue cheese from the valley of Pas in Cantabria that can be found all over Spain.

THE WINE

Galicia is the only area in the Celtic north to make wine in any appreciable quantity. Some of this wine is good—very good, in fact—though little of it makes its way outside the area. There are two geographical denominations of origin, the Ribeiro and the Valdeorras. There is also a denomination for the wines made from the Albarino grape, wherever it is grown. The Albariño is the same grape as the Alvarinho of Portugal, from which the delicious low-alcohol, slightly petillant *vinhos verdes* of that country are made.

The red wines are usually light and fruity, low in alcohol, high in acid. The best white wines have been compared to the wines of Alsace and of Muscadet. There is a similarity to the Riesling that has to do more with the climate than the grape. There are dozens of grape varieties, most seldom seen elsewhere. Often, local wines are made from tiny plots by small farmers without the capital to invest in the proper equipment. These wines can be quite good on occasion, but typically the reverse is true. Much of this local wine is sold in unlabeled bottles in local markets or bars and the first sip is often a real adventure.

But the real "wine of the country" throughout these Celtic regions is apple cider. The *sidra* of Galicia and Asturias—like those of País Vasco—is much appreciated throughout Spain and is especially popular in the bars of Madrid. These dry ciders actually make a delicious pairing with grilled fish and shellfish.

The traditional Galician vineyards are much different in appearance from the vineyards of most of Spain. The vines are trained on wires that run across the top of concrete or wooden Ts that look—except for the vines—rather like a long series of outdoor clotheslines. The wires that hold the vines are between five and six feet off the ground.

Grapes are very susceptible to many forms of rot and mildew if heavy rains occur during or near harvest time, so the vines were originally grown high off the ground to allow the wind to go under the vines and blow away the spores of the fungus.

Some twenty to thirty years ago, growers were encouraged to train the vines lower (it is easier to harvest the grapes) on a Y-shaped trellis system. That was about the time when chemical sprays were being introduced in the vineyard to control mildew and rot. Now that chemical sprays seem to be on the way out—because of quite legitimate consumer fears about pollution, as well as the high cost of using them—it probably won't be long before the high wires will be back.

SPANISH DAYS

The road had seemed fine for the first few kilometers—a narrow blacktop ribbon twisting and snaking its way through a green, heavily wooded landscape. Although it had rained all night, there were just a few scattered showers by dawn when we left Orense in a rented car. We were rather happy later that we had spent extra car-rental money on a front-wheel-drive Peugeot.

But for the time, the sun was actually beginning to break briefly through the cloud cover. We were predicting picnic weather by noon. Not only was sunshine in view, but there was a good prospect of supplementing our basket of bread, cheese, sausage, and bottled wine with what we were told was the best Albariño wine in Galicia. We were on a peculiarly Galician search, for we were after wine straight from the barrel. Not that there isn't plenty of bottled wine in Galicia. It is simply that Galicians consider it inferior and "adulterated."

"What they put in the bottles," the man said, making a grimace and pretending to spit on the floor. "It is the dregs, what they sell in bottles. For the real, the true Albariño you must go to where it is made."

The speaker was the owner of a small bar in Orense where we had stopped for our late-afternoon *merianda*—a light snack—and a glass of wine. We noticed that he took the wine—the classic Galician Albariño—straight from the barrel. We complimented him on his wine, which was delicious, one of the best Albariños we had tasted. The flavor was fresh and appealing, a bit like a French Muscadet with a dash of very good Riesling added. Many Galicians believe that the grape was originally brought to the area by pilgrims to Santiago de Compostela in the early Middle Ages—perhaps the eleventh or twelfth century—and that it is actually a true Riesling. There is no California wine quite like it. It is also low-alcohol, so we ordered another glass all around.

The owner-barman nodded his approval of our drinking habits and we told him of our search for the real Albariño—and that we had been told all over Galicia that to get the best wine it is necessary to go to the winemaker. He launched into his own condemnation of any wine in bottles—"you don't know what they might put in it"—and then praised his producer.

But he would not tell us who it was. He simply smiled slyly and said, "He lives so deep in the country, you could never find him. And now," he said, waving at the rain falling steadily outside the open door, "perhaps the road is closed." We couldn't get the information from him, try as we might. Even another round of wine didn't loosen his tongue.

Gallegos are like that. And such silence is quite an un-Spanish trait. In most of Spain, a bar owner would have at once produced the winemaker's name, address, and telephone number and directions to his house. The usual Spaniard is so convinced of the absolute superiority of his baker or his tailor or his wine supplier that he wants to share it with the world.

But that's Mediterranean Spain. As one moves into the Basque-Celtic northeast that openness falls away. Enter the geography and the mindset of northern Europe. Clearly, two passing tourists were no threat to the bar owner's supply of wine. Yet the habit of secrecy was so deeply ingrained that he couldn't break it.

We stayed the night in Orense at the Padre Erjioo on the Plaza Eugenio Montes. Nothing special. A typically nondescript, fairly modern, and overpriced hotel. But since we were only staying the night and it was raining we didn't want to look for a *pensión* in the attractive Old Quarter. We fell into conversation with a young man at the hotel bar. He was from Burgos in Rioja but had married a Galician woman and they had lived now for several years in Orense, where he was an attorney.

"That man is my brother-in-law," he said, laughing. "He is amazing and you have him pegged just right as a typical Galician. I would never dare say this to my wife, but her family is so secretive they hate to tell you the time of day."

He believed it had to do with the widespread Galician belief in witches. Everyone knows, it seems, that the more a witch knows about you, the more damage he or she can do to you. Therefore, tell nothing.

"My wife has cousins out in the country who burn hair and nail clippings so the witches won't find them and have power over them. And, you see, the winemaker who supplies my brother-in-law is married to a witch, so they say. So, of course, my brother-in-law must be especially careful."

He took out a notepad and quickly drew a map showing where the winemaker lives, and gave us his name, which in true Galician fashion (even though he was only adopted Galician) he made us promise not to put in writing. He knew we were journalists but had apparently not heard the maxim "Never trust a writer."

At any rate, we left shortly after dawn, driving northeast on the C546 toward the small town of Monforte de Lemos. Lemos is a lovely town, once the seat of the Counts of Lemos. There is a tenth-century monastery there and some bits and pieces of a castle that once housed the counts. We stopped for a time and I thought how pleasant it would be to live in Monforte de Lemos, where history simply seems to have stopped some time ago.

But we were in search of the perfect Albariño, so we pushed on, taking the narrow paved road toward the village of Sober, an unlikely name for a town noted for its vineyards and wine. Our goal was in the hills above Sober where there lived the winemaker and his witch-wife. About that time, just past midmorning, the sun disappeared for the day and the rain returned in earnest. We also reached the point on the young attorney's hand-drawn map where we were to turn onto a dirt road that led up into the hills. There should be a farmhouse there where local cheese and wine was sold. But that was not the wine we wanted, he said. There, we should stop, buy some of the local blue sheep cheese, and ask if the dirt road was open.

A tiny old man in a shapeless gray sweater met us at the door and led us down a long hallway into a kind of lean-to shed at the side of the main house. There were no windows in the shed, but he switched on a bare overhead bulb. There were cheeses everywhere, hanging from the ceiling and stacked on shelves, cheeses of all shapes and sizes. Most were blue sheep cheeses but there were also goat and cow cheeses. In the dark, almost airless room, it was like being in a cave of cheese.

The smell of the cheese mingled with the sharp, almost acidic smell of wine. There were wine barrels on the floor lining three walls of the room, raised slightly from the floor on a slab of concrete, with a tiled drain running in front of the row of barrels. The drain ran through a screened hole in the wall and into a pigpen outside.

An ancient dark table ran down the center of the room (which was perhaps 20 feet by 25 feet). There was a cutting block and knives on the table, equally dark and stained with generations of cheese.

Yes, we were told. The road was open. But it led to nowhere anyone would want to go. Also, if it continued to rain, high water could close it at any moment. Besides, it was dangerous country. *Muy peligroso.*

Why dangerous? The old man wrapping the cheese shook his head and just repeated that it was dangerous country, rain or no rain.

Larry took a chance. "Witches?" he asked.

The old man looked up at him sharply and tightened his lips, finished wrapping the cheese, and placed it on the table.

Could we taste some of his wine?

Of course. There were several varieties, and as we tasted and talked about the wine, we gradually gained his confidence. Larry made a face at one of the wines, a Garnacha, we thought. "Sour, too thin," Larry said.

The old man nodded. "Yes. I told the fellow I didn't want his wine. But his wife makes good cheese, and if I want the cheese I have to take the wine as well."

"It is Garnacha?"

"Yes. It doesn't grow well here at all. It needs sunshine and we don't have much of that." He waved toward the rain.

"Do you have any Albariño wine?"

His eyes lit up. "Yes, it is my own. But I keep it in the back. It isn't for everyone. Come." He waved us around the table, through a door at the rear of the room, down a rain-spattered gravel path beside the pigpen (which was a model of cleanliness, by the way), and into a small barn behind the house.

There was no electricity in the barn. He left the door open to let in light and also lit several candles that stood on a table.

"Here is my wine," he said.

There were half a dozen barrels arranged in a 3-2-1 pyramid against the rear wall, behind the table that looked like a duplicate of the table in the cheese room. Either of them would probably fetch a year's income for the old farmer in one of the trendy antique shops of London or San Francisco.

He opened a spigot on one of the barrels and poured out three half glasses of the wine. It was stunning. Even better than the wine in the bar the day before.

"This is the best Albariño I have ever tasted," Larry said. We were surprised, but then we had never expected the search for the perfect Albariño to lead us so far inland at all. It is commonly believed that the best Albariño is grown near Pontevedra in the Val de Salnes, only a few kilometers from the Atlantic. In fact, there is a yearly festival (the first Sunday in August) honoring the grape in the seaside village of Cambados.

He thanked us, but not profusely. He knew the wine was good and was clearly very proud of his tiny cellar. "I have been making wine for over fifty years, but last year was my last vintage," he said. He explained that his wife had died the year before and there was simply "no more joy" at his home. He was selling it all and moving to an apartment in Pontevedra to be near the sea.

"I was born there and I want to die there. I brought the cuttings of the Albariño with me when I moved here fifty-five years ago. They originally came with my grandfather from Portugal. I will sit and watch the sea all day and wait to die," he said matter-of-factly, as if talking about the weather.

There was no self-pity in his voice, nor any of that weary self-conscious cynicism found more and more in people of retirement age in Northern Europe or America. Simply an acceptance of the end. His life had finished its circle.

He explained that his *primero* (his cousin) was buying the property from him and would sell the grapes to the local co-op.

"It is a pity to lose such fine wine in the co-op blend."

"It is true, but my cousin is a doctor. He has no time to make the wine. At least my vines will continue to live."

He poured another round. The flowery perfume of the wine was so intense, one could smell it from eight feet away.

"If you like my wines, perhaps you could take them to your country and sell them. You could send me a little of the money? They are the last wines of Marcelino Juan Castroviejo, for that is my name."

We explained to Señor Castroviejo that although we were proud to taste his wines—and that they were, indeed, wonderful—we were not wine importers. We told him we would speak to friends in the wine trade.

But the wines of Galicia are not well known in America, we told him.

He nodded, sipped at his glass, and smiled slightly. "At least my last vintage is a good one."

His mood brightened. "Let me show you the vineyards," and he motioned us into the rain.

Larry has rarely been wetter (Ann thoughtfully said that she would stay behind and finish her wine, as it was far too good to abandon) and would probably have simply drowned but for the fact that the vineyards were rather small.

Larry had started the day wearing hiking boots—Señor Castroviejo wore the knee-high rubber boots commonly seen in the often wet Galician countryside—so at least his feet stayed dry as he slopped down the rows of the vines behind the vineyard owners.

"Look," he seized the end of a vine and pulled it down to face level. "Look, it has begun. And I will not be here to see the finish."

It was a tiny speck of green beginning to form near the end of what appeared to be a dead brown branch. Señor Castroviejo let it go and it swung back up toward the wire, the bursting green tip turned toward where the sun would be if it weren't for the steadily falling rain.

Not surprisingly, none of the importers we contacted in London or the United States were interested in six barrels of Albariño wine from Galicia. We exchanged a few postcards with Senor Castroviejo, but learned that he died only six months after our visit. It would have been about the time of the harvest in Galicia. We know nothing of the circumstances of his death. We'd like to think that he was sitting on a terrace above the sea, watching the endless Atlantic roll onto the coast of Spain, with a glass of his excellent Albariño at hand.

We never made the trip up the dirt road that day. Senor Castroviejo's wine was so good that a further search would have been a waste and an insult. The grail is where you find it.

He was one of those slightly askew Englishmen who turn up in odd parts of the world, absolutely unaware that they are inhabiting a different reality. He was standing near the center of the Plaza de España in Santiago de Compostela, gazing up at the great cathedral of St. James, Santiago.

"I read about it when I was a boy in Yorkshire. The great pilgrim route to Santiago, the 'cockleshell' route we called it in Yorkshire, though the shells are scallops, are they not?"

He must have been at least seventy; a tall, gaunt man with a fringe of gray hair peeking out from under his old felt hat and a full gray beard. His backpack was tattered but he was dressed neatly in old jeans and a sweater, a raincoat was hooked to the backpack and he gripped the traditional pilgrim's staff in his hand. A fine mist was falling.

"I walked all the way, you know, right down from Roncesvalles at the French border. I took what the books call the French route, through Rioja, Santo Domingo de la Calzada," his voice was lively, with only a slight Yorkshire burr peeping through the standard BBC accent.

"How long did it take you?"

"Oh, dear. I quit counting the days some time back. But it's been wet and cold most of the way. Splendid walking weather. I just got in this morning. Something like 800 kilometers, I believe, though I didn't count those either."

He looked up at the sky, as if surprised by the mist. "You don't get much company in winter, that's why I did it now. Didn't want company. Some pack of French students or worse yet Germans marching along. Wanted some time alone with just my own thoughts for company. Good company they were, too."

He smiled slightly as if aware that he was being faintly absurd.

"Are you a religious man?"

"Good heavens, no! Church of England, you know. Hardly a religion, that, is it?"

That same smile. This pilgrim was having a very fine time, playing himself to two wandering Americans in the Galician rain.

And despite the rain and the early prebreakfast hour, a steady stream of tourists walked around the plaza, most coming out of or going back into the Hostal de los Reyes Católicos, the grand luxury hotel that had been founded by Ferdinand and Isabella as an inn and hospital for pilgrims. Now the pilgrims carried American Express gold cards and read the European edition of the Wall Street Journal *over breakfast.*

"No spiritual insights, then, to share with the world?"

"It's best to avoid those things, I think. But I saw some fine country and met some fine people. But spirits I'll leave to the priests and the politicians. I'll stick to the earth myself." He put down his backpack and dug around inside it for a moment, finally fishing out a gleaming Nikon.

"I wonder if you could just spare a moment to snap my picture with the cathedral in the background. I want a snapshot to stick in my tomb. To remind God, you see, that I did this pilgrimage. And if it's all nonsense, then it hasn't done any harm, has it?"

GUIDELINES: CANTABRIA, ASTURIAS, GALICIA

Cudillero

A spectacular village on the Asturian coast with houses perched crazily on the side of a gorge overlooking the sea below. Stop at one of the bars in the port for the excellent sardines. If you want to stay for a day or two, ask in the bar about rooms, or drive a few miles on to the resort of Salinas, where there are a number of hotels on the wide beach.

Santiago de Compostela

HOTELS

The goal of most travelers in Celtic Spain will be Santiago de Compostela, where pilgrims have been arriving for almost a thousand years. There is an excellent *parador* there, but the real crown jewel of all Spain's hotels is also in Santiago:

Hostal de los Reyes Católicos, Plaza España. Tel. (981) 58-20-00. This is one of the few luxury hotels that are worth it. It was ordered built by Isabella in the fifteenth century to shelter pilgrims and converted into a luxury hotel in 1954. A fun one-night blowout.

RESTAURANT

There is one must restaurant in Santiago:

Anexo Vilas, Avenue Villagarcía, 21. Tel. (981) 59-83-87. One of the most extensive Galician menus to be found and outstanding food.

San Vicente de la Barquera

A picturesque village on the Cantabrian coast.

HOTEL

Miramar, Carreta del Faro. Tel. (942) 71-00-75.

RESTAURANT

Maruja, Avenida Generalísimo Franco. Tel. (942) 71-00-77. Seafood specialties.

In the Galician countryside, look for a *fonda* or ask in a bar about local rooms for rent.

Wineries

Cooperativa Vitivinícola del Ribeiro, Valdepereira in the eastern Galician province of Orense. Tel. (988) 47-01-75. Open to the public upon application during normal business hours by calling ahead. This large co-op has a good range of wines for tasting, giving an excellent idea of the possibilities of Galician wines.

Ask in any village to find small producers.

EXTREMADURA

IN FOCUS

Extremadura is a harshly scenic land of mountains and high valleys lying between La Mancha and the Portuguese border. To the south is Andalusia, to the north, Castile. It is a very poor region today, although centuries ago untold wealth in the form of *conquistador* gold flowed into Extremadura from the Americas. It was a battleground for centuries between the Christians, advancing from Castile, and the Moors, falling back on Andalusia.

In the nineteenth century, the entire region was so underpopulated that the government in Madrid encouraged mass immigration from Galicia in an attempt to resettle villages that had been abandoned. But even the Galicians—accustomed, it would seem, to the most grinding poverty—couldn't deal with the harshness of Extremadura. Summer heat may climb over 100 degrees daily. In winter, frigid winds howl through the mountain passes.

Spring—that is, late March or early April to the end of May—is the best time to visit Extremadura. The weather is ideal, with high blue skies and intense green fields crowded with wildflowers, including brilliant displays of a red poppy that seems to grow everywhere in Spain in roadside ditches, kitchen gardens, and in the tracks of wandering shepherds. The hedgerows and trees are thick with birds and the stork may be seen adding a stick to its towering nest.

The name Extremadura means "beyond the Río Duero" and it was the frontier for several centuries in the wars of Reconquest against the Moors. As the Moors fell back to the south, new towns were settled, old towns reclaimed.

During a lull in the years of battle, around 1300, a shepherd near the mountain town of Guadalupe stubbed his toe, so it is said, on a piece of wood sticking out of the ground. He took a closer look, got his shovel, and dug up a small statue, perhaps half life size, of a black virgin who became known as the Virgin of Guadalupe. Her discovery was hailed as a miracle. Doubtless the carved image had been buried at some point to save it from destruction by the Moors.

A few years later, in 1340, King Alfonso XI invoked the Virgin of Guadalupe before a key battle against the Moors at Salado. Alfonso was triumphant; he dealt the Moors a defeat from which they never recovered. He ordered a monastery and church built at Guadalupe, near the field where the statue was found. Today, there is a hostel (the Hospedería del Real Monasterio) and a very good restaurant for local specialties in the monastery (still very much a working monastery and church), which was taken over and restored by the Franciscan order in 1908.

The Black Virgin of Guadalupe's usefulness didn't end with the Moors. She came to represent the mystic concept of the hispanidad, the community of language and culture linking Spain with the New World. Papers were signed in Guadalupe authorizing Columbus's first voyage to the New World, and the first American Indians to be converted to Christianity were brought to the church of the monastery for baptism.

A few hundred yards from the monastery's church there is a modern mural painted on the side of a wall showing the Indians—looking very saintly and noble—being baptized. The mural is not very well painted. The style is naive, simplistic, almost cartoonlike. Yet there is a strength in the simple painting that represents very accurately the spirit of Extremadura.

Inside the church, the Black Virgin herself has a faintly tacky appearance, like an oversized and overdressed doll looking down over the church from her modern enamelwork throne within the *camarín,* the small room high above the altar. The throne turns about (like a tabletop lazy Susan) so the Virgin can be shown to tourists who have paid their hundred pesetas and climbed the narrow stairs behind the altar for a closer look. Despite all these touristic trappings, even to a nonbeliever, there is an air of mystery here and a feeling that somehow one is close to the heart of the Spanish soul. It has to do with an odd combination of fanaticism and fatalism, probably more evident in the Middle Ages, but still to be found in the modern Spaniard. Extremadura seems to lend that spirit to the people with a brooding almost cinematic intensity. In spirit, and very much in appearance, it is akin to the high plateau regions of northern Mexico, the American southwest, and that vast heartland of the American west that runs right up to northern Canada.

In many parts of Spain one can see a geography that the early Spanish explorers and exploiters must have recognized in the Americas; in Extremadura, especially in the Trujillo-Guadalupe area, it seems almost possible to recognize a philosophic kinship as well. There is an underlying hardness, a rocky reality wrapped around a deep spiritual core that has as much to do with the interaction of the people with the land as with the land alone or the people alone.

In the past, the sons and daughters of farmers left for Madrid or Sevilla as soon as they could break away. This was also true in the sixteenth century, when Extremadura was the homeland of the *conquistadores*. Cortés, Pizarro, Balboa, de Soto and their lesser-known ilk were all born in Extremadura. Perhaps economics sent them off to the New World, but Extremadura has a long military tradition, bloodily based in the wars of Reconquest against the Moors.

This tradition of warfare and the search for instant wealth in the form of gold and silver had another effect—common throughout Spain, actually, but especially evident in Extremadura: the development of the *conquistadores* professional soldiers, the "warrior class" that disdained commerce, farming, or any ordinary labor. This attitude, remarkably similar to that of the warrior caste in the High Plains Indian culture—did the Cheyenne and Comanche learn more than how to sit a horse from the Spanish?—contributed to an already impoverished economy and can still be seen today, especially in the attitude toward the commercial world. Huge estates produced nothing but a few hundred sheep or pigs a year, while the owners searched for gold in the New World or fought the pope's wars in Sicily and Italy or the Low Countries.

Sometimes, these often-illiterate warriors struck it rich. The city of Trujillo, which is called the nursery of the *conquistadores*, is filled with the mansions of those who made their fortune as conquerors and colonizers, the most famous being Francisco Pizarro, the conqueror of Peru. Pizarro, the son of a swineherd and butcher, married an Inca princess, only to be murdered a few years later in his palace in Trujillo, the victim of political intrigue within his own command.

The *conquistadores* are still heroes, still remarkable legends to most people in Extremadura. There is little questioning there of what they did or the effect for good or ill on the Indians of the Americas. If there is anything at all critical in the local attitude, it is a faint suspicion. Where did all that gold go, after all? All that Incan silver? There is the nagging feeling that somehow they have been cheated of a legacy.

THE FOOD

There is a schizophrenic aspect to the food of Extremadura. Most is fairly simple—country dishes, very close to their peasant roots—although that, as we shall see, is changing. But there is, surprisingly, a centuries-old tradition of haute cuisine in this ancient territory, a medieval tradition that developed in the many monasteries of Extremadura and is still found at its best in the monasteries and *paradores*. It is more, however, than just a curious relic, because it is now cross-breeding, as it were, with the local country fare and one can see the beginnings of an Extremadura cuisine.

Some of this monastic fare, by the way, made its way into French cookbooks through the famous French chef Auguste Escoffier. It seems that during Napoleon's Spanish war, a Benedictine monastery at Alcantara in Extremadura was sacked by French troops marching toward Portugal. One of the French officers salvaged a cookbook manuscript, which he sent to his wife, who passed it along to Escoffier. It contained such unusual recipes as truffled pheasant and partridge stuffed with duck liver pâté and truffles that have been marinated for days in port. The legend goes that Escoffier declared that recipe alone was worth Napoleon's entire disastrous peninsula campaign.

The truffles were local, a specialty of Extremadura called *criadillas de tierra*, or balls of earth. They are sometimes served chopped and sautéed in garlic.

There is one regional specialty that we did not include in our recipe file. In the town of Plasencia, local gourmets serve *lagarto*, or lizard, in a parsley-based green sauce. The flavor is similiar to frogs' legs.

Dishes of perhaps a wider appeal would include lamb stewed in wine, sautéed lamb, and pork cooked with potatoes, a specialty from Badajoz.

To be honest, the wine and food are not yet quite world-class, but they are in that exciting stage of early self-awareness that can lead to unexpected and delicious results. It's a situation found in many parts of rural Spain: Young chefs are taking traditional dishes and shaping them into new elements. A culinary exploration of Extremadura is for the adventurer, for someone who can travel without the usual gourmet guides and enological maps, for someone willing to risk palate and stomach on dishes and wines that haven't received the slick magazine seal of approval.

There is an abundance of raw materials for the kitchen. In late spring, the garden produce is beginning to fill the market stalls of the towns. There are stalls heaped with tomatoes, peppers, and potatoes, and baskets filled with herbs—rosemary, thyme, marjoram. There are several varieties of freshwater fish, such as *trucha*, and there are tasty local hams, the most famous being the *cerdo ibérico*, the delicious hams from the black Iberian pig. According to the locals, the special flavor of the ham comes from the wild acorns and herbs the pigs feed on in the rough, hilly terrain. One of the best of the regional markets is in Mérida, just a few blocks from the *parador*.

It is this rich and varied local cornucopia that is the instant attraction of the *extremeño* table. Almost any nameless corner café or bar —what the Italians would call a trattoria, the Spanish *un restaurante casere*—can be counted on for the kind of tasty, honest fare normally eaten by *extremeños*. (*Casero* means "homemade"—*comida casere* is probably derived from *cazuela*, the all-purpose peasant clay cooking dish used in much of Spain.)

THE WINES

There have been wines made in Extremadura for at least two thousand years, or since the Romans arrived. Until recently, the wine attracted very little attention outside the area.

One of the most common wines in Extremadura—like elsewhere in Spain—is *clarete*. Grapes used in this rosé-style wine vary from region to region, but in Extremadura it is made mostly from white wine grapes, including Palomino (the principal grape of Jerez), and for color, Morisco (a common red grape throughout central and southern Spain and Portugal). Other winemakers might add Garnacha, Palomino Negro, or Tinto Fino to boost the color of the *clarete*. Extremadura winemakers use what is available and are more concerned with where the grapes grow than with the names of the grapes. There are some outstanding white wines made from Palomino, Pedro Ximénez, Alarija, Bomita, Airén, and Marfil.

Both the white and red wines (but more frequently the white) develop a *flor* somewhat similar to the *flor* that blooms on the Jerez wines that become sherry. The *flor* is visible on the surface of the wine in the vats and looks brown rather than white, like the *flor* of

Jerez. The wine (which is clear for the first twelve to fifteen months of its life) suddenly becomes clouded and muddied in the casks, but it does clear again after three or four months, when it is bottled. No one can explain this but odds are the wine is undergoing some sort of delayed fermentation, either alcoholic or malolactic, perhaps having to do with a peculiar life cycle of the local wild yeasts. The wine has a fairly high alcohol content of 13 to 15 percent and a definite sherrylike appearance and flavor, yet it has none of the sherrylike fruitiness.

Typically, the small wineries of Extremadura ferment the wines in open cement vats that are sometimes sunk into the floor of the winery. Following fermentation, the wines are drained off into five-hundred-liter oak casks—usually American oak—where they are aged for eighteen to twenty-four months.

The best red wines of Extremadura by far come from the winegrowing area of Badajoz, a few kilometers from Portugal. Near the town of Almedralejo is Extremadura's only classified wine-growing district, the Tierra de Barros. As the name implies, the soil is a heavy clay that retains water well—which is a good thing, because the rainfall is low, about what it is in Los Angeles. Clays from this remote area are shipped all over Spain for potters, although now less than in the past.

Most of the wine production is from a white varietal called locally Cayetana, a high-yielding grape from which a low-acid but high-alcohol wine is made. Most of these wines are sold in bulk for blending or for brandy distillation, and if this were the only wine in Tierra de Barros, it wouldn't be worth a second glance.

But there is a wine made here from Spain's workhorse red wine grape, the Garnacha. Around the town of Salvatierra de Barros in the south of the district, a small quantity of a very flowery, intense red wine with deep rich colors is produced. Over the past decade it has gained a loyal following in Spain, and a tiny amount is being imported into the United States under the Lar de Barros label.

There was a flurry of interest in winegrowing possibilities around Cañamero in the 1920s, when many of the current small wineries were opened and new vineyards planted. But the wine of Cañamero, in common with most of Extremadura, remains virtually unknown outside the immediate area and a few places in Madrid, where the white wines have become somewhat trendy.

Locally, Cañamero wines can be found in the Parador Nacional Zurbarán and the Hospedería del Real Monasterio in Guadalupe.

The parador in Mérida has a better kitchen than the one in Guadalupe, but a much less adventuresome wine list, with heavy homage paid to Rioja at the expense of local wines.

The more trendy *madrileños* have also discovered wines from the remote mountain village of Montánchez, north of Mérida. The town is famous for its hams, but there is a red wine that also grows a *flor* as sherries do. Most of it is still made in the huge clay *tinajas* or *conos*. The Montánchez has a very sherrylike character, which is startling to the palate: the eyes are seeing red and the taste buds are saying, "No way. This is sherry."

THE VINEYARDS

Late spring is pleasant in the vineyards. The cold rains and mud of winter have disappeared but the hot summer sun hasn't yet arrived. The vines, old and thick, are close to the ground and look as if they had been there for centuries. There is little to do in the vineyards now. Pruning, of course, is finished; the young leaves are bursting out and it is still a few weeks before flowering. The most up-to-date farmers might spend a few hours walking the vineyards to cut off suckers (the new shoots that spring up at ground level but will not produce fruit) or perhaps cut back on excess young-vine growth to encourage a smaller but more intensely flavored crop of grapes. These alert viticulturists are still rare in Extremadura, where tradition dies hard and the goal of most growers is a larger crop, not smaller. At any rate, it's a good time to walk along and enjoy the warm air and the dozens of varieties of birds. And keep an eye out for wild pigs.

SPANISH DAYS

Atop a small rise in the road deep in the springtime green countryside of Extremadura you may need to brake for a formation of storks —those birds from the mists of childhood—marching across the road in the here and now. It's an unsettling experience. They stand between three and four feet tall and are quite formidable-looking. We felt happy to be inside a car, and not face to face in their preferred habitat, a bog.

The storks nest in the bell towers and on roofs of houses and hotels in towns and villages all through Extremadura. It is possible to watch a male and female white stork go calmly about the business of feeding nestlings within a few feet of a huge iron bell clanging away in a church tower.

But then there are birds everywhere in Extremadura. Even on a casual drive-by through the open countryside, half a dozen birds can be added to a life list. The Spanish no longer net small birds, as is common in Italy and parts of France. It is illegal everywhere now in the European Economic Community, but in some areas the practice is still followed. In Spain, King Juan Carlos is an ardent conservationist, which may have had some effect on the practice there. Once not too long ago, a small bird roasted whole was a common tapa.

We were on our way to lunch at a restaurant in Trujillo called La Troya. We had driven in the day before from Sevilla. National Route 630 climbs over an easy pass through the Sierra Morena, down into Extremadura, and into another Spain. Extremadura seems remote and mysterious, a bit unexpected after the Arab fantasies of the south.

Driving up from Andalusia may not be the most scenic way to approach this lonely, sometimes stunningly lovely countryside. (The scenic route would be through the high mountain passes traveling west out of Madrid-Toledo on the route of the ancient Roman road to Lisbon.) From Sevilla it's a long flat drive through towns that could be in Kansas or Nebraska, through streets filled with Spanish cowboys instead of the American kind, driving pickup trucks missing only the gunracks. The distance, which looks short enough on the map, begins to stretch out. The highway has two lanes jammed with trucks carrying the gardens of Andalusia north to France and Germany.

Amazingly, we arrived in good order in Guadalupe, in time for a wonderful dinner in the Hospedería del Real Monasterio, where we stayed. The friar-chef there is a fund of knowledge about the local foods; he is intent on preserving the traditional monastery cuisine. When he stopped at our table for a glass of wine after dinner and learned of our interest in the local foods, he recommended La Troya, in Trujillo. La Troya is family-style Spanish dining. There is no menu, although the waiter will offer a choice of entrées if asked.

A bottle of *gaseosa* (a kind of Spanish 7-Up) is immediately plonked on the table, along with a bottle of local red wine called

Vina Zanjo—do-it-yourself wine coolers! It is possible, however, to get other wines once the waiter understands that there is an interest. In fact, by the end of the meal, he is likely to be bringing a bottle of wine that his uncle or brother made; if that passes muster, there will probably be another bottle that he himself made. These are simple wines, to be sure, and one can taste the grape in them; yet at the risk of sounding trite or repetitive, it is honest wine and goes remarkably well with the food. Here, as in much of the countryside of Spain at the simpler restaurants, these wines are never bottled but are taken directly from barrel or carboy.

In some mysterious way, the local winemakers are able to achieve an astounding feat: working in a hot climate, with overripe grapes, they make a wine that is high in acid (remember the rough rule— the hotter the climate, the riper the grape, the lower the acidity of a wine). Perhaps the acidity is the result of the young wines (and they are all young) being exposed to air while fermenting, or perhaps it is simply built into the local, obscure grape varietals.

With the wine came a simple salad and a *tortilla de patatas*, a Spanish potato omelet. Those first two dishes are standard. After they are finished, there is some variation. Last time there we had delicious tuna *empanadas* with very thin wrapping skins, almost like wonton skins.

Whole loaves of bread are set on each table and quickly renewed if there is a need. The bread of Extremadura is a little gummy, because of the quality of the local wheat, but very tasty, with a smooth, velvety crust. Each local baker marks the bread in a different way, like a trademark.

The tuna *empanadas* were followed by white beans with *chorizo* and *morcilla*—basically a *sofrito*. This and the next course, a local version of *gazpacho*, were served in huge bowls in the center of the table from which you could take all you wanted.

But don't take too much! We are just beginning. Next came *caldereta de cordero* (lamb stew and very typical of the region) with potatoes and red peppers. The stew alone was worth the visit.

As a kind of sorbet to clean the palate, there followed *migas* (bread crumbs) with *chorizo*. This is one of the most basic peasant dishes of Spain and is found everywhere with local variations. In Extremadura it is a bit more refined than many. At Trujillo, it is a dish of bread crumbs, chopped red peppers, either sweet or piquant, and *chorizo* fried with garlic in olive oil, sometimes lard. It tastes better than it sounds. It was our second dish of *migas* for the day. We had ordered it for breakfast that morning at the monastery and had been served a *very* traditional *migas* heavy with pork fat.

There followed *cabrito frito*, a simple dish of fried kid served with a green tomato salsa. In Spain, milk-fed baby lamb and kid are often used interchangeably. Outside of Spain it is possible to substitute small lamb chops or sliced leg of lamb for most dishes that call for lamb or kid, since the Spanish usually cut the meat into evenly sized pieces anyway, rarely serving an entire joint. *Cabrito frito* is a traditional market dish served at the end of the day when the market is finished. A group of farmers at the market go together early to buy a goat, which is then butchered and cooked for a joint feast at the end of the day.

Finally, a simple dish of *probar de cerdo* was served. These thin slices of pork are traditionally cut from a freshly butchered pig to test the quality of the meat—should it be cured or cooked fresh?

For dessert, we had a flan served with a sauce made from *bellota y arellanos*, a local liqueur made from acorns. A glass of the liqueur was served with the flan.

The food at the *comida casero* in Trujillo was simple gustatory pleasure on almost an unconscious level. Regular patrons would know what to expect and would certainly want no changes. Yet the quality of the raw materials—the meat, the vegetables—was superb. When we mentioned this to the waiter he seemed surprised that anyone would notice. That kind of quality is simply a given, is taken for granted in most of Spain. Anything less would be remarkable.

The following night we had dinner at the Restaurante Nicolas in Mérida, where they serve a version of *caldereta de cordero* that has left the countryside and come into the city. It is more refined, the flavors are more focused and intense. The wines at Restaurante Nicolas (just down the street and around the corner from the *parador*) come in corked bottles and the waiters can discuss vintages and styles. They do not bring out their own homemade wine at the end of the meal. For sure, something has been gained. But something is also lost.

Perhaps we are sometimes guilty of a kind of reverse snobbism, but young wines served simply (near where they are made) without fuss or pretension often seem to get at a kind of vinous truth that may be lost in a more elaborate setting. There is actually some sound viticultural thinking behind this attitude. The process of blending and filtering or clarifying wines sometimes seems to strip them of their regional or varietal personality. Robert Mondavi in California has, in fact, stopped filtering his red wines (beginning with the 1985 vintage) and feels the wines are now much more representative of the local soils. In bottling, most wines are stabilized by one of several different technical processes; all of them change a wine to some extent. For example, anyone who has tasted a fruity young Beaujolais nouveau fresh from the barrel and the same wine a few weeks later after bottling can attest to that.

We stopped one afternoon in the small town of Cañamero, about halfway between Trujillo and Guadalupe, on a pleasant winding country road that will appear on a detailed Michelin map of Spain as C401. The road twists up, into, and over the Sierra Guadalupe, looping back to the main Madrid-Lisbon road, the N521.

It was late afternoon, the heat of the day had broken, and it was time for a plate of olives and a glass of wine. We fell into small talk with a man perhaps in his seventies sitting at one of the little round tables that crowded the sidewalk. He was a coin collector and we traded him a few American coins dredged from the bottom of purses and knapsacks for a glass of the local wine.

I don't know how the conversation got on to the Civil War, but it did. He said he had fought with Franco.

"Because they were the first to get me. If I hadn't gone with Franco, his soldiers would have killed me." He had been through the whole war, including the horrific siege of Madrid and the street-to-street, house-to-house fighting there.

"I killed many people," he said, shrugging and rolling the wine in his glass, "but I never got accustomed to it."

"Do you think it has made any difference, the Civil War? Does it matter now?"

He thought for a bit and looked carefully around him, "Then, I thought it mattered. I thought it was necessary. But now, I don't know. I don't think it mattered after all. We would still have been doing this," he waved a hand vaguely at the buildings around, the street, the televised soccer game in the dark bar behind him. But he had clearly grown a bit uncomfortable with the subject.

"Do you like our wine?" he asked.

"Very much. It is made nearby?"

He laughed. "It is made right across the street by the man who owns the bar. Come on, I'll introduce you."

The owner was a gentleman named Miguel Valle Gómez, and we

fell at once into deep discussion of his vineyard and winery, which was also his home. It was, indeed, just across the street. His wines were quite good, particularly his whites, which were clean with a good acid balance.

We invited the Civil War veteran to join us for a glass with Señor Valle. We toasted King Juan Carlos. We could see, through the open door of the bar, the man's vineyards across the street and a corner of his house where the wine we were drinking had been made in the basement two years before.

"To the vine." We raised our glasses.

Wandering down a twisting narrow street in Guadalupe, just at dusk. Past houses with signs announcing honey and wine for sale. Old women dressed in black (where are the young women?), sitting stiff-backed, knitting lace on narrow front porches.

At the bottom of the hill, an old man sitting very still doing nothing; thinking we were lost, he explained carefully in slow Spanish how to get back to the main plaza. We thanked him, followed his directions, and found ourselves with a different view of the mural showing the baptism of the Indians. In the half-light of dusk, approached from below, it took on a heroic, otherworldly look.

In a bar across the street from the monastery, the young crowd (sixteen to twenty-five, maybe) was drinking beer and listening to Three Dog Night. They were waiting for the disco to open. Guadalupe has a population of under three thousand. There are three discos. The young women dance to rock and roll while their mothers and grandmothers knit lace to sell to the tourists or to give to the Black Virgin.

Later that night we could hear the goats crying in the hills all around Guadalupe. That day many of the kids had been taken to market. The goats cried until dawn.

Sit in the Plaza Mayor in Trujillo surrounded by the mansions of men who made their fortune by murder and worse in the New World, and gaze at those ponderous, absurd storks nesting in church towers. Calmly contemplate the incredible folly of mankind.

But after a bit, it's time for lunch and a glass or two of wine.

GUIDELINES: EXTREMADURA

Guadalupe

HOTEL/RESTAURANTS

Hospedería del Monasterio, Plaza Juan Carlos, 1. Tel. (927) 36-70-00. This is a must stay. Stunning place. Days could pass by here, the world could slip away and peace would come, on sandled feet, opening the small bar just off the main patio where a small statue of the Virgin watches over your afternoon glass of wine. Price is moderate for both food and room.

Mesón el Cordero, Convento, 11. Tel. (927) 36-71-31. Good local fare but a step down from the Monasterio kitchen. Try for lunch.

There are some excellent bakeries just below the monastery. Try the almond cookies, which are a specialty of the area.

Mérida

HOTELS

There is the *parador*, which is comfortable. Somehow, I find *paradores* a little too-too. Like all those quaint bed-and-breakfast places in California and New England where one is always conscious of being part of a scene. On the other hand, there is something to be said for comfort and reasonable efficiency.

Parador Nacional Vía de la Plata, Plaza de la Constitución, 3. Tel. (924) 31-38-00. High moderate range in keeping with all *paradores*.

If you plan to stay a few days to have a closer look at the remarkable Roman ruins, look for *pensiones* around the Plaza de España.

RESTAURANTS

There are excellent regional dishes in the *parador*.

Restaurante Nicolas, Félix Valverde Lillo, 13. Tel. (924) 31-96-10. Try Nicolas for sure. Very moderate.

Bar Restaurante Briz, Félix Valverde Lillo, 5. Tel. (924) 31-93-07. Good country fare, simple but delicious. Also a fair tapas bar, although tapas are not a big deal in Extremadura.

SIGHTS

Do go to the Parque Arqueológico, which has maybe the best Roman ruins in Spain. It's about an eight-block walk from the Plaza Mayor. There is a theater, an amphitheater, and a stunning Roman museum. Don't miss this.

Trujillo

HOTELS

Hostal Pizarro, Plaza Mayor, 13. Tel. (927) 32-02-55. Cheap, with great views of the Plaza Mayor, which is one of the best in Spain.
 Avoid the local *parador*, which is cold and uninviting.

RESTAURANTS

La Troya, Plaza Mayor, 11. Tel. (927) 32-41-56. See above.
 The restaurant in the Hotel Pizarro serves remarkably good *extremeña* fare. Cheap.

This was long past harvest, another visit to Rioja, another time. It was after midnight when we left Mesón de la Merced, a rather posh restaurant about four blocks from Plaza del Mercado in Logroño. The dinner had been very good but very reserved. We were one of a group of Americans there mostly to taste the delights of Rioja, perhaps a bit too self-conscious about those delights to actually enjoy them. But everyone was tired. It had been a long day, with another long day to follow.

Most had read what the guidebooks had to say about Logroño. "Logroño lacks the charm that might be expected of the major wine-producing region of Spain." The American Express Pocket Guide to Spain. *Even worse, in its way, "Logroño . . . remains a busy provincial capital. It is a manufacturing center (textiles) and still produces its famous coffee caramels . . ."* The Michelin Green Guide to Spain. *How damning is that faint praise? Would anyone want to linger in a city that appeared to be famous only for coffee caramels?*

But we left the restaurant into an extravaganza, a burst, a swarm of music and color. The very streets were being painted. Just past midnight, we had come in at the beginning of the eve of Corpus

Christi. Beginning at midnight, the Calle Mayor had been seized by painters in chalk. For blocks leading to the Cathedral de Santa María de la Redonda, the narrow lane was divided into sections and had become a sketchbook for fantastic scenes, more or less religious, relating to the theme of Corpus Christi. The sidewalks were crowded by onlookers watching the work in progress. Apparently each shop took the section in front of its doors as canvas. There were bright angels with purple wings and violet halos staring down green virgins, each wearing glowing lavender shawls and clutching a golden Jesus to her breast.

On the sidewalk, musicians played the guitar and shouted encouragement to the chalkers, who frequently interrupted their work for a glass of wine offered by friendly sidewalk critics.

I stood amazed. We had entered the Mesón de la Merced about nine-thirty on an apparently quiet evening in late May, eaten our way through a satisfying if rather boring meal, and exited at one in the morning into a fairy kingdom. Fellini out of Disney.

People in the bar next door spilled out onto the sidewalk to criticize, to comment, to offer drinks, to dart back inside for another quickly emptied bottle.

My companions gazed bemused for a moment, then opted for the hotel, bed, and sanity.

We wandered like lost children into the heart of the madness and never looked back.

At three o'clock we were teaching hopscotch to a small tribe of Spanish children on the steps of the cathedral, sharing a bottle of rosada with a young couple who had come from Navarre for the Corpus Christi celebrations.

They were farmers, their first child very visibly on the way. They wanted to know about California. Did we celebrate Corpus Christi in San Francisco? Was the wine as good? (Surely not, the young woman said, giggling.)

The children simply thought we were crazy, which was okay with them. They kept bringing us olives—one by one on toothpicks— from a nearby bar.

In a few moments, the young couple from Navarre were joined by another couple who had made the trip with them.

There was more wine and roast chicken from somewhere.

We made a picnic on the steps of the church while the children swarmed around shouting, "Hopscotch, hopscotch." The chicken was delicious. It had been roasted with sprigs of rosemary and garlic cloves stuffed in the body cavity.

Near dawn, a shower at the hotel. Our bodies were covered in chalk dust, which we didn't want to wash away.

In the Tomb of the Kings at the Monasterio outside of Santo Domingo de la Calzada, two statues of the Virgin stare at each other down a long aisle. One is above the altar where Mass is celebrated, the other is in the Tomb of the Kings. Life and death stare at each other down the long stone-paved aisle.

MADRID

*Madrid is truly a city of
miracles, madame. I do not
know whether there are always
such illuminations here, such
ballets, such lovely women, but
I do know that I feel a
tremendous urge to make
Spain my country and Madrid
my home.*

—ALEXANDRE DUMAS
FROM PARIS TO CÁDIZ

IN FOCUS

Madrid doesn't fit exactly into the seasonal cycle, yet it is a touch-point for all of Spain. We will explore this city near the end of our season, because it is natural to come back to Madrid. In Spain, all the old roads give the distance to Madrid and all roads lead to and from Madrid, which is located near the geographical center of Spain.

Unlike the other areas we have looked at during our Spanish season, Madrid isn't really a regional entity; it is a compilation, in a sense, of all the regions of Spain.

The city is situated on a high plateau, surrounded on all sides by mountains; these alpine barriers serve as some protection against the storms of winter, but on the other hand, very effectively trap the heat of summer and form a barrier against summer rain. In truth, Madrid is not an easy city, either in terms of climate or the infamous traffic. Yet for all its admitted problems, it is worth it.

Madrid is not an ancient capital; it is a young city. Not as glamorous as Barcelona or as fabled as Sevilla, yet there is a charm to Madrid that can't be denied. Despite all its faults—which become very obvious to anyone who spends even a few hours here—Madrid is magical. It easily ranks among the world's most exciting cities—Rome, London, Paris, San Francisco, New York . . . Whatever your favorite city, I believe you'll find Madrid the equal, whether your interests are cultural or gastronomic. It isn't simply the laundry list of great museums, great restaurants, great opera and theater; like all great cities, it is more than the sum of its parts.

Madrid was established as the permanent capital of Spain in 1561 by Philip II. Before then (if one can speak of a national unity called Spain before then, or even now for that matter) the capital of Spain was wherever the court happened to be, although Toledo and Valladolid were favorite royal roosting places.

It isn't clear why Philip chose Madrid. Perhaps, because of its central location, he may have been trying to promote some feeling of unity. Philip also enjoyed the hunting in the area. Whatever his reasons, critics ever since have enjoyed pointing out that it was a sorry choice. Madrid has been described as an obscure village with no history or importance. We suspect that these critics have simply had to spend too many summers in Madrid, because the history of the capital goes back to settlements of prehistoric people along the Manzanares River.

The Moors built a fortress there and called it Majerit. It was captured in 1083 by the Castilian king, Alfonso VI, who promptly discovered a statue of the Virgin just outside a granary, or *almudín*. He converted the local mosque into a church and dedicated it to the Virgin of Almudena, who has been the patroness of Madrid ever since. That's a pretty good start for the city's table, Our Lady of the Granary.

Spanish kings made Madrid a regular stopping point from the fourteenth century, so Madrid seems as sound a choice for the Spanish capital as any other royal way station.

Nowadays a great many people simply cannot take Madrid at any price. They complain of the heat in summer, the cold in winter. They complain of the traffic, which is near gridlock for twelve to fourteen hours a day in the center of the city. They complain of the expensive (compared with the rest of Spain) restaurants and hotels. And this is all true. What you rarely hear anyone complain of is the people, the *madrileños*. One would have to be a prime grouch indeed to find a grouch in Madrid.

And for all its size, for all the appearance of modern urban life the pace in Madrid is reasonable. There is time to stop and look around. There is eye contact between strangers on the broad sidewalks. If people in Madrid are in a hurry, they are probably from New York or Barcelona.

THE FOOD

Whatever the season, if you don't eat well in Madrid, you simply didn't try. So much of the bounty of Spain finds its way to Madrid —like a delicious national smorgasbord—that it would be a pity to ignore the Spanish capital as a gustating entity simply because there are no vines growing in the Prado.

And there are restaurants there that know exactly how to serve forth all the harvest bounty. They range from grimy tapas bars around the Plaza Mayor, to trendy upscale hangouts on the grand avenues, to the unlikely mall-like setting for one of the best restaurants in Europe, Cabo Mayor.

Like most regional capitals, the nation's regional dishes can be found in Madrid. There are restaurants that specialize in all the cuisines of Spain, and other restaurants, a few, that try to bring them together. There is even a tapas bar that calls itself the Museum of Ham.

But besides the many regional foods available in the capital, Madrid has its own special dishes that are worth looking for. The most famous is undoubtedly the *callos a la madrileña*, the well-known veal tripe stew, which is sometimes eaten as a tapa early in the evening or in the wee hours of the morning to settle the tummy before bedtime. Another classic is *cocido madrileño*, a meat and vegetable soup. Another tasty Madrid dish is a variation on the Spanish tortilla that includes asparagus tips, called *tortilla capuchina*.

Again, the best raw kitchen materials in Spain—from the coast, from the garden, from the farms—are sent to Madrid. Whatever the season, the best will be in the Spanish capital.

THE WINE

The white-tablecloth restaurants will lean heavily on Rioja with a scattering of Catalonian wine from the Penedés. Maybe you'll find a few bottles from France—overpriced, of course—and the waiter will probably say that they are not available anyway. In the moderate-priced restaurants and the tapas bars, there will be the honest wines of La Mancha, especially from around Valdepeñas. These are often sold straight out of barrel, and are usually nonvintage and quite drinkable. And very, very cheap. A generous glass (three to four ounces) in a tapas bar will run 30 to 50 pesetas. A good quaff, as the British say. There will also be plenty of sherry on hand. There are also many bar/restaurants where a cooling glass of cider from the northwest can be found.

Much of the red wine in the small bars and cafés of Madrid is made nearby in the denomination of Méntrida, the most northern of the wine districts of La Mancha. The demarcated vineyards lie at the feet of the Sierra de Gredos, in the provinces of Toledo and Madrid. The chief grape—mostly the only grape—is the Garnacha, which covers over 90 percent of the vineyard area. The wines are usually drunk while still very young, with only about one-third sold in bottle, the rest in bulk.

If you have ordered white wine, it is still almost local—75 to 100 kilometers distant—and will almost surely be from the denomination of La Mancha. In direct contrast to Méntrida, 90 percent of production is white wine from the Airén grape, which produces a fairly neutral white wine, used a great deal in blending in other areas of Spain and brandy production for the *soleras* of Jerez.

SPANISH DAYS

Summer—notably, July and August—is a season that many avoid in Madrid—especially the natives, who flee to the nearby mountains. There is absolutely no cooling breeze. The air hangs hot and heavy right through the night, with perhaps some slight relief at five or six in the morning, before even the newspaper kiosks are open. Madrid is ringed by the mountains and the high plains of La Mancha. The summer rains that sweep in from the Atlantic to the north are blocked by the Sierra de Guadarrama, only a few dozen kilometers away.

Yet there are few things in life more pleasant around midnight of a typically hot Madrid summer day than a coffee with brandy (called, inexplicably, *carijillo*, or "small penis") in an outdoor café, watching the lights playing on a nearby fountain (Madrid is filled with fountains) discussing last night's dinner, planning the next night's dinner, and watching people pass back and forth. These post-midnight *paseos* are excellent for the digestion and also prepare the feet for a few hours of dancing to follow. Yes, it is late, but there is always the next day to sleep (or rather try to) in the summer heat.

The best plan is to meet in the afternoon at about five or six in one of the small cafés off the Plaza Mayor. In this older part of the city, the walls of the buildings are thick to keep out the heat or the infidel or the French; inside it will be dim, cooling to the eyes, at least. Do not move too fast. Take a cue from the *madrileños*. This is not Paris or New York, remember. It is only six o'clock. There is the whole night ahead.

One of the most popular meeting places is the Posada de la Villa, an old coach inn that has been remodeled without at all overwhelming the spirit of the original. It is on Cava Baja, one of the little streets opening out in a maze south of the Plaza Mayor. In the seventeenth century, Cava Baja was one of the major routes into the city, just off the Puerta Cerrada and the Calle Toledo, the road to Toledo.

The upstairs restaurant is, to be honest, a bit too palsy-walsy with the tourists who arrive in noisy buses from Germany, Italy, or maybe even Barcelona. (They are a determined lot. There is no bus parking within blocks.) But at the moment, we need not be concerned with them. Up the stairs they go for a dish of roast suckling pig (quite good, actually) and we are left at the street-level bar—still moving slowly, don't raise a sweat—which as it happens is one of the best all-purpose tapas bars in Madrid. There are other places that might have better this or better that, but at Posada de la Villa, everything will be of high quality.

A plate of olives will come with the first glass of wine. Order a light, slightly chilled red wine from La Mancha. It is a wine that need not be fussed over. Not for one moment is it necessary to hold it to the light and admire the color, to swirl it in the glass and admire the nose, to hold it in the mouth, rolling it back and forth like an all-purpose mouthwash. None of the above is necessary. The only job is enjoyment.

Now that we've quizzed the barman about the wine (and, with luck, gotten close to the right answers), soon one of the locals will introduce himself or herself, recognizing a stranger. A curious manifestation of Madrid culture is the effusiveness of the introduction. "You must meet Señor Lopez. He is my tailor. He is the best tailor in all of Madrid." By the third glass of wine, he has become the best tailor in all of Spain—possibly the world; for if one is the best in Spain, there is little else to compare.

At first, being a too-cynical, too-cautious *americano*, you have the tendency to draw back a bit. Why are these people being so friendly? What are they going to try and sell us? Are they planning to steal something? Not to worry. Almost everywhere in Spain, but especially in Madrid, you will meet with honestly friendly folk who will want to talk to you; first of all because they just like to talk, second because you are not Spanish and they are fascinated by anyone who has the great misfortune not to be a Spaniard.

The friendliness, the eagerness to meet and talk to strangers borders on the naive, but *madrileños* are not naive. They are quite sophisticated people who live in a time warp or an alternative universe where the greatest joy imaginable is to eat, drink, and talk.

Before very long, someone will suggest a change of scene perhaps to the bar of the Restaurant Neru on the Calle del Bordabores, only a few streets away from the Posada de la Villa, for an absolutely delicious blue cheese from Asturias in the Celtic north. It is a sharp, acidic cheese, made of an exotic blend of sheep, goat, and cow milk, mixed with Asturian cider to a spreadable consistency and served on bread, with a glass of cider at hand. The cider is spectacularly poured by the barman from a bottle held high above his head so that a small amount splashes into the glass, only a mouthful really. The aeration gives the cider an instant sparkle and you must drink it before you lose the foam and sparkle, or throw it out and the barman will pour another.

About this time, a running discussion will begin about where to eat dinner. It is now past nine. The last three hours have been filled with eating and drinking, but it is possible that a small dinner might be in order. There are those who worry about having too much to drink, but most generally, a careful recounting (and a careful recounting would not be possible if there had been too much) shows that it has been, so far, a fairly moderate evening. The tumblers of wine have been small, and following the Spanish lead, it is easy to make them last.

That is the great secret of a long evening of eating and drinking in Madrid without facing bankruptcy or temporary physical disability. Move slowly, nibble, sip. The evening is long and there are miles to go, and it could be, you are yourself walking the edge of that alternative universe of Spain.

We found ourselves one memorable evening deep in conversation with a man and his wife. He was the minister of tourism in the previous administration but one. His father had been in Franco's government, although he himself was a child when Franco came to power.

Be careful here. Yes, of course, Franco was a dictator; no doubt many terrible things were done by him or in his name during the Civil War. But the Spanish are pragmatists. Many who are quite liberal have found a few good words to say about Franco, although they have learned to be cautious in saying them to Americans. But the Civil War, to many Spaniards, is like a toothache that won't go away. They are constantly probing it, touching it—yes, the pain is still there—and inviting you to share the pain, or at least to look at it.

At any rate, this man, this rather funny-looking little man whose name we would never reveal, is offering to buy dinner at a nearby Galician restaurant called Casa Gallega. It is, he assures you, the best Galician restaurant in all of Spain. Yes, of course it is, but why should he want to buy dinner for two Americans? Because he wants your advice, is the quick answer.

His wife interrupts. She will only go to Casa Gallega, she insists, if afterward we can go for *callos* to Maxi's, a tapas bar on the Cava Alta, also nearby. Of course, yes, that is no problem. Certainly not, since Madrid is famous for this stewed tripe dish, which everywhere else in the world is called *callos a la madrileño*, but in Madrid, just *callos*. The true *callos* of Madrid is made from veal tripe and Maxi's is said to have the best in Madrid.

His wife disappears briefly to find recruits for the grueling two-block march to Casa Gallega and dinner, and our new friend outlines his problem. It seems that he is a bit short of ready cash—here it comes, you think, he is getting ready to try and sell us the family silver—but he has some paintings that he believes might interest an American museum. He is thinking particularly of the Getty Museum in Los Angeles. Later, he says, he will show me the paintings but he doesn't want to bore me with them just now. The question is, should he try and deal directly with the museum, or should he work through an agent, who will take a large commission?

"What are the paintings?"

Picasso, Miró, some minor turn-of-the-century portraits. The paintings, we were told, are in his mother-in-law's apartment (she has recently died) and after dinner we can have a look.

Yes, and we were guessing we would be stuck with the dinner check. As it turned out, we were not, and the paintings (viewed much later, after the *callos* at Maxi's) appeared to be as described.

And the next morning there was a call at the hotel from our host, inviting us to lunch. Of course, he is not on hand, we assume, to meet every American who wanders into the Posada de la Villa ("You can always find me there after six."), but it isn't difficult to meet and talk to people in Madrid. Perhaps more than most places, it is necessary to be a bit open, a bit trusting in Madrid. Yes, the crime rate is up, but it's up everywhere, isn't it? And it's still much lower in Madrid than almost any other world capital. Think of Washington, D.C.

Mountain climbers, downhill skiers, hangliders, and the like understand the joys of taking risks. It is necessary to put yourself at risk to reap the heart-stopping rush of pleasure. Perhaps the same principle should be applied to visiting in a strange land. Madrid, like most great cities, is a state of mind. You cannot *be* in Madrid and act as if you are in Chicago.

In a small bar just off the Plaza Mayor it is after Mass a late Sunday morning. Escaping the already hot sun for a small space of coolness, a glass of chilled wine.

A few moments before there had been only three or four people at the bar; one man read a newspaper at a bench in the corner. The bar is called Los Cuevas de Luis Candelas. The caves of Luis Candelas. He was a seventeenth-century Spanish Robin Hood who shared his booty with the poor. The bar was the entrance to a series of caves where he would hide from the king's soldiers.

That Sunday it looked very respectable, perhaps even a bit dull. But within minutes it was filled with well-dressed families, from an infant in a carriage to an old grandmother, who set herself firmly at the bar, turning her back on her grandchildren, who were arranged by the mother around one of the few tables in the bar. Coloring books, notebooks, and reading books were spread out. Large glasses of fruit juice were handed about, along with bowls of nuts and olives.

The children were fairly quiet, though active; an older boy trod on the newspaper reader's toes as he went for more juice.

The parents stood at the bar, eating, sipping wine, exchanging news of the week. Occasionally the mother or the father would take a look at the baby, sleeping in a carriage, blocking most of the narrow aisle.

No one seemed concerned. People edged past the baby, smiling at it, taking care not to awaken it.

If it had been a thieves' den three centuries before, the old bandit was nowhere in sight. The wine was only thirty pesetas a glass. No robbery there. A television set was tuned to a soccer game, the volume very low.

A young couple—perhaps sixteen or eighteen—came in, hand in hand; they stopped and smiled at the sleeping baby, the young woman greeting some of the adults, some of the children at the table. Perhaps she was an older sister, a cousin, or an aunt.

Her soft holas *were like a blessing.*

Inevitably, we ended up in the Plaza Mayor. Almost inevitably, we were having grilled prawns and looking out the window at not much of anything. It was a slow day. A tourist asked to use the bathroom and the barman waved him up the stairs, adding, "If it is still there." A little joke, we thought, and went back to our prawns.

A few moments later, the tourist returned, assuring the barman that it was, indeed, still there. "No, no," the barman explained. "It was not a joke."

It seems that a few weeks before, during a very busy evening, two Gypsies who had been drinking at the bar created a bit of a disturbance. Eventually, it was all sorted out peacefully, but in the meantime there had been, of course, much shouting and to-ing and fro-ing.

In a short time, someone went upstairs to use the bathroom. They found that most of the essentials were missing. Sawed right off at the wall and hauled away.

The barman could only guess that during the disturbance, other Gypsies, friends of the two at the bar, had slipped upstairs and taken away the toilet and the sink.

He shook his head in disbelief. "And there is no other way in or out except right through that door," he said, indicating the front door.

In Spain, Gypsies are blamed for everything, but I had never before heard them blamed for stealing the bathroom.

The wall of water at the marvelous, cooling fountain in the Plaza Colon. On a hot afternoon, it cools the eyes.

GUIDELINES: MADRID

Madrid

HOTELS

I won't even pretend to offer a guide to Madrid. The standard guides are quite good at major cities like Madrid. The following hotel and *pensiones* are good for long, economical stays.

Hotel Inglés, Calle Echegaray, 8. Tel. (91) 447-40-00. Ask for room 402. It has a separate sitting room and a lanai at a moderate price, and it's on a quiet street!

If you plan on staying for a time in Madrid, and you should, check out the *pensiones*. I like the *Hostal Residencia Pinaiega* on Calle Santiago, 1. Tel. (91) 248-08-19. The location is excellent, between the Plaza Mayor and the Opera House, not far from the Puerta del Sol and Palacio Real. Cheap.

There are lots of other inexpensive hotels and *pensiones* in Madrid, and a good thing, too, since many of the hotels are quite expensive. Begin your search near the Puerta del Sol and the Plaza Mayor; you are very near the center of Madrid here and can walk or take a quick subway ride to the Prado. It tends to be a noisy area, so ask for a room at the back. The Gran Vía area (Madrid's major east–west avenue) is a high-traffic area, so the rooms are noisy—but very cheap. Some of the best rooms in town are between Puerta del Sol and the Atocha rail station, including a marvelous place called the Hotel Sud Americana, which is right across the street from the Prado. The closer you get to the Atocha station, the cheaper the rooms and the riskier the area. Be streetwise here and keep your back covered. But it's still safer than Oakland. Also bear in mind that the higher you go, the less expensive the room. It is critical in renting a *pensión* or a *residencia* that you check out the room first—the accommodations vary wildly, even in the same establishment. Look under the bed (a good indication of how thoroughly the rooms are cleaned) and look inside the shower stall. Stand still and listen. Do you hear traffic or the guy next door bouncing off the wall?

RESTAURANTS

Cabo Mayor, Calle Juan Ramón, 37. Tel. (91) 250-87-76. A world-class restaurant in both food and service. Dishes from all of

Spain, lovingly perfected. Expensive and a long taxi ride from downtown.

Casa Paco, Puerta Cerrada, 11. Tel. (91) 266-31-66. Good manchego fare, also Asturian special dishes. Good tapas bar, popular hangout.

RECIPES

BASICS, TAPAS, SOUPS, AND SALADS

ALAS DE POLLO DIABLO
Deviled Chicken Wings

When we first brought this recipe back from Spain, many years ago now, our middle son, Jude, was delighted. There is a similar American fast-food creation, Buffalo wings, to which he was addicted. No blue cheese sauce and celery with these but they are a popular tapa in our home anyway.

SERVES 6 AS A TAPA.

¼ cup olive oil
12 whole chicken wings, split
  and tips removed
1 teaspoon salt
3 garlic cloves
½ cup dry white wine

1 teaspoon paprika
1 teaspoon thyme
1 teaspoon marjoram
1 teaspoon oregano
¼ teaspoon hot red pepper
  flakes

Preheat the oven to 400°F.

Heat the olive oil in a large ovenproof skillet. Cook the chicken pieces until they are lightly golden, sprinkling with the salt as they cook. Pour off the excess oil.

Add the garlic cloves. Pour in the wine and stir in the remaining ingredients. Place the skillet in the oven and bake for 30 minutes.

Return the skillet to the top of the stove and cook until the liquid is reduced. Toss the pieces of chicken as they cook so they don't burn.

Serve immediately or cooled to room temperature.

ALCACHOFAS REBOZADAS RELLENAS
Deep-Fried Stuffed Baby Artichokes

These artichokes are a great tapa or an interesting first course if served in a pool of fresh tomato sauce. Remember when planning a menu that artichokes really alter the taste of other foods, and especially wine. They make the other foods taste somewhat sweet and the wine slightly metallic.

SERVES SIX AS A FIRST COURSE OR SEVERAL MORE FOR TAPAS.

½ lemon
16 to 20 very small baby artichokes (about 1 pound)
½ tablespoon unsalted butter
½ cup minced shallots
⅔ cup (about 3 ounces) minced baked ham
All-purpose flour

½ cup cold milk
2 tablespoons grated Parmesan cheese
Salt and white pepper to taste
2 eggs
1½ cups fine dry bread crumbs
Oil for frying

Bring a pot of salted water to a boil with the lemon.

Cut away the stems and about half an inch from the bottoms of the artichokes. Cut a third off the tops and remove the tough outer leaves. Immediately plunge the artichokes into the water and cook over medium heat until tender, about 20 minutes. Drain well and cool.

Melt the butter in a small pan and sauté the shallots until golden. Stir in the ham and cook 2 minutes. Sprinkle 2 teaspoons of flour over the ham. Stir and cook for 1 minute. Pour the milk in all at once and stir until thickened. Add the cheese and salt and white pepper.

Barely open the artichokes, gently removing a few of the inner leaves to form a cavity. Divide the ham mixture among the artichoke openings.

Beat the eggs with a tablespoon of water. Place 1 cup of flour and bread crumbs in separate bowls. Dip the filled *tops* of the artichokes first into the flour, then the egg, and then the bread crumbs. (The whole artichoke is not breaded, just the tops. This can all be done ahead and refrigerated until time to cook.

Heat 2 inches of oil to 380°F. Drop in a few of the artichokes at a time and fry until golden. Drain on paper towels.

The artichokes stay very hot so can be done a little ahead of serving, or even reheated briefly in the oven or microwave.

BUÑUELOS DE BACALAO
Salt Cod Puffs

Salt cod puffs and croquettes are popular all over Spain. Often in restaurants they are presented as a little plate for sustenance until the first course arrives. Usually they are fried light, lovely, and greaseless. But we tasted these baked versions in Madrid and found the flavor was still wonderful. Baking might be a lot easier for the home cook who would like to be a part of the party and not in the kitchen doing last-minute frying. However, if you would like to taste them fried, this same recipe works perfectly.

SERVES 6 AS A TAPA.

Begin preparation 24 hours in advance.

½ pound boneless skinless salt cod	¼ cup butter
2 tablespoons olive oil	⅔ cup all-purpose flour
1 medium onion, minced	4 eggs
1 tablespoon minced fresh parsley	Salt and white pepper

Soak the cod in cold water for 24 hours, changing the water several times. Drain the cod, squeeze dry, and chop medium-fine.

Preheat the oven to 400°F.

Heat the oil in a skillet. Add the onion and sauté over medium heat until golden. Add the cod and parsley and cook, stirring, for 2 minutes. Drain off any liquid and place the cod mixture in a bowl.

Bring ⅔ cup of water and the butter to a boil in a medium saucepan. When the butter has melted, stir in the flour and continue to stir until it pulls away from the sides of the pan and forms a ball.

Place this mixture in the bowl of the food processor. With the motor running, add the eggs. Whirl until the eggs are fully incorporated into the dough. Add salt and pepper to taste.

Stir the dough into the cod mixture and combine well.

Drop by heaping teaspoons onto greased baking sheets. Leave about an inch between them. Bake until golden and puffed, about 15 to 20 minutes.

Serve immediately.

HUEVOS DUROS CON CHORIZO
Hard-Boiled Eggs with Sausage

Every Spanish tapas bar is sure to have at least a couple of egg tapas. The most famous, of course, is the Tortilla Española, *page 131. The ingredients of this particular egg tapa vary from area to area. It is sometimes served cold and sometimes hot. We prefer it warm as a tapa or as a light supper dish.*

SERVES 6 TO 12 AS A TAPA.

6 eggs
2 tablespoons olive oil
5 garlic cloves, sliced
1 onion, minced
¾ pound mild, dry *chorizo* or
  similar sausage, thinly sliced
1 cup dry white wine or
  Chicken Stock, page 147

1 tablespoon sun-dried or
  regular tomato paste
1 cup fresh shelled or frozen
  tiny peas
Salt and freshly ground black
  pepper to taste

Place the eggs in a saucepan and cover with cold water. Bring to a boil, lower the heat, and cook for 5 minutes. Remove from the heat, pour off the hot water, and cover with cold water.

Meanwhile, heat the oil in a skillet. Cook the garlic over medium heat until golden. Add the onion and cook until soft. Add the *chorizo* and cook for 3 minutes. Stir in the wine or stock and tomato paste. Cook until the sauce begins to thicken.

Peel the eggs and add to the sauce. Cook for about 5 minutes. Cut the eggs in half and baste with the sauce. Sprinkle with the peas. Cook for a few more minutes until the peas are hot. Season with salt and pepper.

Serve immediately with the sauce.

REVUELTOS DE SALMÓN CON PASAS
Scrambled Eggs with Fresh Salmon and Raisins

The Spanish are fond of scrambled egg dishes as first courses or as part of their light, late suppers. The combination of raisins and salmon is unusual and very delicious.

SERVES 4 TO 5.

2 tablespoons butter
¼ cup black raisins
3 garlic cloves, minced
4 ounces fresh salmon fillet, shredded

8 eggs, beaten
2 tablespoons milk or cream
Salt and white pepper to taste

Heat the butter and sauté the raisins and garlic until golden. Add the salmon and sauté until barely done.

Combine the eggs with the milk or cream and stir into the salmon. Sprinkle with a little salt and pepper and stir and cook until fluffy and barely set.

Serve immediately.

ENSALADA DE HABAS CON COCHOS
Squid and Fava Bean Salad

We had this salad as a tapa in northern Spain but we have also served it as a salad on a bed of mixed greens. Either way it has a refreshing flavor and very interesting texture.

SERVES 6 AS A SALAD AND 10 AS A TAPA.

Begin preparation 5 or more hours in advance.

- 3 garlic cloves
- 3 anchovy fillets
- ½ cup minced fresh parsley
- ½ cup olive oil
- 1 teaspoon salt
- ½ teaspoon freshly ground black pepper
- ¼ teaspoon hot red pepper flakes
- 3 tablespoons fresh lemon juice
- 3 tablespoons wine vinegar
- 2½ pounds fava beans in their shell
- 1 bay leaf
- 3 whole cloves
- 1½ pounds cleaned squid, tentacles left whole and tubes cut into ½-inch rings

Combine the garlic, anchovies, and parsley in a blender or food processor and blend to a paste. Add the oil, salt, pepper, pepper flakes, lemon juice, and vinegar and whirl to combine well. Set the dressing aside.

Shell the fava beans. Place the shelled beans, bay leaf, and cloves in a pan and cover with water. Bring to a boil and cook the beans until tender. The time for this will vary with the age of the beans. Young ones will only take about 7 to 10 minutes.

Drain the cooked beans and remove the bay leaf and cloves. Combine the beans with the dressing.

Bring another pot of salted water to a boil. When the water is at a furious boil add the squid and cook for 30 seconds and drain.

Toss the squid with the beans and coat well with the dressing.

Allow to cool and refrigerate for at least 5 hours before serving.

MEJILLONES RELLENOS
Stuffed Mussels

*We have had these in San Sebastián at several of the wonderful tapas
bars in the Old Quarter. There they are deep-fried. Frying does keep
you in the kitchen, so if you want to be with your guests while these
are cooking, bake them as we do here. They are just as delicious.*

SERVES 6 OR MORE.

30 mussels (about 2 pounds)
 1 cup dry white wine
    Olive oil
 1 medium onion, minced
 2 garlic cloves, minced
    Pinch of hot red pepper
    flakes
    Pinch of dried or fresh
    thyme

 1 tablespoon all-purpose flour
    Salt and freshly ground black
    pepper to taste
 1 red bell pepper, roasted and
    peeled, see instructions for
    Peppers Stuffed with Crab,
    page 394
 ⅓ cup fine dry bread crumbs

Wash the mussels and debeard, if necessary. Bring the wine to a boil
in a pot, preferably a spaghetti cooker with an insert to make it easy
to remove the mussels. Put the mussels over the boiling liquid,
cover, and steam open—it will take only a few minutes. Remove the
mussels as they open. Reduce the cooking liquid to ½ cup. Pour the
reduced liquid through a fine strainer or through cheesecloth or a
coffee filter to remove any grit. Set aside.

Remove the mussels from the shells, reserving half of the shells.

Heat 2 tablespoons of oil in a small pan and cook the onion and
garlic until golden. Stir in the red pepper flakes, thyme, and flour.
Cook 1 minute.

Add the reduced cooking liquid and stir until smooth and thickened. Season with salt and pepper.

Coarsely chop the roasted red pepper and mussels and stir them
into the sauce.

Fill the reserved mussel shells with the mussel mixture. Refrigerate until firm.

Preheat the oven to 400°F.

Pour the bread crumbs onto a plate. Coat the filled side of the
mussels with the crumbs and place them on a baking sheet filled side
up. Sprinkle the tops with olive oil.

Place the mussels in the oven and bake for 5 minutes. Remove from the oven and place under the broiler until golden.

Serve immediately.

NOTE: If serving as an appetizer, serve with tiny appetizer forks. As a first course, divide them among 6 plates.

ENSALADA TEMPLADA DE GAMBAS
Y ESPARRAGOS CON
VINAGRETA DE JAMÓN
Warm Asparagus and Prawn Salad with Ham Dressing

*A warm salad can sometimes be intimidating, since you want to be
with your guests and in the kitchen at the same time. Don't be put off.
Much of this salad can be done ahead, and the last-minute cooking
really does just take a couple of minutes, especially if timed so that all
three cooking procedures are done simultaneously.*

SERVES 6.

18 prawns, (about ¾ pound)	2 tablespoons olive oil
½ onion, sliced	2 ounces ham or prosciutto,
Sprig of parsley	thinly sliced and shredded
1 celery stalk, quartered	3 garlic cloves, peeled and
10 peppercorns	thinly sliced across
2 teaspoons salt	½ teaspoon freshly ground
2 pounds asparagus, pencil	black pepper
thin, ends trimmed and tops	1 tablespoon vinegar
sliced diagonally	

Shell the prawns and reserve the shells. Devein the prawns and set
aside.

Bring 3 cups of water to a boil. Add the onion, parsley, celery,
peppercorns, and salt. Cook for 5 minutes. Add the prawn shells and
cook for 10 minutes over medium heat. Strain the stock into another
saucepan and discard the shells and vegetables. Bring the stock to a
boil. Taste for salt; it should taste a little salty. (The recipe can be
prepared ahead to here. Refrigerate the stock if kept more than a
couple of hours. Bring it to a boil and proceed.)

Boil the prawns in the stock until pink. Remove the prawns to a
bowl and keep warm.

Meanwhile, steam the asparagus over boiling water until just
tender—this will depend on their size. Combine the asparagus in
the bowl with the prawns.

Heat the oil in a small skillet and cook the ham with the garlic
until the ham begins to crisp and the garlic is golden. Stir in the

pepper and the vinegar. Heat through and pour the ham sauce over the prawns and asparagus. Toss well.

Divide the salad among 6 heated plates and serve immediately.

ENSALADA DE BREVAS Y ANCHOAS
Fresh Fig and Anchovy Salad

This is one of the best salads we've ever eaten. Its success depends simply on the very best ingredients.

Brevas is the name given to the first crop of Spanish figs, plump and black. Use the figs that ripen at the end of June. And you oh so lucky ones with your own fig trees, just pluck them from the tree and slice and serve them still warm from the sun.

SERVES 6.

1 large head curly endive, torn apart

12 fresh figs, stemmed and, if you like, peeled

1 2-ounce can good-quality anchovies, drained and rinsed

3 ripe but firm medium tomatoes, peeled, seeded, and cut into tiny dice

Best-quality extra-virgin olive oil

Freshly ground black pepper

Divide the endive among 6 plates. Cut the figs into quarters and arrange in the center of the plates. Crisscross 2 fillets of anchovies over the figs and scatter the tomatoes over all.

Drizzle the oil over the tops and sprinkle with pepper.

Serve immediately.

SOPA DE TOMATE EXTREMEÑA
Tomato Soup with Bread Extremadura-Style

We were told that this is a "very old recipe," but it can't be really ancient since the tomatoes in Spain date only from the time of the discoveries of the Americas. When grapes or figs are in season they are served in a bowl beside the soup and added to each bite.

SERVES 4.

2 tablespoons olive oil
1 large onion, minced
½ celery stalk, thinly sliced
3 tomatoes
3 cups Chicken Stock, page 147
1 bay leaf

2 cloves
Salt and freshly ground black pepper
1 cup ½-inch cubes day-old bread

Heat the oil and slowly cook the onion and celery until very tender but not colored. Puree 2 of the tomatoes and stir them into the onions. Cook quickly until the tomatoes form a paste.

Pour in the stock and add the bay leaf, cloves, and salt and pepper to taste. Cook over low heat for 30 minutes.

Peel, seed, and cube the remaining tomato. Add it to the soup just before serving and heat through. Stir in the bread cubes and serve immediately.

PURÉ DE PATATAS CON AJO
Garlic Potatoes

These potatoes are a heavenly variation on that homey American tradition "mashed potatoes." They are a wonderful accompaniment to winter stews of all sorts.

SERVES 6.

2½ pounds Idaho or yellow
    Finnish potatoes
  2 large garlic bulbs, cloves
    separated and peeled
¼ cup (½ stick) unsalted
    butter, softened at room
    temperature

½ cup warm half-and-half
Salt and white pepper to
  taste

Bring a large pot of salted water to a boil. Peel and quarter the potatoes and add to the pot with the whole, peeled garlic cloves. Lower the heat and cook until tender.

Drain the potatoes, reserving the cooking liquid.

Force the potatoes and garlic through a food mill or mash them. Using a hand mixer for best results, whip in the butter and half-and-half. If necessary, add some of the reserved cooking liquid to achieve a smooth, fluffy mixture. Season with the salt and pepper.

Serve immediately.

NOTE: Leftover potatoes are excellent for making Potato Puffs, page 128.

VERDURAS A LA PLANCHA
Grilled Vegetables

*In Spain, simple grilled vegetables are served either as a course them-
selves or as an accompaniment to the main course. Two such grilled
vegetable preparations have their own surnames: escalivada and calçots. Indeed, calçots even have their own festival, see page 188.*

MIXED GRILLED VEGETABLES
Select several vegetables that are visually appealing, like squash (cut
into slices), asparagus (whole), Japanese eggplant (cut in half), tomatoes (whole), onion (thick slices); whole assorted sweet peppers,
or any others you like and think will work on the grill.

Salt **Lemon, optional**
Extra-virgin olive oil

   Use a lidded barbecue and heat the coals until they are uniformly
white, then spread them evenly over the bottom grill. Brush the grill
with olive oil. Lay the vegetables on the top grill, cover, and cook
covered until they are just tender. You won't need to turn them.
Remove the vegetables to a platter, sprinkle with salt, and drizzle
with the oil. Sprinkle with lemon juice if desired. When we enjoy
wine with the meal we skip the lemon, which interferes with the
taste of the wine.

ESCALIVADA
Escalivada refers to an assortment of vegetables grilled whole over a
fire, then peeled and pulled apart, arranged on a platter and drizzled
with extra-virgin olive oil and salt and pepper. The mix usually consists of eggplant, peppers, and onions. We have had this as an appetizer on toast, as a first course, as part of a main dish, and as a tart
(see Tarta de Escalivada, page 262). After grilling, put the peppers
into tightly closed paper bags for 15 minutes to cook them further
and to ease the peeling.

CALÇOTS
Calçots are a type of large scallion or small leek that has more white
than green and a milder flavor. We buy the biggest scallions or baby
leeks we can find and grill them over hot coals or a combination of

coals and vine cuttings. Sprinkle them with salt as they cook. When thoroughly charred all around, remove them from the grill and wrap them in paper—in Spain they use newspaper. They will steam in the paper and complete their cooking. They are brought to the table still wrapped in their paper. When the paper is opened the air is perfumed with the sweet-acrid smell of the *calçots*. They are served with *romesco* sauce, see page 278.

MENESTRA DE VERDURAS
Vegetable Stew

Every region of Spain has a version of menestra for every season of the year. I've tasted it flavored with salt pork, with lamb, with clams, and with vegetables alone.

I can hardly call this a recipe; use what follows as a rough guide. Menestra can be a first course, a side dish, or a light main dish.

It is very different from the vegetable stir-fries, in which the vegetables remain crisp. As the vegetables cook together they soften and the flavors of the menestra mingle in a very satisfying way. Play with this. Try lots of different combinations.

SERVES 6 TO 8.

¾ pound each of 4 or 5 compatible, seasonal vegetables (green beans, artichoke hearts, carrots, turnips, and zucchini)
2 tablespoons olive oil

1 onion, minced
¼ pound slivered ham, preferably prosciutto
Salt and freshly ground black pepper to taste

Prepare the vegetables for cooking, peeling those that need to be peeled. Keep the vegetables separate. Cut the larger ones into easy-to-eat pieces. Bring a large pot of lightly salted water to a boil. If you have a spaghetti cooker with an insert, use it; it makes it a lot easier to remove the vegetables after cooking.

Cook a vegetable at a time in the water until tender but not mushy. Set aside. Reserve the cooking liquid. The vegetables can now be combined.

Heat the oil in a large pan and cook the onion and ham until golden. Stir in the vegetables and 1 to 2 cups of the reserved cooking liquid. Season with salt and pepper and cook the vegetables over medium heat for about 10 minutes.

Serve immediately in flat soup plates.

HABAS CON ALMEJAS
Fava Bean Stew with Clams

*Probably the most famous Asturian dish is the traditional bean prep-
aration* fabada asturiana. *Here is another wonderful bean dish but
much lighter and perhaps more suitable to American palates, since
this uses clams instead of pork sausages.*

SERVES 6 TO 8.

Begin preparation 12 hours in advance.

2 pounds dried fava beans (available at Italian markets)	1 garlic clove, peeled
	1 tablespoon olive oil
1 pound small clams in their shells	1 cup dry white wine
	1 teaspoon salt
2 bay leaves	1 teaspoon freshly ground black pepper
1 large onion, minced	

Cover the beans with cold water and soak overnight. The next day,
scrub the clams, place in cold water, and set aside. Drain the beans
and place in a large pot. Add the bay leaves, onion, garlic, and oil.
Cover well with cold water. Bring to a boil, remove the surface
scum, lower the heat, and cook the beans until tender. Test the
beans after 45 minutes by removing a bean and blowing on it. If the
skin cracks, the beans are done.

While the beans are finishing cooking, prepare the clams. Place
the clams in a pot with the wine. Cover and steam until the shells
open. Remove the clams, discarding any that do not open, and
reserve the cooking liquid.

Preheat the oven to 350°F.

When the beans are tender, drain them and reserve the liquid.
Place the beans in an ovenproof casserole and top with the clams.
Place the reserved bean liquid in a separate pot and pour the clam
liquid through a fine sieve into the pot. Reduce the liquid by half.
Season with the salt and pepper. Pour over the beans and clams and
heat in the oven just until hot.

Serve immediately in flat soup plates.

FISH, ETC.

SOPA DE MARISCOS AL PASAJE
DE SAN JUAN
Fish Soup Pasaje de San Juan Style

Fish soups vary from region to region. Some have saffron, some have cream, some have orange zest. This particular one we had in a charming fishing village just 20 minutes east of San Sebastián in the Basque country. All the shellfish was as fresh as the sea breeze blowing across our table. Buy the freshest ingredients possible—crucial always, but particularly with fish and shellfish.

SERVES 6.

¼ cup olive oil
2 onions, minced
4 garlic cloves, minced
5 medium tomatoes, chopped
1 cup dry white wine
1 recipe Fish Stock, page 149
   Salt and white pepper

18 small clams (about
   1½ pounds)
12 mussels (about ½ pound)
12 prawns (about ½ pound), in
   their shells
6 lemon wedges

Heat the oil in a pot and cook the onions and garlic until they begin to color. Add the tomatoes and cook until dry. Stir in the wine and cook until the pot is dry. Add the stock, bring to a boil, and lower the heat to medium. Cook for 20 minutes and strain, discarding the solids. Return the stock to the pot and cook to reduce to 8 cups.

Add the shellfish to the stock: first add the clams and cook 1 minute, then add the mussels and prawns. Cook until the clams and mussels have opened and the prawns have turned pink. Remove the shellfish with a slotted spoon to a serving bowl, discarding any clams or mussels that do not open. Garnish with the lemon wedges.

Strain the stock into a terrine through a fine strainer to remove any grit.

Serve at the table by dividing the shellfish among soup bowls—preferably large flat ones—and pouring the stock over the shellfish. Garnish each bowl with a lemon wedge and have your guests squeeze the lemon juice over the soup before eating.

MARMITAKO
Basque Tuna with Potatoes

Marmitako is a very simple fishermen's dish from the Basque country. Before the discovery of the Americas, fishermen prepared their "catch of the day" with bread, onions, and water—pretty basic!

Later they added the potatoes and tomatoes brought from the New World—still a simple dish but a very satisfying one. This recipe does not call for tomatoes but green peppers, another treat from America.

SERVES 6 TO 8

- 3 tablespoons olive oil
- 1 large onion, minced
- 2 green peppers, stemmed, seeded, and cut into chunks
- 2 pounds white potatoes, peeled and quartered
- 1 teaspoon salt
- ½ teaspoon white pepper
- 3 pounds bonito or fresh tuna, cut into 6½-ounce servings

Preheat the oven to 400°F.

Heat the olive oil in a sauté pan large enough to hold all the ingredients. (We like to use a clay casserole that we can cook in and serve from.) Add the onion and green pepper and cook over medium heat until soft but not golden. Add the potatoes to the pan, season with the salt and pepper, and pour in enough water just to cover the ingredients. Place the casserole in the oven and cook until the potatoes are tender but not falling apart, about 20 minutes. Place the fish pieces on top of the potatoes and return to the oven for another 10 minutes. Taste for seasoning, adding more salt and pepper if needed. Serve hot, placing the fish on the plate and pouring the potatoes and sauce over the fish.

PAELLA AL WEBER
Mixed Seafood and Meat Paella Weber-Style

The proper making of paella is an art form in Spain, with just the right wood selected for the outdoor fire where the traditional paella is cooked. In Valencia, the wood must be trimmings from the orange groves, it's said; in other parts of Spain, vine prunings are usually preferred. We are sure this method of cooking the paella on a covered barbecue would bring howls of outrage from Spanish purists, but it works quite well, and most of us haven't access to vineyards or orange groves to stoke our wood fires anyway.

SERVES 6.

3 tablespoons olive oil
1 medium onion, minced
3 garlic cloves, minced
½ pound tomatoes, chopped
½ pound cleaned squid, tubes sliced into rings
1½ pounds meaty chicken pieces, cut with a cleaver into chunks (use all dark meat for more flavor)
¼ pound boneless pork or *linguiça*, chopped
2 teaspoons salt, or more to taste

6 cups Chicken Stock, page 147, Fish Stock, page 149, or water
½ teaspoon saffron threads
3 cups short-grain rice, preferably Valencian or Italian
1 pound cleaned mussels, in their shells
1 pound prawns, in their shells
1 cup fresh peas or 1 pound asparagus tips, optional
2 lemons, cut into wedges

Light the coals in a covered Weber-type barbecue. When the coals are white hot, heap them in the center of the barbecue. Place the paella pan on the grill above the hot coals and pour in the oil. When hot, add the onion and garlic and cook until limp. Stir in the tomatoes and cook until dry. Push the vegetables to the side of the pan. Add the squid, chicken, and pork or sausage. Sprinkle with the salt. Grind the saffron threads to a powder in a mortar and add or just rub the threads between your palms and sprinkle over the chicken.

Cook, turning the pieces over, until the chicken begins to color, about 5 minutes. Add the stock or water. At this time you may need to stoke the fire with a few sticks of kindling to bring the stock to a boil. Taste for salt. The broth should taste slightly salty. Cook the broth at a rapid boil for about 5 minutes.

Stir in the rice, turning the chunks of chicken over so all the rice is submerged in the broth, and cook the paella for about 10 minutes.

Arrange the prawns over the top of the paella and the mussels, hinge side down, around the edge of the paella. If you wish, add the peas or asparagus now. Cook another 5 minutes. Close the cover of the barbecue. Cook another 5 minutes.

To serve, remove the paella to the table and cover with a cloth. Allow to rest for about 5 minutes, then decorate the top of the paella with lemon wedges. Garnish each portion with a lemon wedge and have your guests first squeeze the lemon juice over before eating.

PIMIENTOS RELLENOS DE TXANGURRO
Peppers Stuffed with Crab

The classic presentation of this delicious crab dish is to serve it in the hollowed-out Dungeness crab shell—one shell served to each guest. We find that is just too much to eat. Juan Marí Arzak, at his restaurant in San Sebastián, sometimes presents the dish in a fashion similar to that given here, and we love it.

SERVES 6.

2 fresh Dungeness crabs, cooked, or ¾ pound crabmeat
7 red bell peppers
2 tablespoons olive oil
1 small leek, cleaned and white part chopped
1 small onion, peeled and minced

1 carrot, minced
1½ pounds tomatoes, peeled, seeded, and pureed
¾ cup Fish Stock, page 149
1 cup cream
Salt and white pepper

Preheat the oven to 400°F.

Crack the crab and remove the meat from the legs and body. Carefully pick over the crab to remove any shell or cartilage. Set aside.

Oil the peppers and place them, whole, on a baking sheet. Bake until the skins are blistered and charred, about 30 minutes. Remove from the oven and place the peppers in a paper bag. Close it tightly and let steam for 15 minutes. Stem, seed, and peel the peppers. Try to keep them whole. Set aside. (Do not rinse the peppers with water, it dilutes the flavors.)

Heat the oil and cook the leek, onion, and carrot slowly until very tender. Stir in the tomatoes and cook to a paste. Pour in ½ cup of the stock and ½ cup of the cream. Cook until reduced and thick. Stir in the crabmeat and season with ½ teaspoon of salt and ½ teaspoon of pepper.

Stuff 6 of the peppers with the crab mixture and arrange them in a circle with the open ends pointing up in a round clay casserole or other baking pan. Heap any excess filling in the center where the peppers meet.

Puree the remaining pepper with the remaining ¼ cups of stock and ½ cup of cream. Season to taste with salt and white pepper. Pour over the peppers and bake until hot through and bubbling, about 25 minutes.

Serve immediately.

RAPÉ CON PUERROS Y CALABACINES
Monkfish with Leeks and Zucchini

Juan Maríe Arzak is generally considered one of the best chefs in Spain. And rightly so. Among so many good and great restaurants in the Basque country, his Arzak stands out as the best. Although he is very inventive, his dishes stay true to the fundamentals of Basque cooking.

This is a very simple dish that allows all the component flavors to come through distinct, uncluttered. Arzak had wrapped each scallop of fish in a large slice of zucchini. You might want to prepare it that way when you have larger zucchini. The following adaptation is easier for home preparation.

SERVES 6.

2 medium leeks	½ teaspoon white pepper
4 small zucchini	1 cup Fish Stock, page 149
3 tablespoons unsalted butter	½ cup cream
1 teaspoon salt	2 pounds monkfish

Preheat the oven to 400°F.

Cut off the green part of the leeks. Cut the leeks in half and wash thoroughly. Peel off several folds of the leek, roll into a bundle, and then thinly slice with the grain. You will have long, thin strips of leek. Repeat with the remaining leeks and set aside.

Remove the tops and tails of the zucchini. Cut each zucchini into fourths lengthwise. Then thinly slice each quarter diagonally. There will be little slivers of white with green tips at each end. Set aside.

Heat the butter in an ovenproof skillet. Braise the leeks and zucchini in the butter until they begin to soften. Sprinkle with the salt and pepper. Pour in the fish stock and cream. Increase the heat and cook until the vegetables are soft and the sauce has begun to thicken.

Meanwhile, prepare the monkfish. Remove any of the thin gray membrane and cut the monkfish into 18 round scallops.

Add the monkfish to the sauce and place the skillet in the oven. Cook for 10 minutes. Remove from the oven. Remove the fish and vegetables to a serving platter and keep warm. Reduce the sauce over high heat to a medium thickness. (The sauce should not be too thick or it will take away from the fresh flavor of this dish.)

Pour the sauce over the fish and serve immediately.

MAINS

POLLO AL AJILLO
Chicken with Garlic

We had a memorable version of this dish in a small country restaurant near Murcia, south of Valencia. It's a dish common in the country throughout Spain or wherever comida casera, *or home cooking, is found.*

Here, whole nuggets of garlic nestle among the chicken pieces in a wine-and-herb sauce.

SERVES 6.

½ cup olive oil
15 large garlic cloves, peeled and
    left whole
 1 3½-pound chicken, cut into
    8 serving pieces
 1 teaspoon salt

½ teaspoon freshly ground
    black pepper
½ teaspoon dried thyme
½ teaspoon dried oregano
 1 cup dry white wine

Heat the oil in a large, heavy nonreactive skillet. Add the garlic and sauté until golden, gently turning the cloves often. Remove the garlic and set aside.

Add the chicken to the hot oil in the pan and sprinkle with the salt and pepper. Cook until lightly browned. Carefully pour off the excess oil.

Return the garlic to the pan. Add the thyme and oregano. Pour in the wine and bring to a boil. Cover the pan and simmer for 30 minutes.

Remove the chicken and garlic cloves to a platter and keep warm. Raise the heat to high and boil the juices in the skillet until they are thick. Pour the sauce over the chicken and serve immediately.

PAELLA DE MONTAÑA
Duck and Chicken Paella

Ask most people what they know about Spanish food and the first thing they'll say is paella. Practically everyone has tasted a paella, usually the kind with shellfish and chicken. But there are many paella variations, as we discovered in Valencia one evening when our host prepared no fewer than six. This particular one was served to us in the mountains near Malaga and there it contained snails. We were told to eliminate the rosemary, since the snails would already be seasoned from nibbling rosemary themselves!

SERVES 6.

2 tablespoons olive oil
6 ounces boneless pork, cut into small cubes
6 chicken thighs
   Salt
1 4- to 5-pound duckling
1 medium onion, minced
3 garlic cloves, minced
3 large tomatoes, chopped
   Sprig of fresh rosemary

½ pound green beans, ends removed and cut in half
1 cup cooked large white lima or Great Northern beans
5 cups unsalted Chicken and/or Duck Stock, page 147
½ teaspoon saffron threads
2 cups short-grain rice, preferably Valencian or Italian

Heat a paella pan or other wide, flat-bottomed pan and add the oil. Sauté the pork until golden, remove from the pan, and set aside. Using a heavy knife or cleaver, cut each of the chicken thighs in half. Sprinkle lightly with salt and sauté the thighs quickly in the hot oil until golden but still underdone. Remove and set aside.

Cut the duck into serving pieces, reserving the backs, wings, and neck for another use. Remove excess fat from the remaining pieces and cut the pieces into smaller chunks with the cleaver.

Remove all the fat from the paella pan and sprinkle the duck lightly with salt. Sauté in the pan until golden. Remove and set aside. Pour off all but 3 tablespoons of the fat.

Sauté the onion and garlic in the fat until tender. Add the tomatoes and rosemary and cook quickly until all the liquid is gone. Meanwhile, bring the stock to a boil.

Scatter the meats and beans over the tomato mixture in the pan and stir in 1 cup of the stock. Cook quickly until all the liquid has cooked away.

Toast the saffron threads 1 minute in a hot, dry pan, then pulverize in a mortar and pestle or with the back of a spoon.

Stir the rice, 1½ teaspoons of salt, and the saffron into the meat mixture. Pour in the remaining stock and bring to a boil. Lower the heat to medium and cook, moving the pan around on the burner from time to time so that all parts of the bottom of the pan receive heat, until the rice has absorbed almost all the liquid and is tender but still a little firm, about 20 minutes. (Alternatively, after bringing the paella to a boil place it on the floor of a preheated 400°F. gas oven or on the lowest shelf of an electric oven and cook for 20 minutes.)

To serve, remove the paella from the heat, drape a clean, dry cloth over it, and allow it to rest for 5 to 10 minutes. Paella, traditionally, is not served piping hot from the oven. It really does taste better after it has cooled slightly.

CONFIT DE PATO
Preserved Duck

French maybe in origin but the Spanish Basques have made it their own—both at home and at the simplest and grandest restaurants. Cooks care little for mere man-made borders. With confit, the main concern was preserving the meats without refrigeration. This method not only does that but also creates a new and wonderful flavor of the meats confitado, *whether duck, goose, or pork.*

This recipe might look a bit intimidating, but actually it goes together easily and the flavors at the end certainly justify the effort.

Getting together enough duck fat is sometimes difficult. Ask your butcher if he can order some duck fat for you from his supplier. Otherwise, just pull off as much fat as possible from any ducks you cook, render it, strain it, and refrigerate it. It will keep at least a year, refrigerated. Add good-quality lard to the duck fat to arrive at enough to cook the duck pieces. The fat can be used several times within a year for preparing confit.

Begin preparation 24 hours in advance.

2 whole ducks	12 black peppercorns
⅓ cup kosher salt	2 pounds duck fat or a
3 bay leaves	combination of duck fat and
Several sprigs of fresh thyme	good-quality lard
or 2 teaspoons dried thyme	1 medium onion studded with
leaves	whole cloves

Remove the fat from the duck. Place the duck fat in a pan and cook over medium-low heat to liquefy it, or render it. Refrigerate when cool.

Disjoint the ducks, reserving the backs, wings, and necks for another use. Place the whole legs and breasts in layers in an enamel or glass pan and sprinkle each layer with the salt, bay leaves, thyme, and peppercorns. Refrigerate, covered, for 24 hours. (If desired, use only the legs for the confit and keep the breasts for other recipes. But breasts are delicious *confitado* too, and we particularly like the breast confit in salads.

Preheat the oven to 300°F. Heat a large nonreactive pan over medium-low heat and add enough of the duck fat to cover all the duck pieces. Slowly melt the fat. Add the clove-studded onion. The fat should be only about 200°F.—so as not to fry the duck. A quick-read thermometer is useful here.

Wipe off the duck pieces and slide them into the fat so that they are entirely submerged. Return the fat to 200°F. and place the uncovered pan in the oven, baking the duck until it exudes no juice when pierced. This usually takes 1½ to 2 hours.

Meanwhile, thoroughly clean a nonporous container that can hold both the duck and the fat. Cover the bottom of the container with something to raise the duck off the bottom so it will be completely encased in the fat. You can use sterilized sticks, cooked duck bones, or sterilized marbles—they are inexpensive, reusable, and easy to use.

Gently lift the duck pieces from the fat and put them in layers in the prepared container. Ladle the fat through a strainer over the duck pieces, completely covering them. Leave behind any meat juices at the bottom of the pan.

When the fat has set, cover the top with foil, closely fitting it to the top of the fat. Keep in a cool place. Since American homes are usually much warmer than a "larder," we keep our confit in the refrigerator just for safety. (The confit will keep covered in fat and refrigerated for at least six months.)

To use the confit, bring to room temperature so the fat liquefies and gently lift out as many pieces as you wish. Remove any fat adhering to the pieces. Use the pieces whole or shredded, prepared as in the following recipes. Cover the unused confit with fat and return it to the refrigerator.

DISHES WITH CONFIT DE PATO

Once you have begun to make confit, your imagination will guide you to all sorts of wonderful presentations.

Duck confit can be substituted for the regular duck in any of the recipes for duck in this book. Simply brown the duck pieces and set aside. Then prepare the sauce and reheat the confit in the sauce before serving.

Here are a couple of ideas using confit to get started.

ENSALADA DE CONFIT DE PATO A LA VINAGRETA DE NUECES
Duck Confit Salad with Walnut Oil Dressing and Fresh Herbs

Many modern markets now carry mixed salad greens of several different kinds of lettuce, endive, escarole, radicchio, and so on, all washed and expensively priced. My produce supplier refers to this as "yuppie leaf." We think it's one of the greatest new food products to come along in a while, and it really isn't that expensive considering there is no waste and no preparation time. (How many times do we throw away half a lettuce trying to get a few decent leaves for a salad?) Quality varies greatly; only buy the salad really fresh and complain hotly if it's not absolutely clean. If you do not have such a lettuce assortment available, simply create your own.

This delicious salad is good as a first course or a light supper dish. Experiment, adding other favorite vegetables to the mix.

SERVES 6.

3 tablespoons walnut oil	2 whole legs duck confit (page 400)
1 tablespoon olive oil	
1 tablespoon lemon juice	1 whole breast duck confit, halved
1 teaspoon Dijon-style mustard	Mixed greens (lettuces, spinach, endive spears, escarole, and radicchio)
1 garlic clove, crushed	
1 tablespoon sherry wine vinegar	
1 teaspoon salt	3 tablespoons mixed chopped fresh parsley, marjoram, and sage
¼ teaspoon freshly ground black pepper	

Combine the oils, lemon juice, mustard, garlic, vinegar, salt, and pepper and set aside.

Skin and shred the leg meat and place in a bowl. Skin the breasts and cut into 3 diagonal slices each. Place in a separate bowl.

Attractively arrange the greens on a platter or individual plates. (We like to use dinner plates, strewing the salad over a large part of the plate and using the endive spears as a point of drama.)

Add the chopped herbs to the dressing and immediately divide the dressing between the 2 bowls of meat. Toss with the meat.

Arrange the shredded leg meat on top of the salad and garnish the edge of each plate with 1 slice of the breast.

Serve immediately.

CONFIT DE PATO CON SALSA DE ACEITUNAS
Duck with Olive Sauce

We have found duck with olive sauce in Catalonia and Andalusia, both olive-producing areas.

SERVES 4 TO 8.

1 tablespoon duck fat
4 breasts and 4 legs duck confit (page 400)
1 medium onion, finely minced
3 tomatoes, grated (discard skin)
½ cup dry white wine

2 cups Duck, Chicken, or Veal Stock, pages 147 and 149
1 cup good-quality green olives
Salt and freshly ground black pepper to taste

Heat the fat in a large skillet and cook the duck, skin side down, until browned. Remove from heat, discard all but 1 tablespoon of the fat, and set aside.

In the fat, cook the onion until it begins to color. Add the tomatoes and cook to a paste. Stir in the wine and stock and cook to reduce to 1 cup. Add the olives and season with salt and pepper if needed. Return the duck to the pan and heat through in the sauce.

Serve immediately.

CALDERETA DE CORDERO MÉRIDA
Lamb Casserole Mérida-Style

One night in Mérida we ate this lamb stew twice. Yes, the dish is worthy of two helpings, but we didn't really do it on purpose. We had arranged to meet friends at a certain restaurant for dinner. We went to the restaurant and waited. When they didn't show, we went ahead and ordered. The lamb came and it was good, but not as wonderful as we had been led to expect. In walk our friends, who explain that they are waiting in the restaurant next door and have ordered for us. We hastily talk to our perplexed waiter, pay, and go on to yet another, and really better, caldereta at Bar Nicolas.

Incidentally, both restaurants are owned by the same people.

SERVES 6.

2 tablespoons olive oil
3 pounds leg of lamb, cubed
2 onions, peeled and sliced
3 tomatoes, chopped
1 green pepper, stemmed, seeded, and quartered
4 garlic cloves
2 bay leaves
10 sprigs of parsley
2 sprigs of thyme

1 cup dry white wine
1 1-inch-thick slice white bread
1 tablespoon white wine vinegar
8 peppercorns
2 teaspoons paprika
1 whole clove
1 teaspoon salt

Heat the oil in a large pot with a cover. When hot, cook the lamb pieces in small batches until golden. Pour off the excess fat. Return all the lamb to the pot. Add the onions, tomatoes, green pepper, garlic, bay leaves, parsley, thyme, and white wine. Bring to a boil, lower the heat, and cover. Simmer until the meat is tender, about 45 minutes.

Meanwhile, prepare the *picada:* Soak the bread in the vinegar with water to cover until soft. Squeeze dry and puree in the blender or food processor with the peppercorns, paprika, clove, and salt. Add some of the cooking juices to obtain a smooth puree.

Remove the meat to a platter. Puree the vegetables and pour back into the pot through a sieve, pushing down on the solids to extract as much juice as possible. Stir in the *picada*. Cook to reduce and thicken. Return the lamb to the pot and heat through, adding more salt if necessary.

Serve immediately.

PIERNA DE CORDERO GUISADA CON JUDÍAS BLANCAS
Lamb Shanks with White Beans

An abundance of lamb and cold nights have helped inspire some wonderful stews in the north of Spain. This combination of white beans and lamb appears on both the Spanish and French sides of the Pyrenees.

SERVES 6.

Begin preparation 24 hours in advance.

½ pound Great Northern white beans

¼ cup olive oil

4 pounds lamb shanks, cracked by your butcher

2 teaspoons salt

1 teaspoon freshly ground black pepper

6 garlic cloves, minced

1 large onion, minced, plus 1 small onion studded with 8 whole cloves

2 carrots, chopped

3 cups dry white wine

4 bay leaves

Sprig of rosemary

Sprig of thyme

Soak the beans overnight.

Heat the oil in a large, deep skillet. Brown the shanks in the oil, sprinkling with 1 teaspoon of the salt and the teaspoon of pepper as they cook. Remove the shanks. Pour off all but 1 tablespoon of the oil. Cook the garlic, minced onion, and carrots until tender.

Return the lamb shanks to the pan. Pour in the wine. Add 2 of the bay leaves, and the rosemary and thyme. Bring to a boil, lower the heat, and cover. Simmer for 1½ hours.

Meanwhile, drain the beans and place in a pot. Add cold water to cover 2 inches above the beans. Add the clove-studded onion and remaining 2 bay leaves. Bring to a boil and skim off the foam. Lower the heat and cook, uncovered, for 45 minutes. Add the remaining teaspoon of salt and continue to cook until tender. Remove the onion and bay leaves. Drain the beans, reserving the liquid.

Preheat the oven to 375°F.

Remove the lamb from its cooking liquid. Remove the bay leaf, rosemary and thyme, and discard. Puree the solids. Return the liquid and puree to the pan and boil quickly to reduce by half.

Pour half of the beans into a clay casserole or other ovenproof casserole and arrange the lamb on top of the beans. Cover with the remaining beans. Pour the reduced cooking liquid over the beans and place in the oven to bake for 30 minutes. Check after 15 minutes. If the beans have become too dry add some of the bean cooking liquid. Remove the casserole from the oven and let rest 10 minutes.

Serve in flat soup plates.

CORDERO PASTORIL
Lamb Shepherd-Style

Rosemary and mint that grow wild in the mountains season this simple lamb stew. The flavors are so pure you can almost smell the smoke from the shepherd's campfire.

SERVES 6.

Begin preparation 3 to 12 hours in advance.

3 pounds boneless leg of lamb, cut into 2-inch cubes	3 tablespoons wine vinegar
4 garlic cloves	2 to 3 medium-size new red potatoes per person
2 tablespoons fresh rosemary	1 tablespoon olive oil
3 tablespoons fresh mint leaves	2 cups dry white wine
Freshly ground black pepper	Salt

Place the lamb cubes in a nonreactive pan. In a mortar, grind together the garlic, rosemary, and mint and 1 teaspoon of pepper. Stir in the vinegar to form a paste. Rub this into the lamb. Cover and refrigerate for several hours or overnight.

Parboil the potatoes in boiling salted water for about 10 minutes. Drain and discard the water. Cut the potatoes in halves or quarters depending on size.

Heat the oil in a clay casserole or skillet. Add the lamb, potatoes, and wine. Bring to a boil and lower the heat to medium-low. Cook until the lamb is tender and the potatoes have browned, about 45 to 60 minutes. There will be no sauce left. Season to taste with salt and pepper.

Serve immediately.

PROBAR DE CERDO TRUJILLO
Marinated Pork Tenderloin

"Taste of the pork" is the name of this recipe and refers to the custom of seasoning a little of the freshly butchered pork and cooking it to see if that particular pig should be made into ham and sausages or eaten fresh. Or so the story goes. It makes a great tapa, anyway.

SERVES 6 TO 8 AS A TAPA.

Begin preparation 48 hours in advance.

1 pound pork tenderloin	1 teaspoon salt
3 garlic cloves	1 teaspoon freshly ground black
2 teaspoons paprika	pepper
1 teaspoon oregano	1 tablespoon red wine vinegar

Cut the pork tenderloin into 4-inch pieces.

In a mortar, crush the garlic and grind into a paste with the remaining ingredients. Rub this paste into the pork tenderloins. Place the pork in a glass or stainless steel container, cover, and refrigerate for 2 days.

Remove the pork from the refrigerator and let it come to room temperature.

Preheat the oven to 400°F.

Bake the pork until it registers 145°F., about 25 minutes. Let rest 10 minutes.

Slice and serve with or on top of a slice of bread. The pork is also very good cold. In that case, let it cool and refrigerate it before slicing.

EMPANADA DE LOMO
Pork Tenderloin Pie

The empanadas of Galicia are large, flat oval or round double-crusted pies with ropelike edges and dough-decorated tops. You'll find them filled with meat, vegetables, and fish as a snack in tapas bars and as a take out meal in bakeries.

SERVES 6 AS A MAIN COURSE AND 12 AS A TAPA.

DOUGH

2 teaspoons yeast
2 cups all-purpose flour

1 tablespoon olive oil
1 teaspoon salt

FILLING

¾ pound pork tenderloin
2 garlic cloves
1 teaspoon paprika
1 teaspoon oregano
½ teaspoon salt
½ teaspoon freshly ground
    black pepper

2 tablespoons olive oil
3 medium onions, chopped
2 red peppers, chopped
3 large tomatoes, chopped
2 hard-boiled eggs, chopped
1 egg, beaten

To prepare the dough—Mix ¾ cup of warm water, the yeast, and ¼ cup of the flour together and let stand in a warm place for 20 minutes. The mixture will become foamy.

Stir in the remaining flour, oil, and salt. If desired, this can all be done in the food processor. Whirl until the mixture pulls away from the sides of the bowl. Gather into a ball and place the dough in an oiled bowl. Turn the dough so all sides are coated with the oil. Cover with a cloth or plastic wrap and leave in a warm place until the dough doubles in size.

Meanwhile, prepare the filling—Slice the pork loin into ¼-inch-thick rounds and place in a bowl. With a mortar and pestle, make a paste of the garlic, paprika, oregano, salt, and pepper. Rub this mixture into the pork pieces.

Heat the oil and sauté the pork just until it is no longer pink. Remove.

Add more oil to the pan if necessary and sauté the onions and peppers until soft. Add the tomatoes and cook until it is a thick paste.

Preheat the oven to 425°F.

Punch the dough down and divide in half.

Lightly oil a 12-inch pizza pan. Stretch half of the dough over the bottom of the pan. Spread half of the tomato mixture over the dough and top with the pork slices. Sprinkle the pork with the chopped eggs and cover the eggs with the remaining tomato mixture.

Roll out the remaining dough to cover the filling. Position the dough and trim off any excess. This trim can be rolled into a rope to decorate the top of the *empanada*. Roll the bottom crust up over the top crust to form a neat seal around the edge of the *empanada*.

Brush the top of the *empanada* with the beaten egg and bake for 20 minutes. If desired, decorate the top with the excess dough. Brush with the egg.

Serve immediately or cool on a rack to serve later at room temperature.

ALUBIAS ESTOFADA
White Beans with Sausage and Chard

The paradores of Spain can not only be counted on for a comfortable bed, often in a spectacular setting, but they offer typical local dishes as well. Sometimes, in an effort to cater to what they imagine to be the tastes of tourists, these get a bit bland and/or overrefined. But when you are on a limited travel schedule, it is possible to explore the local cuisine with some gusto this way. The parador in Mérida has an especially good reputation for local dishes. This wholesome, full-flavored bean-and-sausage stew, the perfect companion for a cold and rainy night, is a good example.

SERVES 6.

Begin preparation 24 hours in advance.

1 pound Great Northern white beans
1 pound ham hocks, cracked
1 whole medium onion, plus 2 medium onions, minced
2 bay leaves
Salt
3 tablespoons olive oil
3 garlic cloves, minced

½ pound *chorizo*
½ pound *linguiça*, Italian, or blood sausage
3 large tomatoes, peeled, seeded, and chopped
1 small bunch red chard, washed well and chopped
½ teaspoon freshly ground black pepper

Soak the beans in cold water to cover overnight.

Drain the soaked beans and place in a large pot with the ham hocks, whole onion, and bay leaves. Add cold water to cover 3 inches above the beans. Bring to a boil, lower the heat to moderate, and cook the beans until tender. This may take as long as 2 hours. Season the beans during the last 30 minutes of cooking with 1 to 2 teaspoons of salt. Don't season them at the beginning or they will be tough no matter how long you cook them.

Remove the ham hock, onion, and bay leaves from the beans. Discard the onion and bay leaves. Cut the tough outer skin from the ham hocks and discard. Tear the meat into small pieces and set aside. Discard the bones.

Heat the oil in a clay casserole and cook the garlic and minced onions until soft. Add the sausages. (They can be added whole if they are the kind that will fall apart if cut into pieces, then cut into rounds after they have firmed during the cooking.) Cook for about 5 minutes.

Stir in the tomatoes and cook for another 5 minutes but not to a paste—they should still be juicy. Stir in the chard and cook until the chard has wilted. Season with 1 teaspoon of salt and the pepper.

Add the beans and any of their liquid and the meat. Cook for another 30 minutes for all the flavors to mingle. Add water if the beans begin to dry or raise the heat if the beans are too soupy.

Serve immediately in flat soup plates.

ENTRECOT AL QUESO DE CABRALES
Steak in Blue Cheese Sauce Cabo Mayor–Style

The foundation for this dish is cabrales, *a dark-leaf-wrapped blue cheese of Asturias that is absolutely delicious. We would rank it right up there with Stilton, Roquefort, and Gorgonzola. Unfortunately, it is not available at this time in the United States. Substitute one of the other great blues for this dish. Do not use a dried-out cheese.*

SERVES 6.

½ teaspoon salt
6 5-ounce steaks
1 cup dry red wine
1 cup Veal Stock, page 148

4 ounces good-quality blue cheese
¼ cup cream

Heat a heavy-bottomed skillet until very hot and add the salt. Brown the steaks well on both sides but do not cook all the way through. Remove the steaks and set aside. Add the wine and cook to reduce to 2 tablespoons. Stir in the stock and reduce by half. Crumble in the cheese and pour in the cream. Stir to combine. When the cheese has melted and the sauce has bubbles all over the surface, return the meat and any accumulated juices to the pan, turn the meat to coat with the sauce, and cook to desired doneness. Remove the steaks to a platter. Taste the sauce for seasoning, adding more salt if needed. The sauce should not be thick and gooey, but about the consistency of heavy cream. Pour the sauce over the steaks and serve immediately.

SWEETS

TARTA DE SANTIAGO
Almond Tart, Galician-Style

We first encountered this tart in Madrid where several restaurants serve a tarta de Santiago that is really a very good almond torte. Later when we visited Santiago de Compostela we again tasted tarta de Santiago but as a tart. Both are delicious. A thin slice of this tart, accompanied by some fresh fruit, is a truly great dessert.

SERVES 8.

1 recipe Tarta de Músico pastry, page 310, plus ½ teaspoon almond extract mixed with the ice water
½ pound whole almonds

4 large eggs
1 cup sugar
½ teaspoon cinnamon
Grated zest of 1 lemon
Powdered sugar

Preheat the oven to 350°F.

Roll out and prebake the crust according to the directions.

Raise the oven temperature to 425°F.

Slice 15 of the almonds and set aside. Very finely grind the remaining almonds.

Beat the eggs, granulated sugar, cinnamon, and lemon zest until thick. Stir in the ground almonds.

Pour the filling into the prepared tart shell and scatter the sliced almonds over the top.

Bake until the filling is uniformly golden, about 25 minutes. A toothpick should test clean when inserted in the middle. Allow to cool for 15 minutes, then sprinkle lavishly with powdered sugar.

Serve warm or at room temperature.

GATEAU BASQUE
Basque Cake

The Basque sheepherders took this cake (or variations) to the American West, where it is very popular in the Basque restaurants of Nevada and California. The creamy custard center is baked right in the cake.

SERVES 8 TO 10.

CUSTARD

12 pitted prunes, cut into pieces	½ cup sugar
2 tablespoons rum	2 egg yolks
1½ cups half-and-half	2 tablespoons all-purpose flour

CAKE

4 eggs	1¾ cups flour
1½ cups sugar	1 tablespoon rum
1 teaspoon baking powder	½ teaspoon vanilla extract
Grated zest of 1 orange	1 beaten egg
7 ounces (1¾ sticks) unsalted butter, melted	

To prepare the custard—Combine the prunes, 1 tablespoon of the rum, and ½ cups of water in a small saucepan. Cook over medium heat until the prunes are tender and the juice is reduced to 1 tablespoon. Set aside.

Heat the half-and-half and sugar in a saucepan. In a separate bowl, beat the egg yolks with the flour and remaining tablespoon of rum. Whisk in a little of the hot half-and-half to temper the eggs. Pour this mixture into the saucepan of milk. Cook and stir over medium-low heat until thickened.

Combine the prunes and their juice with the hot custard. Cool and then refrigerate until cold.

Preheat the oven to 350°F.

To prepare the cake—Beat the eggs with the sugar, baking powder, and orange zest until light. Gradually add the cooled melted butter and the flour. Do not overmix. Stir in the rum and vanilla.

Butter a 9-by-2-inch round springform pan. Pour half of the batter into the pan. Spoon the custard over the batter, leaving a 1-inch border around the edge. Drizzle the remaining batter over the custard to cover completely.

Bake for 20 minutes. Remove from the oven and brush with the beaten egg. Return to the oven and bake until the cake springs back when you touch it with your finger, about another 10 minutes. It will still jiggle because of the custard filling. Cool to room temperature and then refrigerate. (Refrigeration is necessary if you keep it for any length of time at all.)

Serve cold.

PERRUNILLAS DE GUADALUPE
Almond Cookies from Guadalupe

Just down the hill from the monastery in Guadalupe on the right is a small bakery that specializes in these cookies. They are soft and delicious inside with a crunchy top. They offer another local specialty, muegado, that we think you would have had to have grown up eating in your grandmother's kitchen to appreciate. No doubt the roots of this sweet are Moorish. It consists of tiny balls of flour and egg, deep fried and mixed with a honey syrup and formed into a ring. We think it's better to stick with the perrunillas.

MAKES 36 TO 48 COOKIES

Begin preparation 2 hours in advance.

½ pound butter
Sugar
2 eggs
1 cup ground almonds
Grated zest of 1 orange
½ teaspoon vanilla extract
½ teaspoon almond extract
2½ cups all-purpose flour
2 egg whites, beaten stiff

In a food processor, cream the butter with 1½ cups of sugar until smooth. Beat in the eggs until light. Add the almonds, orange zest, vanilla, and almond extract and whirl until smooth. Add the flour and combine well. Refrigerate in a covered bowl for at least 2 hours.

Preheat the oven to 375°F.

Scoop walnut-size balls out of the dough. Roll each between your palms to form a smooth ball. Place about ⅓ cup of sugar in a deep, small bowl and roll the ball to coat with sugar. Put the ball on a buttered baking sheet and flatten with the heel of your hand. Repeat with the remaining dough, spacing the balls 2 inches apart. (If you don't bake the cookies immediately, refrigerate the prepared cookies. They will be too flat if left at room temperature for long).

Baste the tops of the cookies with the beaten egg white and bake until tops and bottoms are golden, about 12 minutes.

CLOSING CIRCLES

We had to get to Jerez de la Frontera in five days for the beginning of the *vendimia*, the harvest festival. This was a true "had to be," since José Ignacio Domecq was taking the time to have lunch with us and show us around the Domecq bodega, or at least one of them. We hadn't yet decided whether to turn in our rental car and fly or take the coast-hugging *autopista* to Murcia, then cut across the bottom of Andalusia to Jerez.

We had a late lunch with friends in Tarragona and in the first cool breeze of late afternoon had walked out to the partially restored ruins of the Roman arena. The setting of the arena could never have been lovelier. It's high up a steep hillside above the sea, in a flower-splashed park above the Playa del Milagro.

From our perch high in the upper reaches of the arena, it was obvious that the origins of Tarragona go far back in antiquity—to at least 2000 B.C. Rome took the city from Carthage in 218 B.C., and for a time it was the Roman capital of all Spain and one of the major cities in the empire. In fact, the citizens of Tarragona possessed imperial rights granted only to the citizens of Rome.

Today it has a slightly decayed air of forgotten power. The best days are in the past, but no regrets. Standing on the steps of the cathedral, looking down through the medieval section of town toward the Ramblas, one imagines it as a just-the-right-size city to call home. With a population of about 125,000, it is more manageable than bustling Barcelona, where perpetual hurry is the rule.

Perhaps, because the city's archeological past is so evident, Tarragona seems a step back in time, to a slower, more thoughtful Mediterranean world. In a few blocks, it is possible to walk past the ruins of thirty centuries, from the Iberians to nineteenth-century fortifications. In contrast, only about 100 kilometers north, Barcelona, even though it is on the Mediterranean, has a northern spirit. It is a restless place—part bravado, part adventure—ready to take on new projects, to accept new ideas, to embrace new philosophies.

All that is quite wonderful. But there are times we would simply like to sit in the sun.

Or rather in the shade (especially in late August), high on the west rim of the arena. Hundreds of sailboats dot the Mediterranean, tacking and turning slowly, trying to catch the light wind from the north. Below, Playa del Milagro is crowded, although the real beach scene in Tarragona is a few kilometers south at La Pineda and Salou. A group of Japanese tourists, managing to look fresh and interested despite the late afternoon heat, filed onto the floor of the amphitheater, staring up at our group as if we were imperial judges, ready to give thumbs up or thumbs down. Far out on the Med, a few puffs of white cloud drifted slowly south toward Africa.

We were with old friends who lived in Arboc, a few kilometers north of Tarragona. We shared the contented feeling that comes after good food, a few glasses of wine, and good company. We were idly discussing lunch, trying to settle on what our favorite dish had been. Had it been the snails sautéed with sausage or perhaps the lamb chops in a stew of baby onions, carrots, and fried morels?

While sitting in the arena, gazing out over the sea, searching our palates' memories for the best of lunch (and occasionally straying back to dinner the night before—deer in red wine sauce), we made up our minds not to forsake the coast for an airplane. We wanted to drive, even though it would take longer. We wanted to soak ourselves in Spain. Most of all, we wanted to plunge back into the Mediterranean south.

Three days later, on a mountainside above Málaga at the edge of an old vineyard, looking south toward Africa, we were visiting with a man whose hands were as gnarly and twisted as the vines in the field he had worked for half a century. It was an old Moscatel vineyard that was alleged to have been planted in the early days of the Arab conquest. (The individual vines would, of course, have been replanted many times over since then.) The harvest would begin early next week. We all sampled some of the grapes. That intensely sweet Moscatel taste filled our mouths and the perfume of the grapes permeated the afternoon.

This whole hillside had been vines only a hundred years ago, when Málaga was one of the most popular wines in the world. Now Don Rodríguez's vines were the only ones in sight.

The man, Don Diego Rodríguez, was patiently laying a bed of

vine cuttings from the winter before inside a framework of fire-scorched loose brick, stacked three bricks high, with one side open. The frame was just the right size for a paella pan to sit on.

"No one wants good wine anymore," he said, as he carefully broke sticks into the right length to fit inside the portable brick fireplace he had constructed on a flat, blackened gravely area where many fires had clearly been made in the past.

"Now it is all beer. Beer and gin that the young people drink." He shook his head and spat.

"I see them drunk now in the streets of Málaga, standing outside those beer clubs. I knew their fathers, too. I worked this hillside with some of them. But they sold their oceanfront land to the English for those great ugly buildings and abandoned the land. You should not abandon the land." He spat again. "If you take care of the land, the land will take care of you."

There is no ready explaining why the young people, or at least some of the young people, of Spain have taken to beer and certain spirits. Spanish-made gin and rum are cheap, but so is wine. Beer is much the same price as wine. It isn't a price thing.

Some blame television. Beer and spirits look more glamorous, especially in the American, German, and English shows. Many teenagers believe that wine is the "old way." It's what their parents and grandparents drink, and is considered old-fashioned by the trendy teen set. The beer-drinking set is most evident along the coasts, in areas where there are a lot of foreigners. It seems evident that it is connected with the desire of a lot of younger people to reject their "Spanishness" in favor of an indefinite, ambiguous "European" attitude.

On the other hand, the fascination seems to fade when school is finished and regular work begins. We would hate to offer any arm-chair universal insight into trends about Spanish youth based on their switch from wine to beer, gin, and rum. Maybe Spanish teen-agers, like teenagers all over Europe (and the United States), have become more affluent. And with money to spend, they prefer to spend it with their peers rather than stay at home with Mom and Dad, watching the telly and sipping a little wine with dinner. At any rate, teenage drinking patterns had nothing to do with the decline of the great vineyards of Málaga, whatever Don Rodríguez believed.

The sweet wines of Málaga drew high praise from the Romans. Pliny, Virgil, and other Roman writers wrote in glowing terms about them. The Moors, who were not the strict prohibitionists that many believe, made at least two sweet wines from Málaga, the Xarab al Maqui and the Zebibi, which, according to Jan Read in *The Wines of Spain*, were made from sun-dried grapes. Málaga wine was very popular in Victorian England, and it has been written that Catherine the Great of Russia kept a good store of Málaga on hand.

The best Málaga is made from Moscatel vines that grow on the steep mountain slopes inland from the city. In the nineteenth century it was called Mountain Wine and was very highly regarded.

What killed the market for Málaga was the decline in the fashion for sweet wines. Yet, curiously enough, one of the most popular wines in the world today is the light-bodied, sweet Lambrusco from Italy.

And certainly the sweet wines of Oporto and Madeira have held their own in the modern age, perhaps even advanced a bit. We fear that Málaga somehow simply missed the boat when it took the wines to market.

Don Rodríguez had laid the fire to his satisfaction. He waved away all offers to help. There were six of us gathered on the hillside for a "country" paella. In the house behind, Don Rodríguez's daughter was lighting the oil lamps that he insisted on in the evening, even though electricity had come to the area a few years before. The oil lamps fit well with the house, which was stone and tile. Don Rodríguez didn't know how old it was. He had been born there but he thought the house was "not very old. Perhaps three hundred years." The interior was all dark wood, worn and cracked tile and odd little hidden corners where a tiny shelf supported a few wineglasses or an image of the Virgin.

A winery representative had introduced us to Don Rodríguez only a few hours before. For some reason, he had taken an instant liking to us, had insisted when he learned that we had no dinner plans that he would make a real "mountain paella" for us, his daughter and son-in-law, and a young granddaughter who was visiting from Madrid.

"I must do it, you see, because I know you have been to Valencia and they have made you paella there. The whole world thinks the Valencian paella is true paella. Well, that's nonsense. I've been to Valencia and had the paella." Don Rodríguez paused, struggled briefly with his good intentions, and decided to be polite in front of the visitors. "It is quite good paella, you understand, and they are very good with rice, the *valencianos*, but they don't know how to make paella from the *país*, the country. Paella with rabbit, chicken, and sausage, like you will have tonight."

Don Rodríguez explained that the vine cuttings gave just enough heat. "You mustn't cook the paella too fast or too slow. This way, over a wood fire, that is the best way," he said.

It was a beautiful dish, finished by lamplight as darkness fell over the mountainside. Don Rodríguez carried the paella carefully inside and set it on the table "to rest" for ten minutes or so. He opened a bottle of dry Málaga and we went back outside, into the cool night, to drink it. A truly dry Málaga is seldom found and almost never exported. It has the quality of a very nutty *amontillado* or a dry Madeira but with a bit more bite.

The coast was lit up by miles of lights, the brick and concrete apartments of retired British civil servants or army officers, or the vacation villas of the rich, both Spanish and English, and maybe German. Beyond the glaring slash of the coast there was blackness all the way to Africa—that night there was not even the light of a fishing boat.

Behind us, over the ridge of the mountaintop, there was a faint glow where the moon would be rising soon. But before it broke above the ridgeline, we were enjoying an outstanding paella—perfectly done rice and tender, juicy rabbit and chicken with a slight spiciness from the sausages echoing through the dish.

And most delightful, a taste of the burnt rice for everyone—the *quemado*—which Spaniards consider to be the mark of a perfectly made paella or any other rice dish. It sounds a bit odd to talk about burnt rice as a special taste treat, but it does add a remarkable flavor. Don Rodríguez had got it just right by throwing on a double handful of cuttings at the last minute, creating a burst of heat and blackening a handful of rice in the center of the pan.

We quickly polished off a bottle of light, fruity Valdepeñas with the first plate of paella. The granddaughter murmured something in her grandfather's ear, went to the kitchen, and came back in a moment with a carafe of red wine. I saw Don Rodríguez frown slightly, but Carmen, his granddaughter, simply smiled and passed the carafe around, paying no attention to him. (She was a doctor, just starting with a family practice in one of the poorer areas of Madrid, and like many late-twentieth-century Spanish women, was thoroughly liberated.)

Don Rodríguez said gruffly that the wine his granddaughter had bought was not a true Málaga.

"It is something some French people have made. A few years ago they came from Algeria and bought an old vineyard farther up the mountain. They pulled out the old vines, good Moscatel it was, and planted some other stuff. I don't know what it is. I don't know why Carmen wants to bring it here."

Carmen shot me a quick smile. "I'm sure you know the grape, and so do you, Grandpapa," she said. "It is Cabernet Sauvignon. They have built a small winery. Two brothers. The younger one is unmarried." She blushed and saw that we had noticed. She smiled a quick secret smile again and shrugged slightly. "Grandfather likes to say they are crazy to plant anything here but Moscatel, but many of the English like what they make. They have sold some to local restaurants. They do not even put it in bottle yet. You have to bring your own jugs and they take it straight from the barrel. I stopped on my way to get a big jug of it for tonight. I am curious to know what you think."

By the time she had finished speaking she had got over her blush and looked defiantly at her grandfather. This was going to be a bit tricky, so we stalled a bit, sniffing the wine, rolling it in the glass and holding to the lamp to get the color, which was a lovely, rich purple. "Surely, this is a very warm climate for Cabernet."

It was Don Rodríguez who answered. "That is what the foreigners say, but they do not know Málaga. We can grow anything here. The Moors knew that. That is why they fought so hard to keep Málaga.

"They say in the old days, the Mongol Tamerlane the Great sent to Málaga for his wine. There is nothing wrong with this wine." He too held it to the light. "You see the color? That is the soil of Málaga. And they had the good sense to go high up the mountain, where the nights are cold. My father himself knew that. And his father. That is why we planted up here. The grapes like to get cold at night. We can grow anything we want in Málaga."

Don Rodríguez set the glass down carefully. He seemed to realize that he had been tricked out of his curmudgeon role.

"At least," he said, "it is something to keep the English happy, and where there are vines, there cannot be concrete."

We tasted the wine. It was lovely, partaking much more of the character that Cabernet Sauvignon develops in California than in France. It had an intense, brambly fruitiness typical of a young California Cabernet from Mendocino or Lake county, north of San Francisco.

We decided at last that it was quite nice and certainly went well with the paella.

Don Rodríguez nodded and asked for another plate of paella and a glass of wine.

Later, as we sat around the fireplace with a small fire lit against the postmidnight chill, Don Rodríguez agreed that he knew a bit more about the Algerian winegrowers than he had admitted earlier.

"They have worked hard, and if the wine they make is not the wine I would make, well, it is their day not mine. I wish them well," he said.

Later Carmen took us aside and offered to take us to see the Algerians' winery the next day. We quickly agreed. She said that both brothers had been trained in France, but when they left Algeria, they decided they wanted to go to Spain, not France, because they felt they had more freedom to experiment, to try something new in Spain.

"I am very proud of my grandfather, you know. He tries to be hard, but he has actually helped them. He gave them some old barrels and talked to them about the local weather conditions, of which they were ignorant. In the end, I believe he is simply happy to see the possibility of wine returning to Málaga. He said it is not his life, and that is true, but he welcomes the new life."

We raised a glass of sweet Málaga, an old bottle from a small store Don Rodríguez kept in his cellar. "Viva España."

"Viva España."

"Viva," she answered.

FIESTA

The Spanish take play seriously, joyfully observing holidays and fiestas, both on a local and national basis.

There is nothing more exciting than to arrive in a small Spanish town and discover it is some kind of holiday. That can only be a problem if you need to go to the bank or the post office, since they are likely to be closed or at least on restricted hours.

The following selection of fiestas is intended only as a short guide. I am convinced that it would be possible to find a village somewhere in Spain having a fiesta on just about any day of the year.

Many, if not most, of the local fiestas are rooted in religion, a saint's day, or a pilgrimage to some local shrine, church, or holy spot (these pilgrimages are known as *romerías*.) Religion, or at least the forms of religion, are part of the very fabric of Spanish life. It is impossible to imagine living in Spain for any length of time without being aware of the church calendar.

There are also special foods for fiestas, and sometimes the entire fiesta might be built around a particular food, such as the spring snail festival in Lérida or the annual *romesco* festival and contest in Tarragona. Others, such as saint's-day festivals or the many harvest festivals throughout Spain, will simply bring out the best a particular region has to offer.

Even blindfolded it would be obvious when some sort of fiesta is going on because of the smell of chickens roasting, often over a wood fire in a half barrel. No matter what the fiesta, there is sure to be grilled chicken.

It cannot be emphasized often enough that food, the sharing of food, is a part of the life of a Spaniard. It is true that many of the dishes of Spain are basic peasant gleanings from a sparse larder—such as *cocido*, the meat stew, or the many rice dishes—but when those dishes are put on the Spanish table, they are treated with respect. Truly, we believe that famous cliché can be said of the Spaniard—that he or she lives to eat, rather than eating to live.

CHRISTMAS

It is Christmas Eve that gets the biggest play in most of Spain. Christmas Eve is family time with huge dinners that draw family members from all over Spain. It is interesting in the past few years to find many Andalusian Christmas Eve customs being celebrated in the north, especially in Catalonia, because so many Andalusians have come north to work. The Christmas Eve dinner is interrupted by midnight Mass, where special songs or even plays are sometimes performed. After Mass, weather permitting, everyone takes to the streets for several more hours of music, dancing, Christmas pageants, and food, often continuing straight through until dawn.

The Christmas Eve dinner—*la cena de nochebuena*—is likely to feature a roast turkey (Americans would be right at home), since that bird has been a naturalized citizen of the Spanish kitchen since the sixteenth century. Some of the oldest cookbooks in Spain give recipes for turkey. In the Celtic north, if it isn't turkey on the table, it is likely to be *lacón con grelos*, cured pork shoulder boiled with turnip greens. Anywhere in Spain, a baby kid or lamb may be roasted for the feast. In Andalusia and La Mancha, *sopa de almendras*, almond soup, is often served on Christmas Eve.

There are a few traditional sweets at Christmas, notably *turrones*, an almond nougat candy. If one is lucky, someone has made a trip to a local convent for a range of delectable Christmas *dulces* (sweets) traditionally made by the nuns. Most of these sweets trace back to the Arabs, who introduced sugar to Spain in the eighth century. Each convent is likely to have its own specialty, which is normally sold only at the convent.

Although the Christmas tree is sometimes seen in Spain, the center of the Yule decor is still the marvelous *belén* (crèche), the Nativity scene. Some of the public *belenes* are works of art carved from clay, fired, and painted. In the home they are often passed down through generations, with an occasional new piece winning a place in the belén. You can tell how close Christmas is, because each night the three kings are moved a bit closer to the cradle, as they journey through the desert.

I recall one particularly wonderful outdoor *belén* at Olite, south of Pamplona. It occupied about half of a city block in a plaza in front of the *parador*. It was complete with rivers, bridges, lakes, forests, everything one could wish in a landscape. The figures were about Hobbit-size, as I recall, and beautifully carved and painted. Many of these figures are made of cork so they can be easily moved about.

December 28, the Day of the Holy Innocents, has some of the aspects of April Fools' day. It is a day of practical jokes and general unruliness, which could be a survival of the Roman Saturnalia. When the victim of a joke realizes what has happened, the cry of "*Inocente!*" goes up.

New Year's Eve celebrations tend to be loud and noisy, much like the rest of Europe and America, when held in public. We recall one utterly awful New Year's Eve dinner in a village near Barcelona. Through a series of dreadful misunderstandings, we were forced to cancel reservations at one of our favorite restaurants—Celler del Penedés in Vilafranca—to dine at a place that served dish after dish obviously copied from a color feature in a food magazine. The topper came when the main course included a garnish of green mashed potatoes piped around the side of the plate! Why? Also, all the waitresses were splendid in glittery fairy dresses complete with not-so-gossamer wings.

The Spanish do their own thing quite well but they are not great adapters of international culture. New Year's Eve is often, at least for older Spaniards, an at-home celebration. Wherever you find yourself on New Year's Eve, it is important to have a bunch of grapes at hand. As the clock begins to strike midnight, pop a grape in your mouth at each chime. If you get all twelve grapes in, you'll be lucky all year long; if not, well, you'd best watch out.

Day of the Three Kings is January 6 (Twelfth Night), and on the eve of Twelfth Night, the three kings come on camels to give gifts to the children. In many villages and cities, there are parades with floats, dancers, and dozens of bands. The parade in Sevilla is the best known and one of the most spectacular. In many parts of Spain, from Murcia in the south to Navarre in the north, there are also plays performed in the churches or the *plaza mayor*, telling the story of the kings.

In a small village on the plains of La Mancha, a donkey bedecked with more Christmas decorations than the average American Christmas tree is drawing a small cart. Three kings are standing in the cart, each wearing long flowing robes and crowns that sparkle and amaze with cut glass and other "precious" jewels. They are followed by a mob of small children, barking dogs, and a local newspaper photographer. The kings are throwing small bags of candy to the children.

After one tour around the plaza, the kings dismount and step into a handy bar. In a few minutes, refreshed, they resume their journey toward Bethlehem, in this case the village belén set up in the yard before the church. Their supply of candy appears inexhaustible.

SAINTS AND SINNERS

San Sebastián Day on January 20 is, naturally, a major fiesta in San Sebastián. It takes a curious turn in Cáceres. As the saint is paraded through town, men dressed in hideous masks and animal skins follow along, frequently stopping to bow to the saint. We've never found anyone with a good explanation for this.

Saint Agueda's Day is February 5. Agueda is the patron saint of married women and on that day many towns, including Segovia, elect an *alcaldesa*, or mayoress, to run the town for a day or sometimes a week.

Carnaval, a pre-Lenten riot, was banned by Franco as being "pagan and immodest." He was undoubtedly right on both counts, and luckily carnival time has returned since his death.

Major celebrations are held all over Spain. Some of the best are in Cádiz, Orense, Galicia, and Sitges, the beach resort just south of Barcelona. One of the more interesting ritual events takes place in Villanueva de la Vera near Cáceres, where a huge wooden figure, dressed in a black suit and a black hat, is beaten, beheaded, and buried. It is said to be a very old ritual and undoubtedly is a survival from a pre-Christian spring festival.

Fallas, a spectacular Valencian festival, begins on March 12 and lasts for a week, climaxing with huge fires. It is sheer madness and incredible fun, but there is no special food connected with it.

Holy Week begins the spring fiesta season and is unrivaled for its pageantry and flamboyance. The Holy Week celebrations in Sevilla are probably the best known. Almost anywhere you go in Spain from Palm Sunday until Easter, it is like stepping back centuries to a time of faith that we can never know. Some of the sights may not sit well with the modern tourist, because the various mortifications of the flesh are not merely symbolic gestures in Spain. In many cities there are scenes that we're sure would be edited right out of any television documentary.

One can see minor acts of mortification any time of the year in Spain. There is a man on the lower *ramblas* in Barcelona who spends hours—we don't know how many, we've never watched and somehow didn't want to ask—kneeling with his arms stretched out in the attitude of Christ on the cross. An old cardboard box on the sidewalk in front of him fills up with pesetas during the long day. There is another man there who spends the day crying, presumably for the sins of us all. During Holy Week, there are worse sights to be seen.

As everywhere in the Mediterranean, lamb is the center of the Easter table. Although the Spanish eat lamb much younger than in England or the United States (often barely two weeks old), they will accept a lamb up to about four months old. Most of the year, the favorite is the *corderos de leche,* or *lechazos*—suckling lambs. These lambs are confined and not allowed to eat grass. Some of them may be fed by two ewes, which produces a superior-quality meat. They are called *lechazos de dos madres.* The older lamb is called a *cordero pascual* and is often the choice at Easter.

Feria de abril in Sevilla (why does Sevilla end up with so many of the good things?) started out centuries ago as a typical horse fair and was held weekly, usually just outside the walls of the city. (Our expression to "get a fair price" or a "fair shake" comes from the bargaining that went on at the fairs.)

The April fair in Sevilla is now a picture-book Spanish fiesta. There are dozens of dazzling booths filled with food and drink. There are endless parades of handsome men and beautiful women on superb horses. The fireworks go on all night and the flamenco dancing doesn't really get started until a few hours before dawn, which should find you having coffee with anise at a tapas bar overlooking the river. If you are in luck and the day is clear, the river will turn golden in the dawn sun, catching fire as if the old Guadalquivir itself were joining the party. Food? Well, I guess. After all, Sevilla is the best tapas town in Spain.

(And if you miss the Sevilla *feria* in April, Jerez de la Frontera, only a few kilometers down the *autopista,* has its own *feria de caballo* in May that may not be as full-tilt insane as Sevilla but will do quite well.)

Saint Jordi's Day comes on April 23 and is one of the most important of the Catalan festivals. It features mock battles between Christians and Moors (a common element in many fiestas) and, a particularly Catalan touch, the men present a rose to the women and the women give a book to the men. A special food for Saint Jordi is the *brazo del gitano* (arm of the Gypsy).

THE WARM DAYS

Getting into May the fiesta pace picks up. This is the season when many of the old pagan festivals—which have survived so well in Spain, wearing a poorly fitting Christian disguise—are celebrated. Since these fiestas are almost always open-air pilgrimages, or *romerías*, the outdoor grill comes into great play. Often the *romería* begins in town and wends its way, even over the course of several days, to a shrine at least superficially dedicated to the Virgin Mary. In most of these celebrations it is easy to see the face of the old Mediterranean earth goddess smiling behind Mary's correct Christian countenance.

One of the most famous of these is the *Romería de la Nuestra Señora del Rocío* (Our Lady of the Dew), held near the end of May in Almonte in the province of Huelva in the south. There, in the deserted marshlands near the Doñana wildlife reserve, as many as a million pilgrims from all over Spain (but especially Andalusia) come riding on horseback or in ox-drawn or mule-drawn carts, seeking the shrine of the Señora.

It is a major food and wine festival where one hears the old *sevillanas* being sung (and danced) far into the next day. Because Huelva is an area famed throughout Spain (and Europe) for its fresh vegetables and fruit, there are some outstanding foods on offer by Our Lady of the Dew, including, if your luck is in, some of the delicious Huelva strawberries, served from huge wooden baskets.

We remember an early visit to Spain, standing puzzled with little Spanish and maybe fewer pesetas in the market at Barcelona just off the Ramblas. We were standing before a booth that fairly exploded with strawberries—it was a riot of strawberries. There was a tall Catalan woman of indeterminate age behind the booth. Her face was grim, with deep lines. Here is a woman, we thought, who has suffered life. She has been through many things. (There was a copy of *Homage to Catalonia* in our backpack.) She looked at us for a time. "These strawberries," she said, "are the best strawberries in Spain. They are strawberries from Huelva." Somehow, in our confusion, we understood her to say, "They are strawberries from hell."

We promptly bought a quarter kilo of them and walked back up the Rambla, eating strawberries from hell.

Corpus Christi is a major festival everywhere in Spain, dating back to at least the fourteenth century. It is a movable feast, coming near the end of May. For reasons that are not clear, it often involves painting on the streets or displays of colored sand or carpets of flowers. There are no special foods for Corpus Christi, only the usual grills of chicken, fish, and lamb.

The season of summer festivals begins with the summer solstice, the longest day of the year and the official beginning of summer. There are fire festivals held all over Spain, featuring fire walkers who dash through hot coals, often carrying the more tenderfooted piggyback. In Barcelona, huge bonfires are made of elaborate papier-mâché or wooden structures, very like the *fallas* of Valencia. These are called the *Hogueras de San Juan*, or bonfires of St. John. These midsummer fires go far back into European history and were originally fertility rites celebrating the produce off the fields and gardens, which were in full growth by midsummer.

Only a few days later on June 29 comes *Día de San Pedro*. Peter is the patron saint of fishermen, so there are some marvelous feasts in coastal towns and villages. You can sometimes still see seagoing parades of fishing boats in the harbors. There will be *romescos*, of course, and the traditional grilled sardines, the sardines stuck on sticks that are thrust into the sand around a small fire. The delicious grilled fish—which is scaled and gutted before being spitted—is eaten directly off the stick. The best ones have been marinated in olive oil and herbs before cooking.

There is a curious inland festival in honor of Saint Peter, which is held in Haro in La Rioja and known locally as the *Batalla del Vino*. We've never found a good explanation for its origins or what Saint Peter has to do with it. We suspect that the good citizens of Haro, seeing what fun their coastal cousins had, simply decided to have their own party. We've never actually been on hand for the battle itself, but everyone seems to go in the street with jars, buckets, or *botas* of cheap wine and throws it or squirts it on everyone else. Needless to say, quite a lot of the wine gets taken internally as well. At any time of the year, the entire town of Haro smells like the interior of a winery. It is a small town with several large wineries, so one should imagine with the streets running wine for Saint Peter's Day, the impression is merely intensified.

Perhaps the best known of Spain's summer fiestas is *La Corrida de los Toros* in Pamplona. The fiesta is held the week of the feast day of San Fermín, which falls on July 7. It is a marathon week of eating and drinking, with the daily highlight being the running of the bulls through the streets. The bulls are released from pens and teased and goaded by what looks to us like very foolish young men (and the odd foolish young woman). The animals are more or less herded through the streets to the Plaza de Toros. It's a kind of warmup for the afternoon bullfights and is counted a great success if there are at least a few minor injuries. And, of course, anyone who has been even slightly gored by a bull becomes the hero for the day.

Pamplona, thanks in part to Hemingway, has the most famous running of the bulls, but there are many others. In some of the coastal villages, the bulls chase their tormenters into the sea.

There are countless summer festivals all over Spain and anyone attempting a complete fiesta calendar would need years of on-the-ground research. It would be a fine idea and would get you in shape for the many fiestas de la *vendimia*, the grape harvest festivals that begin in late August or early September.

In autumn, the *Día de los Difuntos* (Day of the Dead) is the start of the hog-butchering season. In Mollo near Gerona, this has been turned into a riotous celebration with the pig butchering taking place in the Plaza Mayor and the meat offered up at auction. The drink of the day is rum, which seems rather out of place until you remember that the Catalans have traded extensively with Cuba and other Caribbean ports for centuries and rum is a common article of commerce.

The *Fiesta de Santa Lucía* on December 13 marks the beginning of the Christmas season. This is about the time the traditional Spanish Christmas candies and other goodies start appearing in the shops.

There, we've circled the year.

BIBLIOGRAPHY AND FURTHER READING

Andrews, Colman. *Catalan Cuisine*. New York: Atheneum, 1988.

Asher, Gerald. *On Wine*. New York: Random House, 1982.

Atkinson, William C. *A History of Spain and Portugal*. London: Penguin Books, 1960.

Begg, Desmond, ed. *Wine Buyers' Guide to Spain*. London: Wine Buyers Guides Ltd., 1988.

———. *Travelers' Wine Guide: Spain*. New York: Sterling, 1990.

Boyd, Alastair. *The Companion Guide to Madrid and Central Spain*. New York: Prentice Hall, 1986.

Braker, Flo. *The Simple Art of Perfect Baking*. New York: William Morrow, 1985.

Brown, Edward Espe. *Tassajara Bread Book*, Berkeley: Shambala, 1970.

Burns, Tom. *Spain: Everything Under the Sun*. Madrid: Passport Books, 1988.

Busquets, Jordi. *Sardinas*. Barcelona: Ediciones Baussán, 1983.

Casas, Penelope. *Tapas*. New York: Alfred A. Knopf, 1986.

Cervantes, Miguel de. *Don Quixote*, trans. Peter Motteux. New York: Modern Library Edition, 1950.

Crow, John A. *Spain: The Root and the Flower*. Berkeley: University of California Press, 1985.

David, Elizabeth. *Italian Food*. London: Penguin Books, 1954.

Del Conte, Anna. *Gastronomy of Italy*. New York: Prentice Hall, 1987.

Delgado, Carlos. *Diccionario de Gastronomía*. Madrid: Alianza Editorial, 1985.

Duijker, Hubrecht. *The Wines of Rioja*. London: Mitchell Beazley, 1985.

Dumas, Alexandre. *From Paris to Cádiz*, trans. A. E. Murch. London: Peter Owen Ltd., 1958.

Edwards, John. *The Roman Cookery of Apicius*. Point Roberts, Wash.: Hartley & Marks, 1984.

Gray, Patience. *Honey from a Weed*. New York: Harper & Row, 1986.

Greene, Graham. *Monsignor Quixote*. New York, Simon & Schuster, 1982.

Grunfeld, Frederic V. *Wild Spain*. New York: Prentice Hall, 1988.

Hooper, John. *The Spaniards*. London: Penguin Books, 1986.

Hornedo Christina. *Come y Calla*. Madrid: Ediciones Akal, S. A., 1984.

Isusi, José María Busca. *Traditional Basque Cooking*. Reno: University of Nevada Press, 1987.

Jeffs, Julian. *Sherry*. London: Faber & Faber, 1982.

Lang, Jennifer Harvey, ed. *Larousse Gastronomique*. New York: Crown Publishers, 1988.

Lichine, Alexis. *New Encyclopedia of Wines & Spirits*. New York: Alfred A. Knopf, 1985.

Livesey, Herbert Bailey. *The American Express Pocket Guide to Spain*. New York: Prentice Hall, 1988.

Lladonosa, Josep. *I Giro el Libro de la Cocina Catalana*. Madrid: Alianza Editorial, Madrid: 1988.

Luján, Néstor and Tin. *La Cucina Moderna a Catalunya*. Madrid: Espasa-Calpe, S.A., 1985.

Luján, Néstor, et al. *Allegro Vivace*. San Sadurní de Noya: Freixenet, n.d.

Manjón, Maite. New York: Prentice Hall, 1990.

McConnell, Carol and Malcolm. *The Mediterranean Diet: Wine, Pasta, Olive Oil, and a Long, Healthy Life*. New York: W.W. Norton, 1987.

Mey, Wim. *Sherry*. The Netherlands: Asjoburo Press, 1988.

Morton, H. V. *A Stranger in Spain*. New York: Dodd, Mead & Co., 1955.

O'Brien, Kate. *Farewell Spain*. London: Virago Press, 1987.

Pritchett, V. S. *Marching Spain*. London: Hogarth Press, 1988.

Read, Jan. *The Wines of Spain*. London: Faber & Faber, 1982.

Read, Jan, and Maite, Manjón. *The Wine and Food of Spain*. Boston: Little, Brown, 1987.

Root, Waverly. *Food*. New York: Simon & Schuster: Fireside Books, 1980.

Sagarriga, Cristina Cebrian. *El Vino Albariño: Hijo Legítimo del Valle del Salnes*. Madrid: Self-published, 1988.

436   *Bibliography and Further Reading*

Scarlett, Elizabeth, ed. *Let's Go: The Budget Guide to Spain, Portugal, & Morocco*. New York: Harvard Student Agencies, Inc., 1991.

Stamm, James R. *A Short History of Spanish Literature*. New York: Anchor Books, 1967.

Tannahill, Reay. *Food in History*. New York: Crown Publishers, 1988.

Torres, Marimar. *The Spanish Table*. New York: Doubleday, 1986.

Torres, Miguel A. *The Distinctive Wines of Catalonia*. Barcelona: Servicios Editoriales, S. A., 1986.

———. *Wines and Vineyards of Spain*. Barcelona: Editorial Blume, 1982; San Francisco Wine Appreciation Guild, 1985.

Vélez, Carmen. *El Libro de los Pescados*. Madrid: Alianza Editorial, 1987.

Walker, Ted. *In Spain*. London: Secker & Warburg, 1987.

SPANISH WINE GRAPE VARIETALS

The international wine market is increasingly dominated by a handful of what are called the "classic" wine grapes. What that means to most is the grapes associated with French wine. Chardonnay, Sauvignon Blanc, Cabernet Sauvignon, Pinot Noir, Merlot, and to a lesser degree, Chenin Blanc, are all grapes that have been grown for centuries in France. Along with the German varietals Gewürztraminer and Riesling, these grapes constitute for most the entire world of wine grapes.

That is a pity, for there are delightful wines made from dozens of other grapes. The wine grapes found in Spain belong to that class of grapes that some have called meridional, or southern. The southern French winegrowers in the Rhône and Provence share many grape varietals with the Spanish, sometimes under other names.

As mentioned in the text, the entire question of nomenclature for Spanish grapes is a cloudy area, but the following is a brief summary of the Spanish wine grapes—where they are grown and some synonyms.

RED WINE GRAPES

Bobal is grown in the Levante and can be made into a refreshing red wine for early consumption. It is also often made as a rosé.

Cariñena is widely planted in Aragón and Catalonia where it produces highly tannic wines that are very rich in color and high in alcohol. It is known as the Mazuelo in Rioja, where it is used as a blending grape with lighter Riojas.

Garnacha is grown all over Spain and well up into southern France. It is sometimes called Garnacha Tinta to avoid confusion with the Garnacha Blanca. It is occasionally spelled Garnacho, undergoing a mysterious sex change for no apparent purpose. When properly made, Garnacha can produce fruity, very attractive young red wines and rosés. It is an important blending element in the Rioja red wines.

Graciano is planted almost entirely in Rioja and is important in the blend for Rioja reds. It has a delicate, perfumy aroma and is very flavorful.

Monastrell is widely planted over most of Spain, probably exceeded only by Garnacha. It is especially important in the Valencia area, Catalonia, and Aragón. It is used chiefly as a blending grape, contributing alcohol and body.

Tempranillo is Spain's most important—from the standpoint of wine quality—red wine grape. It is planted in Rioja, Navarre, and in some limited areas of Catalonia, where it is called Ull de Llebre. In La Mancha it is called Cencibel. It produces an elegant, perfumy wine with many of the aroma and flavor characteristics of the Pinot Noir of Burgundy and California.

WHITE WINE GRAPES

Airén is grown chiefly in La Mancha-Castilla, Extremadura, and to a limited degree, Valencia. Always regarded as a blending grape, vintners are discovering that properly made it can produce pleasant, fruity wines for early consumption.

Palomino is the chief grape of Jerez for sherry production. It is grown in small quantities elsewhere in Spain, producing unremarkable wines.

Parellada is an important grape in Catalonia, where it produces light, rather delicate table wines. It is an important part of the *cava* sparkling-wine blend.

Viura is fast becoming the most important white table wine grape of Spain. It is grown in Rioja, where it produces crisp, refreshing, fruity white wines for early drinking. It is being planted in Valencia, Navarre, Aragón, and Catalonia, where it is called Macabeo.

Xarel-lo is important in Catalonia as part of the *cava* blend. It is pronounced Char-el-o.

INDEX

Recipes appear in boldface type.

About the Authors

Ann and Larry Walker live in Stinson Beach, California. Ann is a caterer and cooking teacher who opened the first Spanish tapas bar on the West Coast. She writes about food for a number of publications. When not in the kitchen, she enjoys surfing, hiking, reading, and listening to music with her husband, Larry, who writes on wine and food for several U.S. and European publications.